Powers of the Prosecutor in Criminal Investigation

This comparative analysis examines the scope of prosecutorial powers at different phases of criminal investigation in four countries: the United States, Italy, Poland, and Germany. Since in all four the number of criminal cases decided without trial is constantly increasing, criminal investigation has become central in the criminal process. The work asks: who should be in charge of this stage of the process? Prosecutors have gained tremendous powers to influence the outcome of criminal cases, including powers once reserved for judges. In a system in which the role of the trial is diminishing and the significance of criminal investigation is growing, this book questions whether the prosecutor's powers at the early stage of the process should be enhanced.

Using a problem-oriented approach, the book provides a parallel analysis of each country along five possible spheres of prosecutorial engagement: commencing criminal investigation; conducting criminal investigation; undertaking initial charging decisions; imposing coercive measures; and discontinuing criminal investigation. Using the competing adversarial–inquisitorial models as a framework, the focus is on the prosecutor as a crucial figure in the criminal process and investigation.

The insights of this book will be of interest and relevance to students and academics in criminal justice, criminology, law, and public policy, as well as policymakers, government officials, and others interested in legal reform.

Karolina Kremens, LL.M., Ph.D. works as an Assistant Professor at the Department of Criminal Procedure at the Faculty of Law, Administration, and Economics, University of Wrocław, Poland. She served as an Assistant Prosecutor at the District Prosecutor's Office in Wrocław (2009–2012).

Dr Kremens is the recipient of the 2016–2017 Fulbright Scholarship (University of Connecticut Law School, USA) and 2006–2007 Edward Barry McDougall Scholarship (University of Ottawa, Canada). She was awarded the Scholarship for the Outstanding Young Scholars granted by the

Polish Ministry of Science and Higher Education (2017–2019). She was a visiting scholar at the Aberystwyth University (UK), University of Exeter (UK), University of Toledo (Spain), and University of Bologna (Italy). As the McDougall Memorial Professor, Dr Kremens taught Comparative Criminal Procedure at the University of Ottawa (2014–2020).

She has led and participated in many national and international research projects. Currently she leads a project titled "Reasonable Search—Between Effective Investigation and Rights of Individual" funded by the Polish National Science Center and leads the Polish team in a project "Knowledge, Advisory and Capacity Building Information Tool for Criminal Procedural Rights in Judicial Cooperation" (CROSSJUSTICE) funded by the European Commission (Justice Programme 2018).

Her research focuses on comparative and international criminal procedure, human rights, and women rights during criminal proceedings and the role of the prosecutor in criminal process.

Directions and Developments in Criminal Justice and Law

https://www.routledge.com/Directions-and-Developments-in-Criminal-Justice-and-Law/book-series/DDCJL

The ways in which crime is constructed in society is of time-honored interest to criminologists across the globe. The ever-changing landscape of what is criminal and what is not affects scholars and policymakers in their approach to the body of law defining prohibited conduct, how that law evolves, and the modes by which it is administered. Rule of law cannot exist without a transparent legal system, strong enforcement structures, and an independent judiciary to protect against the arbitrary use of power. Critical consideration of the mechanisms through which societies attempt to make the rule of law a reality is essential to understanding and developing effectual criminal justice systems. The *Directions and Developments in Criminal Justice and Law* series offers the best research on criminal justice and law around the world, offering original insights on a broadly defined range of sociolegal topics in law, criminal procedure, courts, justice, legislation, and jurisprudence. With an eye toward using innovative and advanced methodologies, series monographs offer solid social science scholarship illuminating issues and trends in law, crime, and justice. Books in this series will appeal to criminologists, sociologists, and other social scientists, as well as policymakers, legal researchers, and practitioners.

1. **Criminal Law and Precrime**
   Legal Studies in Canadian Punishment and Surveillance in Anticipation of Criminal Guilt
   Richard Jochelson, James Gacek, Lauren Menzie, and Kirsten Kramar

2. **Manufacturing Crime**
   The Market's Role in Crime Control
   John Brent and Peter Kraska

3. **The Evolving Role of the Public Prosecutor**
   Challenges and Innovations
   Edited by Victoria Colvin and Philip Stenning

4. **Powers of the Prosecutor in Criminal Investigation**
   A Comparative Perspective
   Karolina Kremens

Powers of the Prosecutor in Criminal Investigation

A Comparative Perspective

Karolina Kremens

Routledge
Taylor & Francis Group
NEW YORK AND LONDON

First published 2021
by Routledge
605 Third Avenue, New York, NY 10158

and by Routledge
2 Park Square, Milton Park, Abingdon, Oxon OX14 4RN

Routledge is an imprint of the Taylor & Francis Group, an informa business

Library of Congress Cataloging-in-Publication Data
Names: Kremens, Karolina, author.
Title: Powers of the prosecutor in criminal investigation : a comparative perspective / Karolina Kremens.
Description: New York, NY ; Milton Park, Abingdon, Oxon : Routledge, 2021. | Includes bibliographical references and index.
Identifiers: LCCN 2020032430 (print) | LCCN 2020032431 (ebook) | ISBN 9780367862947 (hardback) | ISBN 9781003018247 (ebook)
Subjects: LCSH: Public prosecutors–United States. | Public prosecutors–European Union countries. | Criminal procedure–United States. | Criminal procedure–European Union countries. | Criminal investigation–United States. | Criminal investigation–European Union countries.
Classification: LCC K5425 .K74 2021 (print) | LCC K5425 (ebook) | DDC 345.4/01262–dc23
LC record available at https://lccn.loc.gov/2020032430
LC ebook record available at https://lccn.loc.gov/2020032431

ISBN: 978-0-367-86294-7 (hbk)
ISBN: 978-0-367-65558-7 (pbk)
ISBN: 978-1-003-01824-7 (ebk)

Typeset in Bembo
by Newgen Publishing UK

This work is a result of the research project no. 2014/15/D/HS5/00658 financed by the Polish National Science Center entitled "The Role of the Prosecutor in Criminal Investigation – comparative perspective".

For Adam – the IRONMAN

Contents

Preface and Acknowledgments xv
List of Abbreviations xviii

1 Introduction **1**
1.1 Vanishing Trials 1
1.2 State of the Art on the (Almost) Unlimited Powers of the Prosecutor in Criminal Proceedings 5
1.3 Aim of the Study 9
1.4 Scope of the Study 13
1.5 Methodology of the Study 17
1.6 Structure of the Study 19

2 Prosecution Systems Compared **27**
2.1 General Considerations 27
2.2 The Prosecution Service in Germany 32
2.2.1 Sources of Law Governing the German Prosecution Service 32
2.2.2 The Position of the German Prosecution Service in relation to the Judiciary and Executive 34
2.2.3 The Internal Independence of the Prosecutor within the Structure of the German Prosecution Service 36
2.3 The Prosecution System in Poland 38
2.3.1 Sources of Law Governing the Polish Prosecution Service 38
2.3.2 The Position of the Polish Prosecution Service in relation to the Judiciary and Executive 40
2.3.3 The Internal Independence of the Prosecutor within the Structure of the Polish Prosecution Service 42
2.4 The Prosecution System in Italy 45
2.4.1 Sources of Law Governing the Italian Prosecution Service 45

2.4.2 The Position of the Italian Prosecution Service in relation to the Judiciary and Executive 46
2.4.3 The Internal Independence of the Prosecutor within the Structure of the Italian Prosecution Service 48
2.5 The Prosecution System in the United States of America 51
2.5.1 Sources of Law Governing the US Prosecution Service 51
2.5.2 The Position of the US Prosecution Service in relation to the Judiciary and Executive 54
2.5.3 The Internal Independence of the Prosecutor within the Structure of the US Prosecution Service 60
2.6 Summary 66

3 Criminal Investigations Compared 74
3.1 General Considerations 74
3.2 Criminal Investigation in Germany 75
3.2.1 The Notion and Outline of Criminal Investigation 75
3.2.2 Prosecutorial Discretion 77
3.2.3 Prosecutorial Objectivity 80
3.3 Criminal Investigation in Poland 81
3.3.1 The Notion and Outline of Criminal Investigation 81
3.3.2 Prosecutorial Discretion 83
3.3.3 Prosecutorial Objectivity 87
3.4 Criminal Investigation in Italy 88
3.4.1 The Notion and Outline of Criminal Investigation 88
3.4.2 Prosecutorial Discretion 91
3.4.3 Prosecutorial Objectivity 94
3.5 Criminal Investigation in the United States of America 95
3.5.1 The Notion and Outline of Criminal Investigation 95
3.5.2 Prosecutorial Discretion 101
3.5.3 Prosecutorial Objectivity 104
3.6 Summary 107

4 Powers of the Prosecutor over Initiation of Investigation 116
4.1 General Considerations 116
4.2 Initiating Investigation in Germany 117
4.2.1 Threshold for Initiating Investigation 117
4.2.2 Procedure for Initiating Investigation 119
4.2.3 Authority Responsible for Initiating Investigation 121
4.3 Initiating Investigation in Poland 122
4.3.1 Threshold for Initiating Investigation 122
4.3.2 Procedure for Initiating Investigation 124
4.3.3 Authority Responsible for Initiating Investigation 127
4.4 Initiating Investigation in Italy 128
4.4.1 Threshold for Initiating Investigation 128

4.4.2 Procedure for Initiating Investigation 131
4.4.3 Authority Responsible for Initiating Investigation 133
4.5 Initiating Investigation in the United States of America 134
4.5.1 Threshold for Initiating Investigation 134
4.5.2 Procedure for Initiating Investigation 137
4.5.3 Authority Responsible for Initiating Investigation 139
4.6 Summary 141

5 Powers of the Prosecutor over the Conduct of Investigation 145
5.1 General Considerations 145
5.2 Conduct of Investigation in Germany 147
5.2.1 The Relationship between Prosecutor and Police 147
5.2.2 The Prosecutor's Supervisory Authority over Investigation 149
5.2.3 The Investigative Authority of the Prosecutor 153
5.2.4 The Role of the Parties in the Conduct of Investigation 155
5.2.5 The Judicial Involvement in the Conduct of Investigation 156
5.3 Conduct of Investigation in Poland 158
5.3.1 The Relationship between Prosecutor and Police 158
5.3.2 The Prosecutor's Supervisory Authority over Investigation 160
5.3.3 The Investigative Authority of the Prosecutor 163
5.3.4 The Role of the Parties in the Conduct of Investigation 165
5.3.5 The Judicial Involvement in the Conduct of Investigation 167
5.4 Conduct of Investigation in Italy 168
5.4.1 The Relationship between Prosecutor and Police 168
5.4.2 The Prosecutor's Supervisory Authority over Investigation 171
5.4.3 The Investigative Authority of the Prosecutor 173
5.4.4 The Role of the Parties in the Conduct of Investigation 175
5.4.5 The Judicial Involvement in the Conduct of Investigation 176
5.5 Conduct of Investigation in the United States of America 179
5.5.1 The Relationship between Prosecutor and Police 179
5.5.2 The Prosecutor's Supervisory Authority over Investigation 181
5.5.3 The Investigative Authority of the Prosecutor 187

5.5.4 The Role of the Parties in the Conduct of Investigation 193
5.5.5 The Judicial Involvement in the Conduct of Investigation 195
5.6 Summary 197

6 Powers of the Prosecutor over the Preliminary Charging 207
6.1 General Considerations 207
6.2 Preliminary Charging in Germany 210
6.2.1 General Considerations concerning Charging Decisions 210
6.2.2 Threshold for Preliminary Charging 214
6.2.3 Procedure for Preliminary Charging 215
6.2.4 Authority Responsible for Preliminary Charging 219
6.3 Preliminary Charging in Poland 221
6.3.1 General Considerations concerning Charging Decisions 221
6.3.2 Threshold for Preliminary Charging 225
6.3.3 Procedure for Preliminary Charging 227
6.3.4 Authority Responsible for Preliminary Charging 231
6.4 Preliminary Charging in Italy 233
6.4.1 General Considerations concerning Charging Decisions 233
6.4.2 Threshold for Preliminary Charging 236
6.4.3 Procedure for Preliminary Charging 237
6.4.4 Authority Responsible for Preliminary Charging 240
6.5 Preliminary Charging in the United States of America 241
6.5.1 General Considerations regarding Charging Decisions 241
6.5.2 Threshold for Preliminary Charging 247
6.5.3 Procedure for Preliminary Charging 249
6.5.4 Authority Responsible for Preliminary Charging 252
6.6 Summary 254

7 Powers of the Prosecutor over Imposition of Coercive Measures 262
7.1 General Considerations 262
7.2 Imposition of Coercive Measures in Germany 266
7.2.1 General Considerations on Search and Arrest 266
7.2.2 Procedure for Imposing Coercive Measures 268
7.2.3 Authority to Impose Coercive Measures 270
7.3 Imposition of Coercive Measures in Poland 272
7.3.1 General Considerations on Search and Arrest 272
7.3.2 Procedure for Imposing Coercive Measures 274

7.3.3 Authority to Impose Coercive Measures 276
7.4 Imposition of Coercive Measures in Italy 278
7.4.1 General Considerations on Search and Arrest 278
7.4.2 Procedure for Imposing Coercive Measures 280
7.4.3 Authority to Impose Coercive Measures 282
7.5 Imposition of Coercive Measures in the United States of America 284
7.5.1 General Considerations on Search and Arrest 284
7.5.2 Procedure for Imposing Coercive Measures 287
7.5.3 Authority to Impose Coercive Measures 290
7.6 Summary 292

8 Prosecutor's Powers to Discontinue Investigation 299
8.1 General Considerations 299
8.2 Discontinuation of Criminal Investigation in Germany 301
8.2.1 Threshold to Discontinue the Investigation 301
8.2.2 Procedure for Discontinuation of Investigation 303
8.2.3 Authority for Discontinuing Investigations 305
8.3 Discontinuation of Criminal Investigation in Poland 307
8.3.1 Threshold to Discontinue the Investigation 307
8.3.2 Procedure for Discontinuation of Investigation 309
8.3.3 Authority for Discontinuing Investigations 312
8.4 Discontinuation of the Criminal Investigation in Italy 313
8.4.1 Threshold to Discontinue the Investigation 313
8.4.2 Procedure for Discontinuation of Investigation 315
8.4.3 Authority for Discontinuing Investigations 318
8.5 Discontinuation of Criminal Investigation in the United States of America 319
8.5.1 Threshold to Discontinue the Investigation 319
8.5.2 Procedure for Discontinuation of Investigation 324
8.5.3 Authority for Discontinuing Investigations 327
8.6 Summary 329

9 Redefining Prosecutorial Powers during Criminal Investigation 335
9.1 Criminal Investigation Remastered 335
9.2 Prospects for Shaping Prosecutorial Powers during Criminal Investigation 336
9.3 Concluding Remarks 350

Index 353

Preface and Acknowledgments

This book is the result of a very long, sometimes overwhelming, but eventually very fulfilling and satisfactory period of research. Therefore, the list of institutions and people that I am indebted to is extremely long. The study was carried out with the financial support of the Polish National Science Center (Narodowe Centrum Nauki) that granted me funds that allowed my ideas and dreams to come true (research project no. 2014/15/D/HS5/00658 entitled "The Role of the Prosecutor in Criminal Investigation – comparative perspective"). Three universities have welcomed me generously and allowed me to conduct the research on their premises and provided me with hospitality and support: The University of Bologna, the University of Cologne, and the University of Connecticut.

This book would not have been possible without the constant support and assistance of Professor Thomas Weigend (University of Cologne), Professor Michele Caianiello (University of Bologna), and Professor Todd Fernow (University of Connecticut). It is difficult to find the appropriate words to express the gratitude I feel toward these three remarkable scholars that devoted their free time, wise advice, and—I hope I can say—friendship that allowed me to finish the book. Without you, Thomas, Michele, and Todd, this would have never happened.

There is also a long list of people whose words and insights echoed in my head long after our meetings and discussions ended. Some of them have supported my research directly and some may not even know what our brief discussions brought me to. Therefore, I wish to thank Mike Gailor, Paul Narducci, Marcia Pilsbury, James R. Turcotte, Tim Everett, Jenia I. Turner, Giulio Illuminati, Giulia Lasagni, Giuseppe di Giorno, Claus Kreß, Bettina Weisser, Elisa Hoven, Jacqueline Hodgson, Jenny McEwan, Andrea Ryan, Sabine Gless, Frank Verbruggen, Vanessa Fransen, Cezary Kulesza, Hanna Kuczyńska, Patrycja Matusz, Anna Śledzińska-Simon, Agnieszka Frąckowiak-Adamska, Marta Kłopocka-Jasińska, Jarosław Zagrodnik, and Dariusz Adamski. Thank you for shedding light when I was in the dark.

I also want to express gratitude to the McDougall Family and late Anne McDougall for the support that they offered me with the generous Edward Barry McDougall Memorial Scholarship, which allowed me to study in Ottawa in 2006. Even though this happened long before I started thinking about writing this book the experience that I had, thanks to them, marks the beginning of my amazing journey through the academic world, for which I will always be thankful. Canada and the University of Ottawa have always treated me in a very special way. Bruce Feldthusen, Adam Dodek, and especially David Paciocco—thanks to you also.

Carrying out this comparative study was an extremely demanding challenge for me. Thus, I would like to apologize in advance for providing a result that will certainly have a number of deficiencies. I am conscious that mistakes are always a part of comparative research. And even though I have spent endless hours on research and consultations, I am sure that the book is not free of errors. Moreover, I am fully aware of the limits of my language abilities. Writing an entire book in English certainly required skills that went far beyond my command of that language, and so I am very grateful to Dave Harrold and Martin Barr for providing excellent editing. All errors and flaws are entirely mine.

I am extremely grateful to my colleagues and fellow researchers at the Department of Criminal Procedure at the Faculty of Law, Administration, and Economics (University of Wrocław), who provide me with the unique opportunity of a daily exchange of ideas and thoughts. I take this opportunity to thank my boss Professor Jerzy Skorupka for inviting me over eight years ago to the Department and for his constant support, the trust, all the wise words, guidance, and direction throughout my journey. The research team that I am a proud part of is built on his idea. I hope that with this book, I am at least to some extent repaying my debts.

Now my special thanks go to my beloved and the one and only #teamkpk, especially Dorota Czerwińska and Dominika Czerniak my closest supporters in whom I could always confide and without whom all the exciting projects in which we engage in the Department would not be possible. To other colleagues, Kazimierz, Krzysztof and Artur, our PhDs, and students with whom we build the community on which I could always rely: my achievements are the result of our teamwork.

But there are no words in which I could express my gratitude to my dearest friend and remarkable research fellow Wojciech Jasiński. Without his encouragement, kind words, and priceless advices this book and everything that led me up to this point would never have happened. Wojtek—I still owe you!

I end by thanking my whole family, especially my parents Ella and Zdzichu, who gave me all my special powers, wings bigger than life, and who are without doubt the source of my self-confidence that allowed me to believe that I could write this book. I also would like to thank my two amazing children Karolinka Junior and Adaś Junior, who always keep me smiling and entertained. Thank you for putting up with my writing and editing. Also my amazing friends on both continents have played an important role in writing this book: Królik, Maja, Kluska, Marcin, Kaziu, Paulinka, Lara, Kurtis, Agusia, and others to whom I must apologize, as I am unable to name you all here: thank you so much for always believing in me. It means the world to me.

My final thoughts and the biggest and most sincere gratitude go to Adam—the fantastic Ironman to whom this book is dedicated. He constantly shows me what devotion and commitment to a goal mean. Adam: without your limitless support and your faith in me, this work and everything else that happened to me over the past 15 years, would not have been possible. This one is for you.

Abbreviations

CCO	*Gerichtsverfassungsgesetz* [Code of Court Organization]
CGS	General Statutes of Connecticut (Connecticut General Statutes)
CPB	Connecticut Practice Book
c.p.	*Codice Penale* [Italian Code of Criminal Law]
c.p.p.	*Codice di Procedura Penale* [Italian Code of Criminal Procedure]
DFS	ABA Criminal Justice Standards for the Defense Function
ECHR	European Convention on Human Rights and Fundamental Freedoms
FRCP	Federal Rules of Criminal Procedure
FRE	Federal Rules on Evidence
ICCPR	International Covenant on Civil and Political Rights
k.k.	*Kodeks karny* [Polish Code of Criminal Law]
k.p.k.	*Kodeks postępowania karnego* [Polish Code of Criminal Procedure]
NPS	NDAA National Prosecution Standards
PSA 1985	*Ustawa o Prokuraturze Polskiej Rzeczypospolitej Ludowej* [Polish Prosecution Service Act of 1985]
PSA 2016	*Ustawa Prawo o prokuraturze* [Polish Prosecution Service Act of 2016]
SPF	ABA Standards for Criminal Justice for the Prosecution Function
SPI	ABA Standards for Criminal Justice. Standards on Prosecutorial Investigations
StGB	*Strafgesetzbuch* [German Code of Criminal Law]
StPO	*Strafprozessordnung* [German Code of Criminal Procedure]
USC	Code of Laws of the United States of America

Chapter 1

Introduction

1.1 Vanishing Trials

The most popular image of criminal proceedings captured in the public imagination refers to the courtroom, where the guilt of the defendant is decided, in the presence of the curious, and even eager for revenge, audience gathered in that hall, with the meaningful participation of the prosecutor and defense counsels. Depending on the system of law where one was born and raised, this image may be complemented by a jury burdened with the obligation of deciding on the guilt of the accused, or a mixed tribunal in which jurors adjudicate together with a professional judge, while in other cases the judge sits alone. The location of actors of this peculiar theatre may move along the courtroom. The parties may sit at right angles to the bench or facing the judge. The testifying witness may be standing in the middle of the room in front of the judge or sitting next to her facing the interrogator and the public. Sometimes even the costumes—the gowns, the wigs, become an important part of the play and in other environments just nice suits and ordinary clothes are enough. In any case, however, the courtroom, an impartial decision maker, witness testimonies, presentation of evidence, as well as prosecution and defense arguments remain in the collective imagination as an image of the criminal process.

It also seems that in minds of those who write and teach about the law this picture remains equally valid. All academics begin their tale of the criminal justice system by explaining the importance of the trial, as it is the leading feature of the criminal process. Of course, at some point they will also pay attention to violations of individual rights during the process, methods of collecting evidence during investigation, or the available remedies and manners in which the judgment can be appealed. But eventually, the central point of any criminal procedure academic course will be the structure of the trial, the procedural roles played by its actors, admissibility of evidence, and issues related to the presence of the accused in the courtroom. It will be presented as having the most significant impact on the criminal justice system as a whole. Frequently, among the compulsory courses to be tackled by young adepts of law are moot courts and mock trials, where they may practice their oratory skills, as well as the ability to question witnesses or submit motions. Such activities are looked forward to and are strongly desired by young lawyers wishing to enter the real world of legal practice. This happens regardless of the latitude in which their school of law is situated and system of criminal process in which young lawyers take their education.

Apparently, only practitioners who have spent enough time outside the courtroom are under no illusions. They very clearly perceive the changes that have taken place in criminal justice systems in which the importance of the trial as a venue where the fate of the defendant is decided has vanished. One might smile when Daniel Kaffee played by Tom Cruise enters the courtroom as a young but already experienced JAG lawyer in one of the scenes of the iconic movie *A Few Good Men* and says with unfailing delight mixed with fear "So this is what a courtroom looks like!" This indicates that he had never been in a courtroom before, since his reputation as a successful and tenacious lawyer had been built on the exploitation of plea-bargaining mechanism and not his litigation skills that would require courtroom experience. This scene was filmed more than 30 years ago and even though it refers to the military proceedings there is no doubt that it is a good example of what became an everyday reality not only in the US courthouse, but it is increasingly becoming the unfortunate truth for all criminal justice systems.

The comparative law literature has noted and broadly described the phenomenon of criminal cases decided out of trial through the negotiations leading to conviction and all other distinct forms of avoiding this form of adjudication.[1] The trend originated in the USA and has spread to the other common-law countries.[2] The statistics are merciless. A study from 2008 shows that in the USA almost 90 percent of all criminal cases are resolved in plea bargaining.[3] Some older works report that only about 3 percent of cases in that country are dealt with by the way of trial and that judges are conducting only about two trials each month on average.[4] And even more striking are data for the federal courts system providing that 97.3 percent convictions are a result of guilty pleas.[5] This is a result of many years of trying to overcome an overload of criminal cases entering the court system.

On the other hand, in Continental European countries, these mechanisms are perceived as relatively new. In 2010 when Wade presented the results of

1 Langer (2004); Turner (2009); Thaman (2010); Hodgson (2015).
2 Turner (2012); Vogel (2019).
3 Gramckow (2008), p. 390.
4 See the studies from 1983 and 2003 cited by Jacoby and Ratledge (2016), p. 88.
5 Brown (2019), p. 544.

a collective comparative study on the issue, the so-called negotiated case-settlement procedures were treated as a "new trend."[6] At that point she was not even able to gather statistical data from all researched countries. But even then, it was clear that this was the direction in which the criminal process had been moving for some time. The current data gathered among the European countries prove that the "new trend" became solid and develops further.[7] Currently, the majority of criminal cases are resolved without trial. In 2009 in Germany only 10 percent of cases in which the police referred an identified suspect to the prosecutor went to trial.[8] In 2012, 77 percent of cases involving known suspects were dismissed for lack of sufficient evidence or for policy reasons and 52 percent of the remaining cases were disposed of by penal order.[9] In Poland more than 54 percent of cases filed yearly with the court are resolved without a trial, as a result of plea-bargained agreements and other forms of trial-waiver procedures.[10] In Italy the popularity of the Italian version of plea-bargaining called *pattegiamento* is distinctively lower, yet other forms of adjudicating out of trial or in a shortened form of proceedings appear to make up for it.[11]

It should not go unnoticed that the disappearance of the trial is not only the result of negotiated agreements concluded by the court's decision to convict and sentence the defendant without a trial. The legal inventions are much broader. As has been presented in various studies, the variety of options in that regard encompasses e.g. conditional disposals, penal orders, and discontinuation of proceedings based on public interest grounds.[12] These decisions to some extent are made by an impartial adjudicator with the prosecutor's consent but in case of discontinuations based on public interest usually they remain purely within the scope of prosecutorial powers. One can therefore notice a common ground for these decisions. First of all, they all add to the replacement of the trial with some other form of adjudication. This results in a major reinforcement of the significance of the criminal investigation as the only phase of criminal process where the defendant is faced with the criminal justice system machinery and where evidence

6 Wade (2010), p. 83.
7 Cf. Fair Trials (2017).
8 Weigend (2012), p. 384.
9 Weigend and Turner (2014), p. 84 note 14.
10 See the most recent data from 2019 regarding Poland in *Sprawozdanie z działalności powszechnych jednostek organizacyjnych prokuratury za rok 2019*, https://pk.gov.pl/wp-content/uploads/2020/03/PK-P1K.pdf (accessed 12.05.2020), p. 6. Note that in 2019, while 302,668 cases were filed with court, at the same time as many as 406,770 were dismissed by the prosecutor (Cf. Jasiński and Kremens (2019), p. 42).
11 Panzavolta (2004), p. 621; Gialuz (2017), p. 46–51.
12 See in comparative perspective especially Luna and Wade (2010); Jehle and Wade (2010). Cf. very recent work by Langer (2020).

is gathered and to some extent tested. As a consequence the defendant is exposed for the sake of those actors that dominate the criminal investigation i.e. police and prosecutor.

The concept that the criminal investigation has gained tremendous importance at the expense of the trial is not a novel observation. Caianiello noted in 2016 that

> in the past two decades the trial phase has lost its relevance and that the crucial decisions for the outcome of criminal proceedings are made more and more frequently during the investigation and pretrial phase, where the prosecutor can operate with greater discretion.[13]

This has been concluded based on the Italian system but should be considered as equally valid for other countries. It has also been observed by Huber that trials should be considered as diminishing in their importance not only due to the constantly growing number of decisions regarding the criminal liability of defendant taken out of trial; it is so also because "the outcome of the criminal process today is in fact determined to a large extent during the pre-trial phase."[14] Even if the process is ultimately taken to the courtroom and decided in an adversarial atmosphere by the trier of fact, the final decision that is to be made has already been largely predetermined by what has happened during criminal investigation. This is in part because the complexity of many investigative measures has reached such a level of professionalization that the presentation of evidence is often just a repetition of what has been done during criminal investigation. And as Elsner and Peters observed of the German system "[t]he investigative stage and the quality of evidence found in it will influence the procedural path and result of the main proceedings; it is therefore a focal point of criminal proceedings."[15] These tendencies were also recognized by Weisser, who suggested that the reduction of criminal proceedings to the pretrial process calls for reinterpretation of guarantees as applied at this stage.[16]

The trials are gone. And they are not likely to ever come back. Only a small number of carefully selected cases is nowadays perceived as deserving a full trial. We can all keep dreaming about the system where the emphasis in taking evidence is put on trial and where the cases are decided publicly in an open court by an impartial adjudicator. We can also try to fix the system

13 Caianiello (2016), p. 3.
14 Huber (2008), p. 357.
15 Elsner and Peters (2010), p. 227.
16 The author refers to conventional guarantees as prescribed in the ECHR but this is so also in the context of legal systems remaining outside of the Council of Europe (see Weisser (2019) p. 113).

by depenalizing over-criminalized behavior and probably we should keep trying. But we should also be aware that such dreams most likely will never come true and that the populistic narrative calling for criminalization of more and more far-reaching areas of human life is not easy to overcome. Hoping that we will come back to the model of criminal justice to which we all once aspired seems utopic. Therefore, we should rather try to find a way to consciously deal with the criminal process in the form to which it transformed. In this model, the criminal investigation constantly grows in importance. Wade is definitely right when she states that:

> our criminal justice systems have departed from the ideals with which they were framed in far more humdrum ways. Day to day challenges and practicalities, as well as overloading, have led to pragmatic practices [...] This can be seen particularly well in relation to prosecution services and the means they use to drive efficient case-ending practices.[17]

And since the prosecutor has gained the position of the powerful master, influential leader, and the dominant ruler of this stage of criminal process, looking into her responsibilities and powers during criminal investigation seems to be indispensable.

1.2 State of the Art on the (Almost) Unlimited Powers of the Prosecutor in Criminal Proceedings

Thus, over the last century the prosecutor became perhaps the most powerful figure within criminal justice systems, considered as "the centerpiece of the process."[18] The rise of her powers has taken a longer period of time, but the recent decades have shown an even more dramatic increase in the attention that this process has deserved. Naturally the role that prosecutors play in the criminal justice system has been grabbing the attention of scholars for some time now and it has been tackled from distinct perspectives, including the comparative one.

A classic comparative work on the prosecution systems in twenty-five EU states edited in 2004 by Tak covered an interesting range of issues such as the relationship between the public prosecution and the police, between the public prosecution and the executive as well as the role of the prosecutor in court and with regard to execution of sanction.[19] The methodology adopted for this work can be described as a country-related approach, where

17 Wade (2016), p. 66.
18 Gilliéron (2014), p. vii.
19 Tak (2004).

regulations of each state were presented separately according to the adopted scheme by different authors usually originating from the country on which they had written. Based on the same structural premises a 2006 study, edited by Jehle and Wade had a much stronger focus on statistical data and an aim to discover methods by which prosecution services in six countries deal with a backlog of criminal cases.[20] A similar approach was also applied in an analysis of prosecution services of nine states from 2008 funded by the Open Society Institute in Sofia with a stronger focus on structure of the prosecution service as well as description of the accountability of prosecutors and their independence.[21] The most recent study of this kind, edited in 2013 by Ligeti, provided an analysis of 24 legal systems of EU Member States with a focus on the investigative and prosecuting stages of criminal proceedings as well as the rights of the accused during the criminal process.[22] This was done with a further aim of providing a draft set of model rules for the procedure of the European Public Prosecutor's Office.[23]

Likewise, single-authored books approaching the position held by public prosecutors from a comparative perspective can be found very easily. One of the classic works is a book authored by Fionda discussing English and Welsh, Scottish, Dutch, and German systems with a particular focus on the discretionary powers of the prosecutor.[24] Research by Marguery focused on the history and organization of the prosecution services, in particular with relation to the executive in Czechia, Netherlands, France, and Poland.[25] A more recent study by Gilliéron analyzed the public prosecution services in the USA, Switzerland, France, and Germany with a focus on the case-ending decisions in each country.[26] Another work by Kuczyńska, devoted to the position of the prosecutor in the International Criminal Court, provided comparative analysis of public prosecution systems in the USA, Poland, and Germany.[27] In fact, for many years, scholars conducting research primarily on international criminal procedure have produced marvelous works on comparative criminal procedure including on the issue of prosecutorial powers.[28]

Though the descriptive form of analysis, usually followed by critical evaluation and some reform proposals, seems a style of choice for the discussion on various roles that the prosecutor serves in criminal justice systems,

20 Jehle and Wade (2010).
21 Open Society Institute Sofia (2008).
22 Ligeti (2013).
23 Ligeti (2016).
24 Fionda (2003).
25 Marguery (2008).
26 Gilliéron (2014).
27 Kuczyńska (2015).
28 See e.g. Orie (2002); Keen (2004); Ambos and Bock (2012).

one can find in recent years a rise of the problem-related approach in edited volumes. One such major work, edited by Luna and Wade, concentrated on the convergence of prosecutorial functions among states in Europe and the USA.[29] More recently the changes in the role of the prosecutor both during investigation and while prosecuting cases has been discussed by scholars in a work on countries not considered before such as Australia, Nigeria, Finland, and Denmark.[30] A similar approach was adopted for another work edited by Langer and Sklansky devoted to analysis of the relationship between the prosecutor and democracy also from the perspective of prosecutorial discretionary powers.[31]

The presented state of the art of the current discussion on the growing powers of the prosecutor in criminal justice systems should not be perceived as covering all topics within that subject to the same extent. Naturally, for the reasons discussed in the previous section, the vast majority of conducted research focused on the issue of prosecutorial discretion and the results of prosecutorial decision-making.[32] Indeed, during the past decades, plea bargaining became a "hub of comparative scholarship on the prosecutorial functions."[33] This seems to be a legitimate choice since the impact of the prosecutor on the outcome of criminal investigation when undertaking the decision whether to drop a case or to file it with a court is undeniable, regardless of normative limitations imposed on the system. Moreover, with the enormous overload of cases that the criminal justice systems experienced in the last decades, prosecutors have gradually begun to obtain unique abilities to undertake some case-ending decisions, even without any involvement of the court; the powers once reserved only for judges.[34] This change in the role of the prosecutor must be perceived as particularly empowering if one understands that the primary role of the prosecutor was to prosecute cases—where the word "prosecutor" comes from—and not to decide on them. Therefore, it is no wonder that by allocation of these powers to prosecutors, these actors have grown into the main players dominating the criminal process. Obviously, this issue has been most extensively tackled from the US perspective where the US understanding of discretion gives the prosecutor extraordinary scope of powers,[35] but this has been also analyzed

29 Luna and Wade (2012a).
30 Colvin and Stenning (2019).
31 Langer and Sklansky (2018).
32 See among many others Pizzi (1993); Gershman (2011); LaFave (1970); Luna and Wade (2010); Wade (2013).
33 Luna and Wade (2012b), p. xvi.
34 Cf. Luna and Wade (2010).
35 It is argued that US prosecutors enjoy powers that are "unique and unparalleled elsewhere in the world" (Anderson (2001), p. 3).

from the Continental viewpoint focusing on case-ending choices made on the European continent.[36] And, obviously, if the system is overloaded and not every case reaches public trial it is necessary to examine who undertakes decisions in such process and selects cases to be decided without trial, and how. The observed secrecy of negotiations conducted between a powerful prosecutor and defense counsel representing the accused especially calls for public scrutiny. As an example, recently some scholars even argued for the involvement of judges in plea bargaining to enhance the transparency of this process and making it fair and procedurally just.[37]

Another very current discussion focuses on the various issues involving the misconduct of prosecutors, miscarriages of justice, and wrongful convictions. The attention has concentrated on such issues among others as proper evidence disclosure and prosecutorial accountability for mistakes.[38] Also, the activity of the Innocence Project initiative,[39] working on exoneration of wrongfully convicted individuals, has made the issue of prosecutorial misconduct an important subject in public discussions among societies. This debate, however, was slowly replaced, at least in USA, by the research relating to the mass incarceration and pressing need for bail reforms.[40] This is closely related to the role that the prosecutor plays within the charging process and regarding available alternatives to pretrial detention.

At the same time, considerably less attention has been paid to the role that the prosecutor plays during criminal investigation and the powers that are vested in her at this stage of criminal process. One of the reasons for such reduced interest might be that criminal investigation and collecting evidence are seen as a part of the police agenda, which seems not to give too much space for prosecutorial involvement. This is somewhat understandable in common-law countries where there is a widely accepted presumption that the prosecutor in those systems is actually nonexistent during criminal investigation.[41] But not enough attention is paid to this problem even in

36 See among many others Langbein (1974, 1979); Weigend (2008); Turner (2009); Rauxloh (2011); Turner (2012); Caianiello (2016). Note that for instance in Germany this problem was detected long ago. Exactly 40 years have passed since Erhard Kausch published his book on the growing role of the prosecutor in the German criminal process, posing a striking question of whether this official is in fact "a judge prior to the judge" (Kausch (1980)), a topic picked up by Weigend (2012).

37 Turner (2006); King and Wright (2016).

38 See e.g. Zacharias and Green (2009); Mosteller (2012); Soubise and Woolley (2018); Roach (2019).

39 www.innocenceproject.org

40 See among many others Alkon (2015); Barkow (2019); Bazelon (2019).

41 An interesting example is England and Wales where until 1985 the prosecution service did not even exist (Lewis (2012), p. 214–219).

Continental countries that usually provide for stronger prosecutorial supervision over formal and official investigation.[42]

1.3 Aim of the Study

As discussed above, the trial has lost its importance. And regardless of the system of law in question, comparable, if not greater significance should be attached to the stage preceding the trial—investigation. Theoretically, the investigation remains subordinate to court proceedings, aimed at gathering material that will be presented as evidence during trial. However, due to the dramatic increase in the number of procedural agreements where the judgment or other case-ending decision is based solely on the findings of the investigation, the relevance of that phase of the criminal process has substantially increased.

Therefore, it is crucial to look closer at how investigation is being conducted, who controls it, what decisions are undertaken at this stage of the criminal process, and how they are influenced. The basic issue to be answered in this work, is the question of how to shape the investigation and in particular what should be the role of the prosecutor during this stage of the criminal process in a system in which trials have largely vanished. The aim is to find a solution for a system in which the assessment of evidence no longer takes place during a public trial where evidence is directly examined and analyzed, but rather when it is done in camera on the basis of limited evidence gathered during the investigation. In this work I will argue that while increasing the participation of the prosecutor in the investigation improves the quality of the investigation and allows for more careful scrutiny of police behavior, this involvement should have its limits, so as to not adversely affect the prosecutor's objectivity, necessary when decision to prosecute is about to be made. For that reason, this work aims to explore the ways in which prosecutorial powers are visible at different phases of criminal investigation and to provide limits to the level of involvement that the prosecutor should have during investigation.

To that extent two extreme models can be denoted which can be easily associated with two commonly discussed systems of criminal procedure: inquisitorial and adversarial. It should be noted that the use of these two terms must be considered as imprecise.[43] The term "inquisitorial" is used to describe the Continental system of law (i.e. civil law system), while those

42 But see as a good example of works focusing at least partially on that issue by Jehle and Wade (2010) and Ligeti (2013). Another example of comparative scholarship in that sphere is a work based on examples of France and Sweden (Taleb and Ahlstrand (2011)); see also Braum (2012).

43 See comprehensive analysis of the use of those terms in Ambos and Bock (2012), pp. 488–491.

used in Anglo-American parts of the world, are "adversarial," "accusatorial," or "common law." It should be noted that the term "inquisitorial" is often associated with a system that prevailed in Europe until the first half of the nineteenth century and it references proceedings that once allowed secret preliminary investigations and torture as employed by the Holy Inquisition.[44] Therefore, the use of such terms as "mixed" or "reformed" instead of "inquisitorial" may be sometimes observed.[45] But it is no longer accurate to think of the modern inquisitorial system as a system of organized repression in which suspects have no rights and all power is concentrated in the hands of a single official who is quite prepared to abuse this power to secure convictions.[46] This is also a result of adoption of the broadly recognized principle of fair trial that excludes the possibility of objectification of the suspect through such international instruments as the European Convention on Human Rights[47] and International Covenant on Civil and Political Rights.[48] Some scholars also assert that the terms "accusatorial" and "adversarial" should not be used synonymously.[49] But despite those arguments, since the terms seem to have an adopted meaning and they are widely used, for the purpose of this work, "inquisitorial system," "civil law system" and "Continental system" are used synonymously, as are "adversarial system," "common law system," and "Anglo-American system," respectively.

Notwithstanding the continuous criticism of the use of this distinction in the context of comparative criminal justice and accepting that there is no strict dichotomy between Continental and common-law legal traditions,[50] these two models may be presented as containing features that allow differentiating one another and they may also work as a framework for the discussion on the role of the prosecutor during criminal investigation and problems that arrive with distinct approaches within each model. The way in which the relations between the individual participants in the process are set

44 Damaška (1973), p. 556.

45 For an explanation on differences between these terms from a historical perspective, see Esmein (1913), p. 11.

46 Keen (2004), p. 769.

47 Convention for the Protection of Human Rights and Fundamental Freedoms adopted on November 4, 1950, entered into force on September 3, 1953 (hereafter ECHR).

48 International Covenant on Civil and Political Rights adopted on December 16, 1966, entered into force on March 23, 1976, 999 UNTS 171 (hereafter ICCPR).

49 Goldstein (1974), pp. 1016–1017 (the author explains that "'[a]dversary' refers to a method of resolving disputes and takes its contours from the contested trial" while "accusatorial ... is a classic procedural model that encompasses not only an adversary trial procedure but also other fundamental premises").

50 This traditional classification has been criticized in literature including by Damaška (1973), 556 and more recently by Langer (2014), pp. 887–912. Cf. Bradley (1996), p. 474 where the author claims that the differences between the Anglo-American and the Continental system have begun to diminish.

is of great importance in any legal system, regardless of whether it is inquisitorial or adversarial. Similarly, criminal proceedings must be structured in a way that allows for sentencing the guilty and acquitting the innocent but equally important is respect for the rights of the individual which remains true for all systems.

Obviously, as with every presentation of extremes and models, this one is oversimplified. But this also means that between these two there is a space that may constitute a common ground. This can be reduced to the question of whether the inquisitorial or adversarial way of conducting a criminal trial determines the shape of criminal investigation, which would govern the level of engagement of the prosecutor during the first phase of the criminal process. This book argues the opposite; that the shape of the criminal process whether inquisitorial or adversarial is not determinative of the role that the prosecutor should play during criminal investigation. This naturally leads us to question how the system should be construed.

The adversarial model is built upon the assumption that the outcome of investigation will be verified during court proceedings. The long, public, oral trial with direct presentation of evidence in an adversarial environment is aimed at careful evaluation of evidence collected during criminal investigation. When such tenets of the criminal process are met, the prosecutorial engagement during criminal investigation is not necessary. Here, the investigation may be short, informal, unofficial, and conducted only by the police with no external control, since the trial in such a system becomes a scene where police investigative actions are checked as to whether they were justified and conducted lawfully. The mechanisms adopted for such trial, with exclusionary rules and strict admissibility conditions, serve as sufficient deterrence mechanisms. Here the criminal investigation is focused only on finding enough material to bring charges against an individual. In this model the prosecutor receives a case from the police and evaluates the chances of conviction and does not engage herself in any way in directing the police during investigation. The prosecutor's task is to prosecute, thus becoming an agent of the state against the individual.

The only problem is that such a model no longer exists. As Brown suggested "when pleas replace trials, most of the systemic components of public adjudication that serve the objectives of factual reliability and accurate normative judgment are missing."[51] As a consequence, this leads to the lack of any scrutiny of police activities within the scope of the criminal process in a way to which the adversarial system has got us used to. Therefore, the disappearance of criminal trials moves attention to criminal investigation as the scene of ultimate state–individual interaction, and asks how this stage of the criminal process should be controlled and by whom. If the outcome of criminal

51 Brown (2012), p. 204.

investigation is not to be verified during the trial and, virtually unquestioned, sets a basis for a plea-bargained judgment or any other concluding decision, should it be just the police taking part in investigation, or should this phase be supervised by another official, namely public prosecutor? And, more importantly, how should the decision-making process during certain crucial phases of criminal investigations be made and by whom?

This is where the inquisitorial model, distinguished by the strong involvement of the prosecutor in criminal investigation, comes into its own. Here, the trial is frequently reduced and aimed just at the confirmation of the pretrial findings. Instead of careful examination of evidence during the trial, official and formal investigation is being conducted when all of the evidence is being tested for its admissibility. In that system the public prosecutor, perceived as an objective figure and representing the public interest, oversees all police actions. Here the prosecutor maintains full control over investigation and police actions, frequently actively participating in the conduct of investigative measures alongside the police. In this model the prosecutor is seen as an objective figure obliged to look both for incriminating as well as exonerating evidence as early as during investigation. This is the result of the assumption that official investigation into the crime should be carried out to establish the truth under the scrutiny of a neutral official.

The question that needs to be answered is whether, as the adjudication at the trial disappears, the Continental approach should become the benchmark for the investigation in the new reality that we face. This appears as a tempting scenario since the Continental countries seems to have found a solution for the lack of adversarial trial—an intense prosecutorial engagement in the criminal investigation and prosecutor's intense control over the police work. Perhaps we should call for the same answer also for these systems that just recently resigned from trials.

But the model in which the prosecutor remains active during criminal investigation has another side to it. Early engagement of the prosecutor in the investigation creates the risk that the decision to prosecute will be infected by subjectivity leading to inaccurate decisions. The strong impact of the prosecutor on the criminal investigation makes her less capable of making an objective decision when evaluating evidence and deciding whether to bring charges, due to the tunnel vision often observed in such cases. Moreover, a close relationship developed between police and prosecution service makes the matter even worse. Therefore, it is rather necessary to balance the adequate prosecutorial control over criminal investigation without causing a threat to the objectivity of its outcome.

This leads to and even more delicate problem. For it is not only an issue of adequately collected evidence during investigation that may or may not constitute the basis for conviction or acquittal. There is also the problem of building adequate mechanisms protecting an individual during the course of criminal investigation, which concerns in particular the suspect but also the victim. The danger of abuse in conducting criminal investigation for the sake of effectiveness remains a legitimate concern. While efficiency of criminal proceedings is crucial, it has been known for centuries that there is no efficiency without implementation of procedural guarantees.[52] Taking into account that other forms of reaction against improper police behavior, such as disciplinary proceedings or civil actions undertaken against officers, are usually rare and frequently ineffective, prosecutorial involvement in criminal investigation and accepting this type of scrutiny might be considered as an appealing choice. This, however, raises important questions, as to whether the public prosecutor may be suitable to protect society from such abuses; if so, how to define such a role. Is the answer to constant abuse of individuals' rights within criminal proceedings a system where the prosecutor makes all the decisions, especially those that infringe individuals' rights, such as search or arrest? Many countries differ on that matter, by either allowing only the judge to undertake such decisions or investing such powers in the prosecutor. Thus, much weight should be attached to the problem of striking a balance between the need for increased protection of the suspect during the course of investigation—including the investigation's transparency—while ensuring the effectiveness of criminal proceedings.

Therefore, this study aspires to give an answer to the question of **to what extent the engagement of the prosecutor in criminal investigation could be a response to changes that the criminal process encounters in its drive to diminish trials for the sake of efficiency and expediency of criminal proceedings**. Since a change in the way investigations are conducted seems inevitable, the engagement of the prosecutor during criminal investigation may work as a safeguard enhancing the quality and, most of all, fairness of the criminal process when cases are not being subjected to the careful scrutiny of a judge during trial. As there are definitely pros and cons to such resolution the limits of such engagement should be explored.

1.4 Scope of the Study

Primarily, the scope of this work is determined by the focus on the prosecutor as the main actor and central figure in criminal proceedings and investigation. Both concepts—prosecutor and investigation—at first blush seem to have an adopted meaning. However, since this work focuses on

52 Braum (2012), p. 68, quoting Carl Joseph Anton Mittermaier, *Deutsches Strafverfahren*, Band I (1845), p. 164.

the comparative method, such assumption may be inherently false. The belief that certain legal concepts are understood in the same way regardless of the state and legal system in which they are rooted, usually leads to misunderstandings and confusions. Therefore, how the term "prosecutor" is understood in the researched countries will be analyzed in Chapter 2 and the same will be done for "investigation" in Chapter 3. This will be done with an aim of finding common ground for analysis before engaging in further discussions on the prosecutorial role during criminal investigation.

Second, the scope of this work has been determined through selection of countries that are subjected to the analysis. Four countries have been chosen for this research: Germany, Poland, Italy, and the USA. The approach adopted in preliminary research that led to the selection of states was to provide the diversity and fair representation of models of prosecutorial activity during criminal investigation. Despite the problem of classifying national laws into legal families according to taxonomic criteria, the aim was to choose countries representing both the adversarial and inquisitorial systems of law.[53]

At one end of the line leading from inquisitorial systems to adversarial ones, literature traditionally positions *Germany*. With well-developed criminal procedure laws dating from the nineteenth century with a mode of a trial led by an active judge, Germany is considered as a mother system for many Continental countries. Surprisingly, in some ways the German system departed from some typical inquisitorial features such as prosecutorial ability to issue arrest or search warrants.[54] Nevertheless, some traditional inquisitorial mechanisms such as the judge's awareness of the contents of the dossier before the commencement of the trial, active judicial participation during trial, and the judge's obligation to establish the truth makes it impossible for this system to be considered more adversarial than inquisitorial.

The second country selected for this analysis is *Poland*. It has been a natural choice because of the nationality of the author of this book. However, this is not the only reason for its selection. The intention was to choose a country that is less frequently picked in the comparative law debate, to broaden the scope of comparative discourse in the field of criminal procedure. Poland is also a country that for many years remained under the Soviet regime, which made an impact on its criminal procedure. For this reason, Poland is to some extent representative of those countries that formed part of the old Eastern bloc. Moreover, despite 2019 celebration of the thirtieth anniversary of Poland's move from communism to democracy, the drive to democratize

53 See critically on taxonomy of states, Glenn (2008).

54 This leads some scholars to highlight the "hybrid" nature of criminal procedure in this country as e.g. Huber (2008), p. 283. But see Boyne who from the perspective of a US researcher consistently calls the German system "inquisitorial" ((2014), pp. 14, 16).

state authorities has not always been successful, which is particularly true of the prosecution service. This is evidenced by the fact that the current shape of the Polish prosecution service has not been significantly modified since 1989, and the changes introduced in 2016 seem even to be going back to old patterns. It should also be mentioned that Poland has a short but interesting history of departure from the inquisitorial model, when the law based on the adversarial system was enforced for a period of only eight months (July 2015–April 2016).[55] This should be also taken into account when the discussion on the convergence between systems takes place.

An almost natural choice for the comparative legal analysis in the field of criminal procedure is *Italy*. This state serves as a great point of reference since it is a fascinating example of a country that, being traditionally associated with an inquisitorial system, has shifted toward the adversarial model through an almost epic change of the Code of Criminal Procedure in 1988.[56] Therefore, it is worth examining how this new approach has changed the Italian model of criminal investigation and whether the position of the prosecutor and other actors at this stage of criminal process resemble the adversarial example to which Italy had been aspiring when adopting the new model of criminal process.

Finally, the *United States* has been chosen as exemplar of the adversarial model. With a long-established tradition of jury trial, strong discretionary powers of the prosecutor, and the concept of active parties during trial, the USA seems a good starting point for the discussion on the position and role that the prosecutor plays during criminal investigation. Due to the large number of legal regimes provided by 50 states together with the federal system, one state (Connecticut) has been chosen as a reference point of specific legal provisions and case law. One of the reasons for this choice was that prosecutors in that state are appointed and not chosen in general elections, and this was one of the first US states to introduce the prosecution service as far as in 1704. It shall be added that choosing the USA might be seen as out of place within this work, not only because the adversariality is so foreign to the other selected states, but because the USA is perhaps the most "extreme" form of adversariality. But this is exactly what makes it the best choice for contrasting the features of the Continental system in an interesting perspective.

Selecting countries for comparative analysis is always subjective. Restricting ourselves to a certain group of states will always be burdened with an error. The number of legal systems under analysis can be extended endlessly and always

55 See Kremens (2020), pp. 126–129.

56 See on the Italian reform of the criminal process, e.g. Amodio and Selvaggi (1989); Panzavolta (2004); Illuminati (2005).

the question can be asked why, for instance, France or Canada should not be included. Analyzing more countries will always enhance the quality of analysis and conclusions. However, there are two reasons for limiting the choice to the selected four.

First, the intention was to make an in-depth analysis of certain legal institutions at various stages of investigation. This requires not only describing their shape, but also understanding the environment in which they operate. The comparative research conducted for the purpose of this work over the years in relation to the USA, Italy, and Germany, not to mention Poland allowed me to understand more deeply the relations between legal institutions within each system and to draw conclusions of a far-reaching nature which would not be the case with other countries I am less familiar with. It is also not without significance that I had the opportunity to observe the operation of the criminal justice systems in these four countries in practice, to talk to practitioners, including numerous prosecutors, judges, and private practitioners, and to observe their daily work. As a result, these four countries seemed the most natural choice for conducting a thorough comparative research.

Second, I acknowledge that in some inquisitorial countries for many centuries, the investigation was vested not in the prosecutor but in the investigating judge (*juge d'instruction*). As an independent magistrate the investigative judge is responsible for conducting investigation by determining its direction and executing certain investigative actions such as interrogating the suspect and witnesses, as well as ordering searches and seizures.[57] For this reason, readers might expect to see included here one of the countries using this institution. However, in recent years, Continental systems still using this institution either have abolished the investigative judge completely (usually splitting her competencies between the prosecutor and the judge for preliminary investigation)[58] or significantly have limited her engagement in criminal proceedings.[59] As a result, the investigating judge participates in the investigation only occasionally, in a small fraction of cases and her importance and influence on the criminal justice system is constantly decreasing. Given this including such discussion seems of limited value.

57 See on the discussion regarding the investigating judge in US literature, Luna and Wade (2010), pp. 1432–1435. See also extensively on the French investigating judge, Hodgson (2005), pp. 65–85; Soubise and Woolley (2018), pp. 609–619.

58 Germany abolished the investigative judge (*Untersuchungrichter*) in 1975 by introducing the judge of the investigation (*Ermittlungsrichter*). Italy did the same in 1989 replacing the investigative judge (*giudice istruttore*) with the judge for preliminary investigation (*giudice per le indagini preliminari*). In Poland the abolishment of the investigative judge (*sędzia śledczy*) took place in 1949 but was not replaced with a judicial figure devoted to controlling the coercive measures undertaken during investigation.

59 According to French statistics less than 2 percent of cases are dealt with by the investigative judge (Soubise and Woolley (2018), p. 610).

1.5 Methodology of the Study

The methodology of this book follows the comparative method. It is believed that this allows for showing distinct perspectives and different resolutions to the same problem that all societies encounter. To enable comparative analysis the law of four chosen states will be discussed. To overcome some obstacles of comparative research being conducted by one researcher on four countries, three means have been employed simultaneously. First, the methodology adopted in this work combines a classic study based on legal acts and case law as well as literature that provide in-depth justification and explanation of legal solutions as adopted in each state. Second, the choice of countries as used in this work has been, to some degree, determined through the fairly extensive number of scholarly works written in English language that facilitates comparative research. This is particularly needed when terminological problems come into play. Finally, the research has included consultations with scholars and practitioners from all four states. The meetings and discussions have significantly improved understanding of how legal provisions are employed in practice. They allowed for filling gaps, clarifying interpretation of certain provisions, and opening new areas of analysis not previously visible.

The structure of this book is informed by adopting a comparative perspective. This demands some broader explanation. One of the established methods of research and a proven way of constructing works on a comparative law is to start with presenting separate reports for each of the chosen countries.[60] According to this method, the objective reports, free from critical evaluation, should be presented as being just a preliminary step before making an actual comparison.[61] This method, which may be called a country-related approach, seems to be a generally accepted method of presenting comparative research on the role of the prosecutor[62] as well as more generally in the field of criminal procedure.[63] Not all cited works, however, after presenting objective reports on each country are followed by actual comparative analysis.

Despite the recognition and popularity of said method of conducting comparative research, for the purpose of this work a method that may be called a *problem-related approach* has been adopted. Instead of presenting a descriptive analysis of the role of the prosecutor during criminal investigation country by country followed by comparative analysis at the end, each

60 Zweigert and Kötz (2011), p. 43.

61 Zweigert and Kötz (2011), p. 43–44.

62 E.g. Tak (2004); Open Society Institute Sofia (2008); Ligeti (2013); Gilliéron (2014).

63 E.g. Bradley (1999); the first part of the book by Delmas-Marty and Spencer (2002); Vogler and Huber (2008).

chapter of this work will be devoted to one of the problem-oriented topics. In each of these chapters the regulations as adopted in all four states will be discussed one after the other and concluded with summary containing critical analysis and observations. It is believed that this allows for a clearer and deeper analysis of the book's topic. It also permits avoiding repetition of legal provisions as adopted in each state when conclusions are presented in the last chapter. Instead, the analysis of the identified issue provided at the end of each chapter devoted to that topic makes the discussion clearer, more focused, and comprehensive. Most importantly the proposed approach forces a focused parallel analysis of legal provisions on each of the selected issues for every chosen country. Concentration on a given problem prevents discussing topics for one country which are not covered in the part where another state is analyzed.

The decision to study the prosecutorial impact on criminal investigation in comparative perspective also requires some difficult choices regarding priorities among possible topics and problems. Where should it begin if the law and literature in some states does not provide for the formal opening of criminal investigation and does not describe in a theoretical framework the role of the prosecutor in it? To what extent can the prosecutorial role in conducting certain investigative actions and coercive measures be described? Should just interrogations, arrest, and search be examined as measures most typically used, or also crime scene investigations, autopsies, and secret surveillance be included? There are no satisfactory solutions to these questions and decisions which had be made will nonetheless be arbitrary. Therefore, *five themes were identified to shape the present work.* They reflect crucial moments during criminal investigation and possible spheres of prosecutorial engagement. These are the:

- initiation of criminal investigation;
- conducting of criminal investigation;
- preliminary charging of a suspect with a crime;
- imposition of coercive measures during criminal investigation; and
- discontinuation of criminal investigation.

Some of these topics are strictly associated with formal decision-making, in particular when it comes to discontinuation of proceedings. Others are of a factual character, e.g. taking a part in investigative actions such as interrogating the suspect or overseeing crime scene investigations and autopsy as is done by the prosecutor in some countries. These five topics have been selected for the significance that they have for every criminal investigation. Therefore, the analysis of the prosecutorial engagement in each of these spheres allows for determining whether her involvement is essential, useful, or unnecessary. This speaks to the important question of how much power the prosecutor should retain during the course of criminal investigation.

As was stated earlier, this work focuses on the criminal investigation and the impact that prosecutors maintain during that stage of the criminal process. As a result, this work acknowledges a scholarly research regarding negotiated justice mechanisms and extensive analysis of a variety of case-ending decisions as available in the discussed countries. It is not the purpose of this book to repeat it.

Finally, a word on the book's terminology, particularly in relation to the translation of legal terms. The challenges of translation and arriving at equivalents between jurisdictions, includes understanding of such notions as "discretion," "charging," and "coercive measures."[64] The discussion regarding use of these terms will be futher carried out in the relevant chapters of this work.

1.6 Structure of the Study

The book is divided into nine chapters. The first three chapters are of an introductory character, while the last one will contain concluding remarks, observations, and suggestions for the development of the role of the prosecutor in the criminal process.

It was never the objective of this research to provide an exhaustive analysis of the criminal procedure during its investigative stage in each of the chosen legal systems, although it was not always easy to resist this temptation. Nor was it the intention to investigate all aspects of the prosecution systems in each country to the fullest, including the structure of prosecution offices and the shape of disciplinary proceedings. Instead the aim was to examine the scope of prosecutorial powers within each country at the first critical stage of the criminal process before the case reaches court. Consequently, the focus of this work remains on legal provisions as employed with regard to the prosecutorial actions undertaken during criminal investigation that are described in Chapters 4–8. Nevertheless, it is necessary to provide at least a brief overview of the researched legal systems discussed within this book, both when it comes to the prosecution systems as employed in each country as well as the structure of the criminal investigation accordingly. As Giulio Illuminati aptly suggested, the position of the public prosecution service is always influenced by its relation to other institutions, particularly the government and police, as well as through internal relations within the office.[65]

64 See a marvelous piece on challenges regarding translation of Italian criminal procedure-related terms into English in Scarpa, Peruzzo, and Pontrandolfo (2017). On the structure of interpretation and meaning in procedural language, see Langer (2004), pp. 9–11.

65 See Illuminati (2004), p. 305.

He also subsequently noted that another important factor is the approach toward the principle of legality and its flip side—prosecutorial discretion.

Therefore, Chapter 2 provides a short presentation of the structure of the four prosecution systems. There is a particular focus on the position of the prosecution service in relation to the judiciary and the executive to mark the scope of the external independence. Also, the internal independence of each prosecutor in her daily work is analyzed, which adds to the freedom in undertaking decisions in the most obvious way. The aim was to provide a proper understanding of the position of the prosecutor within each of the respective criminal justice systems. This part of the book does not necessarily aim to add novelty to current scholarship but rather to feed on the exhaustive findings presented in other works.

The general considerations end with Chapter 3 presenting the shape of the criminal investigation of the selected countries. It is particularly important to discuss what is considered in each country as the "investigation" given the unclear terminology used to describe the first stage of criminal proceedings. The analysis will show that grasping the time frame of this phase of the criminal process is far from simple. For that reason, a brief outline of the criminal investigation as adopted in each country will be presented and two main overarching principles will be discussed: the principle of legality and the principle of prosecutorial objectivity. This allows for a full framework in which the powers of the prosecutor at this stage of criminal process are to be presented.

The next five chapters form the core of this work. Since the methodological decision was to build the book in a problem-related way, there are no separate chapters devoted to each selected country. Instead, each chapter contains an analysis of the approach as adopted in each country toward one of the book's five themes followed by comparative analysis and concluding remarks. This makes for a more clear and comprehensive analysis. It also paves the way for the book's conclusions and recommendations in the final chapter.

Accordingly, Chapter 4 is devoted to a presentation of the power of the prosecutor over the commencement of criminal investigation. This chapter answers the question of whether the prosecutor retains control over commencement of investigation, and, if so, to what extent. In fact, this is a question of whether the prosecutor shall be able to force the police to react in an adequate manner in the event of a report that an offense has possibly occurred. The chapter considers whether the prosecutor should be involved from the outset of criminal investigation in systems that provide for prosecutorial control over investigation. Chapter also looks at the decision not to open investigation, and the ways that such decision is controlled and reviewed.

Chapter 5 focuses on the scope of the prosecutor's activities during the course of investigation. The prosecutor–police relationship is discussed. Moreover, the scope of the powers of the prosecutor with regard to investigative actions is analyzed since in some of the chosen countries certain actions may be conducted only by the prosecutor or also by her. The chapter also analyzes the prosecutor's power to conduct interrogations as well as the right to participate in crime scene investigation and during autopsies. This allows for drawing conclusions regarding the pros and cons of a system in which the prosecutor could (or should) engage in investigative actions and the related extent of same.

Chapter 6 focuses on the power to initially charge an individual with a crime. The information on initial charges allows the suspect to employ her right to defend herself, start actively preparing for any possible future trial, as well as undertake possible actions to convince the competent authority to discontinue criminal proceedings against her. Therefore, the right to information regarding the status of an individual as a suspect as well as on the initial charges laid against her becomes a crucial element in the scope of the suspect's rights. The major focus of the chapter is how much influence the prosecutor has and should have on initial charging decisions in the light of her almost exclusive powers to charge a person with a crime later on in the course of a criminal process. This is crucial, since the initial charging decision, even an informal one, moves investigation in a certain direction, shaping the scope of the investigation and determining further steps that will be likely undertaken by criminal justice authorities in the course of criminal investigation against the suspect. Therefore, theoretically unimportant information given some time during the arrest or when interrogation first takes place, is of crucial importance and may have a tremendous impact on the prosecutor's further decisions.

Chapter 7 is devoted to the analysis of the scope of prosecutorial powers regarding the measures that infringe the rights of the individual during the course of criminal investigation, sometimes called the coercive measures. The limits of acceptable interference with rights and freedoms of an individual during criminal proceedings is the main issue here. Without doubt the prosecutorial competence to impose such measures is crucial to determination of the level of influence that the prosecutor maintains over criminal investigation. The most important question is which authority should be qualified to issue warrants and what should be considered as the minimal features of such authority. Even though the practice shows that the rule understood as prior authorization to impose coercive measures has become the exception, it is still important as giving the most protection to the individual. Making a prior decision to impose a coercive measure raises additional concerns, i.e. whether such decision becomes final and remains unverified until the evidence obtained during such search is to be introduced at trial or shall it be subject to some form of control. And if yes, who should undertake such decision and when it should be undertaken. Unwarranted decisions to conduct coercive measures are also examined to establish the role that the prosecutor may play in it. For the purpose of discussing coercive measures the search and the arrest were chosen as those most commonly used during investigation.

Chapter 8 outlines the decision to discontinue a criminal investigation. Discussion focuses on the reasons that allow discontinuation of a case, and the time frame for doing so. The main focus is again on the ability of the prosecutor to undertake the independent decision to discontinue proceedings and the role that the judicial authority plays with regard to it. Therefore, the controlling mechanisms are discussed, i.e. confirmation of such decision by the judge or the possibility of questioning the prosecutorial decisions in that regard. The amount of discretion given to the prosecutor in this area is of particular importance and analysis of lack of public interest as a reason to drop investigation, as formally and informally introduced within distinct criminal justice systems and employed in practice, are presented.

Chapter 9 offers a summary overview of the main findings of the book. It also provides suggestions and recommendations, building on the conclusions of Chapters 4–8 in the light of considerations provided in Chapters 2–3.

References

Alkon C (2015) An Overlooked Key to Reversing Mass Incarceration: Reforming the Law to Reduce the Prosecutorial Power in Plea Bargaining. *University of Maryland Law Journal of Race, Religion, Gender and Class* 15:191–208.

Ambos K, Bock S (2012) Procedural Regimes. In: Reydams L, Wouters J, Ryngaert C (eds) *International Prosecutors*. Oxford University Press, Oxford, pp. 488–541.

Amodio E, Selvaggi E (1989) An Accusatorial System in a Civil Law Country: The 1988 Italian Code of Criminal Procedure. *Temple Law Review* 62:1211–1224.

Anderson S (2001) The Changing Role of the Prosecutor. In: *The Prosecutor's Deskbook. Ethical Issue and Emerging Roles for the 21st Century Prosecutors*. American Prosecutors Research Institute, Alexandria, VA.

Barkow R (2019) *Prisoners of Politics: Breaking the Cycle of Mass Incarceration*. Belknap Press, Cambridge, MA.

Bazelon E (2019) *Charges: The New Movement to Transform American Prosecution and End Mass Incarceration*. Random House.

Boyne SM (2014) *The German Prosecution Service. Guardians of the Law?* Springer, Heidelberg.

Bradley CM (1996) The Convergence of the Continental and Common Law Model of Criminal Procedure. *Criminal Law Forum* 7:471–484.

Bradley CM (1999) *Criminal Procedure: A Worldwide Study*. Carolina Academic Press, Durham.

Braum S (2012) Prosecutorial Control over Investigations in Europe: A Call for Judicial Oversight. In: Luna E, Wade M (eds) *The Prosecutor in Transnational Perspective*. Oxford University Press, Oxford, pp. 67–81.

Brown DK (2012) American Prosecutors' Powers and Obligations in the Era of Plea Bargaining. In: Luna E, Wade M (eds) *The Prosecutor in Transnational Perspective*. Oxford University Press, Oxford, pp. 200–213.

Brown DK (2019) Evidence Discovery and Disclosure in Common Law Jurisdictions. In: Brown DK, Turner JI, Weisser B (eds) *The Oxford Handbook of Criminal Process*. Oxford University Press, Oxford, pp. 543–561.

Caianiello M (2016) Increasing Discretionary Prosecutor's Powers: The Pivotal Role of the Italian Prosecutor in the Pretrial Investigation Phase. In: *Oxford Handbooks Online*, Oxford University Press, Oxford.

Colvin V, Stenning P (eds) (2019) *The Evolving Role of the Public Prosecutor. Challenges and Innovations*. Routledge, New York.

Damaška M (1973) Evidentiary Barriers to Conviction and Two Models of Criminal Procedure: a Comparative Study. *University of Pennsylvania Law Review* 121:507–589.

Delmas-Marty M, Spencer JR (eds) (2002) *European Criminal Procedures*. Cambridge University Press, Cambridge.

Elsner B, Peters J (2010) The Prosecution Service Function within the German Criminal Justice System. In: Jehle J-M, Wade M (eds) *Coping with Overloaded Criminal Justice Systems. The Rise of Prosecutorial Power Across Europe*. Springer, Heidelberg, pp. 207–236.

Esmein A (1913) *A History of Continental Criminal Procedure with Special Reference to France*. Little Brown and Company, Boston.

Fair Trials (2017) The Disappearing Trial Report. www.fairtrials.org/sites/default/files/publication_pdf/Report-The-Disappearing-Trial.pdf. Accessed 20 June 2020.

Fionda J (2003) *Public Prosecutors and Discretion: A Comparative Study*. Clarendon Press, Oxford.

Gershman BL (2011) Prosecutorial Decisionmaking and Discretion in the Charging Function. *Hastings Law Journal* 62:1259–1284.

Gialuz M (2017) The Italian Code of Criminal Procedure: A Reading Guide. In: Gialuz M, Lupária L, Scarpa F (eds) *The Italian Code of Criminal Procedure. Critical Essays and English Translation*. Cedam, Milan, pp. 17–55.

Gilliéron G (2014) *Public Prosecutors in the United States and Europe*. Springer, Cham.

Glenn HP (2008) Comparative Legal Families and Comparative Legal Traditions In: Reimann M, Zimmermann R (eds) *The Oxford Handbook of Comparative Law*. Oxford University Press, Oxford, pp. 421–440.

Goldstein AS (1974) Reflections on Two Models: Inquisitorial Themes in American Criminal Procedure. *Stanford Law Review* 26:1009–1025.

Gramckow H (2008) Prosecutor Organization and Operations in the United States. In: Open Society Institute Sofia (ed) *Promoting Prosecutorial Accountability, Independence and Effectiveness*. Open Society Institute Sofia, Sofia, pp. 386–429.

Hodgson J (2005) *French Criminal Justice. A Comparative Account of the Investigation and Prosecution of Crime in France*. Hart Publishing, Portland.

Hodgson J (2015) Plea Bargaining: A Comparative Analysis. In: Wright JD (ed) *International Encyclopedia of the Social & Behavioral Sciences*. Elsevier, Oxford, pp. 226–231.

Huber B (2008) Germany. In: Vogler R, Huber B (eds) *Criminal Procedure in Europe*. Duncker & Humblot, Berlin, pp. 269–371.

Illuminati G (2004) The Role of the Public Prosecutor in the Italian System. In: Tak PJP (ed) *Tasks and Powers of the Prosecution Services in the EU Member States*. Wolf Legal Publishers, Nijmegen, pp. 313–324.

Illuminati G (2005) The Frustrated Turn to Adversarial Procedure in Italy (Italian Criminal Procedure Code of 1988). *Washington University Global Studies Law Review* 4:567–581.

Jacoby JE, Ratledge EC (2016) *The Power of the Prosecutor. Gatekeepers of the Criminal Justice System*. Praeger, Santa Barbara.

Jasiński W, Kremens K (2019) *Criminal Law in Poland*. Kluwer Law International, Alphen aan den Rijn.

Jehle J-M, Wade M (eds) (2010) *Coping with Overloaded Criminal Justice Systems. The Rise of Prosecutorial Power Across Europe*. Springer, Heidelberg.

Kausch E (1980) *Der Staatsanwalt: Ein Richter vor dem Richter? Untersuchungen zum § 153a StPO*. Duncker & Humblot, Berlin.

Keen PC (2004) Tempered Adversariality: The Judicial Role and Trial Theory in the International Criminal Tribunals. *Leiden Journal of International Law* 17:769–781.

King NJ, Wright RF (2016) The Invisible Revolution in Plea Bargaining: Managerial Judging and Judicial Participation in Negotiations. *Texas Law Review* 92:325–397.

Kremens K (2020) The New Wave of Penal Populism from a Polish Perspective. In: Hoven E, Kubiciel M (eds), *Zukunftsperspektiven des Strafrechts*. Symposium zum 70. Geburtstag von Thomas Weigend, Nomos, Baden, pp. 123–136.

Kuczyńska H (2015) *The Accusation Model Before the International Criminal Court. Study of Convergence of Criminal Justice Systems*. Springer, Cham.

LaFave WR (1970) The Prosecutor's Discretion in the United States. *American Journal of Comparative Law* 18:532–548.

Langbein J (1974) Controlling Prosecutorial Discretion in Germany. *The University of Chicago Law Review* 41:439–467.

Langbein J (1979) Land Without Plea Bargaining: How the Germans Do It. *Michigan Law Review* 78:204–225.

Langer M (2004) From Legal Transplants to Legal Translations: The Globalization of Plea Bargaining and the Americanization Thesis in Criminal Procedure. *Harvard International Law Journal* 45 (1): 1–64.

Langer M (2014) The Long Shadow of the Adversarial and Inquisitorial Categories. In: Dubber MD, Hörnle T (eds) *The Oxford Handbook of Criminal Law*. Oxford University Press, Oxford, pp. 887–912.

Langer M (2020) Criminal Convictions. *Annual Review Criminology* 4:1.1–1.35.

Langer M, Sklansky DA (eds) (2018) *Prosecutor and Democracy. A Cross-National Study*. Cambridge University Press, Cambridge.

Lewis C (2012) The Evolving Role of the English Crown Prosecution Service. In: Luna E, Wade M (eds) *The Prosecutor in Transnational Perspective*. Oxford University Press, Oxford, pp. 214–234.

Ligeti K (ed) (2013) *Toward a Prosecutor of the European Union, Volume 1:A Comparative Analysis*. Hart Publishing, London.
Ligeti K (ed) (2016) *Toward a Prosecutor of the European Union, Volume 2: Draft Rules of Procedure*. Hart Publishing, London.
Luna E, Wade M (2010) Prosecutors as Judges. *Washington and Lee Law Review* 67:1413–1532.
Luna E, Wade M (eds) (2012a) *The Prosecutor in Transnational Perspective*. Oxford University Press, Oxford.
Luna E, Wade M (2012b) Preface. In: Luna E, Wade M (eds) *The Prosecutor in Transnational Perspective*. Oxford University Press, Oxford.
Marguery T (2008) Unity and diversity of the public prosecution services in Europe. A study of the Czech, Dutch, French and Polish systems. Dissertation, Groningen.
Mosteller RP (2012) Failures of the Prosecutor's Duty to "Do Justice" in Extraordinary and Ordinary Miscarriages of Justice. In: Luna E, Wade M (eds) *The Prosecutor in Transnational Perspective*. Oxford University Press, Oxford, pp. 408–423.
Open Society Institute Sofia (ed) (2008) *Promoting Prosecutorial Accountability, Independence and Effectiveness*. Open Society Institute Sofia, Sofia.
Orie A (2002) Accusatorial v. Inquisitorial Approach in International Criminal Proceedings. In: Cassese A, Gaeta P and Jones JRWD (eds) *The Rome Statute of the International Criminal Court. A Commentary*, vol. 2. Oxford University Press, Oxford, pp. 1439–1496.
Panzavolta M (2004) Reforms and Counter-Reforms in the Italian Struggle for an Accusatorial Criminal Law System. *North Carolina Journal of International Law & Commercial Regulation* 30:577–624.
Pizzi WT (1993) Understanding Prosecutorial Discretion in the United States: The Limits of Comparative Criminal Procedure as Instrument of Reform. *Ohio State Law Journal* 54:1325–1373.
Rauxloh R (2011) Formalization of Plea Bargaining in Germany: Will the New Legislation Be Able to Square the Circle? *Fordham International Law Journal* 34:296–331.
Roach K (2019) Regulating the Prosecutorial Role in Wrongful Convictions. In: Colvin V, Stenning P (eds) *The Evolving Role of the Public Prosecutor. Challenges and Innovations*. Routledge, New York, pp. 249–265.
Scarpa F, Peruzzo K, Pontrandolfo G (2017) Methodological, terminological and phraseological challenges in the translation into English of the Italian Code of Criminal Procedure. In: Gialuz M, Lupária L, Scarpa F (eds) *The Italian Code of Criminal Procedure. Critical Essays and English Translation*. Cedam, Milan, pp. 57–112.
Soubise L, Woolley A (2018) Prosecutors and Justice: Insights from Comparative Analysis. *Fordham International Law Journal* 42:587–626.
Tak PJP (ed) (2004) *Tasks and Powers of the Prosecution Services in the EU Member States*. Wolf Legal Publishers, Nijmegen.
Taleb A, Ahlstrand T (2011) The public prosecutor, its role, duties and powers in the pre-trial stage of criminal justice process – a comparative study of the French and the Swedish legal systems *Revue internationale de droit pénal* 82:523–540.
Thaman S (ed) (2010) *World Plea Bargaining: Consensual Procedure and the Avoidance of the Full Criminal Trial*. Carolina Academic Press, Durham.

Turner JI (2006) Judicial Participation in Plea Negotiations: A Comparative View. *American Journal of Comparative Law* 54:501–570.

Turner JI (2009) *Plea Bargaining Across Borders*. Aspen Publishers, New York.

Turner JI (2012) Prosecutors and Bargaining in Weak Cases: A Comparative View. In: Luna E, Wade M (eds) *The Prosecutor in Transnational Perspective*. Oxford University Press, Oxford, pp. 102–115.

Vogel M (2019) Plea Bargaining Under the Common Law. In: Brown DK, Turner JI, Weisser B (eds) *The Oxford Handbook of Criminal Process*. Oxford University Press, Oxford, pp. 730–760.

Vogler R, Huber B (eds) (2008) *Criminal Procedure in Europe*. Duncker & Humblot, Berlin.

Wade M (2010) The Power to Decide—Prosecutorial Control, Diversion and Punishment in European Criminal Justice Systems Today. In: Jehle J-M, Wade M (eds) *Coping with Overloaded Criminal Justice Systems. The Rise of Prosecutorial Power Across Europe*. Springer, Heidelberg, pp. 27–126.

Wade M (2013) The Januses of Justice: How Prosecutors Define the Kind of Justice Done across Europe. In: Albrecht H-J, Klip A (eds) *Crime, Criminal Law and Criminal Justice in Europe. A Collection in Honour of Prof. em. dr. dr. h.c. Cyrille Fijnaut*. Martinus Nijhoff Publishers, Leiden/Boston, pp. 595–617.

Wade M (2016) Why Some Old Dogs Must Learn New Tricks: Recognising the New in EU Criminal Justice. In Colson R, Field S (eds) *EU Criminal Justice and the Challenges of Diversity*. Cambridge University Press, Cambridge, pp. 65–81.

Weigend T (2008) The Decay of the Inquisitorial Ideal: Plea Bargaining Invades German Criminal Procedure. In: Jackson J, Langer M, Tillers P (eds) *Crime, Procedure and Evidence in a Comparative and International Context*. Hart, Oxford, pp. 39–64.

Weigend T (2012) A Judge By Any Other Name? Comparative Perspectives on the Role of the Public Prosecutor. In: Luna E, Wade M (eds) *The Prosecutor in Transnational Perspective*. Oxford University Press, Oxford, pp. 377–391.

Weigend T, Turner JI (2014) The Constitutionality of Negotiated Criminal Judgments in Germany. *German Law Journal* 15:81–105.

Weisser B (2019) The ECHR and the Right to a Fair Trial. In: Brown DK, Turner JI, Weisser B (eds) *The Oxford Handbook of Criminal Process*. Oxford University Press, Oxford, pp. 89–114.

Zacharias FC, Green BA (2009) The Duty to Avoid Wrongful Convictions: A Thought Experiment in the Regulation of Prosecutors. *Boston University Law Review* 89:1–59.

Zweigert K, Kötz H (2011) *Introduction to Comparative Law*. Clarendon Press, Oxford.

Chapter 2

Prosecution Systems Compared

2.1 General Considerations

The powers of the prosecutor during criminal investigation is determined by the model of criminal justice system as adopted in the state in question. The tasks and duties assigned to a prosecutor in the course of investigation affect her competencies toward initiation of an investigation, decisions on search and arrest, and of course the charging process. Also, the role that the prosecutor plays at this early stage of criminal process results from her position during the trial. But it is also strongly influenced by the position of the prosecution system in the structure of state powers. Links between the prosecution service and executive authority affects not only activities of individual prosecutors in politically sensitive cases but also have an impact on the social perception of the prosecution service as being subordinate to, or independent of, politicians. The actions of the prosecutor as undertaken during criminal investigation are also influenced by her subordination to persons holding managerial and supervisory positions in relation to her.

This chapter analyzes the position of the prosecution services in Germany, Poland, Italy, and the USA. It addresses the shape of investigation as prescribed on the normative level and as it is employed in practice in these legal systems. This is discussed in light of the concept of prosecutorial independence in its external and internal aspects and influences that other entities have on the prosecutor that may have an impact on her decision-making during criminal investigation shall be answered

The first issue, external (institutional) independence, is understood as going beyond the individual prosecutors and as applying to the office as a whole and viewed as an institution.[1] It "deals with the question to what state power the prosecution service is subordinated or related."[2] This form of prosecutorial independence is of utter importance since allocating the prosecution

1 Côté (2012), p. 324.
2 Tak (2004), p. 3.

service within the executive or the judicial branch will shape of the relationship that the prosecutor has with other actors in criminal proceedings. On one hand, this may impact the prosecutor's relationship with the police as an authority obviously subordinated to the executive. Where the prosecution service is situated within the executive means it has real influence on police investigations in criminal proceedings, thereby taking over responsibility for it. And where the prosecution service is positioned within the judiciary, the prosecutor is granted competencies usually available only to judges and courts, which opens up the discussion regarding prosecutorial competence to issue decisions interfering with the rights and freedoms of an individual.

The issue of external independence of the prosecution service has been addressed on the international level. The Guidelines on the Role of Prosecutors adopted in 1990 in Havana by the Eighth United Nations Congress on the Prevention of Crime and the Treatment of Offenders underlined that states shall ensure that prosecutors are able to perform their professional functions without intimidation, hindrance, harassment, improper interference, or unjustified exposure to civil, penal, or other liability.[3] According to the Standards of Professional Responsibility and Statement of the Essential Duties and Rights of Prosecutors adopted in 1999 by the International Association of Prosecutors, the use of prosecutorial discretion, when permitted in a particular jurisdiction, should be exercised independently and be free from political interference.[4] Both rules have also been repeated in the Guide on the Status and Role of Prosecutors adopted in 2014 jointly by the United Nations Office on Drugs and Crime, and the International Association of Prosecutors, where it was also underlined that "[i]ndependence of prosecutorial decision-making is recognized as being necessary as prosecutors play an important role and functions in relation to the executive branch."[5]

On the European level the external independence of prosecutors has been addressed directly by Recommendation Rec(2000)19 on the Role of the Public Prosecution in the Criminal Justice System, adopted by the Committee of the Ministers of the Council of Europe in 2000, providing that states should take appropriate measures to ensure that public prosecutors are able to perform their professional duties and responsibilities without unjustified interference or unjustified exposure to civil, penal, or other

3 Rule 4. www.ohchr.org/EN/ProfessionalInterest/Pages/RoleOfProsecutors.aspx. Accessed July 12, 2020.

4 Standard 2.1. www.iap-association.org/getattachment/Resources-Documentation/IAP-Standards-(1)/IAP_Standards_Oktober-2018_FINAL_20180210.pdf.aspx. Accessed July 12, 2020.

5 www.unodc.org/documents/justice-and-prison-reform/14-07304_ebook.pdf Accessed July 12, 2020, p. 8.

liability.[6] In other provisions of this document, the relationship between the executive and the prosecution service has been regulated to further the idea of prosecutorial independence.[7] Also, the European Court of Human Rights has strongly stated "that in a democratic society both the courts and the investigation authorities must remain free from political pressure."[8] Finally, the need to preserve the autonomy of prosecutorial decision-making and to assure that performance of their duties is free of external pressure or interference, having regard to the principles of separation of powers. Accountability was addressed by the Consultative Council of European Prosecutors on European norms and principles concerning prosecutors in 2014 in Opinion No. 9.[9] It has been also clarified that

> the independence of prosecutors is not a prerogative or privilege conferred in the interest of the prosecutors, but a guarantee in the interest of a fair, impartial and effective justice that protects both public and private interests of the persons concerned.[10]

The second issue, that is the internal independence of the prosecutor, may be understood as "providing the prosecutor with an environment free from fear of personal reprisals of any kind in the exercise of his professional duties."[11] It refers to the hierarchical structure being a common feature of many prosecution systems.[12] All documents mentioned above refer to this issue. For example Recommendation Rec(2000)19 provides that

> with respect to the organization and the internal operation of the Public Prosecution, in particular the assignment and re-assignment of cases, this should meet requirements of impartiality and independence and maximize the proper operation of the criminal justice system, in particular the level of legal qualification and specialization devoted to each matter.[13]

The internal independence of the prosecutor is discussed here first through the analysis of the structure of the prosecution services in each of the four selected countries. In particular, the focus will remain on the issues of the

6 Recommendation 11. https://rm.coe.int/16804be55a. Accessed July 12, 2020.
7 Recommendation 13 and 14 Rec(2000)19.
8 *Guja* v. *Moldova*, no. 14277/04, February 12, 2008, § 86.
9 § V. https://rm.coe.int/168074738b Accessed July 12, 2020.
10 § 35 of the Opinion No. 9.
11 Côté L (2012), p. 341.
12 Tak (2004), p. 4.
13 Recommendation 9 Rec(2000)19.

prosecutor's independence specifically in decision-making process during the investigation. The key issue is competence to issue instructions to the prosecutor by her superiors within the structures of the prosecution service.

However, before discussing external and internal prosecutorial independence, each of the sections on selected states sets out relevant sources of law as relating to the position of the prosecution system and to the role that the prosecutor serves in criminal proceedings. The presentation of these sources will also make it possible to determine whether and how the position of the prosecution service is reflected in the national constitutions.

Finally, a word on how the term "prosecutor" is used in this work is in order, and in particular how the notion of the prosecutor operates in the respective countries. This term is commonly associated with a public official who brings criminal action against an individual. But the more precise and legal understanding of it might be quite different depending on the system. For example, Langer argues that in the adversarial system, the word "prosecutor" means a party in a dispute with an interest at stake in the outcome of the procedure—(with a focus on the trial part of criminal process). While in the inquisitorial system prosecutor signifies an impartial magistrate of the state whose role is to investigate the truth (with a focus on criminal investigation).[14] However, when in inquisitorial systems the trial role of the prosecutor is being considered she is perceived as a party to the court proceedings. Similarly, in the adversarial system the prosecutor during investigation is not a party in a dispute against the suspect but an objective evaluator of the gathered evidence. This shows that the problem is more complex than it appears at first sight.

Moreover, the terms used to describe the figure that we call in English "the prosecutor" should be addressed at this point. The prosecutor is referred to by various names.[15] In Germany, the prosecutor is called *Staatsanwalt*, being a civil servant of the German prosecution service—*Staatsanwaltschaft*. This name is used regardless of whether the prosecutor is organized within the federal or Länder structure. But it should be also noted that German law does not usually speak of the prosecutor (*Staatsanwalt*) as an individual but rather refers to the office that she holds (*Staatsanwaltschaft*). However, the conventional approach in the relevant legal literature is prosecutor, which the present work will follow.[16]

In Polish, the word *prokurator* is most typically translated as a "prosecutor" and is commonly understood closely to its general meaning without necessity

14 Langer (2004), p. 10.
15 E.g. in the Netherlands the prosecutor is called *schout* (Tak (2012)), and in France this is *procureur* or *procureur publique* (Hodgson (2005)).
16 Weigend (2013) p. 266.

for additional explanations. However, another word is used in Polish law to describe a person that decides to bring charges against a person understood as decision to prosecute a case. In such cases, the term *oskarżyciel* is used, which can be translated as the "accuser" or "person that accuses." And the law makes it clear that it is *prokurator* who holds the primary responsibility to prosecute (accuse) in the majority of cases. But that competence is also given to some criminal justice agencies, such as the Border Guard (Straż Graniczna), or a fiscal inspection office (urząd kontroli skarbowej), although not to the police. This means that what is normally associated with the prosecutorial function, i.e. prosecuting a case, is done in Poland by the *oskarżyciel* who, in the overwhelming majority of cases is the *prokurator*.

In Italy, the prosecutor is called the *pubblico ministero* which is understood as a magistrate without judicial power.[17] She has a monopoly in initiating the criminal action and representing the state during a criminal trial, but also plays a significant role during criminal investigation.[18] The Italian term highlights the "public" (*pubblico*) element of the prosecutorial function. This is also true for other European countries and can be explained by fact that there are also private prosecution practices in all three Continental states analyzed here.[19] Even though private prosecutions have been rejected in the USA on the federal level[20] such practices are also known in the common-law system[21] and some states still adhere to such an idea, allowing interested parties to pursue their own prosecutions in the absence of the prosecutor.[22] Therefore, the adjective "public" signifies the prosecutor's public function. In this work, "prosecutor" and "public prosecutor" will be used interchangeably, with no difference in meaning attached to either term, in doing so.

The understanding of who is a prosecutor seems quite obvious in the US system, since this word in the English language has an adopted meaning. *Black's Law Dictionary* defines a prosecutor as "a legal officer who represents the state or federal governments in criminal proceedings" making this term

17 Corso (1993), p. 226.

18 Di Amato (2013), p. 158.

19 The private prosecution is available in Germany (Section 374–394 StPO), in Poland (Article 59–61 and 485–499 k.p.k.) and in Italy although to a limited extent, based on Decreto Legislativo, August 28, 2000 n. 274 (d.lgs. 274/2000).

20 See *Linda R.S.* v. *Richard D.*, 410 US 614 (1973) confirmed by *Leeke v. Timmerman*, 454 US 83 (1981).

21 See also the historical perspective on private prosecution in the USA proving that this institution is rooted in that system by Ireland (1995) and Worral (2008), pp. 5–6.

22 See for discussion on states allowing and prohibiting private prosecutions in the USA, John Bessler, "The Public Interest and the Unconstitutionality of Private Prosecutions," 47 *Arkansas Law Review* 1994, pp. 529–543.

equal to "public prosecutor," "state's attorney," and "public commissioner."[23] A more precise definition provides that "prosecutor" means

> any attorney, regardless of agency, title, or full or part-time assignment, who acts as an attorney to investigate or prosecute criminal cases or who provides legal advice regarding criminal matter to government lawyers, agents, or offices participating in the investigation or prosecution of criminal cases.[24]

But when details come into play the situation becomes more complex. Thus, instead of the term prosecutor, most commonly such terms as "district attorney," "state's attorney," "prosecuting attorney," or "US Attorney"[25] are used. This is closely related to the distinction between the state system and the federal system in the US case and the structure of the prosecution systems discussed below.[26]

This book, and especially this chapter, does not aim at providing an exhaustive analysis of all aspects of the position and structure of the prosecution service in the selected countries. Therefore, the focus shall remain on the external and internal independence of the prosecutor. In view of the detailed and current considerations available in the legal literature, concerning in particular the organization of the prosecution service, the selection of prosecutors, their further training, as well as the scope of prosecutorial accountability also in the form of disciplinary proceedings, these issues have been touched upon only briefly in this chapter and for the rest, the reference should be made to the extensive literature on the subject already quoted in Chapter 1.

2.2 The Prosecution Service in Germany

2.2.1 Sources of Law Governing the German Prosecution Service

The major source of German criminal process regulating, among others, the duties and competencies of the prosecutor in criminal investigation and trial remains the German Code of Criminal Procedure.[27] It dates from 1877, but since then has been amended countless times, although it retains its

23 Black's Law Dictionary (2009), p. 1341.
24 American Bar Association, *Standards for Criminal Justice on the Prosecution Function*, § 3-1.1 (4th ed. 2018) [hereafter PFS].
25 Kamisar et al. (2015), p. 4 footnote c.
26 Cf. Sections 2.5.2. and 2.5.3.
27 *Strafprozessordnung* [German Code of Criminal Procedure] of April 7, 1987, I BGBl – 1987, 1074 (hereafter: StPO).

original structure. The second source is the German Criminal Code,[28] which contains provisions on substantive criminal law. There is also the German Constitution: the Basic Law of 1949[29] that to a limited extent contains direct regulations relating to the prosecution service and its powers during criminal process. Among these are norms referring to deprivation of liberty[30] and privacy.[31] In this context, the case law of the Federal Constitutional Court (Bundesverfassungsgericht) is of utmost importance, as it interprets the rules of criminal procedure in the light of the German Constitution. In the last decades, the Court has particularly often shaped criminal policy and influenced the behavior of authorities in the course of criminal proceedings. For example, in recent years the Court has played an important role in accepting the practice of out-of-court settlements.[32]

The Federal Constitution declares that Germany is a state based on the rule of law (*Rechtsstaat*). This means that legislation must comply with the constitutional order and that the executive and judiciary must comply with laws and statutes.[33] As a result, the legislative branch has the exclusive competence to define crimes as well as criminal sanctions for them. This builds the foundation for the principle of mandatory prosecution in the criminal justice system, particularly relevant to the actions undertaken by prosecutors during the criminal process.

The Court Constitution Act[34] is also of relevance, as it regulates the status and functions of the prosecution service. This act primarily sets out the structure of national civil and criminal courts at all levels establishing their jurisdiction and organization. The Tenth Title of CCO entitled "Public prosecution office" contains provisions on the position of the prosecution service. These regulations are stated in rather general terms, e.g. indicating that every court should have a prosecution office within its structure[35] or determining that prosecutors cannot perform judicial functions.[36] Between them, however, there are also more detailed provisions concerning both the territorial jurisdiction of a given prosecutor's office[37] and the internal organizational

28 *Strafgesetzbuch*, [German Criminal Code] of November 13, 1998, BGBl – 1998, 3322 (hereafter: StGB).

29 *Grundgesetz* [Basic Law, German Constitution] of May 23, 1949, I BGBl 1949, 1 (hereafter: German Constitution).

30 Article 104 German Constitution.

31 Articles 10 and 13 German Constitution.

32 March 19, 2013, Case No. 2 BVR 2628/10.

33 Article 20 (3) German Constitution.

34 Gerichtsverfassungsgesetz [Code of Court Organization] of May 9, 1975, I BGBl 1975, 1077 (hereafter: CCO).

35 § 141 CCO.

36 § 151 CCO.

37 §143 CCO.

structure of each office, in particular with regard to the relationship between chief prosecutors and their subordinates.[38]

2.2.2 The Position of the German Prosecution Service in relation to the Judiciary and Executive

No clear answer can be given to the question of whether the prosecution service in Germany belongs to the executive or judiciary.[39] On one hand there are several arguments why the public prosecution service can be treated as a part of the judiciary rather than the executive. First, prosecutors in Germany are seen as neutral and objective officials holding a quasi-judicial role in fact finding, whose duty during criminal investigation is to examine the facts regardless of whether they support the initial suspicion.[40] This normatively expressed obligation to search both for incriminating and exonerating evidence[41] positions them as civil servants dedicated to establishing the truth of the case and not simply charging the suspect by taking all measures possible to charge the suspect regardless of exonerating evidence.[42] Moreover, during the investigation the position of the prosecutor can be considered as similar to the position held by the judge during the trial. In this sense the prosecution service is seen as equivalent to the courts and both groups are equally responsible for the provision of justice. Indeed, it is true that both judges and prosecutors are "required by law to clear up the offence in question in full, taking into account all incriminating and exonerating circumstances. In other words, by law the public prosecutor is not a party, and equally he is not the opponent of the defendant."[43]

Moreover, every prosecutor undergoes exactly the same training as judges.[44] Both groups are trained together, for the same period of time, with no distinction to the form and scope of training, including taking a part in a two-step state examination.[45] And at the end of the training each of them may decide to choose either professional career. Moreover, advanced, noncompulsory training for those who access the office is provided, jointly again, by the German Judicial Academy (Deutsche Richterakademie).

38 §§ 144–146 CCO.
39 Elsner and Peters (2010), p. 208; cf. Trendafilova and Róth (2008), p. 236.
40 Weigend (2013), p. 266.
41 § 160 (2) StPO.
42 This unique position is additionally strengthened at the federal level by § 148 CCO providing that the Federal Prosecutor General and federal prosecutors are civil servants.
43 Siegismund (2003), p. 64.
44 See interesting analysis on how students in Germany are taught as early as in law schools to perceive the law "like a judge" and through the lens of judges when compared to training of young future lawyers in the USA by Boyne (2014), pp. 37–38.
45 Gilliéron (2014), p. 265.

Finally, pay and pensions are also always at the same level for both judges and prosecutors.[46] These features make the German prosecution service, at least on a normative level, lean toward independence and impartiality that makes it possible to associate it with the judicial branch. It is also rather clear that this connection should not be considered as a form of subordination or even dependency, as it is clearly emphasized in § 150 CCO that the public prosecution office shall be independent of the courts in the performance of its official tasks.

But despite these strong ties between prosecution and judiciary the prosecution service in Germany is not considered as being fully independent of the executive. The organization of the prosecution service with the Minister of Justice on the top both at the federal and state levels[47] gives a clear impression of dependence on the executive branch.[48] Moreover, since prosecutors must obey the orders of their superiors,[49] that is also from the Minister, they should not be regarded as enjoying the same level of independence as judges.[50] Indeed, it is reported that due to the broad powers vested in the Minister of Justice she might impermissibly influence prosecutors, in particular, in cases of political interest.[51] This eventually led the German Federal Constitutional Court to conclude that prosecution is a part of the executive.[52]

Notwithstanding the position expressed by the Constitutional Court, the issue of the allocation of the German prosecution service within state powers remains open. As Trendafilova and Róth report, in practitioners' views, prosecutors remain within the executive but exercise their powers in a nonpolitical fashion.[53] Scholars also argue that German prosecutors are independent organs in the administration of justice, remaining somewhere in between judicial and executive authority, while not being part of any of those two or even holding the position of a separate organ of the criminal justice system (*Organ der Rechtspflege*).[54] Regardless of which of these views dominates, there is no doubt that the German prosecution service is not a part of the judicial branch and therefore prosecutors cannot be characterized by independence and impartiality, which is an obvious attribute of judges.

46 Trendafilova and Róth (2008), p. 214.
47 § 147 CCO.
48 Weigend (2004), p. 212.
49 § 146 CCO.
50 Bohlander (2012), p. 55.
51 Gwladys Gilliéron, *Public Prosecutors in the United States and Europe*, Heidelberg: Springer 2014, p. 283.
52 BVerfGE 32, 216 and BVerfGE 103, 142, 156.
53 Trendafilova and Róth (2008), p. 236.
54 Siegismund (2003), pp. 64–65.

2.2.3 The Internal Independence of the Prosecutor within the Structure of the German Prosecution Service

One of the most visible features of the German prosecution service is its organization on two independent levels: federal and state. Their structure is strongly determined by the fact that Germany is a federal state constituted of 16 separate *Länder*. As a result, each *Bundesland* has its own criminal justice system with its own public prosecution service. Above that, there is a federal criminal justice system with a federal public prosecution service, which works independently from the offices in each *Länder*. On the federal level the Federal Prosecution Service (*Bundesanwaltschaft*) led by the Prosecutor General (*Generalbundesanwalt*) is responsible for investigating and prosecuting certain serious crimes falling under the jurisdiction of Higher Regional Courts.[55] Accordingly, each *Länder* has its own prosecutor's office, which is completely independent from the federal prosecution service in terms of both structure and jurisdiction.

The territorial competence of the public prosecutor's office remains parallel to the jurisdiction of the court where the public prosecution office has been established. This is so, since § 141 CCO provides that each court should have its own public prosecutor's office.[56] On the federal level each Federal Supreme Court (*Bundesgerichtshof*) has the Federal Public Prosecution Office attached to it. On the state level each of 25 Higher Regional Courts (*Oberlandesgericht*) and each of 116 Regional Courts (*Landsgerichte*) has a separate prosecutor's office attached. The prosecutors from the regional public prosecution offices carry out their prosecutorial functions also in local courts (*Amtsgerichte*)[57] with the help of so-called *Amtsanwalt* (assistant prosecutors) who are not qualified to hold judicial offices (which is a requirement for all prosecutors). They work within so-called *Antsanwaltschaften* (assistant prosecutor offices) and are responsible for 40 percent of all proceedings[58] that are considered as being the simplest cases.[59] The group of so-called auxiliary prosecutors (*Ermittlungspersonen*) play an important role, though as police officers and not prosecutors, they remain outside of the scope of prosecution service per se.[60]

55 § 142a CCO.
56 See on the structure of German courts, Bohlander (2012), pp. 36–39.
57 Siegismund (2003), p. 60.
58 Elsner and Peters (2010), p. 209.
59 According to §§ 142 (2) and 145 (2) CCO an *Amtsanwalt* can act only where the local court has jurisdiction and that these must be cases heard by the single judge and not those which are considered as being more complicated and heard by one professional judge and two lay judges – according to OrgStA [*Anordnungen uber Organization und Dienstbetrieb der Staatsanwaltschaft*]
60 This issue will be discussed in detail in Section 5.2.1.

The structure of the public prosecution service is hierarchical, which in fact works both ways. On the one hand, the prosecutor must obey orders given by her superior.[61] But on the other hand, prosecutors act, in their service capacity, as deputies of the head of the office,[62] which in practice means that every decision made by the public prosecutor is valid as if the head of the office had made it, even if it violates the instruction given by the supervisor.[63] At the same time the systems are not interconnected which means that the federal and *Länder* prosecutors as well as prosecutors from distinct *Länder* do not remain in any formal relationship.[64]

This creates an interesting configuration of 17 separate regimes (16 *Länder* and one federal) that are internally organized in separate hierarchical structures. But the shape of the organizational culture of the German prosecutor's offices is determined most significantly by the competence of superiors to give orders (*Weisungsrecht*) to lower-ranked prosecutors subordinated to them.[65] At the top of this hierarchy, both in federal and state systems is the Minister of Justice, while simultaneously higher-level prosecutors have a supervisory role over lower-level prosecutors.[66] This also includes the power to give orders to subordinates. The scope and nature of the orders is quite broad. They can be quite general or may refer to individual cases.[67] They may also remain in relation to the facts of the case or to legal aspect of it but can never go beyond the principle of mandatory prosecution. Therefore, the prosecutor can be given orders regarding further investigation, taking decisions to prosecute, what charges to bring, whether to drop a case, or what conditions to impose.[68] Moreover, the case may be at any time, without any other condition, reassigned to another prosecutor (*Substitutionsrecht*) or be taken over by a higher-ranking prosecutor (*Devolutionsrecht*) at her will.[69] Despite this broad scope of orders that can be given to the prosecutor, there are provisions to refrain from acting against her own convictions. The prosecutor, as a civil servant[70] can refuse to accept

61 § 146 CCO.
62 § 144 CCO.
63 Siegismund (2003), p. 70.
64 On the model structural composition of prosecution offices in Germany, see Trendafilova and Róth (2008), p. 217.
65 § 146 CCO.
66 According to § 147 CCO the right to supervise and direct is granted to (1) the Federal Minister of Justice in relation to the Federal Prosecutor General and the Federal prosecutors; (2) the judicial administration of the *Länder* in relation to all prosecutorial staff of the Land concerned; (3) the highest-ranking prosecutor at the Higher Regional Courts and Regional Courts in relation to all prosecutors in their jurisdictions.
67 Elsner and Peters (2010), p. 208.
68 Wade (2010), p. 103.
69 § 145 CCO. Cf. Juy-Birmann (2002), pp. 299–300.
70 § 148 CCO.

orders that require commission of a crime, may report concerns to her superior, or may withdraw from a case if she believes that the instructions are ill founded.[71] But it is doubtful whether in practice such mechanisms are capable of sufficiently protecting the independence of an individual prosecutor.

The general right of the Minister of Justice to issue orders and instructions is of a slightly different character. Since the Minister of Justice is not a public prosecutor, the orders are more of general and external character directed rather at the Prosecutor General, but as a consequence translated into internal instructions.[72] It is reported that in practice the Minister of Justice rather rarely uses the power to interfere with the handling of individual cases.[73] Yet, other sources reveal that a practice of issuing instructions to prosecutors goes on an informal level.[74] In any case, such broad executive powers, even if transferred informally through another official to the prosecutor, should be seen as problematic in allowing for politically inspired influence.

In order to prevent such informal practices, it has been proposed that a mechanism be put in place over the years to force chief prosecutors to formulate written orders so that they can be subject to external scrutiny, which would also protect prosecutors, especially less experienced ones, from orders which raise doubts about their legality.[75] However, it is true that due to the informal character of such orders, they cannot be completely ruled out. Therefore, most likely, despite the creation of such a mechanism, recourse to softer forms of pressure will not be prevented.

2.3 The Prosecution System in Poland

2.3.1 Sources of Law Governing the Polish Prosecution Service

As in the German system, the Constitution of the Republic of Poland[76] does not refer to the prosecution service.[77] On the other hand, as in the case of other states described in this book as well as many others, constitutional regulations remain particularly important when it comes to the mechanisms of protection of rights to liberty, privacy, property, etc..

71 See broadly Trendafilova and Róth (2008), p. 221.
72 Siegismund (2003), p. 70; cf. Boyne (2014), p. 99.
73 Gilliéron (2014), p. 283.
74 Boyne (2014), p. 99.
75 Siegismund (2003), pp. 71–72. See also Jasch (2019), p. 212.
76 *Konstytucja Rzeczpospolitej Polskiej* [Constitution of the Republic of Poland] of April 2, 1997, Dz. U. 1997, Nr 78, poz. 483 (hereafter: Polish Constitution).
77 See the critical remarks on the lack of regulation of prosecution service in the Polish Constitution in Polish: Iwanicki (1995); Ważny (2009); Szeroczyńska (2017), pp. 111–113 and in English Lach (2005), pp. 599–600.

The Polish Code of Criminal Procedure is the basic source of law governing the prosecution service.[78] It contains provisions that cover the conduct of criminal proceedings including powers vested in the prosecutor. The Code regulates, among others, the functioning of the prosecutor's office through adoption of the principle of objectivity[79] and the principle of legality.[80] As a result of the latter, the Criminal Code,[81] defining crimes, remains crucial among sources of law relating to the work of prosecutors subordinating them to the letter of law.

The organization and functioning of the prosecution service is mainly based on the Prosecution Service Act of 2016.[82] This act covers both the organizational structure of the prosecution service and issues related to the powers of individual prosecutors, especially those managing their units; it also covers promotions and disciplinary proceedings against prosecutors. It should be noted that the current PSA is a completely new act and not an amendment to the PSA 1985,[83] which was heavily amended between 1985 and 2016.[84] Importantly however, both acts remain strikingly similar in terms of their structure and some provisions are even copied directly from the PSA 1985. Therefore, the current shape of the prosecution service in Poland is definitely not a new approach but maintains the preexisting concept of the prosecution service. This strongly supports arguments that in this respect Poland has not fully abandoned the old model of communist prosecution system.

The last source of law governing the activities of prosecutors and their offices are the Regulations adopted by the Minister of Justice in 2016.[85] It provides in greater detail the organization of the prosecutor's offices of all levels, their internal structure, budget, and specifies tasks to be undertaken in criminal proceedings implementing to a certain extent provisions of the k.p.k.

78 *Kodeks postępowania karnego* [Polish Code of Criminal Procedure] of June 6, 1997, Dz.U. 2020, poz. 30 as amended (hereafter: k.p.k.).
79 Article 4 k.p.k.
80 Article 10 k.p.k.
81 *Kodeks karny* [Polish Criminal Code] of June 6, 1997, Dz.U. 2019, poz. 1950 as amended (hereafter: k.k.).
82 *Ustawa Prawo o prokuraturze* [Prosecution Service Act] of January 28, 2016, Dz.U. 2016, poz. 177 (hereafter: PSA 2016).
83 *Ustawa o Prokuraturze Polskiej Rzeczypospolitej Ludowej* [Polish People's Republic Prosecution Service Act] of June 20, 1985, Dz.U. 1985, Nr 31, poz. 138 (hereafter: PSA 1985).
84 See Section 2.3.2.
85 *Regulamin wewnętrznego urzędowania powszechnych jednostek organizacyjnych prokuratury* [Regulation of the Minister of Justice on the internal rules of official conduct of common organizational units of the prosecution service] of 7 April, 2016, Dz. U. 2016, poz. 508 (hereafter: Regulations 2016).

2.3.2 The Position of the Polish Prosecution Service in relation to the Judiciary and Executive

Position of prosecution service in Poland relative to the executive and judiciary is problematic.[86] The fact that the Polish Constitution of 1997 does not mention prosecution service does not help the issue. . On a normative basis, no decision was taken to place the prosecution service in the structure of the state authorities as neither k.p.k. nor the PSA 2016 refers to that matter.

In the past, the prosecution service was considered to be located somewhere between the executive and the judiciary, but leaning toward the latter.[87] The connection with the judicial power was justified through the organizational structure of courts (three levels of courts with the Supreme Court at the top) and the prosecution service (three levels of prosecution offices with the National Prosecution Office at the top),[88] the joint system of education and training of judges and prosecutors within one national school and the same salary and promotion structure in both groups. However, currently there should be no doubt that since 2016 the position of the prosecution service has shifted and remains fully subordinated to the executive power. This is a result of recent changes in law providing that the office of the Prosecutor General is held by the Minister of Justice,[89] who is a full-fledged politician.

This is not the first time that such a personal link between the two positions has occurred in the legal system. After Poland regained independence in 1918, the Minister of Justice led the Prosecution Service, although her influence on day-to-day prosecutorial activities evolved over the course of time.[90] Particularly drastic changes were introduced in 1950 through a general reform of the system and court structures, which, by means of the new Prosecution Service Act of 1950,[91] formally made the prosecutor's office independent of the Minister of Justice, yet subordinating it to the highest state authority available at that time—the Council of State.[92] At the same time, according to Lenin's concept of a prosecution service, this public organ was modeled as an apparatus of repression. Therefore, the position of the Polish prosecution service, shaped on the Soviet model, was to ensure that socialist laws were observed and to react to any violations against the

86 See broadly Kardas (2012).

87 Zięba-Załucka (2016), p. 117 and sources cited in footnote 18.

88 See Section 2.3.3.

89 Article 1 § 2 PSA 2016.

90 See extensively on evolution of Polish Prosecution Service in Polish: Misztygacz (2013); Mazowiecka (2015) and in English Marguery (2008), pp. 139–299.

91 *Ustawa o Prokuraturze Rzeczypospolitej Polskiej* (Prosecution Service Act) of July 20, 1950, Dz.U. 1950, Nr 38, poz. 1346.

92 Lach (2005), p. 599.

communist system.[93] The following years, including the introduction of martial law in 1981, only strengthened the existing model. The new law adopted in 1985 had little significance in this respect. It was the transformation of the state system from a communist to a democratic one that led to changes in the model of the prosecution service aimed at making it independent from the state power. Paradoxically, however, the changes in the law introduced by the 1990 amendment to PSA 1985[94] once again linked the function of the Minister of Justice to the position of the Prosecutor General. Surprisingly, its drafters were looking at these provisions as a way of making the prosecution service independent of the executive. It was considered that the prosecution service should be dependent on someone, it would be better if it was a minister rather than a council of state. Nevertheless, the adoption of such a model has been met with justified criticism, as giving the executive too much influence over prosecutors.[95]

This remained so until the adoption of a reform in 2009[96] that aimed at making the prosecution service fully independent of the executive. Under the new legislation, the functions of the Prosecutor General and Minister of Justice were separated. The amendment was based on the desire to prevent the politicization of the prosecution that leads to instrumental use of the prosecution service for political purposes.[97] The Prosecutor General became an independent body, appointed by the president of the Republic of Poland for a fixed term in office.[98] In fact, the only link between the prosecution service and the executive remained the obligation to present the prime minister with an annual report on the activities of the prosecution service. Despite some criticism, the new law brought a serious change to the prosecution service, giving it for the first time a chance to gain desirable independence.

Unfortunately, it didn't last long. In 2015 the right-wing party won the election using populist slogans on the need for enhanced national security and more control over the prosecution service, perceiving it as an efficient tool for fighting political opponents.[99] The main element of these changes was a return to the merger of the positions of the Minister of Justice and the Prosecutor General.[100] This, in itself, is not, of course, crucial for the

93 Smoleński (1970), p. 22.
94 Ustawa o zmianie ustawy o Prokuraturze Polskiej Rzeczypospolitej Ludowej, Kodeksu postępowania w sprawach o wykroczenia oraz ustawy o Sądzie Najwyższym of March 22, 1990, Dz.U. 1990, Nr 20, poz. 121.
95 See Waltoś (2002); Stefański (2015), p. 795 and literature cited in footnote 194.
96 Act amending the Prosecution Service Act and other acts of October 9, 2009 (J.L. 2009, No. 213, item 1802).
97 Herzog (2009), p. 119.
98 Mazowiecka (2015), p. 162.
99 Cf. Kremens (2020), pp. 126–129.
100 Article 1 § 2 PSA 2016.

assessment of the dependence of prosecutors on the executive. It is feasible to create a system in which functions remain combined, yet the prosecution service remains an independent body. The key issue is the scope of the Minister of Justice's powers with regard to individual criminal cases and her competence to give instructions to prosecutors. This is the issue that truly determines the actual subordination of the prosecution service to executive.

Currently, the Prosecutor General—Minister of Justice, holds, by law, the position of the superior of all prosecutors.[101] Thus, she may give instructions to any prosecutor regarding investigations or prosecutions, including orders on what the person should be charged with and with what kind of decision the individual case must be ended.[102] This heavily violates the external independence of the prosecution service. Thus, since 2016, total subordination of the prosecution service to the state has become an unquestionable fact.[103]

2.3.3 The Internal Independence of the Prosecutor within the Structure of the Polish Prosecution Service

The independence of the prosecutor, at least in theory, is one of the guiding principles of the prosecution service in Poland. It is seen as the prosecutor's ability to undertake activities and make decisions independently without external pressure from superiors.[104] Despite continuous discussions on the scope of prosecutorial independence in Poland this principle has been unceasingly expressed in laws regulating the system of the prosecution service. It is currently provided in Article 7 § 1 PSA 2016 which states that the prosecutor is independent in her actions prescribed by law, although further provisions constitute exceptions to this rule. Moreover, the long-standing principle of hierarchical subordination of lower-level prosecutors to higher-level prosecutors and subordination of each prosecutor to her superior within the unit where she works, clearly contradicts the principle of internal independence of the prosecutor. Yet, it was not until the most recent changes that this concept was destroyed totally. This is reflected by the organizational structure of the prosecution service in Poland, which under PSA 2016 has been as follows.

101 Article 13 § 2 PSA 2016.

102 Article 8 PSA 2016.

103 European Commission for Democracy through Law (Venice Commission), Opinion on the Act on the Public Prosecutor's Office as Amended, No. 892/2017, Strasbourg, December 11, 2017, www.venice.coe.int/webforms/documents/default.aspx?pdffile=CDL-AD(2017)028-e. Accessed July 12, 2020, para. 115 ("[t]his has direct negative consequences for the independence of the prosecutorial system from political sphere, but also for the independence of the judiciary and hence the separation of powers and the rule of law in Poland").

104 Stefański (2015), p. 818.

The prosecution service consists of the Prosecutor General (*Prokurator Generalny*), his deputies including the National Prosecutor (*Prokurator Krajowy*), public prosecutors[105] and prosecutors of the Institute of National Remembrance.[106] The Prosecutor General is in charge of the whole prosecution service, a function that he undertakes in person or through his deputies by issuing a variety of guidelines and instructions.[107]

The structure of the prosecution service reflects the structure of the judiciary. As in the case of criminal courts which operate at four levels,[108] there are four levels of prosecution offices in Poland. The lowest level is the district prosecution office (*prokuratura rejonowa*), headed by the District Prosecutor (*Prokurator Rejonowy*), responsible for investigating and prosecuting the vast majority of crimes.[109] The second level is the provincial prosecution office (*prokuratura okręgowa*), led by the Provincial Prosecutor (*Prokurator Okręgowy*), responsible for investigating and prosecuting cases considered to be too serious to be taken care of on the district level.[110] In turn, the regional prosecution office (*prokuratura regionalna*), led by Regional Prosecutor (*Prokurator Regionalny*), conducts the most serious investigations concerning economic and financial crimes.[111] At the same time, both regional and provincial prosecution offices conduct extensive supervisory activities over the lower-level prosecution offices and prosecutors subordinated to them. Actually, the activity concerning supervision of lower-lever prosecution offices absorbs much more time and energy of provincial and regional offices when compared to their investigative activity.

At the very top of the organizational structure of the prosecution service is the National Prosecution Office, headed by the National Prosecutor. It contains an additional special prosecution unit—the Organized Crime and Corruption Department (*Departament do spraw Przestępczości Zorganizowanej i Korupcji*), responsible for prosecuting organized crime, most serious

105 In the PSA 2016 the term "prosecutors of regular units of the prosecution service" (*prokuratorzy powszechnych jednostek organizacyjnych prokuratury*) is used, which has traditionally made it possible to distinguish between civilian and military prosecutors. With the abolition of the separate military prosecutor's offices, this division lost its importance. In this work a shorter term, "prosecutors" or "public prosecutors" will be used.

106 Article 1 § 1 PSA 2016. The last group of prosecutors has been established to investigate and prosecute crimes committed against Polish nationals or Polish citizens of other nationalities in the period from September 1, 1939 to July 31, 1990 (Article 1 (2) of the Institute of National Remembrance Act of December 18, 1998, Dz.U. 2019, poz. 1882).

107 Article 1 § 2 and 13 § 1 PSA 2016.

108 From the bottom, there are district courts (*sądy rejonowe*), provincial courts (*sądy okręgowe*), appellate courts (*sądy apelacyjne*), and the Supreme Court (*Sąd Najwyższy*).

109 Article 24 § 2–3 PSA 2016.

110 Article 23 § 2–3 PSA 2016.

111 Article 22 § 2–3 PSA 2016.

corruption crime, and terrorist crime.[112] This department and its 11 units formed within each of the Regional Prosecution Offices remains an independent structure, solely subordinate to the National Prosecutor and managed at the national level. The purpose of building up such a separate structure is to preserve the independence of prosecutors conducting investigations and prosecuting cases involving organized crime and corruption.[113]

The degree of internal independence of a prosecutor is primarily impacted by the wide range of methods that allow a superior prosecutor to interfere with the work of their subordinates. Despite the nominally guaranteed independence, the provisions allow the superior prosecutor to issue guidelines, orders, and instructions that must be carried out by the subordinate prosecutor.[114] This situation is further exacerbated by the fact that power to issue such orders and instructions is vested in both the head of the office in which that prosecutor is employed and each prosecutor managing a superior unit over that in which the prosecutor is employed. This means that several people, including the Prosecutor General himself, can influence the shape of investigation and prosecution on all levels including the lowest ones.

The key to understanding how far control over the activities of individual prosecutors reaches is the nature of the instructions that may be given. The scope of these orders is extremely broad and may concern not only technical issues, but also the content of procedural activities, i.e. the decision to initiate an investigation, to discontinue proceedings, to initially charge a person with a crime, or to file a case with a court.[115] Admittedly, such orders must be issued in writing, and, at the request of the prosecutor at whom it is directed, it must be accompanied by justification which must be reflected in the case file.[116] In any case, the prosecutor has the right to request that the order be changed, or that she be excused from executing the order, or even from participating in a case if she does not agree with the content of such order.[117] However, such a mechanism seems to protect the prosecutor only to a limited extent, since a request to be excluded from handling a case simply may be not respected.[118] A superior prosecutor also has the right to

112 Article 19 § 2 PSA 2016.

113 In the past, these units remained a part of the Regional Prosecution Offices and subordinated to Regional Prosecutors, which was criticized as being too exposed to local influences. See this critique by Gabriel-Węglowski (2011), pp. 79–81.

114 Article 7 § 2 PSA 2016.

115 The possibility of giving orders regarding such issues has been criticized in the past. In the PSA 1985, as amended in 2010, orders could only be of an organizational or administrative nature and only to the extent limited by statute, which significantly reduced the possibilities for interference with the independence of an individual prosecutor. See Kremens (2010), pp. 4–5; Herzog (2010), p. 24.

116 Article 7 § 3 PSA 2016.

117 Article 7 § 4–5 PSA 2016.

118 Article 7 § 4 PSA 2016.

amend or revoke any decision of a subordinate prosecutor[119] and to take over their cases and perform their activities in the course of proceedings.[120] Moreover, there are no regulations indicating when such a decision can be made, for what reasons, in relation to what type of proceedings; there is not even a requirement that such a decision be made in writing, nor contain any justification.[121] This leads to the conclusion that prosecutorial independence, declared in Article 7 § 1 PSA 2016, is actually nonexistent and has been effectively replaced by a principle of strict subordination.

2.4 The Prosecution System in Italy

2.4.1 Sources of Law Governing the Italian Prosecution Service

The position and structure of the Italian Prosecution Service is based on several sources of law, including the Constitution of Italian Republic of 1947.[122] This issue will be discussed in more detail below, but it is worth noting at once that both the special status of Italian prosecutors, who are treated equally to judges, as well as the importance of the principle of legality binding prosecutors in their everyday work are directly settled by constitutional provisions. The current status of the prosecution service is a direct result of the disgraceful role it played in World War II. The instrumental use of law and subordination to executive were vivid signs of it. . The adoption of the principle of legality has similar historical roots. It was strongly reinforced in 1947 and aimed at implementing the idea that policies on crime should be defined by Parliament's enacting criminal laws and not by prosecutorial discretion.[123]

As a result, the substantive criminal law is the second most influential source of law regulating the functioning of prosecution service. These regulations can be found in the Criminal Code of 1930,[124] as amended many times. The scope of rights and procedural obligations of the prosecution service is prescribed in the Code of Criminal Procedure of 1988.[125] With adoption of this Code, the criminal process transformed from a traditional inquisitorial system into a much more adversarial one.[126] As a result of strong criticism

119 Article 8 § 1 PSA 2016.
120 Article 9 § 2 PSA 2016.
121 Szeroczyńska (2017), p. 118.
122 *La Costituzione della Repubblica Italiana* [Constitution of Italian Republic] of December 27, 1947 (hereafter Italian Constitution).
123 Illuminati (2004), p. 305.
124 *Codice Penale* [Italian Code of Criminal Law] Regio decreto, October 19, 1930, n. 1938 (hereafter: c.p.).
125 *Codice di Procedura Penale* [Italian Code of Criminal Procedure] Decreto del presidente della Repubblica, September 22, 1988, n. 447 (hereafter c.p.p.).
126 For more information on the main features of Italian criminal process before enforcement of a new CCP in Italy in 1989, see Del Duca (1991), pp. 75–81.

as well as the judgments issued by the Constitutional Tribunal, the c.p.p. has been modified many times. Suffice it to say that, despite the 25-year-long debate preceding the entry into force of the Code, more than 80 changes were made to it over the years.[127] This issue has been thoroughly discussed from a variety of perspectives, so there is no need to repeat it here.[128]

Besides the Constitution and both Codes the organization of the prosecution service in Italy is regulated by Royal Decree no. 12 of 1941.[129] This act generally relates to the structure and organization of the judicial system, but, to some extent, especially Articles 69–84, it also applies to the prosecution service.

2.4.2 The Position of the Italian Prosecution Service in relation to the Judiciary and Executive

The founding premise of the prosecution service in Italy is the normative location of the prosecutors as members of the judiciary. Contrary to the system that existed prior to the Italian Constitution of 1947, when public prosecutors were part of the executive and were accountable to the Minister of Justice, currently prosecutors retain a judicial or at least quasi-judicial function.[130] The reason for this radical change in the prosecutorial position within the system of state powers was the hierarchical subordination to the Ministry of Justice and the executive under the fascist regime.[131] As a result, the new Italian Constitution guaranteed prosecutors the same degree of independence as judges,[132] positioning them collectively within a single group (*magistratura*) as a part of the judicial system.[133] Therefore, the term "judicial authority" now is understood as referring equally to judges and prosecutors alike.[134]

To ensure the independence of the public prosecution service the Constitution provides various institutional and organizational guarantees. First, the Constitution proclaims the judiciary to be autonomous and independent of all other powers.[135] This, by definition, includes prosecutors. Moreover, the law ensures the independence of judges of special courts, of

127 Gialuz (2014), p. 21.
128 See e.g. Amodio and Selvaggi (1989); Grande (2000); Illuminati (2005); Panzavolta (2004), 577.
129 *Ordinamento Giudiziario* [Judicial Regulations] Regio decreto January 30, 1941, n. 12 [hereafter: Judicial Regulations].
130 Illuminati (2004), p. 313. See also Caianiello (2012), p. 250.
131 Ruggeri (2015), p. 61.
132 Article 107 of the Italian Constitution, third sentence.
133 Articles 104–106 of the Italian Constitution.
134 Caianiello (2016), p. 4.
135 Article 104 of the Italian Constitution.

prosecutors of those courts, and of other persons participating in the administration of justice.[136] In order to strengthen the status of prosecutors they are selected and appointed in the same way and upon the same criteria as judges. After recruitment and initial training, successful candidates are assigned to their offices and courts by the Superior Council of the Judiciary (Consiglio Superiore della Magistratura). Further career development remains similar for both groups: the salary and promotion opportunities received are not differentiated and *magistrati* from both groups can be easily transferred between courts and prosecution offices.[137] But despite these structural links, public prosecution offices are not subordinated to judges and remain autonomous and distinct from the courts where they exercise their functions.[138]

The association of the prosecution service with the judiciary is also visible through the position of the prosecutor that she plays during criminal proceedings. Prosecutors are understood to be independent of any other powers and to be bound by the legality principle.[139] Moreover, since according to the theoretical model, prosecutors are supposed to remain objective in the gathering of evidence that includes an obligation to consider evidence, both in favor of and against the accused,[140] their position and status at least during criminal investigation resembles that of a judge.

Finally, the weak relationship between the Minister of Justice and prosecution service is perceived as the ultimate guarantee of the lack of influence of executive power over prosecutors. Despite the fact that the law grants the Minister of Justice responsibility for the organization and functioning of the criminal justice system,[141] delegates to the Minister powers to initiate disciplinary proceedings against all *magistrate*,[142] and allow the Minister to monitor prosecutorial activities[143] these powers are not perceived as a threat to the independence of the prosecution service.[144] Since the selection of prosecutors, their careers and promotions depends solely on the Superior Council of the Judiciary, they feel independent of the Ministry of Justice. The Minister therefore lacks the authority to give instructions to prosecutors and cannot interfere in their prosecutorial functions.[145]

136 Article 108 of the Italian Constitution.
137 Fabri (2008), pp. 3–4. Di Federico (2008), pp. 311–314.
138 Di Amato (2013), p. 37.
139 Article 112 of the Italian Constitution; see also Section 3.4.2.
140 Article 358 c.p.p.
141 Article 110 of the Italian Constitution.
142 Article 107 of the Italian Constitution.
143 Article 69 of Judicial Regulations.
144 Di Federico (2004), pp. 198–199. But see Caianiello (2012), p. 256.
145 Caianiello (2012), p. 255.

This puts the prosecution service closer to the judiciary and further from the executive.[146] But the independence of the prosecution service as prescribed on the normative level does not remain uncontested.[147] Even at the very beginning when the Constitution was adopted in 1947, scholars criticized the approach of associating prosecutors with the judiciary, arguing that constitutionalizing the system without adopting new paradigms was not enough.[148] Scholars also discussed whether the Minister of Justice had influence on the prosecution service, by dint of its ability to trigger disciplinary proceedings.[149] Some also suggested, not without reason, that a system in which judges are structurally more proximate to prosecutors than to defendants can cause a natural tendency to rule in favor of the prosecution, which leads to a clear violation of the equality-of-arms principle.[150] This approach has led in the past to some attempts, unsuccessful so far, to change the law and ultimately separate prosecutors from the judiciary.[151]

Finally, despite the persistent normative attribution of the prosecution to the judiciary, some scholars position the prosecutor as the "fourth power" neither associated with judiciary nor executive.[152] That approach is seen in part as a result of the existence of the principle of legality in Italian law,[153] perceived by some as a principal source from which the subjection of prosecutors to the law is derived, guaranteeing their independence from state powers, including both judiciary and executive.[154] In the light of the above, it is doubtful whether the Italian prosecution service is in fact as closely linked to the judiciary as the system seems to suggest.

2.4.3 The Internal Independence of the Prosecutor within the Structure of the Italian Prosecution Service

The structure of the prosecution office in Italy reflects the structure of the court system. This means that individual prosecution offices are structurally connected with courts of first instance as well other courts. Thus, at each

146 Montana (2012), p. 109.
147 Scaccianoce (2010), p. 6.
148 Caianiello (2016), p. 5.
149 Caianiello (2012), p. 256.
150 Di Federico (1998), pp. 381–382.
151 Illuminati and Caianiello (2007), p. 132 (the authors discuss the lobbying and legislative actions taken to make such a change, but not successfully completed).
152 M. Nobili, "Un quarto potere?," in: Mariella Tirelli (ed.), *Recenti orientamenti in tema di pubblico ministero ed esercizio dell'azione penale*, Milan 1998, pp. 29–43 as quoted by Grande (2000), p. 241.
153 Article 112 of the Italian Constitution.
154 Scaccianoce (2010), p. 7 with cited literature; Caianiello (2012), p. 256; Di Amato (2013), p. 36.

court of first instance (*Tribunali*), there is a public prosecution office (*Procure della Republica*), of which there were 165 in 2008.[155] Depending on the size of jurisdiction, the number of employed prosecutors within each office can vary significantly—reported as being between three and 117.[156] The separate structure of juvenile justice has led to the creation of 29 separate prosecution offices (*Procure della Repubblica presso il Tribunale perii minorenni*), one at each Juvenile Court (*Tribunale dei minorenni*), which are solely responsible for conducting investigations and prosecutions of cases involving juveniles before these courts.

Further prosecution offices (*Procure generali presso le Corti di appello*) exist at the 26 Courts of Appeal (*Corte di appello*) but they do not hold any investigations, being responsible for prosecuting cases in courts to which they are attached.[157] On the top of this ladder the Prosecutor General's Office at the Court of Cassation (*Procura Generale presso la Corte di Cassazione*) exists although with no ability to perform any supervisory functions over the prosecutor's offices at lower levels of jurisdiction.[158]

The prosecution system has a special feature, being a completely separate structure of prosecution offices established for the purpose of increasing the efficiency of conducting proceedings related to organized crime (mafia).[159] Behind its creation stands a constant need to make the activities of the prosecution service independent of politicians who, presumably, might retain close links to organized crime. The creation of a separate structure of prosecution offices was perceived as being more likely to independently fight the Italian mafia's heavily influence on politics. Recently, the powers of these separate prosecutorial units were significantly expanded to include the obligation to deal with terrorist cases.[160]

The National Anti-Mafia and Counter-Terrorism Bureau (*Direzione nazionale antimafia e antiterrorismo* (DNAA)) sits at the top in the centralized structure of the Prosecutor General's Office at the Court of Cassation. It is headed by the National Anti-Mafia and Counter-Terrorism Prosecutor (*Procuratore nazionale antimafia e antiterrorism*) who supervises 26 Anti-Mafia and Counter-Terrorism District Bureaux (*Direzione distrettuale antimafia e antiterrorism*).[161] His responsibility is to act as an impetus to the district

155 Scaccianoce (2010), p. 5.
156 Di Federico (2008), p. 303.
157 Di Amato (2013), p. 37.
158 Di Federico (2008), p. 303.
159 Decreto-legge "Coordinamento delle indagini nei procedimenti per reati di criminalitá organizzata," November 20, 1991, n. 367.
160 Decreto-legge n. 7, February 18, 2015 changed by Legge n. 43, April 17, 2015.
161 The structure of these units is reflecting the 26 districts of the Courts of Appeal where higher-level prosecutor units are located. But all these units are structurally linked to the lowest-level public prosecution office.

prosecutors of these special units in order to make effective the coordination of investigative activities, to ensure the functionality of the deployment of the judicial police in its various articulations, and to ensure the completeness and timeliness of investigations.[162]

Despite the fact that, structurally, prosecution offices are organized on different levels reflecting the structure of courts, there is no hierarchical organization of prosecution offices on a national level.[163] This is also true for the anti-mafia divisions where the independence and autonomy of district offices are protected accordingly, and also in that the National Prosecutor does not exercise hierarchical authority over lower-level units.[164]

Similarly, the structure of individual prosecution offices at all levels is also hierarchical only formally.[165] Each prosecutor's office is led by the chief prosecutor (*procuratore capo*) who is expected to direct the office, organize its activities, and assign cases to prosecutors.[166] Yet, independence of an individual prosecutor is strongly secured and the powers of chief prosecutors heading each prosecutor's office are very much limited.

The most important role in ensuring the independence of prosecutors in their activities during criminal proceedings is played by the Superior Council of the Judiciary. Since 1998 the Council has been responsible for producing the norms regulating internal organization of prosecutor's offices with an aim to reduce as much as possible the discretionary powers of those who lead the prosecutor's offices.[167] The chief prosecutors are also obliged to present to the Council organizational plans of their units, including methods of distribution of cases between individual prosecutors. In particular, during court proceedings prosecutors enjoy full autonomy and may be replaced by another prosecutor only exceptionally, while the justification for such a decision should be sent by the head of the prosecutor's office that made the decision to the Council (Article 70 (4) of Judicial Regulations). This means that a case assigned to a prosecutor remains pretty much her property and she can only be removed from a case by the chief prosecutor.[168]

It should be emphasized that the internal independence of the prosecutor derives from the constitutionally guaranteed principle of legality, which is binding on every prosecutor. If a legal provision requires certain action, e.g. initiating investigation or filing a case with court, a chief prosecutor's

162 Article 371bis c.p.p.
163 Illuminati (2004), p. 313.
164 Fabri (2008), p. 5. But see for example ("No hierarchical organization of prosecution offices exists at a national level").
165 Di Federico (2008), p. 301.
166 Article 70 (3) of Judicial Regulations.
167 Di Federico (2008), pp. 326–327.
168 Di Amato (2013), p. 37 and Di Federico (2008), p. 327.

order to behave otherwise would violate this principle in a significant way. Notwithstanding the clearly expressed views that the principle of legality is not as strongly employed in practice as theory suggests[169] it is still seen as a mechanism that guarantees the independence of every prosecutor making her an extremely powerful figure in the criminal justice system.[170]

2.5 The Prosecution System in the United States of America

2.5.1 Sources of Law Governing the US Prosecution Service

Of all the prosecution systems discussed in this book, a concise description of the US proves most difficult. There are several reasons for this. First, the prosecution service in the USA is decentralized due to the parallel functioning of state and federal law in the USA. It is exceptional, even if compared to the German system which also works under a decentralized federal–*Länder* system. Each of the 50 states, plus the District of Colombia and the federal government, is empowered to decide independently of the others the shape of the criminal law by establishing their own laws in this regard; each state is also entitled to conduct its own law enforcement policies. But distinguishing between what is the federal and the local in law enforcement activities is not an easy task. As former US Attorney General RH Jackson once stated

> outside of federal law each locality has the right under our system of government to fix its own standards of law enforcement and of morals. And the moral climate of the USA is as varied as its physical climate. For example, some states legalize and permit gambling, some states prohibit it legislatively and protect it administratively.[171]

It should therefore be emphasized that both federal and state prosecution systems are completely independent of one other, both in terms of organization and in terms of the competencies entrusted to them.

The decentralization of the prosecution service and the jurisdictional independence of US states, with strictly protected decision-making sovereignty of each state in the criminal policy sphere, makes the structure of prosecution service system even more complex. Each US state identifies its own criminal law, substantively and procedurally, which contrasts with the unified German system in this respect. Differences between prosecution systems in each of the US states is also a result of this tendency. This is to a

169 Cf. Caianiello (2012), p. 255.
170 Di Federico (2008), p. 333.
171 Jackson (1940), p. 6.

large extent a result of the great independence that state governments have always enjoyed in relation to each other. Therefore, it is virtually impossible to identify one state prosecution service that is typical, as differences between the respective states will remain. Yet, as Gramckow confirms, there are sufficient commonalities among the state-level prosecution systems to allow presentation of how they are structured and operate.[172] However, it is not this book's aim to provide a full and detailed analysis of organizational solutions adopted for prosecution services in selected states, but rather what comes from this structure and organization. Therefore, the presentation of the prosecution system of the USA will be limited to elements that will allow for determination of the level of prosecutorial independence from the external and internal perspectives, and in all other respects one should refer to the rich existing literature.[173]

The prosecution service is not mentioned directly in the US Constitution[174] in any way. As part of the executive branch, the prosecution "shall take care that the laws be faithfully executed."[175] At the same time, the Constitution remains the primary source of law, which significantly influences the activities of the prosecution during the criminal process, and during investigation in particular. The most important of its regulations include amendments to the Constitution guaranteeing the right to a fair trial during the criminal process. The Federal Constitution in this regard, by virtue of the Fourteenth Amendment, through its due process clause, extends the validity of these regulations to the US states as well. This shape of the sources of law at the federal level was subsequently supplemented by Federal Rules of Criminal Procedure and Federal Rules of Evidence being legal rules promulgated by the Supreme Court of the USA.[176] The shape of the prosecution service at the federal level is regulated by the Judiciary Act, which has been in force since 1789,[177] defining the structure of the federal judiciary and the Act to Establish the Department of Justice adopted much later,[178] creating the

172 Gramckow (2008), p. 389.

173 See e.g. on the historical evolution of US prosecution service in Worral (2008). See on structure and organization of prosecution service on federal- and state-level among many others e.g. Gramckow (2008), p. 385–407 and Gilliéron (2014), pp. 65–85.

174 Constitution of the USA of September 17, 1787 (hereafter: US Constitution).

175 Article II, Section 3 of the US Constitution.

176 The US Supreme Court under the Rules Enabling Act (Pub.L. 73–415, 48 Stat. 1064) has a statutory authority to promulgate laws. Both Federal Rules of Criminal Procedure (hereafter: FRCP) and Federal Rules on Evidence (hereafter FRE) has been originally adopted this way however the evidentiary rules eventually became a binding federal law on January 2, 1975 upon adoption of An Act to Establish Rules of Evidence for Certain Courts and Proceedings (Pub.L. 93–595, 88 Stat. 1926).

177 Judiciary Act of September 24, 1789, 1 Stat. 73.

178 Act to Establish the Department of Justice of June 22, 1870, 16 Stat. 162.

Department of Justice and its structure. It should be also added for clarification that all general federal statutes and law are jointly compiled in the US Code.[179] For example, FRCP are regulated in Title 18 of the USC and FRE in Title 28.

On the state level each state has its own constitution and set of laws that govern the structure and authority of its prosecution service. Furthermore, the vast majority of US states have created a system in which individual and completely independent prosecutors' offices are established on the county level. The State of Connecticut serving in this work as an example of a state system regulates the position of the prosecution service upon the Connecticut Constitution of 1965.[180] Of particular importance is Article XXIII, being an amendment to the Constitution from 1984 which added regulations relating to the appointment of state attorneys. The Constitution also provides the binding standard referring to protection of the rights and freedoms of individual during criminal process.[181]

Beside these regulations the most important source of law in Connecticut regulating the substantive criminal law, the procedural criminal law as well as the structure of courts are the General Statutes of Connecticut,[182] being a codification of the law of Connecticut similar to the USC on the federal level. The structure and organization of the prosecution service in Connecticut is regulated in Secs. 51–275 to 51–288 CGS. The rules provided in CGS are further supplemented by the Connecticut Practice Book[183] which contain the rules of professional conduct for lawyers and detailed rules of procedure including in criminal matters. The significance of CPB can be compared to some extent to the FRCP and FRE.

One should not overlook the importance that guidelines directed at prosecutors serve in the US criminal justice system both on federal and state level.[184] For the former, the guidelines issued by the US Attorney General in the Justice Manual[185] used by US Attorneys and other employees of the

179 Code of Laws of the USA (hereafter USC).

180 Constitution of the State of Connecticut of December 30, 1965 (hereafter: Connecticut Constitution).

181 Articles 1 (7)–(9) of the Connecticut Constitution.

182 General Statutes of Connecticut (Connecticut General Statutes), revised in 1958 (hereafter: CGS).

183 Connecticut Practice Book adopted on July 29, 1997 by the Superior Court (hereafter: CPB).

184 Cf. Gillieron (2014), pp. 79–89.

185 Section 1–1.100 Justice Manual (2018) available at www.justice.gov/jm/justice-manual. Accessed July 12, 2020 (hereafter as Justice Manual). The JM was previously known as United States Attorney's Manual (USAM). The new version, revised and renamed in 2018, was the first comprehensive review and overhaul of the Manual in more than 20 years, updating it to reflect current law and practice (Department of Justice, Department of Justice Announces the Rollout of an Updated United States Attorneys'

US Department of Justice are crucial. As an internal document it does not have any officially binding force, yet provides guidance for those who conduct prosecutions on the federal level.[186] But a similar function is served by the American Bar Association Standards for Criminal Justice directed at prosecutors for their investigative[187] as well as prosecutorial[188] roles. Finally, the National District Attorneys Association has issued guidelines directed at prosecutors and their functions within the criminal justice system.[189] These guidelines, together with official legal sources and the case law, build the environment in which the prosecutors exercise their roles during various stages of criminal proceedings.

2.5.2 The Position of the US Prosecution Service in relation to the Judiciary and Executive

The formal association of the prosecution service with the executive does not seem to raise any doubts.[190] In a widely noted case *United Sates* v. *Nixon* the US Supreme Court stated that the "Executive Branch has exclusive authority and absolute discretion to decide whether to prosecute a case."[191] Therefore, the prosecutor is the representative of the "state," whether that is understood as a country or as one of the 50 states. But the position of the prosecution service at federal and state level is not uniform in this respect.

First, on the federal level the dependency of the prosecution service on the executive branch is visible through the specific position of the US Attorney General. This public official is a member of federal government and heads the Department of Justice that is the US equivalent of the Ministry of Justice. The Attorney General answers directly to the US president who appoints the Attorney General on the advice and consent of the US Senate.[192] This means that each newly elected US president, as a rule, will immediately replace the person holding the position of the US Attorney General as is done with all other members of the previous government. It is warranted in the US presidential system of governance where the President who heads

Manual, September 25, 2018. www.justice.gov/opa/pr/department-justice-announces-rollout-updated-united-states-attorneys-manual. Accessed July 12, 2020)

186 See broadly on the nature of prosecutorial guidelines by Podgor (2012).

187 ABA Standards for Criminal Justice. Standards on Prosecutorial Investigations, 3rd ed., Washington: American Bar Association 2014 (hereafter: ABA SPI).

188 ABA Standards for Criminal Justice for the Prosecution Function, 4th ed., Washington: American Bar Association 2017 (hereafter ABA SPF).

189 NDAA National Prosecution Standards, 3rd ed., 2009, NDAA, Alexandria (hereafter: NDAA NPS).

190 Gramckow (2008), p. 391. Neubauer and Fradella (2017), p. 192.

191 418 US 683, 693 (1974).

192 28 USC § 503.

the government is the main executive authority of the country.[193] But, due to such close relation between the president and the US Attorney General, the position of the latter remains highly politicized. Federal criminal policy guidelines may vary significantly every four-year period, depending on whether there is a switch from a Republican to a Democratic president, or vice versa.

The US Attorneys responsible for enforcing the federal criminal law within their jurisdictions[194] are perceived as retaining considerable autonomy with regard to the organization of their offices and the cases handled within them.[195] Indeed, the daily work of the US Attorney is not supervised by the Department of Justice, and each US Attorney is able to set her own priorities depending on the needs of the district.[196] There is no requirement of uniformity to that extent. Each of the US Attorneys is also responsible for the shape of the Office that she leads, having exclusive competence to hire and fire the Assistant US Attorneys working for her. All this means the US Attorneys are praised for their discretion and independence.

Nevertheless, the Attorney General has a variety of instruments that allow him to influence the activities of US Attorneys. The daily work of US Attorneys is regulated by the Justice Manual which they are required to follow. Admittedly, it expressly states that US Attorneys act "under the supervision and direction of the Attorney General and his/her delegates"[197] but they contain no rules that specify the scope and nature of this supervision. Usually, the Attorney General will limit the US Attorneys' discretion determining the type of cases in which the death penalty must be sought, as well as adopting instructions in which cases the authorization for issuing the indictment must be obtained by the US Attorney.[198] This, however, refers to certain types of case and not individual cases. Moreover, the Attorney General, as well as her deputies, may issue policy statements in the form of "memorandums" that must be adhered to by all federal prosecutors and that can force certain discovery practices or allow communication with individuals in the absence of their legal counsel.[199] It appears that the Attorney General has a significant influence on the activities of US Attorneys. However, this influence, at least in formal terms, does not extend to the right to interfere in individual cases within the US Attorney's Office. Moreover, the Attorney General does not seem to have a noticeable influence on the activities of

193 Article II, Section 1 of the US Constitution.
194 See Section 2.5.3.
195 See e.g. Beale (2015), p. 33 and Gilliéron (2014), p. 66.
196 Gramckow (2008), pp. 396–397.
197 9-2.001 JM.
198 Gramckow (2008), p. 397.
199 See more on controversial memos of former Attorneys General in: Podgor (2012), p. 13.

individual lower-level federal prosecutors, who remain dependent on the US Attorneys leading the Office.

The independence of federal district prosecutors from politics and politicians has been questioned for a long time. The determinant here is the way in which US Attorneys are appointed. The scale of dependency of the US Attorneys on federal executive authority is also manifested through the unquestioned power of the president of the USA to dismiss them.[200] Moreover, the US Attorney is almost always a member of a ruling political party and candidates for these positions are nominated by senators and members of the House of Representatives from a given state also belonging to the ruling party.[201] The practice confirms it brutally. The scale in which this mechanism impacts the shape of the federal prosecution proving the dependence of the US Attorneys on federal power is visible every time a new president takes office. When President Bush was ending his term, the 77 US Attorneys nominated by him remained in office.[202] The new President Bill Clinton asked all US Attorneys to resign and, as a result, appointed new US Attorneys with political views associated with the party he represented in the elections (the Democrats).[203] An even more extreme example is the Nixon presidency and the circumstances in which the Watergate affair was handled.[204] The most recent case is from 2017, when the Attorney General Joe Sessions requested 46 US Attorneys appointed by Barack Obama to resign.[205] This study is by no means the place to describe the details of these cases but they seem to indicate that the US prosecution service on the federal level has been significantly politicized and does not exclude pressures which may play a crucial role when it comes to decision-making in the course of criminal proceedings. This also gives rise to the important question of how the federal prosecution service is structured, making the US Attorneys loyal to the US president, rather than to law.[206]

The mere existence of the independent counsel (special prosecutor, special counsel) in the federal legal system only confirms the dependence of the US Attorneys on the government.[207] The independent counsel is a public official appointed to investigate high-level executive branch-ranking

200 28 USC § 541 (c).
201 Kamisar et al. (2005), p. 975.
202 Burnham (2011), p. 152.
203 Burnham (2011), p. 152.
204 See Entin (1990), pp. 186–188.
205 "Sessions asks 46 Obama-era US Attorneys to resign," Reuters, March 10, 2017 www.reuters.com/article/us-usa-trump-justice-prosecutors-idUSKBN16H2K8. Accessed July 12, 2020.
206 Perry (1998), p. 130.
207 See on the US tradition to appoint federal prosecutors from outside the Department of Justice in Kavanaugh (1998), pp. 2142–2145.

officials, including the US president himself. The need to establish a completely independent prosecutorial authority in the structure of the prosecution service appears to be justified by the need to indicate such an entity that would remain outside the influence of executive power.[208] Only independent counsel grants full impartiality and authority to exercise all investigative and prosecutorial functions and powers of the Department of Justice and the Attorney General as adopted in 28 USC § 594 (a) is believed to be able to perform her duties properly avoiding any conflict of interest with the executive.

On the state level, the position of the prosecution seems to be of a completely different nature. It can be argued that the state prosecution systems, independent of one another, are generally not controlled by their respective state governments in any manner.[209] Despite the state prosecution service's being part of the executive, their level of independence from the state as well as local government is noticeable. There might be several reasons for that. Even though each state, like the federal government, has its own state Attorney General, it is difficult to compare these state officials to their federal counterpart.[210] But the solutions adopted among states are not in any way uniform in nature. In order to illustrate the heterogeneity of the adopted choices, distinct cases can be described. In three of the 50 US states, namely Alaska, Delaware, and Rhode Island, the state Attorney General has full and exclusive responsibility for prosecuting criminal cases.[211] In all other cases, the state Departments of Justice (also called Offices of the Attorney General) and Attorneys General who manage them, have virtually no influence over the activities of state prosecutors' offices. Given that most state prosecutors in the USA are elected through popular vote within communities where the position will be served, the state Attorneys General do not have any impact on selection of chief prosecutors in their state. The autonomy of state prosecutors and their independence from other state authorities is perhaps the third most important feature of the US state prosecution system,

208 This raises other questions regarding possible interference of the special counsel with constitutional obligations of the US president to observe execution of law. It was also a subject of the debate among scholars as a result of the US Supreme Court judgment in *Morrison* v. *Olson* (108 S. Ct. 2597 [1988]). See more in Dangel (1990).

209 Gramckow (2008), p. 416; Kress (1976), p. 105.

210 The tradition of appointing state Attorneys General is much longer than the US Attorney General. The first appointment of state Attorney General can be traced to 1643 when Richard Lee was appointed in Virginia, still a colony at that time. Shortly afterwards, in 1650, the Attorney General was established in Rhode Island. See more in Department of Justice, *200th Anniversary of the Office of the Attorney General 1789–1989*, Washington 1989, p. 3.

211 Israel (2012), p. 8.

together with the decentralization of the prosecution service and extraordinary discretionary prosecutorial powers that they are granted.

It should be noted at this point that within the 51 US states (including the District of Columbia), only in four of them are chief prosecutors appointed and not elected.[212] There were 2,330 state prosecutors in 2007.[213] This is, however, just the number of chief prosecutors and not the number of *all* attorneys executing prosecutorial functions within offices throughout the USA. The lawyers working for the state's attorneys are appointed to their positions by the state prosecutor herself and will depend on her, as will be discussed below.[214]

But it is specifically the way in which prosecutors are appointed through general elections held by citizens of a given state that seems to be one of those features which makes it possible to regard these elected officials as independent entities. Nevertheless, the election of chief state prosecutors is probably the most disturbing feature of the US state prosecution system.[215] The selection of chief state prosecutors through general election is not a centuries-long tradition. Even in the early nineteenth century, prosecutors in all states that at that time constituted the USA were nominated for their positions in various ways including by judges of local courts, legislative or executive authorities of various kinds.[216]The first election of state prosecutors dates back to 1832 and took place in the state of Mississippi, soon followed by Ohio. This trend can be justified in two ways. First, the disapproval of the selection of public officials (both prosecutors and judges) through vague appointment processes not subject to public scrutiny had significantly increased in that period.[217] Second, and probably more importantly, at the same time the unexpected increase in prosecutorial powers can be noted, by entrusting the prosecutors with a far-reaching discretionary power.[218] The charging decisions, and ultimately prosecuting or discontinuing proceedings against those accused of crimes, became an exclusive competence of local prosecutors.[219] Releasing state prosecutors from appointment processes conducted by local political authorities by introducing general elections seemed, at least at the time, the most appropriate solution strengthening

212 US Department of Justice, *Prosecutors in State Courts 2007*, Bureau of Justice Statistics Bulletin, p. 11, www.bjs.gov/content/pub/pdf/psc07st.pdf. Accessed July 12, 2020.

213 US Department of Justice, *Prosecutors in State Courts 2007*, Bureau of Justice Statistics Bulletin, p. 11, www.bjs.gov/content/pub/pdf/psc07st.pdf. Accessed July 12, 2020.

214 See Section 2.5.3.

215 Even Americans note that for Europeans the idea of appointing prosecutors by general election may be "glaring" (Wright (2009), p. 581).

216 Ellis (2011), pp. 1536–1537.

217 Ellis (2011), p. 1536.

218 Ellis (2011), p. 1539.

219 Ellis (2011), p. 1539.

the prosecutorial independence. In theory, elections promised to control prosecutors' actions, keeping them consistent with public values without resorting to detailed and prospective legal rules.[220]

Soon enough it became clear that the general elections were also not that far from political influence.[221] The appointment of chief state prosecutors in this form is a matter of legitimate critique. First, they may not be able to guarantee the best level of expertise of the elected official—just the most popular or the most skillful. There are cases where candidates for office did not even have to have a legal education, as was the case until 1959 in the state of Utah.[222] Second, after winning the election chief state prosecutors might have a tendency to perform their duties in the shadow of future elections, pleasing the electoral community.[223] Finally, it is doubtful that the election that takes place only once every four years with a low turnout of voters can be considered as an efficient mechanism of accountability. Despite these concerns and criticism, the general election is still perceived as an efficient way to guarantee the independence of the chief prosecutor from executive power. This does not preclude the prosecution service from being openly and unquestionably positioned as a part of the executive.

But the association of the prosecution service with executive power, yet not subordinated to it, is also confirmed by the example of those few states in which prosecutors are not elected but appointed, such as in Connecticut. The current relevant regulations are from 1984, when the Congress of the State of Connecticut voted for the XXIII Amendment to the Connecticut Constitution, introducing a regulation which gives responsibility for investigation and prosecution of criminal cases to a body called the Division of Criminal Justice. This new governmental authority was to include the Chief State's Attorney as responsible for the administrative aspects of its works, and the state's attorneys in the number corresponding to the state's judicial district. At the same time the Division officially became part of the executive.[224]

However, the key issue was a change in how state prosecutors were appointed. Actually, from the beginning of the Connecticut statehood, i.e.

220 Wright (2014), p. 604.

221 Ellis (2011), p. 1564 (the author gives an example of a New York prosecutor's campaign from 1853 in which politicians were strongly involved. thanks to which he won the elections four times and remained in office until 1969. He did so thanks to the election support of German and Irish immigrants, owners of many bars and taverns, often illegally selling alcohol, who were accused of these acts by the prosecutor during his term of office).

222 Kress (1976), p. 105.

223 Wright (2014), p. 604.

224 See Article 23 of the Connecticut Constitution ("There shall be established within the executive department a division of criminal justice which shall be in charge of the investigation and prosecution of all criminal matters").

from 1776, the selection of officials responsible for criminal prosecution was made by the Superior Court judges.[225] Since the beginning, the concept of judges electing prosecutors, unprecedented in other states, was ineffectively combated until its abandonment in 1984.[226] The power to appoint all state prosecutors was entrusted with the Criminal Justice Commission.[227] The reasons for this change were accurately summed up by Joe Lieberman, Attorney General for Connecticut at the time, who during his hearing conducted by the Justice Committee of the Connecticut General Assembly on amendments to the Constitution, explicitly pointed out that "the power to appoint state prosecutors should not be entrusted to the same judges before whom prosecutors appear. Such a system creates a sense of conflict of interest."[228]

Therefore, regardless of whether a state or federal prosecution system, whether the choice of the prosecutor is made by appointment or general election, US law seems to stand behind the concept of making the prosecution service a part of the executive branch. The prosecutor is the state and all actions she undertakes are done in the name of the government. But this allocation of the prosecution system does not make it, at least on normative level, equally dependable on executive wishes and desires. One must agree that on the state level the actual independence of the prosecutors from the state government is achieved by the election process and sustained by withdrawing instruments which would enable local officials to interfere in prosecutorial actions.[229] At the federal level, the situation seems to be quite different. Both the extensive powers of the federal government to appoint and dismiss US Attorneys and the ability to influence their decision-making process through guidelines issued by the Department of Justice and direct and indirect orders make the federal prosecutors visibly subordinated to the executive.

2.5.3 The Internal Independence of the Prosecutor within the Structure of the US Prosecution Service

Freedom of decision-making by US prosecutors is the most well-known trait. US prosecutors are seen as actors in the criminal process that enjoy

225 See Horton (2012), p. 141.

226 See e.g. *State* v. *Moynaham*, 164 Conn. 560, 567–571, 325 A.2d 199 (1973).

227 The Criminal Justice Commission remains part of the Division of Criminal Justice and is composed of the Chief State's Attorney and six members appointed by the Connecticut General Assembly nominated by the Governor, two of whom shall be judges of the Superior Court (Sec. 51-275a CGS).

228 Joe Lieberman, March 5, 1984, HJR No. 35.

229 Green and Zacharias (2008), p. 194.

powers that are unique and unparalleled anywhere in the world, since they are free to apply the law of their jurisdictions to their constituencies as they see fit.[230] This is strongly connected to their extraordinarily wide discretionary powers, as recognized by the US Supreme Court.[231] However, the real question is whether every prosecutor enjoys the same level of independence in the system of US law and what is the extent to which individual prosecutors remain dependent on the attorneys who govern their units. This issue is shaped differently again at federal and state levels and will be discussed in turn.

The federal prosecution system is headed by the Attorney General of the USA (US Attorney General) who leads the Department of Justice. Within the complicated structure of this governmental office, which includes among others a wide variety of law enforcement agencies, such as the Federal Bureau of Investigation (FBI),[232] the US Marshal Service,[233] or the Federal Bureau of Prisons (FBP),[234] are 93 United State Attorneys (US Attorneys)[235] who carry plenary authority with regard to federal criminal matters within their jurisdictions.[236] The powers of US Attorneys, which they hold in their jurisdiction, are clearly defined and include, but are not limited to, prosecuting all offenses against the USA in criminal matters and being a party to all civil and other proceedings to which the state is a party.[237]

Originally the Judiciary Act of 1789, which established the US Attorney General and US Attorneys, did not in any way create a centralized structure.[238] Moreover, the Department of Justice was established just over 80 years later and, therefore, the supervision and control of the US Attorney General was at least very limited. Additionally, at the time of their creation, regulations on US Attorneys were set within the Judiciary Act before the norms constituting the US Attorney General, which could also indicate a relatively high degree of independence of the US Attorneys. The US

230 Anderson (2001), p. 3.

231 "Whether to prosecute and what charge to file or bring before a grand jury are decisions that generally rest in the prosecutor's discretion" (*United States* v. *Batchelder*, 442 US 114 (1979), para. 124).

232 28 USC§ 531–540c.

233 28 USC § 561–575.

234 18 USC § 4041–4049.

235 The number of US Attorneys is dependent on the number of federal judicial districts, which does not necessarily coincide in the size of the state. E.g. in California there are four separate judicial districts (Central, Eastern, Northern, and Southern) each having its own Office of the US Attorney. Two judicial districts of Guam and the Northern Mariana Islands have one US Attorney.

236 9-2.000 JM.

237 28 USC § 547.

238 Seymour (1975), p. 46.

Attorneys were also entrusted with conducting cases before federal courts in both criminal and civil matters, excluding any authority by the US General Attorney to do so until the case reached the US Supreme Court.[239] This all means that originally the US Attorney General did not have power to exercise control over the activities of federal prosecutors in office at the time. In the late eighteenth century, each US Attorney represented the federal government, ran his own legal practice, and for cases conducted in favor of the USA was receiving reimbursement or a percentage of the civil cases that were won.[240] It was not until 1933, in the era of the "New Deal" announced by Franklin D. Roosevelt, that the supervision of the US Attorneys by the Federal Department of Justice was formally confirmed by executive order of the president of the USA.[241]

The dependence of the US Attorneys on the US Attorney General is also visible through their appointment. Despite the fact that they are nominated by the president on the advice and consent of the Senate for a four-year term of office,[242] which might suggest that their position is independent from political turmoil, traditionally, even if the four-year term of office has not yet expired, each of the 93 US Attorneys resign following the election of a new president from a party other than the one that brought them into office.

Each US Attorney has her own Office. The size of each Office varies significantly depending on the size and needs of the jurisdiction[243] including the possibility to create separate branch offices within one judicial district to facilitate work. Within the Offices of the US Attorney, lower-level federal prosecutors named Assistant US Attorneys are hired in the number dependent on the workload. Officially they are appointed by the Attorney General[244] but in practice all decisions are made at the local level involving the relevant US Attorney's views.[245] Therefore, they work at the disposal of the US Attorney and may be removed for cause by her.

Depending on how large their offices are and how many Assistant US Attorneys they employ, the competencies of US Attorneys are distributed differently. Obviously, in smaller federal prosecution offices, the US Attorney will be personally responsible for many litigation activities, including appearing in court, while in larger offices, the duties of the US Attorney will be limited to the efficient organization of work and administrative tasks.[246]

239 Seymour (1975), p. 21.
240 Eisenstein (1978), pp. 9–10.
241 Executive Order No. 6166 of 10 June 1933. Cf. Eisenstein (1978), pp. 10–11.
242 28 USC § 541 (a)–(b).
243 E.g. there are 12 positions in Guam and 360 in District of Columbia (Gramckow (2008), p. 391).
244 28 USC § 542.
245 Gramckow (2008), p. 404.
246 Eisenstein (1978), p. 5.

As a result, the structure of Office of the US Attorney is designed in the hierarchical way. Therefore, each Office can have divisions (e.g. criminal, civil, administrative) and each division can be composed of sections (e.g. general crimes section, violent and organized crime section, criminal appeals section). Each section is led by the Assistant US Attorney ranked as the Chief of Section possessing, together with her deputies, supervisory powers over other Assistant US Attorneys working within section.

The most important question, however, is how far-reaching is the independence of the individual federal prosecutor at the lowest level, with regard to the tasks entrusted to her in respect of each individual case conducted by her? These prosecutors are on an equal footing with US Attorneys according to the guidelines and instructions issued by the Attorney General. If, therefore, the guidelines indicate that approval of the Attorney General should be obtained, this will also bind each federal prosecutor conducting the proceedings. But there are no specific regulations as to the scope of instructions that may be given in individual cases to the federal prosecutor by the head of the office or his immediate deputy. This can suggest that low-level prosecutors exercise full freedom in terms of such decisions. But at the same time each US Attorney in her office has the ultimate authority and discretion to assign and reassign cases.[247] This would mean, in turn, that the US Attorney as well as her deputies and heads of departments within the Office of the US Attorney, and most likely also other senior prosecutors within the Department of Justice, would have full control over the activities and decisions of individual prosecutors in the proceedings, if only theoretically. This can be derived from the hierarchical structure of the Offices of US Attorney, which remains within the complex hierarchical structure of the Department of Justice.[248] And even if it is true that the higher-ranked prosecutors do not frequently use their powers to interfere in the decisions of the subordinate prosecutors and the freedom to undertake decisions is a norm, the mere fact that there are no clearly prescribed restrictions on intervention in decisions of lower-ranked prosecutors seems to be an obvious threat to their independence. It cannot be ruled out that such influence is and will be exerted in key, politicized proceedings.

On the state level the prosecution service may be characterized as being both extremely decentralized and very diverse. Each state is usually divided into bigger or smaller districts and counties within which prosecutorial powers are exercised by district attorneys or county attorneys completely

247 Gramckow (2008), p. 399.

248 See a practical analysis of the structure of the federal prosecution and relations between the Attorney General, US Attorneys and officials within the Department of Justice in Perry (1998), pp. 138–140.

independent from each other. As discussed above, the head of the office is usually an elected official or, rarely, appointed to that position by an external authority. In addition to such elected chief prosecutors the state and county prosecutor's offices may operate employing assistant state or county prosecutors often appointed by their heads, sometimes with the help of independent commissions established within the county.[249] The organization of the prosecutor's office depends greatly on the size of jurisdiction in which such bureau operates. In 22 percent of local state prosecution offices, the local prosecutor has no assistance and take on prosecution functions in that jurisdiction on her own, sometimes even on a part-time basis.[250] But in many other jurisdictions there are bigger offices with ten assistant prosecutors as well as very large offices with a complicated structure hiring hundreds (or even thousands!)[251] of prosecutors and other staff.[252]

It is also true that the US prosecutor possesses wide discretionary powers. However, in practice this applies to chief prosecutors, not necessarily to their subordinates. In result, the decision-making process within each prosecutor's office will be strongly tied to its organizational structure. In small prosecution offices, assistant prosecutors will also prosecute criminal cases, but they will remain entirely dependent on their superiors, leaving office with them when the next election replaces the chief prosecutor. In such units, there is no demand for complicated bureaucratic structures and the assistant state's attorneys retain a close personal relationship with the chief prosecutor. As a result, the supervision over their work does not require issuing any guidelines and the decision-making process may be controlled more informally.[253]

On the other hand, in large city prosecutors' offices, where the workload is much higher than in small suburban prosecutors' offices, the relationship between the chief prosecutor and his hundreds of subordinates is less personal and demands stronger coordination and support. However, distributing cases among lower-level prosecutors and supervising their actions can take different forms.[254] In any case, the structure of the office and channels of communication within it are the sole decision of the chief prosecutor.[255]

249 Kress (1976), p. 105.

250 Kamisar et al. (2012), p. 961.

251 In Los Angeles County District Attorney's Office, the biggest in the USA, there are 1,000 deputy district attorneys responsible for prosecution of crimes. https://da.lacounty.gov/about/office-overview. Accessed July 12, 2020.

252 See broadly on sizes of state and county prosecutor's offices in USA, Gramckow (2008), pp. 390–391 and Kamisar et al. (2012), p. 961.

253 Kamisar et al. (2012), p. 961.

254 See extensively on the structure of decision-making in state prosecutions in Green and Zacharias (2008), pp. 194–196. See also more on so-called vertical and horizontal models of distribution of cases in Kamisar et al. (2012), p. 961.

255 Gramckow (2008), p. 390.

While in smaller offices the state prosecutor is able to personally control the work of all assistant prosecutors, in larger units it will usually be done in a different way, i.e. by adopting common guidelines for given units.[256] In some cases, the standard behavior in certain situations, e.g. negotiating pleas, will be determined by experienced prosecutors allowing free and autonomous application of these rules by junior prosecutors. While in other cases, the rules of conduct will be defined more precisely through guidelines, and some decisions will require the approval of senior prosecutors. Anyhow, few chief prosecutors would allow their subordinates to act entirely independently, without direction through internal policies (either formal or informal) and without supervision.[257]

This may be confirmed by the example of the State of Connecticut. Under Article 23 of the Connecticut Constitution, the Chief State's Attorney and 13 state's attorneys are entrusted with "prosecutorial power of the state." Thirteen state prosecutors' offices, run by 13 state's attorneys, deal with criminal prosecution, one in each state's court district. Each state's attorney's office is managed by a state's attorney, who is assisted by deputy state's attorneys and assistant state's attorneys employed in a number depending on the needs of the particular unit, upon recommendation of the relevant state's attorney.[258] In these units, apart from prosecutors and administrative employees, inspectors are also employed. They are hired to carry out investigations at the direction of the prosecutor in all cases where this is required.[259] Importantly, every inspector is entitled by law to equal rights with police officers,[260] including the right to carry arms. Besides these regulations, the organizational structure of each state's attorney's office remains under the full control of the head of the office. Each state's attorney determines the division of duties between the various assistant state's attorneys and is responsible for their actions.

In the light of the above, the structure of the prosecution service in the state system can be described as decentralized. The prosecutor's offices are independent of each other, not only between states, but also within the state. Each prosecution office is independent from the others and is headed by a, usually elected, chief prosecutor responsible for setting the entire policy for her own office. The degree of their independence and the separation between the offices that they lead is practically absolute.[261] At the same time,

256 See Jacoby (1977), p. 38.
257 Green and Zacharias (2008), p. 196.
258 Sec. 51–278(b)(1)(B) CGS.
259 Sec. 51–286(a) CGS.
260 Sec. 51–286(b) CGS.
261 Which is subject to constant criticism in the USA itself. See e.g. Wright (2009), p. 581 and Kress (1976), p. 105.

the structure of each such office can be characterized as hierarchical and centralized.[262] The chief prosecutor takes full responsibility for her office including the employment of attorneys working within it. Regardless of the size of the prosecutor's office the chief prosecutor sets priorities and give instructions directly or in form of guidelines on handling cases. As a result, all lower-lever prosecutors working within each office are fully answerable to the chief prosecutor and fully depend on her decisions.

2.6 Summary

The position held by the prosecution service in a given state results from the relationship that the prosecution service maintains with other state powers. The external independence of the prosecution service is determined, in particular, by the subordination to the executive and the relation built with the judiciary. The researched countries deliver substantially distinct perspectives on these correlations. The USA seems to provide the most straightforward answer, clearly associating the prosecution service with the executive. Therefore, the US prosecutors represent in their actions the government, whether it is the federal or the state one. Moreover, the connection that the prosecution could have with the judiciary is seen rather as problematic than beneficial, especially for the latter, since the individual facing the criminal justice system should not be under the impression that they are prosecuted and sentenced by the same group. This argument seems valid and should not be quickly forgotten.

At the same time, the European countries have a tendency to claim that the prosecution service is, or should be, a part of the judiciary. Italy goes the furthest, providing that the constitutionally recognized notion of "judicial authority" applies to the same extent to prosecutors and judges. But both Poland and Germany seem to be attracted by the idea of separating the prosecution service from the executive. The arguments in all three cases are similar and relate to the assurance of independence of the prosecution service which, allegedly, can be established only through strong ties with the judiciary. And differently to what is presented in the US system, the proximity to the executive is perceived as an obvious threat to independence. Therefore, in each case the education, training, selection, pension, and promotion for judges and prosecutors are the same. This is understandable if one takes into account the traumatic history that Italy and Germany were faced with before and during World War II and in which the prosecutorial subordination to fascist and Nazi regimes played a significant and infamous role.

262 Gramckow (2008), p. 390.

As a result, the subordination of the prosecution service to the government is perceived as being undesirable.

Yet, the position of the prosecution systems in the researched European countries, as being a part of the judiciary, is continuously undermined. Strong ties with the Ministry of Justice, subordination Minister's orders, possible disciplinary sanctions imposed by her, etc. are, at least for some, proof that the association with the executive is a fact. Germany, in light of the Constitutional Court case law, seems to be the closest to admitting that the prosecution service in the Montesquieu triad is the government's flank.

But there are also some that consider prosecution as not fitting into the traditional separation of powers scheme, claiming that it should be considered rather as "the fourth power." This perception is not absent in US legal doctrine either. For instance, Barkow argues that the conventional formula upon which the separation of powers has been interpreted by the US Supreme Court and scholars is merely compatible in the criminal context, which can have questionable consequences for the institutional checks.[263] Therefore, perhaps, we should not be wasting too much time on identifying where the prosecution service belongs, but rather the focus should be switched to how the prosecutors exercise their powers and who holds them accountable for it.

Indeed, a simple association of the prosecution service either on the normative level or by scholars with one state power or another, is just a first step in the discussion on the level of external independence that the prosecution service possesses. Even international instruments listed at the beginning of this chapter do not provide that the connection between the prosecution service and the executive is a threat. It is rather the level of subordination that is achieved between the government and the prosecution service that might generate the problem. This is visible in a recent reform of the Polish prosecution system where not only the Minister of Justice became the head of the prosecution service—the Attorney General—but also through the introduction of immediate powers vested in ministers' hands toward every prosecutor in every case. This can also be shown by the example of the US system where the federal prosecution service is clearly subordinated to the president while their state counterparts, and not only those chosen in popular elections, maintain a substantial independence from the state's governments. And even though it is clear that the district attorney represents the state and *is* the executive, the lack of influence that the state government exercises over her allows for considerable independence. So, the institutional dependence on the executive may coincide with functional autonomy.

263 Barkow (2006), p. 1053.

Equally important is the issue of the internal independence of the prosecutor. This stems from the organization of the prosecution service in a centralized and decentralized way. To that extent, Italy provides for the strongest guarantees of the independence of prosecutors in exercising their duties in the criminal process. There is no established power of the chief prosecutors to give orders to their subordinates and the institutional guarantees such as the existence of the Superior Council of the Judiciary provides for the protection of freedom in undertaking decisions by prosecutors. Moreover, the existence of the legality principle on the constitutional level is interpreted as a mechanism safeguarding the prosecutorial independence.

On the other hand, both Germany and Poland provide for a hierarchical structure of prosecutor's offices subordinating first-line prosecutors to their immediate supervisors, as well as higher-ranked prosecutors and even, as discussed, to the Minister of Justice herself. The scope of competencies given to the supervisors is broad and includes the power to issue orders including those referring to the final outcome of the case and the power to transfer a case from one prosecutor to the other as per the chief prosecutor's wish. Yet, the difference between execution of these powers is noticeable. The level of trust that the criminal justice system enjoys in Germany is quite high and even though the system is criticized there is not much drive for a change.[264] To the contrary, in Poland, since the changes within the system have been of a strictly political character and the prosecution service is often used as a tool to fight political opponents, it raises much stronger criticism.[265] In both cases, however, it is submitted that the level of interference in individual decisions is excessive, and calls for immediate modification.

In the US case on the federal level the prosecution service organized around the Attorney General is highly centralized, while the state systems toward each other as well as internally are decentralized. However, the relationships within each office is of a hierarchical nature. It is clearly seen on the federal level where subordination of the prosecutors working within each US Attorney's Office is a fact but also within DA's offices and county's or state's attorney offices, the dependency of the frontline prosecutors on the chief prosecutor or her deputies is very strong either through direct orders or guidelines. The proclaimed discretion of the prosecutors is the feature of the head of the office and goes through her to the subordinates.

The analysis of the external and internal aspects of the independence of prosecutors in Germany, Poland, Italy, and United States that shapes the position of the prosecutor in the criminal process, allows us to engage in the

264 Jasch (2019), p. 213.
265 Szeroczyńska (2017), p. 138.

second part of the introductory discussion designed for this book regarding the scope of criminal investigation in each of the researched countries.

References

Amodio E, Selvaggi E (1989) An Accusatorial System in a Civil Law Country: The 1988 Italian Code of Criminal Procedure. *Temple Law Review* 62:1211–1224.

Anderson S (2001) The Changing Role of the Prosecutor. In: *The Prosecutors Deskbook. Ethical Issue and Emerging Roles for the 21st Century Prosecutors.* American Prosecutors Research Institute, Alexandria, pp. 3–23.

Barkow RE (2006) Separation of Powers and the Criminal Law. *Stanford Law Review* 58:989–1054.

Beale SS (2015) Prosecutorial Discretion in Three Systems: Balancing Conflicting Goals and Providing Mechanisms for Control. In: Caianiello M, Hodgson JS (eds) *Discretionary Criminal Justice in a Comparative Context.* Carolina Academic Press, Durham, pp. 27–58.

Bessler J (1994) The Public Interest and the Unconstitutionality of Private Prosecutions. *Arkansas Law Review* 47:529–543

Bohlander M (2012), *Principles of German Criminal Procedure.* Hart Publishing, London.

Boyne SM (2014) *The German Prosecution Service.* Guardians of the Law? Springer, Heidelberg.

Burnham W (2011) *Introduction to the Law and Legal System of the United States*, 5th ed. West, St. Paul.

Caianiello M (2012) The Italian Public Prosecutor: An Inquisitorial Figure in Adversarial Proceedings. In: Luna E, Wade M (eds) *The Prosecutor in Transnational Perspective.* Oxford University Press, Oxford, pp. 250–267.

Caianiello M (2016) *Increasing Discretionary Prosecutor's Powers: The Pivotal Role of the Italian Prosecutor in the Pretrial Investigation Phase.* Oxford Handbooks Online, Oxford.

Corso P (1993) Italy. In: Van Den Wyngaert C (ed) *Criminal Procedure Systems in the European Community.* Butterworths, London, pp. 223–260.

Côté L (2012) Independence and Impartiality. In: Reydams L, Wouters J, Ryngaert C (eds) *International Prosecutors.* Oxford University Press, Oxford, pp. 319–415.

Dangel SAJ (1990) Is Prosecution a Core Executive Function? Morrison v. Olson and the Framers' Intent. *Yale Law Journal* 99:1069–1088.

Del Duca LF (1991) An Historic Convergence of Civil and Common Law Systems – Italy's New "Adversarial" Criminal Procedure System. *Dickinson Journal of International Law* 10:73–92.

Di Amato A (2013) *Criminal Law in Italy.* Kluwer Law International, Alphen aan den Rijn

Di Federico G (1998) Prosecutorial Independence and the Democratic Requirement of Accountability in Italy: Analysis of a Deviant Case in a Comparative Perspective. *British Journal of Criminology* 38:371–387.

Di Federico G (2004) Independence and Accountability of the Judiciary in Italy: The Experience of a Former Transitional Country in a Comparative Perspective. In: Sajó A (ed) *Judicial Integrity*. Brill, Leiden, pp. 181–201.

Di Federico G (2008) Report on the Public Prosecution Service in Italy. In: Open Society Institute Sofia (ed) *Promoting Prosecutorial Accountability, Independence and Effectiveness*. Open Society Institute Sofia, Sofia, pp. 301–339.

Eisenstein J (1978) *Counsel of the United States*. John Hopkins University Press, Baltimore.

Ellis MJ (2011) The Origins of the Elected Prosecutor. *Yale Law Journal* 121:1528–1569.

Elsner B, Peters J (2010) The Prosecution Service Function within the German Criminal Justice System. In: Jehle J-M, Wade M (eds) *Coping with Overloaded Criminal Justice Systems. The Rise of Prosecutorial Power Across Europe*. Springer, Heidelberg, pp. 207–236.

Entin JL (1990) Separation of Powers, Political Branches, and the Limits of Judicial Review. *Ohio State Law Journal* 51:175–227.

Fabri M (2008) Criminal Procedure and Public Prosecution Reform in Italy: A Flash Back. *International Journal for Court Administration*. January:3–15.

Gabriel-Węglowski M (2011), Koncepcja usprawnienia instytucjonalnego prokuratury w zwalczaniu przestępczości zorganizowanej. *Prokuratura i Prawo* 4:73–103.

Garner BA (ed) (2009) *Black's Law Dictionary*. West, St. Paul.

Gialuz M (2017) The Italian Code of Criminal Procedure: A Reading Guide. In: Gialuz M, Lupária L, Scarpa F (eds) *The Italian Code of Criminal Procedure. Critical Essays and English Translation*. Cedam, Milan, pp. 17–55.

Gilliéron G (2004) *Public Prosecutors in the United States and Europe*. Springer, Cham.

Gramckow H (2008) Prosecutor Organization and Operations in the United States. In: In: Open Society Institute Sofia (ed) *Promoting Prosecutorial Accountability, Independence and Effectiveness*. Open Society Institute Sofia, Sofia, pp. 385–432.

Grande E (2000) Italian Criminal Justice: Borrowing and Resistance. American Journal of Comparative Law 48:227–259.

Green BA, Zacharias FC (2008) "The US Attorney Scandal" and the Allocation of Prosecutorial Power. *Ohio State Law Journal* 69:187–254.

Herzog A (2009) Niezależność prokuratury – mit czy nadzieja? *Prokuratura i Prawo* 1:111–129.

Herzog A (2010) *Nowelizacja ustawy o prokuraturze*. Komentarz. Lexis Nexis, Warsaw.

Hodgson J (2005) *French Criminal Justice. A Comparative Account of the Investigation and Prosecution of Crime in France*. Hart Publishing, Oxford and Portland.

Horton WH (2012) *The Connecticut State Constitution*, 2nd ed., Oxford University Press, Oxford.

Illuminati G (2004) The Role of the Public Prosecutor in the Italian System In: Tak PJP (ed) *Tasks and Powers of the Prosecution Services in the EU Member States. Volume I*. Wolf Legal Publishers, Nijmegen, pp. 303–332.

Illuminati G (2005) The Frustrated Turn to Adversarial Procedure in Italy (Italian Criminal Procedure Code of 1988). *Washington University Global Studies Law Review* 4:567–581.

Illuminati G, Caianiello M (2007) The Investigative Stage of the Criminal Process in Italy. In: Cape E, Hodgson J, Pranken T, Spronken T (eds), *Suspects in Europe. Procedural Rights at the Investigative Stage of the Criminal Process in the European Union*. Intersentia, Antwerp, pp. 129–154.

Ireland RM (1995) Privately Funded Prosecution of Crime in the Nineteenth-Century United States. *American Journal of Legal History* 39:43–58.

Israel JH, Kamisar Y, LaFave WF, King N, Primus EB (2012) *Criminal Procedure and the Constitution*. West, Eagan.

Iwanicki S (1995) Prokuratura w nowej Konstytucji. *Prokuratura i Prawo* 2:7–11

Jackson RH (1940) The Federal Prosecutor. *Journal of Criminal Law and Criminology* 31:3–6.

Jacoby JE (1977) *The Prosecutor's Charging Decision: A Policy Perspective*, US Department of Justice Washington.

Jasch M (2019) Prosecution and Politics in Germany: The Struggle for Independence. In: Colvin V, Stenning P (eds) *The Evolving Role of the Public Prosecutor. Challenges and Innovations*. Routledge, New York, pp. 205–219.

Juy-Birmann R (2002) The German System. In: Delmas-Marty M, Spencer JR (eds) *European Criminal Procedures*. Cambridge University Press, Cambridge, pp. 292–347.

Kamisar Y, LaFave WR, Israel JH, King NJ, Kerr OS, Primus EB (2015) *Modern Criminal Procedure. Cases-Comments-Questions*. West, St Paul.

Kardas P (2012) Rola i miejsce prokuratury w systemie organów demokratycznego państwa prawnego. *Prokuratura i Prawo* 9:7–49.

Kavanaugh BM (1998) The President and the Independent Counsel. *Georgetown Law Journal* 86:2134–2178.

Kremens K (2010) *Odpowiedzialność zawodowa prokuratorów*. Warsaw.

Kremens K (2020) The New Wave of Penal Populism from a Polish Perspective. In: Hoven E, Kubiciel M (eds) *Zukunftsperspektiven des Strafrechts. Symposium zum 70.* Geburstag von Thomas Weigend. Nomos Verlag, Bade-Baden, pp. 123–136.

Kress JM (1976) Progress and Prosecution. The Annals of the American Academy of *Political and Social Sciences* 423:99–116.

Lach A (2005) The Prosecution Service of Poland. In: Tak PJP (ed) *Tasks and Powers of the Prosecution Services in the EU Member States*. Volume 2. Wolf Legal Publishers, Nijmegen, pp. 597–616.

Langer M (2004) From Legal Transplants to Legal Translations: The Globalization of Plea Bargaining and the Americanization Thesis in Criminal Procedure. *Harvard International Law Journal* 45 (1): 1–64.

Marguery T (2008) Unity and Diversity of the public prosecution systems in Europe. A study of the Czech, Dutch, French and Polish Systems. Dissertation. Groeningen.

Mazowiecka L (2015) *Prokuratura w Polsce 1918–2014*. Wolters Kluwer, Warsaw.

Misztygacz M (2013) *Ustrój prokuratury w Polsce. Tradycja i współczesność*. Elipsa, Warsaw.

Montana R (2012) Adversarialism in Italy: Using the Concept of Legal Culture to Understand Resistance to Legal Modifications and Its Consequences. *European Journal of Crime, Criminal Law and Criminal Justice* 20:99–120.

Neubauer DW, Fradella HF (2017) *America's Courts and the Criminal Justice System*, 13th ed., Cengage, Boston.

Panzavolta M (2004) Reforms and Counter-Reforms in the Italian Struggle for an Accusatorial Criminal Law System. *North Carolina Journal of International Law & Commercial Regulation* 30:577–624.

Perry Jr. HW (1998) United States Attorneys – Whom Shall They Serve? *Law and Contemporary Problems* 61:129–148.

Podgor ES (2012) Prosecution Guidelines in the United States. In: Luna E, Wade M (eds) *The Prosecutor in Transnational Perspective*. Oxford University Press, Oxford, pp. 9–19.

Ruggeri S (2015) Investigative and Prosecutorial Discretion in Criminal Matters: The Contribution of the Italian Experience. In: Caianiello M, Hodgson JS (eds) *Discretionary Criminal Justice in a Comparative Context*. Carolina Academic Press, Durham, pp. 59–85.

Scaccianoce C (2010) The principle of mandatory prosecution and the independence of public prosecutors in the Italian Criminal Justice System. ReAIDP/e-RIAPL, A-01:1–10.

Seymour Jr. WN, *United States Attorney: An Inside View of "Justice" in America Under the Nixon Administration*. Morrow, New York.

Siegismund E (2003) The Public Prosecution Office in Germany: Legal Status, Function and Organization. In: Effective Administration of the Police and the Prosecution in Criminal Justice. The 120th International Senior Seminar, Visiting Experts' Papers www.unafei.or.jp/publications/pdf/RS_No60/No60_10VE_Siegismund2.pdf. Accessed 12.07.2020, pp. 58–64.

Smoleński J (1970) Rodowód leninowskiej koncepcji prokuratury i jej ustawowa realizacja. *Problemy Praworządności* 7–8.

Stefański RA (2015) Prokurator jako organ postępowania karnego. In: Kwiatkowski Z (ed), *System Prawa Karnego Procesowego, Sądy i inne organy postępowania karnego*, vol. V. Wolters Kluwer, Warsaw, pp. 726–872.

Szeroczyńska M (2017) Międzynarodowy standard statusu i organizacji prokuratury a najnowsze zmiany polskiego porządku prawnego. *Czasopismo Prawa Karnego i Nauk Penalnych* 2:109–139.

Tak PJP (2004) Introduction. In: Tak PJP (ed) *Tasks and Powers of the Prosecution Services in the EU Member States*. Volume I. Wolf Legal Publishers, Nijmegen, pp. 1–15.

Trendafilova E, Róth W (2008) Report on the Public Prosecution Service in Germany. In: Open Society Institute Sofia (ed) *Promoting Prosecutorial Accountability, Independence and Effectiveness*. Open Society Institute Sofia, Sofia, pp. 213–246.

Wade M (2010) The Power to Decide – Prosecutorial Control, Diversion and Punishment in Europe. In: Jehle J-M, Wade M (eds) *Coping with Overloaded Criminal Justice Systems. The Rise of Prosecutorial Power Across Europe*. Springer, Heidelberg, pp. 27–126.

Waltoś S (2002) Prokuratura – jej miejsce wśród organów władzy; struktura i funkcje. *Państwo i Prawo* 4:5–12.

Ważny A (2009) Konstytucja bez prokuratury. *Prokuratura i Prawo* 9:114–117.

Weigend T (2004) The Prosecution Service in the German Administration of Criminal Justice. In: Tak PJP (ed) *Tasks and Powers of the Prosecution Services in the EU Member States*. Wolf Legal Publishers, Nijmegen, pp. 203–222.

Weigend T (2013) Germany. In: Ligeti K (ed) *Toward a Prosecutor of the European Union, Volume 1: A Comparative Analysis*. Hart Publishing, London, pp. 264–306.

Worral JL (2008) Prosecution in America. A Historical and Comparative Account. In: Worrall JL, Nugent-Borakove ML (eds) *The Changing Role of the American Prosecutor*. State University of New York Press, New York, pp. 3–27.

Wright RF (2009) How Prosecutors Election Failed Us. *Ohio State Journal of Criminal Law* 6:581–610.

Wright RF (2014) Beyond Prosecutor Elections. *Southern Methodist University Law Review* 67:593–616.

Zięba-Załucka H (2016) Prokuratura w nowej ustawie z 2016 roku. Eksperyment z podległością władzy wykonawczej. *Przegląd Prawa Konstytucyjnego* 33:111–124.

Chapter 3

Criminal Investigations Compared

3.1 General Considerations

The prosecutor, as the word implies, is connected with prosecution as a discrete stage in the criminal process. In some countries the prosecution seems to commence when the charging of an individual takes place and further actions against the accused are undertaken. Therefore, prosecution of a case before a court of law sounds like the most natural environment in which to find a prosecutor. But even those systems in which the role of the prosecutor during the early stages of the criminal process is limited, the systems provide, as we shall see, a certain role for her during criminal investigation. And it is the aim of this book to explore the ways in which the prosecutor should be engaged during that stage in the criminal process.

Therefore, it is necessary to define at this point the criminal investigation. The chapter offers answers to the following: What are the aims of criminal investigation and what purpose it serves in the context of future trial and criminal process as a whole? What are the boundaries of the criminal investigation? When exactly does the criminal investigation commence—and end? What actions and measures are (or should be) taken while conducting a criminal investigation? And, most importantly: Who has the authority to undertake decisions and take part in the investigatory actions and measures? And finally, who actually controls criminal investigations?

Answers to these questions are crucial to the comparative context of this work. Since comparison is only possible if comparable objects are the subject of this process, determining the common ground between chosen states with regard to what exactly the criminal investigation is the first task of this book. Thus, this chapter is devoted to this kind of analysis and attempts to identify common elements of what is called criminal investigation in Germany, Poland, Italy, and the USA.

There is no common definition of criminal investigation. As discussed by Roberts, criminal investigation has potentially two meanings: (1) it is the stage in criminal process that is prosecution-oriented toward solving unsolved crime, identifying perpetrators, and bringing offenders to justice; (2) it entails collecting intelligence, maintaining order, or undertaking other routine policing tasks.[1] Most commonly the term "investigation" is associated with an early stage of the criminal process during which criminal justice authorities gather information to identify suspects. But legal definitions of investigation are rather hard to find. At the same time other terms, such as pretrial phase or preliminary proceedings, are invoked in similar context although without explanation on the relation that it has toward criminal investigation.[2] Should it be, therefore, assumed that, despite the lack of common definition, in all selected countries "investigation" is understood in the same way? Perhaps, it is the best first to describe how that notion is understood in each country and then—in the summary of the chapter—return to this analysis. Throughout this book, the terms investigation and criminal investigation are used interchangeably in referring to the first stage of criminal process.

Therefore, this chapter focuses on criminal investigation itself as a stage of the criminal process as structured in each of the selected states. The presentation of each legal system is based on normative analysis while all factual and practical distortions from the model prescribed in legal provisions will be discussed throughout the following chapters devoted to stages in the criminal investigation. The chapter commences with a brief outline of criminal investigation in each country. This will be done through the analysis of the aims of criminal investigation, events determining the time frame of this phase of the process, as well as crucial moments in its conduct, in particular, identifying suspects. The main actors in criminal investigations are briefly presented, with a focus on the judicial authority exercised at this stage. The presentation of the course of investigations as adopted in each country is followed by a more specific analysis of the approach that each country takes toward two principles that shape the model of criminal process at this stage and influence the powers of the prosecutor in a most substantial way: prosecutorial discretion and prosecutorial objectivity.

3.2 Criminal Investigation in Germany

3.2.1 The Notion and Outline of Criminal Investigation

In Germany the first stage of the criminal process is called *Vorverfahren* or *Ermittlungsverfahren*. Both may be translated as "preparatory phase"[3] or

1 Roberts (2007), p. 95.
2 See Ligeti (2019), p. 145.
3 Juy-Birmann (2002), p. 310.

"pretrial procedure."[4] Still, some scholars use the term "investigation."[5] The literature lacks a straightforward definition of criminal investigation and it is rather defined through its aims and characteristics or through the time limits separating investigation from the subsequent stages of criminal proceedings.

Generally, the German criminal investigation is aimed at discovering whether an offense can be attributed to the suspect and whether it is possible to institute a prosecution.[6] The investigation is also described as a string of attempts by the police to obtain information that can be used by the prosecution in determining whether the case should be brought to trial, and if so, on what charges.[7] Investigation, however, is not only aimed at enabling the prosecutor to make a final decision on the further course of proceedings but at the same time should allow the prosecutor to collect and record evidence in such a way that will allow for its use during the trial.[8] Moreover, the German criminal process, as a typical inquisitorial system is, at all its stages, aimed at establishing the truth (*Wahrheitserforschung*).[9] To achieve this goal all authorities are obliged to act *ex officio*, which results in obliging the prosecutor to gather evidence both in favor of and against the accused during the investigation.[10] This provision, together with the principle of mandatory investigation and prosecution,[11] has a strong impact on the shape of criminal investigation in Germany.

The investigation starts when the prosecutor or police are informed that a criminal offense may have been committed. It is conducted by the police under the supervision of the prosecutor and, in theory, the prosecutor maintains full control over every investigation in the country, but in practice the actual control of the prosecutor is limited to the most serious cases.[12] Prosecutors maintain very broad investigative powers in terms of the scope of activities undertaken in proceedings, to identify the suspect and the circumstances in which a crime has been committed. And these powers are, almost in full, transferrable to the police. During investigation, prosecutors and police can interview witnesses and suspects, gather real

4 This term is used e.g. by Huber (2008), p. 283; Weigend and Salditt (2007), p. 95.
5 The term "investigation" is used e.g. by Weigend (2013), p. 264.
6 Roxin at al. (2017), p. 317; Juy-Birmann (2002), p. 312.
7 Weigend (2015), p. 188.
8 Elsner and Peters (2010), p. 226.
9 Trendafilova and Róth (2008), p. 230 ("The purpose of the investigation is to discover the objective truth [...]"; Gilliéron (2014), p. 275 ("Preliminary proceedings have the purpose of ascertaining the facts and thus of deciding whether to bring charges or to drop the case for lack of evidence or lack of violation of criminal law").
10 § 160 (2) StPO.
11 § 152 (2) StPO.
12 Frase and Weigend (1995), p. 323.

evidence as well as documents. This may also happen in a coerced manner through summonses, searches, and seizures. Some of these measures are even mandatory. For instance, the interrogation of the suspect must be conducted at least once during investigation.[13] All measures are recorded according to formal rules and become a part of the prosecutorial dossier that subsequently becomes a basis for the court proceedings to which it is transferred together with the indictment. The investigation is therefore conducted in an official and formal way and as a result is relatively time-consuming.

The role of the court can be key at this stage due to the importance of the use of certain coercive measures. Since 1975, Germany no longer has the investigative judge (*Untersuchungsrichter*) who had broad competencies to conduct independent investigations. Instead, the judge of the investigation (*Ermittlungsrichter*) has been introduced into the system, vested with powers relating to authorization of investigatory measures interfering with the rights of an individual during criminal investigation, such as arrests, pre-trial detentions, searches, seizures, and secret surveillance. This also means that the powers of the prosecutor in the course of an investigation will be significantly limited by the powers granted to this authority. Additionally, the *Ermittlungsrichter* may undertake certain investigative measures (interrogations, taking real evidence) so that by the fact of being carried out in the presence of the court, they obtain a similar value of credibility and probative value as such measures carried out during the trial. This is, however, done upon prosecutorial request only and no own initiative of the judge is allowed.

The investigation ends with a decision whether to file a case with the court in the form of written accusation, or whether to discontinue. These decisions remain solely in the hands of the prosecutor, regardless of how engaged she was during the course of criminal investigation.

3.2.2 Prosecutorial Discretion

The principle of legality (*Legalitätsprinzip*) constitutes a foundation of the German criminal justice system.[14] The reinstatement of this principle became a necessary response to the abuse of discretion during the Nazi regime before and during World War II. The experience of abandoning the principle of legality by the National Socialist government, leading to instrumental treatment of the law, that ended with horrific cruelty and violence, necessitated redefinition of the role of the state emphasizing the rule of law (*Rechtsstaadt*). This was directly connected with the idea that it is the parliament, not the judges, who have the power to make laws. As a result, laws

13 § 163a (1) StPO.
14 See Jescheck (1970), p. 245.

were to have a binding effect on all actors of the criminal process, including judges and prosecutors who must obey regulations provided by the legislature and exercise their functions without discretion.

Despite its obvious importance, the principle of legality is not directly reflected in the text of German Constitution.[15] The closest to it seems to be Article 20 (3) of German Constitution providing that "the executive and judiciary shall be bound by law and justice" although this provision does not address the issue in the same way as § 152 (2) StPO, understood as incorporating the principle to German criminal procedure in a normative way. According to this provision the public prosecution office shall be obliged to act in relation to all prosecutable criminal offenses, provided there are sufficient factual indications. This is interpreted as a requirement that the prosecutor is obliged both to investigate[16] and prosecute[17] in every case when sufficient factual basis for commitment of a crime exists. From that perspective, the principle "is thought to imply a principle of compulsory prosecution—a radical attempt directed to eliminate police and prosecutorial discretion altogether."[18] Accordingly, the discretion of the prosecutor is limited to evaluating whether reasonable grounds exist: the process that, at least in theory, should be also objective in nature[19] which, reportedly, leads to a high number of investigations initiated in Germany.[20]

The rigid principle of mandatory investigation and mandatory prosecution should be perceived in light of other legal provisions that put natural boundaries on bringing too many cases into the system. The first mechanism relates to the establishment of the category of least serious offenses (*Übertretungen*) classified as administrative offenses subject to fine, such as some traffic offenses.[21] Second, the category of private crimes (*Privatklagdelikte*)[22] which have a common characteristic of predominantly personal character of the interest involved.[23] This list contains for example defamation, bodily injury, criminal damage to property.[24] It is reported that, due to the nature of

15 Boyne (2014), pp. 2, 30 (the author presents the view that the principle of legality is rooted in a constitutionally expressed principle of rule of law).
16 § 160 (1) StPO.
17 § 170 (1) StPO.
18 Dubber (2006), p. 438.
19 There is a noticeable difference between the grounds necessary to commence investigation and to file charges with the criminal court. See more on this topic in Weigend (2013), pp. 267–268 and in Section 4.2.1 on the threshold necessary to initiate investigation in Germany.
20 Trendafilova and Róth (2008), p. 227.
21 Elsner and Peters (2010), pp. 225–226.
22 Sometimes also called "offenses investigated by the victim."
23 Herrmann (1974), p. 478.
24 § 374 (1) StPO.

the proceedings and costs that private prosecution involves, the numbers of attempted proceedings triggered this way is gradually declining.[25] Another group of crimes is distinguished that narrows down the scope of offenses that the prosecutor has full control over. This is a broad category of offenses investigated upon complaint (*Antragsdelikte*) which are only investigated and prosecuted if the victim requests so.[26] The StGB provides examples of such crimes, including trespass, libel and slander, abduction, and many more. In all these cases the victim has simply a right of veto over investigation and prosecution.[27]

Technically, all the above discussed provisions are not considered as exceptions to the principle of legality.[28] The police and prosecution are not given the discretion to choose the crimes to investigate but are obliged to act always when the victim files the complaint. However, in practice, *Antragsdelikte* limit the scope of legality principle as applicable only upon the victim's approval. This allows the crimes investigated upon complaint to be considered as an exception to the legality principle by reducing the number of offenses subjected to compulsory investigation and prosecution. But the heavy workload of cases carried by prosecutors still required some reaction which allowed for introduction of prosecutorial discretion, or as it is rather termed, the "principle of opportunity" (*Opportunität*).[29] It all started in 1970s when the legality principle began to lose some of its prescriptive force.[30] The compulsory investigation and prosecution are still considered necessary with felonies,[31] because of their serious character.[32] However, in other less serious cases the law provides for other possibilities, among which disposition of a case without conditions, and conditional discontinuations of proceedings are most frequently used. This also includes the discontinuation of criminal investigation based on the lack of public interest even if only in case of minor offenses.[33] So, the introduced mechanisms allow to admit that the observance of the principle of legality in Germany is less strict than the § 152 (2) StPO promises.

25 Frase and Weigend (1995), p. 352.
26 See §§ 77–77e StGB.
27 Frase and Weigend (1995), p. 352.
28 Although see the discussion considering all prescribed mechanisms and many more as forms of prosecutorial discretion in Herrmann (1974), pp. 468–505.
29 See more on the development of discretionary mechanisms in minor cases in Boyne (2014), pp. 65–70.
30 Boyne (2018), p. 148.
31 These are called *Verbrechen*; serious offenses carrying a statutory minimum sentence of one-year imprisonment or more.
32 Herrmann (1974), p. 474.
33 § 153 StPO. See Section 8.2.1.

3.2.3 Prosecutorial Objectivity

As discussed earlier, German prosecutors are perceived as apolitical figures that cannot be easily associated with the executive or the judiciary.[34] They are positioned as independent of the judges and courts, yet nor are they seen as subordinate to the executive. Moreover, certain mechanisms provided in law, including the subordination to legal norms through the adoption of the principle of legality, equips them with a unique level of independence. Therefore, prosecutors are seen as "guardians of the law" (*Wächter der Gesetzes*), tasked with supporting public order and legality.[35] But how this position translates into criminal investigation is a question to be answered.

The German prosecutor is actually seen as a neutral and objective official that holds a quasi-judicial role in fact finding, whose duty during criminal investigation is to examine the facts regardless of whether they support the initial suspicion.[36] By law, the prosecutor is obliged to investigate not only incriminating evidence but to look for evidence that might be of an exculpatory character.[37] This duty makes prosecutors appear to function as second judges devoted to establishing the truth on equal terms.[38] In this sense the prosecution service is equivalent to the courts and both groups are equally responsible for the provision of justice. Indeed, it is true that both judges and prosecutors are

> required by law to clear up the offense in question in full, taking into account all incriminating and exonerating circumstances. In other words, by law the public prosecutor is not a party supporting, and equally he is not the opponent of, the defendant.[39]

This perception of the prosecutor is, moreover, strengthened by the possession of a unique position during the first stage of the criminal process—the "master of the investigation" (*Herr des Ermittlungsverfahren*).[40] The full control granted to the prosecutor from the commencement of investigation and continuing until its very end, resembles the position that the court (judge) serves when assuming control over the trial. It is also enhanced by accompanying competences that the prosecutor is equipped with in the German criminal process e.g. deciding on the admission of evidence and

34 See Section 2.2.2.
35 Trendafilova and Róth (2008), p. 213.
36 Weigend (2013), p. 266.
37 § 160 (2) StPO.
38 See Boyne (2018), p. 141.
39 Siegismund (2003), p. 64.
40 Trendafilova and Róth (2008), p. 225.

taking evidence during criminal investigation. Moreover, the shape of the criminal process in which the German prosecutor performs does not force her to pursue the "win" at all costs. As was long ago discussed by Langbein, and remains true today, the prosecutor is not expected to engage during the trial since the form of evaluation of her performance is not based on the number of cases won by her.[41] It is assumed, at least in theory, that even if the prosecutor has filed an accusation, she retains the neutral stance of an officer of law also shown through the ability to subsequently file an appeal on behalf of the accused.[42]

All these features make German prosecutors as Boyne argues "the most objective civil servants of the world"[43] and at least on a normative level, as having strong regulations toward objectivity in their conduct of criminal investigation. But the duty of objectivity does not make prosecutors immune from political interference.[44]

3.3 Criminal Investigation in Poland

3.3.1 The Notion and Outline of Criminal Investigation

The first stage of the criminal process in Poland is called *postępowanie przygotowawcze* which can be translated as "preparatory proceedings." This is also the title of Section 7 of the k.p.k. containing provisions relating to this phase of the criminal process. The use of this term clearly accentuates the preparatory aspect of this early stage of the criminal process conducted with an aim to undertake the decision whether to bring a criminal action against an individual and a future trial.

The time frame of criminal investigation is specified by law by its beginning and ending moments. The law also specifies the investigative measures that can be undertaken at this stage. Importantly, investigations can be conducted in two separate forms: inspection (*śledztwo*) and inquiry (*dochodzenie*). Inspection is usually conducted in more complicated cases, i.e. in case of all felonies and some misdemeanors that are exceptional, e.g. those in which the suspect is a judge, prosecutor, police officer, but it is also possible to turn any inquiry into an inspection on the prosecutor's decision.[45] As a result, an inspection is deemed to be more formal than an inquiry and the prosecutor plays a more important role in it, being responsible for directly

41 John H. Langbein, "Land without Plea Bargaining: How the Germans Do It?," 78 *Michigan Law Review* 1979, p. 217.

42 Weigend (2013), p. 266.

43 Boyne (2018), p. 161.

44 See Section 2.2.2.

45 Art. 309 k.p.k.

conducting certain actions, e.g. preliminary charging and interrogating the suspect.[46] But from the practical point of view this distinction is of rather diminishing importance.[47]

Note that *śledztwo* is translated as "investigation" and practically all analysis of the Polish criminal process in English use this term instead of inspection.[48] However, for the sake of clarity, this book uses the term investigation to describe the first stage of the criminal process, comprising *śledztwo* and *dochodzenie*. On the other hand *śledztwo*, consequently is called "inspection."

The objectives of criminal investigation closely correspond with objectives of criminal proceedings in Poland as prescribed in Article 2 § 1 k.p.k. Among the aims of the first phase of the criminal process are establishing whether a criminal act has been committed and whether it constitutes an offense, identification of the offender and, if necessary, apprehending him or her, clarifying the circumstances of the case and collecting, securing, and recording evidence for the court to be used during "future trial".[49] The aim of investigation must, therefore, be considered as relatively broad and demanding from the prosecutor, as well as police, full engagement in discovering the truth about the crime in question.

The criminal investigation commences with a formal decision to initiate proceedings. It is always conducted by the prosecutor, or by the police under the supervision of prosecutor. Other agencies may also conduct investigation, again always controlled and supervised by the prosecutor. Importantly, the investigation is divided into two substages: the first is the so-called investigation *in rem* when the suspect has not yet been identified and the second is the investigation *ad personam*, i.e. against an identified person.[50] The division is the result of the adoption of a formal mechanism designating the accused through bringing initial charges against her. This should be considered as the most crucial stage during investigation since such rights as the right to defense or right to remain silent are triggered only when such a formal designation of the suspect occurred.[51]

The collection of evidence during criminal investigation is conducted under formal rules and recorded carefully so the court will be subsequently able to rely on these findings. The parties to the criminal investigation, i.e. both the suspect after her formal designation, as well as the victim, are

46 See Section 5.3.1.

47 De Vocht (2010), p. 429.

48 The words "investigation" describing *śledztwo* and "preliminary proceedings" as *postępowanie przygotowawcze* are used by, among others, Murzynowski (2005), p. 395; Nowak and Steinborn (2013), p. 499; Jasiński and Kremens (2019), p. 208. But see e.g. Kruszyński (2007), p. 181 using "investigation" for *postępowanie przygotowawcze*.

49 Art. 297 § 1 k.p.k.

50 Nowak and Steinborn (2013), p. 498.

51 See Section 6.3.1.

generally allowed to participate in criminal investigation. They may take part in investigatory measures undertaken by the police and the prosecutor and may also request undertaking the investigative measures. Yet, no private investigation by the suspect is allowed.

There is no investigating judge in criminal proceedings. However, the court plays an important role during this stage of the criminal process, since it is accepted that some actions must be vested in the hands of an independent and impartial authority, which calls for raison d'être of judge.[52] Therefore, the measures that interfere with the rights of an individual must be undertaken by the court, including pretrial detention or secret surveillance. Yet, some other measures such as search, seizure, and arrest are imposed by the prosecutor and only subjected to judicial review. Moreover, certain evidentiary measures must be conducted with court involvement. This, in particular, applies to interrogation of vulnerable witnesses in cases of sexual assault. Such decisions during investigation are undertaken by a regular judge who is later not precluded from hearing the case on a trial.

Upon the conclusion of the investigation, the prosecutor decides on discontinuation of proceedings or files a formal, written accusation with a court through indictment or by other form as law prescribes. The decision to drop an investigation at any point in time is subject to judicial review and controlled by the court on the victim's request.

3.3.2 Prosecutorial Discretion

The principle of legality (*zasada legalizmu*) is key in Polish criminal procedure. The law provides that the authority responsible for conducting investigations is bound to initiate and conduct proceedings while the authority responsible for prosecuting cases file an accusation with a court and support it throughout the prosecution.[53] The principle thus formulated is considered to guarantee equality of individuals under the law, perceived as demonstrating its democratic character.[54] And even though the Polish Constitution does not mention the principle of legality directly, its roots can be traced to the principles of equality and material truth and it corresponds with the unacceptability of understanding the concept of legalism as an obligation to punish the perpetrator at all costs.[55]

The wording of Article 10 § 1 k.p.k. means the principle of legality applies to both investigative and prosecuting authorities and should be understood

52 Jasiński and Kremens (2019), p. 213.
53 Art. 10 § 1 k.p.k.
54 Sobolewski (1999), p. 117.
55 Skorupka (2010), pp. 40–41.

very broadly. Therefore, there is not only an obligation to prosecute a case but, first and foremost, a prosecutorial duty to commence and conduct investigation. It applies both to the prosecutor and the police, depending on who undertakes such decision. Perhaps this is also a reason why Polish literature avoids using the term "the principle of mandatory prosecution" and prefers instead "the principle of legality," since the former suggests that the principle applies only at the later stage of the criminal process.

Since the principle of legality is prescribed in such a rigid way, it might seem that the system is faced with having to carry on an enormous number of cases. One may wonder how Polish prosecutors deal with such a huge number of investigations, and whether there are mechanisms to reduce the caseload. It has been acknowledged that it is impossible to sustain in full the concept of the principle of legality without compromising the effectiveness of actions undertaken by law enforcement.[56] Therefore, the principle of legality has its limitations. It applies only to such situations where, first of all, there is reasonable suspicion that crimes have been committed and, second, when conducting investigation and prosecution is, in fact, legally permissible.[57]

Thus, the application of the principle of legality does not apply to all crimes. It is not valid in cases of so-called private offenses or offenses prosecuted by private accusation (*przestępstwa ścigane z oskarżenia prywatnego*). This group is small consisting only of four crimes: causing minor bodily harm or a minor impairment to health,[58] slander,[59] insult,[60] and breach of personal inviolability.[61] Where one of these offenses occurs, the victim is solely responsible for the conduct of proceedings and may file a private indictment with the court.[62] The prosecutor would normally not become involved with the investigation and prosecution of these offenses, since they are considered as not posing a threat to the public interest.[63] In rare cases, however, the prosecutor may decide otherwise and can commence such proceedings or join them.[64]

Second, the limitation on the application of the principle of legality is also seen in cases of so-called offenses investigated *ex officio*.[65] Similar to the

56 Duży (2011), p. 65.
57 Waltoś (2008), p. 293.
58 Art. 157 § 2 and 3 k.k.
59 Art. 212 k.k.
60 Art. 216 k.k.
61 Art. 217 k.k.
62 See Arts. 59–61 and 485–499 k.p.k. regulating the conduct of investigation and court proceedings in case of offenses prosecuted by private accusation.
63 Jasiński and Kremens (2019), p. 206.
64 Art. 60 § 1 k.p.k.
65 Art. 10 § 1 k.p.k. *in fine*.

German law, the Polish criminal procedure differentiates between offenses prosecuted upon complaint (*przestępstwa wnioskowe*) and offenses prosecuted without complaint (*przestępstwa bezwnioskowe*). As provided by law, the criminal justice authorities are obliged to carry out proceedings and undertake actions in every case where a reasonable suspicion that an offense has been committed exists, unless the law provides that a complaint from a victim is required.[66] Therefore, commencing and conducting investigation in cases of offenses investigated upon complaint is possible only if the victim files an official complaint with a criminal investigation authority. Examples of such offenses are criminal threat[67] or theft committed to the detriment of next of kin.[68] The Polish Criminal Code attributes an offense to one group or the other. Since the investigation (and prosecution) of such offenses is possible only upon the complaint of the victim, the criminal justice authorities are in each such case obliged to identify the victim (if this is not the person that reported the offense) and to inform him or her of the consequences of filing or not filing a complaint.[69] But from the moment that the victim expresses her expectation that the investigation should be carried out and the offender subsequently accused, the proceedings must commence and are conducted *ex officio* regardless of the victim's subsequent activity.

The above examples show that the legality principle is certainly not absolute and there are certain limitations to it, since not all criminal offenses fall under it or at least not without the permission of the victim. Additionally, the criminal procedure provides for few other straightforward exceptions to the legality principle. The first is the discontinuation of investigation due to the absorption of an offense by conviction in other proceedings conducted against the same offender.[70] Accordingly, a case might be terminated by the prosecutor if there is no purpose in holding proceedings against the defendant for a lesser offense (a misdemeanor punishable by a penalty of imprisonment for up to five years) in view of another penalty having already been imposed on that defendant for some other offense. The offense for which the defendant has already been sentenced should be of a graver manner and the penalty imposed for that offense would foreseeably most likely absorb the penalty that could be imposed for the offense in which the proceedings were discontinued.[71]

Another exception is the discontinuation of proceedings conducted against a state witness (*świadek koronny*) within 14 days after a judgment against defendants against whom the witness has testified has become final.

66 Art. 9 § 1 k.p.k.
67 Art. 190 k.k.
68 Art. 278 § 4 k.k.
69 Art. 12 § 1 k.p.k.
70 Art. 11 k.p.k.
71 Nowak and Steinborn (2013), p. 501.

This special ground for terminating the case relates to the need to break the loyalty of organized crime groups and is regulated by the State Witness Act of June 25, 1997.[72] Moreover, Polish scholars sometimes identify the discontinuation of investigation against an offender suspected of possession of drugs, if it is proven that the amount of the possessed substance was minor, intended for personal use, and in the light of the circumstances of the case (i.e. first-time offender), the conviction seems inappropriate.[73] Also, the discontinuation of investigation against a juvenile offender if the circumstances of the case do not give grounds for its initiation or conduct, or when the educational and correctional measures are without merit,[74] is considered a form of exception to the principle of legality, although it should be kept in mind that proceedings against juveniles are regulated separately. On the other hand, the decisions reached through the negotiated case settlements allowed for in Polish system are not considered in any way as exceptions to the legality principle.[75]

Interestingly, the Polish system does not provide for the exception from the principle of legality allowing for discontinuation of investigation based on public interest.[76] The reasons for lack of such option can be traced to mistrust of the prosecution service, rooted in perceiving this authority as historically an instrument of political control.[77] The Polish theory of the criminal process accepts the so-called principle of material legality which basically means that the criminal process should be initiated whenever the "social harm of the committed offence is greater than negligible,"[78] which makes it a part of definition of a crime.[79] As a result, the law precludes proceedings from being commenced or continued if the social harm does not reach a certain expected level.[80] This approach creates a situation that, if the social harm is considered more than negligible, the prosecutor has no choice but to commence investigation. Consequently, the nonexistent

72 Consolidated text Dz.U. 2016, poz. 1197.

73 Art. 62a Drug Abuse Prevention Act of July 29, 2005 (consolidated text Dz.U. 2019, poz. 852).

74 See Art. 21 § 2 Juvenile Justice Act of October 26, 1982 (Dz.U. 2014, poz. 382).

75 Skorupka (2019), p. 50. But see the opposite view naming those mechanism as "actual discretion" (*oportunizm faktyczny*) in e.g. Kmiecik (2011), p. 27 and Kulesza (2014), pp. 21–22.

76 See Bulenda et al. (2010), p. 267.

77 See Wade (2008), p. 610.

78 Rogacka-Rzewnicka (2007), p. 257.

79 Art. 1 § 2 k.k. The assessment of the degree of social harm of a prohibited act is carried out through the prism of criteria set out in Art. 115 § 2 k.k. among which are the type and nature of the violated legal interest, the extent of the damage caused or threatened, the manner and circumstances in which the act was committed, the seriousness of obligations breached, the form of intent, perpetrator's motives, etc.

80 Art. 17 § 1 (3) k.p.k.

category of discontinuation of criminal investigation for lack of public interest might be hidden in other categories.

3.3.3 Prosecutorial Objectivity

The Polish k.p.k. accepts objectivity as a leading principle of the criminal process providing that authorities conducting criminal proceedings are obliged to examine and take into account circumstances both in favor of and against the accused.[81] It is considered to be a directive according to which a procedural authority should have an impartial attitude toward the parties and other participants to criminal proceedings and should not be oriented toward the case itself.[82] Interestingly, this provision refers not only to the prosecutor but to all authorities involved in criminal proceedings and, in particular, to the court.[83] In this context, it relates to the principle of judicial impartiality guaranteed primarily by Article 45 § 1 of the Polish Constitution, which in turn does not cover prosecutorial objectivity.[84]

When this principle, as provided in Article 4 k.p.k., applies to the prosecutor who conducts or supervises criminal investigation, it must be interpreted as an obligation to gather both incriminating and exonerating evidence.[85] Moreover, its applicability is not limited to criminal investigation but equally binds the prosecutor during the trial, forcing her to behave objectively also in proceedings before the court.[86] This is supported, inter alia, by the prosecutorial competence to appeal the case also in favor of the accused.[87]

The problem of maintaining objectivity by the prosecutor in the course of criminal investigation was raised in 2015, when criminal procedure, for a short period of time, turned toward adversariality.[88] It was argued at that time that it is impossible to reconcile a situation in which the prosecutor is covered by the principle of objectivity during the course of criminal investigation with her position in the adversarial nature of court proceedings, when the prosecutor becomes an equal party to the trial.[89] In such cases the duality

81 Art. 4 k.p.k.
82 Cieślak (1984), p. 318.
83 Skorupka (2018), p. 160.
84 The rule reads: Everyone shall have the right to a fair and public hearing of his case, without undue delay, before a competent, impartial, and independent court.
85 Jasiński and Kremens (2019), p. 190.
86 Zgryzek (2017), p. 12 and text accompanying fn. 15 (author quotes broad literature presenting this dominant view, nevertheless, brings interesting perspective supporting the claim that when the trial starts the objectivity of the prosecutor changes).
87 Art. 425 § 4 k.p.k.
88 See Kremens (2020).
89 Hofmański and Śliwa (2015), pp. 79–80.

of the prosecutorial function is difficult to maintain, and the prosecutor may feel torn between the obligation to act objectively at the early stage of criminal process and the duty to argue against the accused after the case is sent to trial. As Poland reverted to its traditional inquisitorial form in 2016, the question of prosecutorial objectivity during trial became less important. In any case, whether it is even possible to remain objective during the trial while burdened with the obligation to prove the guilt of the accused, this discussion does not undermine the deeply held belief that, during the course of criminal investigation, the prosecutor must always remain objective.

There are many other provisions both within the k.p.k. and in other legal acts that support this view. For one, it is reinforced by how the objectives of criminal investigation are put together. In particular, the fact that the prosecutor, as the "master of criminal investigation" controlling and supervising the outcome of this stage of criminal process is burdened with an obligation to establish the circumstances of the case[90] shapes the position of the prosecutor in an obvious way. It is, therefore, expected that the prosecutor, as well as law enforcement authorities conducting investigation, will not solely focus on incriminating evidence but will strive to verify all probable versions of events. And most likely confirmation of the neutral position of the prosecutor, regardless of the role that she plays in the criminal justice system or in the system as a whole, is seen in the most explicit way in Article 2 PSA 2016, which confirms that the prosecution service carries out law enforcement tasks and upholds the rule of law. This makes all prosecutors "the guardians of the rule of law."

3.4 Criminal Investigation in Italy

3.4.1 The Notion and Outline of Criminal Investigation

The first stage of the Italian criminal process is the *indagini preliminari* which can be translated as "preliminary investigation." In English literature, it is translated interchangeably as "preliminary investigation phase," "pretrial phase," as well as "investigation phase."[91]

The provisions related to investigation are discussed in Book V of the Italian c.p.p. (from commencement to end of investigation including preliminary hearing).[92] But in fact the investigation should be understood as a

90 Art. 297 § 1 (4) k.p.k.

91 See e.g. Di Amato (2013), p. 162 (in one small paragraph all these terms are used as meaning the same: "Once the prosecutor is informed about the commission of an offence, the preliminary investigation phase commences. During this pre-trial phase, the public prosecutor has a dominant position in carrying out the investigation").

92 Arts. 326–437 c.p.p.

separate phase of the criminal process preceding the preliminary hearing.[93] Regulating in the code the investigation and preliminary hearing separately from the regulation on trial phase was a natural consequence of adoption of the clear separation of stages of process in accordance with adversarial model of criminal proceedings.[94] The aim was to prevent judicial prejudice founded on knowledge of the findings gathered during criminal investigation and revealed during preliminary hearing by withholding them from the trial judge.[95] It was primarily based on the assumption that the probative value of evidence is affected by the manner in which it is collected.[96] This helped to develop strict boundaries for the investigation providing for its end at the time when the prosecutor files a request for trial to the judge (*richiesta di rinvio a giudizio*).

After 1988 the aim of the investigation has also changed noticeably. While the traditional inquisitorial approach under the Rocco Code of 1930 made an objective of criminal investigation to "ascertain the truth,"[97] in the new Code it was decided that the aim of criminal investigation would focus not on collection of evidence, but on seeking to establish elements of the crime in order to file charges against defendants.[98] Under new provisions, the police and the prosecutor would gather facts regarding the event and present that evidence at a preliminary hearing (rather than including it in a dossier that becomes part of the record).[99] This allowed for a shift in focus on taking evidence from investigation to the trial phase and, again, prevented the uncontrolled flow of pretrial findings contained in dossier to the trial. In addition, the criminal procedure did away with the infamous investigating judge (*giudice istruttore*), who, prior to 1988, was fully responsible for the conduct of investigation by collecting evidence, ordering searches and seizures, summoning witnesses, and questioning the accused.[100] This figure has been replaced by a new type of judge, the judge for preliminary investigation (*giudice per le indagini preliminari*, GIP) with limited powers to intervene only upon the parties' request. In particular, the judge for preliminary investigation has been called upon to adopt measures restricting rights of the individual, such as pretrial detention or interception of communications.

93 Grande (2000), p. 232 ("The new code divides ordinary criminal proceedings into three phases: (1) the preliminary investigation, (2) the preliminary hearing, and (3) the trial" [fn. omitted]). Cf. Di Amato (2013), p. 160 (note however that Di Amato considers the preliminary hearing as part of trial stage).
94 Panzavolta (2004), p. 585.
95 Illuminati (2005), p. 571.
96 Caianiello (2012), p. 253.
97 Illuminati (2005), p. 567.
98 Del Duca (1991), p. 82.
99 Del Duca (1991), p. 82.
100 Panzavolta (2004), p. 579.

Though, it is worthy of note that the power to order a search remained in hands of the prosecutor.

Investigation commences with registering notification of a crime called *notitia criminis* in the special register maintained by the prosecutor.[101] The law prescribes for only one form of criminal investigation, regardless of the gravity of a crime, yet informally differences in their severity may and will influence the outcome of criminal investigation. The prosecutor retains control over investigation having a constitutional prerogative to avail himself of the police, which is perceived as an inevitable implication of the mandatory prosecution principle.[102] This makes the prosecutor, at least on normative level, fully responsible for the criminal investigation from beginning to end.[103] But the prosecutor is not free in determining how long the investigation will be carried on. The prosecutor is constrained by the very strict rules regarding an expiration of investigation that should be concluded within six months from the registration of the name of a suspect in the prosecutorial register.[104]

The collection of evidence may be conducted both by the prosecutor and by judicial police, since both authorities retain extensive powers over investigative acts. Investigative measures are limited both by the scope of investigation determined by its aim and prohibition of admitting evidence gathered during criminal investigation during the trial. Nevertheless, it was accepted that instruments should be available providing for the gathering of evidence during the criminal investigation when there is either a risk of losing such evidence e.g. the witness might die before the trial commences or that are not repeatable during the trial e.g. search or phone interception. For this purpose, the law provides for the evidential hearing (*incidente probatorio*) aimed at allowing the gathering of evidence before the judge for preliminary investigation which will be admissible at trial.[105] During the hearing the same rules as those for receiving evidence at trial apply, which allows the trial judge to have access to it.[106] Therefore, while control of the investigation is largely in the hands of the prosecutor, the judge serves as a check on prosecutorial powers.[107] Moreover, the defense is permitted to conduct independent investigation[108] to equalize the position of the parties.[109]

101 Art. 335 § 1 c.p.p.
102 Caianiello (2012), p. 257.
103 Art. 327 c.p.p.
104 See Arts. 405–407 CCP-Italy. See Section 5.4, for extensive discussion on this issue.
105 Di Amato (2013), p. 164.
106 Grande (2000), p. 233.
107 Marafioti (2008), p. 83.
108 Art. 327bis c.p.p.
109 See also Art. 391-bis and 391-decies CCP-Italy.

The criminal investigation ends with a decision to prosecute or discontinue the case. Both decisions are undertaken by the prosecutor, but the latter must be confirmed by the judge for preliminary investigation.

3.4.2 Prosecutorial Discretion

The principle of legality[110] was introduced into the criminal process, together with provisions of the Italian Constitution of 1948 for the same reasons that stood behind the decision to make the prosecution part of the judiciary. It was believed that, by binding prosecutors with the legality principle, they could avoid future possible unfair treatment of crimes in accordance with the needs of the current political powers, as happened during the times of Italian fascism.[111] Together with the prescribed full independence of the prosecution service from the Ministry of Justice's orders, the introduction of the principle of legality was therefore intended to ensure that criminal justice authorities treat all defendants equally.[112] The founding fathers clearly believed that "independence and mandatory prosecution [are] two faces of the same coin."[113] Moreover, when the new adversarial c.p.p. of 1988 came into force this rule surprisingly remained in place despite its obvious contradiction with the prosecutorial discretion present in traditional adversarial systems. It was a clear signal that the move toward adversariality does not entail changes regarding that sphere and that some features of the traditional Continental model were to be retained.[114]

According to Article 112 of the Italian Constitution, the public prosecutor has an obligation to institute criminal proceedings. This should be understood as obliging prosecutor both to initiate an investigation and to prosecute a case against charged individual. This provision was paired up with Article 109 of the Italian Constitution giving prosecutors full control over judicial police conducting investigation.[115] Moreover, it led to limiting and subsequently to removing any hierarchical powers of the Minister of Justice over the prosecution service with an aim to allow the full application of the mandatory prosecution principle.[116]

110 This term is traditionally used in the literature, but some scholars suggest using the expression "compulsory criminal action" which acknowledges that the prosecutor is bound by the obligation to act not only when the case is prosecuted but also earlier when the criminal investigation is to be commenced (Di Federico (2008), p. 302). Some other translations are used in the literature, i.e. "mandatory penal action" and "compelling initiative of criminal proceeding" (Fabri (2008), p. 9, and seem to confirm this approach).
111 Grande (2000), p. 240.
112 Illuminati (2000), p. 115.
113 Di Federico (1998), p. 375.
114 Panzavolta (2004), p. 591.
115 Caianiello (2012), p. 257.
116 See Di Federico (2008), pp. 322–323.

The compulsory criminal action has been incorporated into the new Code of 1988 through various provisions although the principle itself is not found in the articles. The basic rule forces both prosecutor and police to conduct the investigations necessary to decide on criminal prosecution.[117] To achieve that goal, the prosecutor is obliged to carry out all necessary activities including carrying out ascertainments on the facts and circumstances in favor of the accused.[118] To complete this picture, another provision forces the prosecutor, upon receiving notice of a crime, to register it and by doing so commence the investigation.[119] The prosecutor must also proactively seek information about commitment of crimes[120] and not to rely only on *notitia criminis* as transferred by the police or victims and witnesses. That provision is perceived as adopted in accordance with the principle of mandatory prosecution preserving prosecutorial independence from the executive that controls the police to make sure that no crime goes unpunished.[121] Alongside this, the prosecutor is expected to pursue prosecution when the case must not be dropped.[122]

But, as Di Federico notes, the idea of prescribing mandatory criminal prosecution for all criminal violations to avoid the discretionary or arbitrary use of prosecutorial powers was "somewhat naive."[123] And, as Caianiello concludes, the fixed principle is also both "inefficient" and "impracticable."[124] As a result of adoption this principle, the criminal justice system faced a growing backlog of cases as it has been difficult to process all reported offenses.[125] It should come as no surprise that some exceptions, both normative and factual, eventually emerged in Italian criminal procedure.

First, not all cases fall under the rigid construct of the legality principle. Offenses investigated and prosecuted upon complaint (*reati perseguibili a querela dell'offeso*), examples of which are rape and minor personal injury, do not automatically trigger the reaction of the prosecutor. In cases of crimes from this group for commencement of investigation the complaint (*querela*) filed by the victim of a crime is needed.[126] Unless authorities are able to obtain the complaint, criminal investigation cannot be subsequently prosecuted.

117 Art. 326 c.p.p.
118 Art. 358 c.p.p.
119 Art. 335 § 1 c.p.p.
120 Art. 330 c.p.p.
121 Caianiello (2016), p. 11.
122 Art. 405 § 1 c.p.p.
123 Di Federico (2008), p. 321 (see also Di Federico's description of legislative process in which some ideas to enhance the accountability were rejected [p. 321, fn. 57 together with quoted literature]).
124 Caianiello (2012), p. 260.
125 Di Amato (2013), p. 36.
126 Art. 336f c.p.p.

Obviously if the information on commitment of a crime has reached the prosecutor first, the investigation will be commenced by registering such information. It will, nevertheless, be subsequently discontinued upon the victim's refusal to file the complaint. But if it will be officially known before investigation commences that the victim does not wish to file a complaint, the *notitia criminis* will not even be registered.

Moreover, recently important change has been introduced on a normative level, aimed at loosening the principle of legality. The law of 2015[127] introduced into the c.p.p. a provision allowing the prosecutor to discontinue proceedings of a minor nature.[128] This power of the prosecutor, however, is not absolute and, as any other decision to discontinue the investigation is subject to judicial review at the request of either the person under investigation or the victim.[129] Nevertheless, it constitutes a visible change in so far inviolable principle of legality being a long overdue response to the impossibility of coping in practice with the rigidity of the compulsory criminal action principle. Before this provision was introduced, prosecutors were forced to make choices, since it was impossible to properly react to each and every reported crime. In view of the over-criminalization of the Italian system, the prosecutors were simply unable to initiate investigation in every reported case, while the system gave them leeway to choose which proceedings to prosecute first.[130] For once, prosecutors intentionally were failing to register many notifications of crimes.[131] Another solution was to prolong the completion of proceedings on time, since the delay resulted in expiry of the period allowed for this stage of the criminal process[132] and was releasing the prosecutor from the obligation to take action.[133] In the light of the lack of a mechanism to verify these choices, leading to prosecutorial unaccountability for their decisions, some scholars, and eventually legislators, started to discuss the possibility of setting the official priority criteria, but such attempts up to 2015 produced unsatisfactory results.[134]

To sum up, the principle of legality in the Italian criminal process definitely has a very strong normative foundation as a constitutional rule. But taking into account all normative exceptions, including especially Article 411 § 1bis c.p.p. as well as the factual approach, it is fair to say that the

127 Decreto-legge n. 28, Mar. 16, 2015.
128 Art. 411 § 1bis c.p.p. Criteria regarding the minor nature of a crime are provided in Art. 131bis c.p.
129 Mangiaracina (2019), p. 235.
130 Di Amato (2013), p. 158.
131 Caianiello (2012), p. 256.
132 Illuminati (2005), p. 317.
133 Caianiello (2012), p. 261.
134 See comments in Caianiello (2012), pp. 260–261.

prosecutorial discretion in the Italian system exists and arises from potential legal interpretations and application to case facts.[135] Therefore, as aptly concluded by Marafioti, the "compulsory prosecution [...] is a little more than a dogma [and] prosecutors exercise discretion without any checks and balances at a hierarchical or political level."[136]

3.4.3 Prosecutorial Objectivity

The position of the prosecutor during criminal proceedings cannot be considered as unequivocal. From a normative standpoint, it seems to be clearly defined, since Article 358 c.p.p. indicates that the prosecutor is obliged to investigate exculpatory as well as inculpatory evidence. This nonpartisan position is also supported in Article 73 of the Judicial Regulations providing that the prosecutor shall ensure observance of the law. As a result, the prosecutor is seen by the Italian Constitutional Court as a "mere prosecutor, but also an organ of justice that is obliged to search for all elements of evidence that are relevant for the correct verdict, including any elements in favor of the accused."[137] Moreover, in a number of subsequent judgments, it was held that the prosecutor does not represent a particular interest but simply acts in order to guarantee adherence to the law.[138] This means that the prosecutor in Italy should be seen as strong in the categories of neutrality and objectivity.[139] This perspective is also reinforced by the inclusion of the prosecutor's position in the Constitution as having an equal status to the judge associating with her the attribute of independence.[140]

On the other hand, the objectivity of the prosecutor seems to have been severely compromised. First, the aim of the new c.p.p. was to give the prosecutor the characteristics of the participant in the trial that she enjoys in adversarial criminal procedure. Therefore, the traditional inquisitorial position of the prosecutor was taken away from her and currently she is seen much more as a party to the proceedings.[141] That means that the prosecutor is no longer required to search for the truth during investigation and, moreover, is even expected or at least allowed to be partisan during the trial.[142] Furthermore, Article 358 c.p.p. cannot be interpreted in isolation from the

135 Caianiello (2012), p. 256.
136 Marafioti (2008), p. 95.
137 Corte Costituzionale [Italian Constitutional Court], Feb. 15, 1991, n. 88.
138 Italian Constitutional Court's decisions quoted in Di Amato (2013), p. 159.
139 See e.g. Corso (1993), pp. 226–227 ("The Italian prosecutor is a public party but with a task to act objectively, in the sole interest of preserving law and justice").
140 Arts. 104–106 Italian Constitution. See Section 2.4.2.
141 Lupária and Gialuz (2019), p. 43; Perrodet (2002), p. 361.
142 Grande (2000), p. 235 together with literature cited in fn. 20.

Code's other provisions. As pointed out by Grande, this provision, as read together with Article 326 c.p.p.

> has been interpreted as asking the prosecutor to collect the evidence in favor of the suspect only for the very limited purpose of deciding whether to prosecute or not [...] The prosecutor, having determined that his case is strong enough to go forward to trial, is consequently under no obligation to look for exculpatory evidence.[143]

Therefore, one may ask which of the two perspectives dominates. Is the prosecutor indeed an objective and neutral figure seeking for both incriminating and exonerating evidence, or is she simply a party to the criminal proceedings? Apparently, the latter approach can be considered as being employed in practice. At the trial stage the prosecutor is explicitly partisan and during investigation the duty of the prosecutor to act impartially is considered a "ghost provision."[144] It is also reported, based on empirical research, that prosecutors hardly ever seek evidence in favor of the accused.[145] It seems that the ability to conduct separate investigations by defense[146] only strengthens in prosecutors the sense of lack of obligation to collect evidence in favor of the suspect and to act objectively. This also seems to comply with the objective of criminal investigation which does not require, at this stage, clarification of the entire circumstances of the case but only a decision whether to prosecute the accused.

3.5 Criminal Investigation in the United States of America

3.5.1 The Notion and Outline of Criminal Investigation

The term investigation does not seem to have a precise definition or an adopted meaning in the US legal literature. Even *Black's Dictionary* does not define the term. The expression is used rather inconsistently and an explanation of what this notion encompasses is rarely provided. Moreover, it is not used in the US criminal process in a way that enables describing a coherent and defined stage of the criminal process. Instead, books separately recite such measures as "arrest," "search and seizure," or "interrogations" as early events in the criminal process that, in the case of Continental states, are

143 Grande (2000), p. 235.
144 Caianiello (2012), p. 251.
145 Di Federico (2008), p. 332.
146 Art. 327bis c.p.p.

part of investigation. Or they are prescribed, still inconsistently, as a part of "pretrial process"[147] or "preliminary proceedings."[148] Therefore, one has the impression that the investigation is rather associated with police practices, while at the same time possibly being a part of the pretrial process or preliminary proceedings when the court becomes involved.

At the same time, the US system focuses to a larger extent on constitutional protection of a suspect at an early stage of criminal proceedings, built upon the provisions of the Fourth and Fifth Amendments, rather than on the structure and steps of the process during criminal investigation. This is most likely the result of extensive Supreme Court jurisprudence from the 1930s and 1960s accentuating the importance of due process while searching and arresting, therefore preventing abusive police behavior.[149] This might be also be down to the fact that Anglo-Saxon legal scholarship is overall less focused on classification than its European counterparts, and aims at resolving problems, focusing to a larger extent on the practical perspective. This makes US legal scholars less inclined to develop complex definitions, which remains pertinent also to the notion and structure of criminal investigation.

Providing an outline of US criminal investigation is therefore difficult, given that there is no clear demarcation of when an investigation begins or ends. Some sources describe the criminal investigation as "the initial administrative step in the processing of what eventually will become a prosecution" and an ongoing process that continues after the arrest and beyond the filing of charges.[150] However, while the commencement of investigation can be more or less precisely narrowed down to filing a complaint by the witness to a crime or making an arrest on a spot,[151] the identification of the end point of investigation is difficult, if not impossible. The termination of investigation cannot be marked with either formally charging a person with a crime, accepting prosecution through preliminary hearing, or even commencing a jury trial. At none of these moments do the law enforcement authorities and the prosecutor lose their powers to carry on investigative measures. This is

147 See e.g. Hall (2009) identifying "The Pretrial Process" (ch. 14) combining arrest, complaint, initial appearance, pretrial release, preliminary hearing, formal charge, discovery, etc. Cf. Worrall (2012), pp. 32–34 who combines all that happens at the beginning of criminal process from filing a complaint until filing charges under one notion of "pretrial." But see e.g. Scheb and Scheb (1999) identifying "The Pretrial Process" (ch. 5) as what happens after the initial appearance and discussing separately "Search and Seizure" and "Arrest, Interrogation, and Identification" (chs. 3–4).

148 See Title II of the Federal Rules of Criminal Procedure which is named "preliminary proceedings." This part of the FRCP consists of five provisions pertaining to the complaint, arrest warrant, summons, initial appearance, and preliminary hearing.

149 See Boyce et al. (2007), p. 1207.

150 Kamisar et al. (2012), p. 5.

151 See Section 4.5.1.

also partially due to the nature of the criminal investigation not treated in the US system as a first step in preparation of the case, becoming eventually a basis for the court's final judgment, but rather as a form of building up the case against the accused even if still continuously carried on during trial.

It is bit easier to understand this through the objectives of the criminal investigation. Even though they are not clearly prescribed in legal acts, some guidance may be found in other nonbinding sources. According to the ABA Standards on Prosecutorial Investigations, the purpose of criminal investigation is primarily to develop sufficient factual information to enable the prosecutor to make a fair and objective determination of whether and what charges should be brought and to guard against prosecution of the innocent and, second, to develop legally admissible evidence, sufficient to obtain and sustain a conviction of those who are guilty and warrant prosecution.[152] It is further clarified that the aim of criminal investigation "is not to inflict punishment or damage reputations."[153] Therefore, even though the criminal investigation does not seem to be aiming at establishing all circumstances of the case it also cannot be limited only to finding information incriminating the suspect but, rather, should be guided by facts.

But it is necessary to point out that the aim of criminal investigation should also be discussed in the light of the inquisitorial character of this stage of the criminal process. While the adjudicative stage is conducted in an adversarial environment, where two equal parties argue in front of an impartial entity, the criminal investigation is conducted by the executive authority *ex parte*.[154] This means that, even though its aim is broader than just obtaining incriminating evidence against the suspect,[155] the police and prosecutor conduct the investigation independently of formal influence of the suspect (or victim). The suspect may only suggest but never demand undertaking investigative measures from the criminal justice authorities. However, to retain the equality of arms in the course of criminal proceedings, the suspect is allowed to carry on her own investigation to find evidence supporting the case.

Moreover, what makes the presentation of the scope of investigation difficult is the fact that, in practice, the US system provides for a great variety of procedural paths that cases may follow. This will partially depend on the seriousness of the crime under investigation.[156] In case of grave

152 Standard 26–1.2 (c) SPI.

153 ABA Standards for Prosecutorial Investigations, Commentary to Subdivision 26–1.2(h), p. 60.

154 Boyce et al. (2007), p. 1347.

155 See Section 3.5.3.

156 Kamisar et al. (2012), p. 3 fn. a (generally the law distinguishes between misdemeanors and felonies, the latter concerning crimes punishable by imprisonment exceeding one year).

crimes, the proceedings are more complex and time-consuming, involving more obligatory steps and procedural measures. Investigations conducted in cases of minor offenses tend to be fast-tracked through the courts.[157] Even though the separate legal schemes for conduct of criminal proceedings depending on the gravity of a crime have not developed formally, in practice the procedure for felonies differs considerably to the one employed for misdemeanors. Moreover, the specifics of the criminal procedure may also vary from state to state and from federal to state. Therefore, it is impossible to speak about one common regime of criminal investigation in the USA.

As discussed in the literature, investigation may be conducted before an arrest has been made (pre-arrest investigation) as well as after an arrest has taken place (post-arrest investigation). This division overlaps with another classification of this stage of criminal proceedings since the investigation can take a reactive form (commitment of a crime triggers the reaction of law enforcement authorities), or a proactive form (aimed at uncovering criminal activity).[158] This should not be considered as different from what can be observed in European countries but has strong consequences in the US legal system, especially for the prosecutor and her engagement in the process. Depending on how the investigation was triggered and whether the arrest occurs immediately at the very beginning of investigation, or at some later point in time, the course of proceedings may vary significantly. In some cases (prearrest investigations in a proactive form) the decision to arrest a person may be preceded by the prosecutorial decision to charge a person with a crime and encompass some investigatory actions conducted with the help of grand jury.[159] In other cases, when the investigation takes a reactive form and arrest happens immediately, the decision to charge may take place *post factum* and preliminary activity of the police in such case is most likely conducted without prosecutorial influence.

In any case there are certain steps in the criminal investigation that US law provides for. The arrest seems to be an almost inevitable element of the investigation when the suspect has been identified.[160] In case of minor offenses, the arrest can result in the release of the detainee by the police and summoning the suspect to appear before the court at a later date. But in cases of more serious offenses, the detainee is immediately transferred to court and the initial appearance takes place. This hearing is held in an adversarial environment, in the presence of the prosecutor and defense counsel,

157 Worrall (2012), p. 35. See also considerations in Kamisar et al. (2012), pp. 17–19.
158 See Kamisar et al. (2012), pp. 6–9 (the authors report that the reactive type of investigations take place in about 90 percent of cases).
159 See Section 5.5.
160 Neubauer and Fradella (2019), p. 13 (author reports that the police make more than 12 million arrests for non-traffic offenses every year).

aimed at presenting preliminary charges brought by the prosecutor against the arrested or summoned individual and informing him or her about the rights that attach at this point.

The nature of the initial appearance hearing varies significantly depending on the state system in question as well as whether the person is detained or summoned. In particular, it may also be combined with the bail hearing, during which the judge determines whether the arrested person may be released on bail pending the proceedings, or whether they should remain detained. But in many cases a separate bail hearing may also take place. The next step in the process is the arraignment that again may be combined with an initial appearance hearing as well as with the bail hearing. During arraignment the defendant is presented with charges that can be significantly modified after their first version and most importantly the defendant is for the first time called to enter the plea.

A charging decision is therefore made before the court of law although the decision as to who is charged, and with what offenses, belongs exclusively to the prosecutor.[161] The case then comes under the court's supervision and control, even though the prosecutor retains far-reaching powers to shape it further, e.g. by gathering evidence supporting the accusation and being able to negotiate with the defendant through plea bargaining the final outcome of the process. A long time may pass before trial commences, depending on the outcomes of plea negotiations, discovery, as well as the number and nature of pretrial motions filed with court. Meantime, the prosecutor may not only decide on changes in charges, but also decide to discontinue the case although usually upon the judicial approval. The most problematic issue in this context is that the prosecutor maintains a tremendous advantage over the defendant up to this stage of criminal process, which makes for severe inequality in negotiations. Despite the availability of constitutional requirements of evidence disclosure, as well as many statutory regulations regarding discovery, they do not apply until the plea is entered,[162] making the negotiating position of the defendant much weaker.

And because charging a person with a crime happens quite early in the course of investigation and, even more importantly, involves the court, the proceedings immediately after arresting the suspect become a part of the court proceedings. It is moved into the stage where the control over the case is taken over by the court (pretrial) while the investigation is still very much developing. Therefore, the line separating investigation and pretrial is described as indistinct yet important.[163] The pretrial and investigation usually

161 Jacoby and Ratledge (2016), p. 61.
162 Brown (2012), p. 203.
163 Boyce et al. (2007), p. 1347.

do coexist, and they cannot be simply distinguished by the engagement of the court in pretrial, since while the case already hangs on the docket the prosecutor can continue to gather evidence. It is hard to present a consistent outline of steps in the process since there is no timeframe set for investigation.

The role of the judge during criminal investigation can also be described as profound.[164] Although it is true that the criminal investigation for the most part remains in the hands of the criminal justice authorities and, as will be discussed, also in the hands of prosecutor, the judge plays a crucial role at this stage of the process. Most significantly, it is the court that, in all cases, decides on interference with rights of individuals when warrants on arrest, search, seizure, etc. are issued. At the same time the role of the court is limited or even nonexistent when it comes to evidentiary measures. It is worth noting that there is no history of associating the judge with a position of "investigating judge" as the Continental systems sometimes do (or rather did) and the role of interrogating witnesses and gathering evidence is generally outside of the scope of judicial competencies. Yet the US judge may also serve an important role in collection of evidence during criminal investigation when allowing for the depositions to be taken which provides for the possibility to obtain statements from witnesses prior to trial.[165]

Finally, it is worth mentioning that in the federal system and in some states, in cases of felonies, the law provides for an exceptional form of conducting investigation involving a so-called grand jury. This extraordinary organ[166] founded upon the Fifth Amendment and composed of 16 to 23 laypersons is primarily designed to approve the indictment that the prosecutor seeks to file with the court. The purpose is to prevent the abuse of prosecutorial powers in accusing individuals ("shield power").[167] But the grand jury has also a second role, more relevant for this discussion, aimed at gathering the evidence that will form the basis of indictment ("sword power"). In such a case the grand jury is allowed to subpoena witnesses to come and testify during secret proceedings where certain rights do not apply in full, and to force seizure of documents. These powers form a unique opportunity to obtain testimonies and documents that normally are not available during investigation.

164 See briefly on the judicial intervention in criminal investigation, Davis (2019), pp. 34–38.

165 See Section 5.5.

166 See comprehensively on the institution of grand jury in US system, Goldstein and Witzel (2016). On the investigative powers of the grand jury, see Section 5.5.

167 In the event there is no grand jury (in cases concerning crimes other than felonies, and in states that abandoned this institution) the US system provides for a preliminary hearing held before the pretrial judge as a mechanism checking against unwarranted prosecutions establishing whether the probable cause standard has been met.

In this context, the State of Connecticut is an atypical example of a grand jury system. The Connecticut version of a grand jury, most often referred to as a "one-man investigatory grand jury,"[168] grants the powers that the grand jury would normally possess to a single professional judge and not a group of laypersons.[169] This might give the impression that the institution of the Continental "investigative judge" is not totally foreign to the common law system.

3.5.2 Prosecutorial Discretion

Most commonly the position of the prosecutor in the US system is defined by three features. The most widely discussed is the extremely broad prosecutorial discretionary power with regard to the charging function. Second, prosecutors are considered to be influential actors in the criminal process, focusing mostly on the adjudicating stage of the criminal process, passing on competencies almost entirely to police during the investigative phase of the criminal process. Third, as a result, they are seen as cruel opponents of the accused, completely devoid of any objectivity, determined to bring about convictions. Of those features, discretion is seen as the "key characteristic of American prosecutors,"[170] which allows them to play the most prominent role in the US criminal justice system.[171] And it is the scope of discretion and the freedom to apply the law of their jurisdictions to their constituencies as they believe best, that makes their powers "unique and unparalleled elsewhere in the world."[172] However, as with every generalization, this characterization of the US American prosecutor is not wholly accurate.

The US prosecutor's powers of discretion include not only the decision as to whether a criminal action is brought against an individual, but also the decision as to what the individual will be charged with, and the decision whether the proceedings against the individual will be terminated.[173] It is also up to the prosecutor to negotiate with the defense, as well as to recommend the sentence. It is true that the US criminal process rests and relies on prosecutorial discretion. It seems an almost inevitable element of the US criminal justice system. Prosecutors, even when criticized for the amount of power vested in them,[174] can be sure that the discretion keeps the system sustainable. This is partially due

168 *Connelly* v. *Doe*, 213 Conn. 66, 70 (1989).
169 See comprehensively on the Connecticut grand jury system, Gailor (2015), pp. 141–161.
170 Neubauer and Fradella (2019), p. 171.
171 Davis (1969), pp. 17–18; Hanley et al. (1987), p. 15.
172 Anderson (2001), p. 3.
173 *Wayte* v. *United States*, 470 US 598 (1985); *Petite* v. *United States*, 361 US 529 (1960).
174 Luna and Wade (2010), pp. 1417–1420. See also in this context the famous case *Bordenkircher* v. *Hayes*, 434 US 357 (1978) and its critical analysis by Stuntz (2005).

to the fact that the decision to prosecute is seen as such that "cannot be a mere mathematical application of criminal statutes to evidence of criminal wrong-doing,"[175] and prevents overloading the system with too many cases.[176]

But as one district attorney from Maine, stated "[t]his discretion is (virtually) unreviewable, clothed with (virtual) immunity, and remains (virtually) absolute."[177] This means that even though prosecutorial discretion seems overwhelming and uncontrolled, since the positive law does not provide visible limitations, there are certain restrictions to it arising from institutional arrangements.[178] These constraints are difficult to grasp due to the fragmentation of the US system and the variety of options that state and federal laws provide for, in particular, on the line between the federal and the state systems. Nevertheless, the general mechanism provides that prosecutors are required to select cases for prosecuting by evaluating in which of the reported cases "the offense is the most flagrant, the public harm is the greatest and the proof the most certain."[179]

A vital role is in turn played by various guidelines seeking to limit the scope of prosecutorial discretion. On the federal level these include the Justice Manual[180] and Department of Justice policies and memoranda.[181] From this perspective, the provisions of 19–16.000 of the Justice Manual, that implement and specify Rule 11 FRCP, concerning acceptance of pleas in federal criminal cases, are of particular importance. Furthermore, the grounds for commencing or declining prosecution are provided. The commencement of federal prosecution is based on belief that the person's conduct constitutes a federal offense and that the admissible evidence will probably be sufficient to obtain and sustain a conviction, unless the prosecution would serve no substantial federal interest, the person is subject to effective prosecution in another jurisdiction or there exists an adequate noncriminal alternative to prosecution.[182] The "substantial federal interest" seems to be key to evaluating the necessity to prosecute and is to be assessed based on further factors such as the federal law enforcement priorities, the nature and seriousness of the offense, the deterrent effect of prosecution, culpability, prior criminal activity and personal circumstances, willingness to cooperate in the investigation or prosecution of others, the interests of any victims, as well as the probable sentence or other consequences if the person is

175 Wallace (2001) p. 85.
176 Jackson (1940), p. 5 ("one of the greatest difficulties of the position of prosecutor is that he must pick cases, because no prosecutor can even investigate all of the cases in which he receives complaint").
177 Anderson (2001), p. 3.
178 Brown (2012), p. 200.
179 Jackson (1940), p. 5.
180 See Section 2.5.1 for more on the nature of Justice Manual.
181 Podgor (2012), p. 9.
182 109.27–220 JM.

convicted.[183] Additional limits to prosecutorial discretion on the federal level are given by the nature of federal crimes, giving less space for negotiations leverage.[184]

Similar constraints, although of distinct impact, are available for state prosecutors. Although generally available standards and guidelines, such as NDAA Standards and ABA Standards do apply, they have a distinct influence on the day-to-day work of elected state and district attorneys, since it is true that the limits on discretion are derived rather from the limited resources that each state's prosecutor's office has.[185]

The scope of prosecutorial discretion at state level may be analyzed using the example of the State of Connecticut. Generally, the state's attorney "has broad discretion in determining what crime or crimes to charge in any particular situation."[186] Of the numerous potential procedures for compelling a prosecutor to charge a person with a crime and prosecute—such as mandamus, grand jury indictment, private prosecution, or directive by the Attorney General[187]—none are available in Connecticut. This does not mean, however, that the prosecutors in Connecticut have unfettered discretion to charge and prosecute individuals. As clearly stems from the case law, every prosecutor, when deciding whether to charge a person with a crime or not, has a duty to: (1) determine that there is reasonable ground to proceed with a criminal charge; (2) see that impartial justice is served for the guilty as well as the innocent; and (3) ensure that all evidence tending to aid in the ascertaining of the truth be laid before the court, irrespective of whether it be consistent with the contention of the prosecution that the accused is guilty.[188]

It should be also clear that, both at federal and state levels, the scope of discretion is limited by the ban on selective and vindictive prosecution.[189] The former may be understood as prosecuting some individuals while others similarly situated are not prosecuted.[190] Although the selective prosecution claim may be considered as valid only if the decision not to prosecute was made with the intention to violate the equal protection clause derived from the Fourteenth Amendment. On the other hand, vindictive prosecution purports to punish the defendant for exercising a statutory or constitutional

183 9–27.230 JM.
184 See Brown (2012), p. 210.
185 Brown (2012), p. 211.
186 *State* v. *Haskins*, 188 Conn. 432 (1982), 473–474.
187 The State Attorney General has no jurisdiction over criminal matters in Connecticut (Sec. 3–125 CGS).
188 *State* v. *Haskins*, 188 Conn. 432 (1982), 473.
189 See broadly regarding the State of Connecticut, Tomasiewicz (2015), pp. 291–295.
190 See *Yick Wo* v. *Hopkins*, 118 US 356 (1886) and *Oyler* v. *Boles* 368 US 448 (1968).

right.[191] But these rules are not considered as restrictions that in either federal or state systems impose on prosecutorial discretion sufficiently strong restraints. This leads some scholars to call for the judicial review of prosecutorial decisions in order to effectively combat selective prosecutions.[192]

Concluding this brief reflection on prosecutorial discretion in the US criminal process, it should be noted that until this point the focus has been on how the "discretion" is understood in US legal literature. This term seems to be generally limited in the literature to describe the power of the prosecutor to make the decision whether to charge a suspect with a crime with all the complexity that comes with this decision. But its meaning should be understood in a much broader sense. Put simply, it is "the power to make decisions"[193] and more precisely "an authority conferred by law to act in certain conditions or situations in accordance with an official's [...] considered judgment and conscience."[194] Therefore, this is a power that cannot be limited only to the decision to prosecute, but should be considered as applying also to the earlier stage when the decision whether to investigate is undertaken. And even more importantly it applies not only to prosecutor but also to other actors in the criminal process, including the jury, the court, and the police.[195] And this is exactly the discretion maintained by the police during criminal investigation, especially the one unsupervised by an external entity, that raises questions regarding the fairness of the process and the role that the prosecutor should play in this context.

3.5.3 Prosecutorial Objectivity

Objectivity[196] is a characteristic of the US prosecutor, who is expected to seek justice rather than victory, is an obvious component of the US criminal justice system. On the normative level the system lacks an explicit obligation targeted at the prosecutor to search for the truth and gather both incriminating and exonerating evidence, in a way European systems commonly offer. But the case law in this respect seems to be clear that the prosecutor must be objective. As long ago as 1935, the US Supreme Court issued a landmark judgment in *Berger* v. *United States* where the justices held that:

191 See *Blackledge* v. *Perry*, 417 US 21 (1974) and *United States* v. *Goodwin*, 457 US 368 (1982).
192 Heller (1997), p. 1325.
193 Jacoby and Ratledge (2016), p. 1.
194 Pound (1960), p. 926.
195 See discussion in Kamisar et al. (2012), pp. 911–915.
196 Note that in the US literature the discussion is conducted referring to prosecutorial neutrality, rather than objectivity (see broadly on the issue, Zacharias and Green (2004), p. 837).

> The United States Attorney is the representative not of an ordinary party to a controversy, but of a sovereignty whose obligation to govern impartially is as compelling as its obligation to govern at all, and whose interest, therefore, in a criminal prosecution is not that it shall win a case, but that justice shall be done. As such, he is in a peculiar and very definite sense the servant of the law, the two-fold aim of which is that guilt shall not escape or innocence suffer [...] It is as much his duty to refrain from improper methods calculated to produce a wrongful conviction as it is to use every legitimate means to bring about a just one.[197]

Similarly, in *Brady* v. *Maryland* it was argued that it is the prosecutor's main role "not to achieve a victory but to establish justice."[198] Therefore, the role of the prosecutor is described differently than that of the defense. As stated in *US.* v. *Wade*, the prosecutor, contrary to the defense counsel, has an obligation to ascertain or present the truth surrounding the commission of the crime.[199] As a result, the prosecutor is not expected to seek convictions at all costs. The position of the prosecutor should be therefore understood as that of the "administrator of justice, a zealous advocate"[200] and as an officer of the court, which means that she has a duty to see that justice is done. Yet, "unlike private attorneys who advocate for the interests of their individual clients, the prosecutor has a broader clientele, the entire community, which must be served with the highest ethical and professional standards."[201] Therefore, it is a central mission of the prosecutor "to promote truth and to refrain from the conduct that impedes truth."[202]

This approach stems from numerous regulations and guidelines that bind prosecutors in their daily work. The NDAA National Prosecution Standards provide that the prosecutor is an independent administrator of justice whose primary responsibility is to seek justice, which can only be achieved by the representation and presentation of the truth, while this responsibility includes ensuring that the guilty are held accountable, that the innocent are protected from unwarranted harm, and that the rights of all participants, particularly victims of crime, are respected.[203] Similarly, the ABA Criminal Justice Standards for the Prosecution Function, building on above-quoted case law, are direct in providing that the primary duty of the prosecutor is to seek justice within the bounds of the law, not merely to convict,[204] as well as

197 *Berger* v. *United States*, 295 US 78, 88 (1935).
198 *Brady* v. *Maryland*, 373 US 83, 87 n. 2 (1963).
199 *United States* v. *Wade*, 388 US 218, 256 (1967).
200 Standard 3–1.2 (a) ABA SPF.
201 Charron (2001), p. xix.
202 Gershman (2001), p. 313.
203 Standard 1–1.1 NDAA NPS.
204 Standard 3–1.2 (b) ABA PFS.

positioning the prosecutor as an administrator of justice, a zealous advocate, and an officer of the court.[205]

These regulations apply to the "prosecution function." However, the obligation to remain objective should be no different when the prosecutor engages in investigation. According to ABA Criminal Justice Standards on Prosecutorial Investigations, the individual prosecutor, although not being an independent agent herself, but a member of an independent institution, has a primary duty to seek justice.[206] This is subsequently strengthened by establishing that the prosecutor's client is the public, not particular government agencies or victims.[207] Moreover, the prosecutor should ensure that criminal investigations are not based on premature beliefs or conclusions as to guilt or innocence, nor on partisan or other improper political or personal considerations including discriminatory ones.[208] The very purpose of criminal investigation is to develop sufficient factual information to enable the prosecutor to make a fair and objective determination when charging a person and to guard against prosecution of the innocent.[209] In comments to ABA Standards, it is clarified that even though when conducting investigation some hypothesis must be formed, "the prosecutor should follow the facts wherever they go" and in doing so must follow the truth as "the investigative lodestar."[210]

In the light of the above, the US system might suggest the prosecutor is objective, striving to achieve justice. But this theoretical framework does not seem to be the case in practice. Despite this view, it is argued, that "the principal objective of the prosecutor is to convict offenders."[211] It is also perceived that most US prosecutors' offices are less committed to carrying out an objective quasi-judicial assessment of defendants' guilt than seems to be the case in many Continental public prosecution services.[212] And the number of prosecutorial misconducts revealed and studied in the US system[213] shows systemic failure in providing tools for reassuring objectivity in prosecutorial decision-making. Without engaging, at this point, in

205 Standard 3–1.2 (a) ABA PFS.
206 Standard 26.1–1.2 (a) ABA SPI.
207 Standard 26.1–1.2 (b) ABA SPI.
208 Standard 26.1–1.2 (d) (i)–(ii) ABA SPI.
209 Standard 26.1–1.2 (c) (i) ABA SPI.
210 ABA Standards for Criminal Justice. Prosecutorial Investigations, 3rd ed., Washington: American Bar Association 2014, pp. 60–61.
211 Forst et al. (1977), p. 65.
212 Brown (2012), p. 201.
213 Epps (2016), p. 765 ("too many [prosecutors] shirk their ethical duties, sometimes doggedly pursuing defendants despite compelling evidence of innocence—and in far too many cases have been responsible for serious injustice"). See also broadly on wrongful convictions in US system, Zacharias and Green (2009), pp. 1–59.

discussion which system provide for prosecutorial objectivity during the course of criminal proceedings, it should be noted that the US system is, indeed, more eager to admit that "[p]rosecutors need not be entirely 'neutral and detached'" because "[i]n an adversary system, they are necessarily permitted to be zealous in their enforcement of the law."[214] But this approach may be the result of the adversarial role that prosecutors play during the criminal trial, rather than a feature of the functions that the prosecutor serves in a criminal justice context.[215] As a result, it may be anticipated that during criminal investigation when the case is still developing the approach toward objectivity is perceived differently than during the trial stage.

3.6 Summary

Having outlined the scope of each of our four countries' criminal investigation, we return to the question of what should be understood as the criminal investigation.

Generally speaking, the criminal investigation is devoted to establishing whether a criminal act has taken place, identifying perpetrators, and gathering enough evidence to enable the decision-maker to file a case with the court in whatever form it may be, or not. However, it is now clear that there are noticeable differences when it comes to certain features of investigations. First, they differ in the aims of what the criminal investigation must achieve, which subsequently influences the investigative measures undertaken during the course of criminal investigation. In some cases, it is enough to do as little as to decide whether it is sufficient to charge a person with a crime and in some others the investigation aims further to answer more questions regarding the circumstances of the case. Second, the time frame of the investigation may be strictly established by clear delineation of its beginning and end, or it can be loosened and less formal. Finally, the way in which the judge may be engaged during criminal investigation may take distinct forms, including taking decisions on interference with the rights of the individual, participating in taking evidence and reviewing the validity of decisions undertaken by the prosecutor or the police. Moreover, the relationship between the prosecutor and the police may be of a distinct character, as well as the roles played by the parties to proceedings. All of this will be explored further in detail throughout the next five chapters of the book.

But one question should be answered directly; that is, where the discussion on the investigation in this book will start and, most importantly,

214 *Marshall* v. *Jerrico*, 446 US 238 (1980), 248.

215 See Zacharias (1991), pp. 107–108 (author argues that the prosecutorial obligation to "do justice" is impossible to achieve in competitive environment of adversarial trial).

when it ends. In the case of the European countries, the official closing of the investigative stage (being marked by discontinuation of proceedings or sending a case for the court's decision) ultimately ends the opportunity to continue with investigative measures such as interrogating witnesses, searching premises, etc. Therefore, the charging decision in Continental systems, being understood as a decision to prosecute a person with a crime, ultimately ends the investigation. This is the moment when the prosecutor loses entirely the control over the investigative actions which is a result of the concept of investigation being an official and formal stage of criminal process led by the prosecutor. At the same time, in the US system, charging happens much earlier in the course of the criminal process and is neither final nor terminates the investigatory activities of the prosecutor and the criminal justice authorities. Instead, after filing a case with a court which leads to a trial, during the preparation of a case or even when a case is already prosecuted, investigatory actions may still occur and the prosecution is free to look for evidence that will advance its case during the trial. This again makes it impossible to find in this case a common definite ending point of investigation in researched countries.

Precisely because investigation in the US system has no clearly defined ending point, it is crucial to accept that the scope of this book's analysis must be based on elements other than the time frame. Therefore, the "criminal investigation" shall be understood for the purpose of this work as a stage in the criminal process where criminal justice authorities and the prosecutor may take the various investigative measures and undertake certain decisions as to initial charges, or regarding coercive measures. In the case of European countries this will concentrate only on that part of the criminal process that ends with the prosecutor's decision to formally charge a person with a crime, but in the US system the discussion will refer also to post-charging investigations. Interestingly, in the USA this is usually also the moment when the prosecutor becomes heavily engaged in the conduct of criminal investigation.

The approach toward the principle of prosecutorial discretion and, its flip side, the principle of legality is often deemed to shape the role of the prosecutor in the most profound way. First of all, it should be noted that these principles come into play most often when the prosecutor decides whether to bring a case against an individual to court. This is particularly underlined in the US debate as to what a suspect is to be charged with. However, the charging process and negotiations that may accompany this decision are not of the main importance for this research as has been stated clearly in Chapter 1. The scope of freedom in decision-making is as important during criminal investigation as at its outcome. Whether the prosecutor is bound by an obligation to commence the investigation of all crimes or is free to pick and choose cases to pursue is of equal importance. The adoption of certain model also impacts the criminal justice authorities. The police and other investigating agencies may be either bound by the same obligation as vested with prosecution or allowed to act with more freedom when selecting cases at their very initial stage. Hence, the approach toward prosecutorial discretion is also of crucial relevance for the criminal investigation and actions undertaken during its course.

Such an approach on the principle of legality applicable both to investigation and prosecution is visible in all three Continental countries. This is also expressed through refraining in these systems from using the expression "mandatory prosecution" and resorting to such notions as "compulsory criminal action." The laws of all three states contain clearly stated normative regulations aimed toward assuring the legality of the proceedings; in Italy this is even provided for in the Constitution. Germany, Poland, and Italy also have measures to limit the scope of the legality principle (i.e. as an obligation to investigate and prosecute all crimes). Such mechanisms include most of all, establishment of the group of offenses investigated upon complaint that make the police and prosecutor's action fully dependent on the will of the victim of the crime. Additionally, Germany and, since quite recently, Italy have introduced mechanisms allowing for a discretionary decision of the prosecutor to discontinue criminal investigation based on public interest grounds. Even though in both states it is possible only for a selected group of minor offenses, it visibly undermines the rigidity of the legality principle. In the case of Poland, the system lacks a similar provision since the discontinuation of proceedings based on "social harm of the committed offense being negligible" cannot be treated as such. However there are some mechanisms that even in that country should be perceived as exceptions toward discretion.

But in all three countries more or less explicitly the need to provide the prosecutor with even more discretion can be observed. Regardless of rigidity of the legality principle it may be claimed that full adoption of that principle is not attainable in any country. Each state must sooner or later introduce some ways to include the discretionary mechanisms. It is reported that some cases discontinued for public interest reasons might be hidden in a broad group of discontinuations based on lack of evidence. One of the reasons for this is the inefficiency and time-consuming nature of the system, in which every crime, even the smallest, is supposed to attract the same attention from criminal justice authorities. Faced with excessive pending proceedings, authorities seek solutions to alleviate the obligation to pursue all cases, especially in large prosecutor's offices burdened with many cases of differing importance.

To that regard the USA seems to be most open in admitting that discretion is an inevitable feature of the prosecutorial decision-making although its applicability to the investigative stage is not pronounced that clearly. But the voices that relate this principle to the investigative stage and to the police are also not that hard to find. Therefore, undoubtedly, both criminal justice agencies and prosecutors exercise broad discretion also at the very first stage of criminal process. But no one should be under the impression that this discretion is absolute. As discussed recently by Gilliéron, "it would be difficult to ignore clear evidence of a serious crime or to prosecute in the absence of any conclusive evidence" and one should be rather afraid of the risk of disparity that the US prosecution system establishes and not the discretion as such.[216] The US system recognizes this problem and provides for guidelines and less formal regulations limiting the conduct of discretionary decisions as much at the outcome of criminal investigation as during its course.

It can obviously be argued that the applicability of general guidelines to all cases is quite doubtful and that they do not provide for the full equality between suspects in different regions of the USA. But the answer to that problems is definitely not the principle of legality. As Marafioti aptly notes "[t]he medicine (that is, the principle of compulsory prosecution) is worse than the disease (that is, the risk that the prosecutor does not act independently) that we would like to cure."[217] And if in the end all four countries accept that "some" discretion is necessary, the question should rather be how to make the process transparent, the prosecutor objective, and criminal justice authorities accountable for their decisions and how the review of their solutions to the occurrence of the crime should be conducted even if, or especially when, decided at the very early stage of criminal process.

At the same time, prosecutorial objectivity is linked to prosecutorial discretion. It is submitted that elements of discretion are acceptable so long as the prosecutor remains objective in undertaking her decisions. This is a crucial feature of the prosecutor when making the decision not to prosecute based on the public interest test but equally important when pushing charges forward. In Germany, the objectivity of the prosecutor as the "guardian of the law" (*Wächter der Gesetzes*) is established by imposing on her an obligation to search for both inculpatory and exculpatory evidence. In Poland a similar rule is less clearly pronounced, being addressed to all authorities exercising their role during criminal investigation. But its interpretation leaves no doubt that the prosecutor should refrain from looking only for incriminating evidence. The Italian case is more nuanced, since the objectivity principle should be interpreted in the light of the principle of adversariality which calls for limiting the criminal investigation only to gathering enough material to decide on whether to charge an individual with a crime or not.

216 Gilliéron (2014), p. 321.
217 Marafioti (2008), p. 95.

In the US case, the adversariality of the court proceedings where the prosecutor becomes the defendant's opponent seems to also impact her position during the conduct of investigation. This, however, does not exclude that standards and guidelines anticipate that the prosecutor will be neutral, fair, and objective in all determinations during the criminal process.

Despite such provisions obliging prosecutors to be objective in their decisions, all four systems fail to do so in practice. Whether these provisions are provided in law (Poland, Italy, Germany) or just in guidelines and confirmed by jurisprudence (USA) the objectivity of the prosecutor seems not to be entirely respected. This might be partially due to the use of such an ambiguous term as objectivity (neutrality) that potentially encompasses various meanings to describe the expectations toward the appropriate prosecutorial conduct.[218] Perhaps it is even unreasonable to expect the full objectivity from the prosecutor since her decisions must always encompass a certain level of subjectivity. Therefore, the focus should rather remain on transparency of the process of prosecutorial decision-making and the effective reviewing mechanism instead of objectivity.

References

Anderson S (2001) The Changing Role of the Prosecutor. In: *The Prosecutors Deskbook. Ethical Issue and Emerging Roles for the 21st Century Prosecutors*. American Prosecutors Research Institute, Alexandria, pp. 3–23.

Boyce RN, Dripps DA, Perkins RM (2007) *Criminal Law and Procedure. Cases and Materials*. Foundation Press, New York.

Boyne SM (2014) *The German Prosecution Service. Guardians of the Law?* Springer, Heidelberg.

Boyne S (2018) German Prosecutors and the Rechtsstaat. In: Langer M, Sklansky DA (eds) *Prosecutor and Democracy. A Cross-National Study*. Cambridge University Press, Cambridge, pp. 138–174.

Brown DK (2012) American Prosecutors' Powers and Obligations in the Era of Plea Bargaining In: Luna E, Wade M (eds) *The Prosecutor in Transnational Perspective*. Oxford University Press, Oxford, pp. 200–213.

Bulenda T, Gruszczyńska B, Kremplewski A, Sobota P (2010) The Prosecution Service Function within the Polish Criminal Justice System. In: Jehle J-M, Wade M (eds) *Coping with Overloaded Criminal Justice Systems. The Rise of Prosecutorial Power Across Europe*. Springer, Heidelberg, pp. 257–284.

Caianiello M (2012) The Italian Public Prosecutor: An Inquisitorial Figure in Adversarial Proceedings. In: Luna E, Wade M (eds) *The Prosecutor in Transnational Perspective*. Oxford University Press, Oxford, pp. 250–267.

Caianiello M (2016) *Increasing Discretionary Prosecutor's Powers: The Pivotal Role of the Italian Prosecutor in the Pretrial Investigation Phase*. Oxford Handbooks Online, Oxford.

218 See Zacharias and Green (2004), pp. 847–850.

Charron T (2001) Introduction. In: The Prosecutors Deskbook. Ethical Issue and Emerging Roles for the 21st Century Prosecutors. American Prosecutors Research Institute, Alexandria.

Cieślak M (1984) *Polska procedura karna*. Państwowe Wydawnictwo Naukowe, Warsaw.

Corso P (1993) Italy. In: Van Den Wyngaert C (ed) *Criminal Procedure Systems in the European Community*. Butterworths, London, pp. 223–260.

Davis FT (2019) *American Criminal Justice. An Introduction*. Cambridge University Press, Cambridge.

Davis KC (1969) *Discretionary Justice. A Preliminary Inquiry*. Louisiana State University Press Baton Rouge.

Del Duca LF (1991) An Historic Convergence of Civil and Common Law Systems—Italy's New "Adversarial" Criminal Procedure System. *Dickinson Journal of International Law* 10:73–92.

De Vocht D (2010) Poland. In: Cape E, Namoradze Z, Smith R, Spronken T (eds) *Effective Criminal Defence in Europe*. Intersentia, Antwerp, pp. 425–488.

Di Amato A (2013) *Criminal Law in Italy*. Kluwer Law International, Alphen aan den Rijn.

Di Federico G (1998) Prosecutorial Independence and the Democratic Requirement of Accountability in Italy: Analysis of a Deviant Case in a Comparative Perspective. *British Journal of Criminology* 38:371–387.

Di Federico G (2008) Report on the Public Prosecution Service in Italy. In: Open Society Institute Sofia (ed) *Promoting Prosecutorial Accountability, Independence and Effectiveness*. Open Society Institute Sofia, Sofia, pp. 301–339.

Dubber MD (2006) Criminal Law in Comparative Context. *Journal of Legal Education* 56:433–443.

Duży J (2011) Zasada legalizmu a cele procesu karnego. *Państwo i Prawo* 2:65.

Elsner B, Peters J (2010) The Prosecution Service Function within the German Criminal Justice System. In: Jehle J-M, Wade M (eds) *Coping with Overloaded Criminal Justice Systems. The Rise of Prosecutorial Power Across Europe*. Springer, Heidelberg, pp. 207–236.

Epps D (2016) Adversarial Asymmetry in the Criminal Process. *New York University Law Review* 91:762–854.

Fabri M (2008) Criminal Procedure and Public Prosecution Reform in Italy: A Flash Back. *International Journal for Court Administration*. January:3–15.

Forst B, Lucianovic J, Cox S (1977) *What Happens After Arrest?* Government Printing Office, Washington DC.

Frase RS, Weigend T (1995) German Criminal Justice as a Guide to American Law Reform. *Boston College International and Comparative Law Review* 18:317–360.

Gailor MA (2015) Grand Jury, Arraignment, Transfers from Juvenile Court, Bail and Probable Cause Hearings. In: Schuman CJ (ed) *Connecticut Criminal Procedure*. Connecticut Law Tribune, Hartford, pp. 141–232.

Gershman BL (2001) The Prosecutor's Duty to Truth. *Georgetown Journal of Legal Ethics* 14:309–354.

Gialuz M (2017) The Italian Code of Criminal Procedure: A Reading Guide. In Gialuz M, Lupária L, Scarpa F (eds) *The Italian Code of Criminal Procedure. Critical Essays and English Translation*. Cedam, Milan, pp. 17–55.

Gilliéron G (2004) *Public Prosecutors in the United States and Europe*. Springer, Cham.
Goldstein HW, Witzel SM (2016) *Grand Jury Practice*. Law Journal Press, New York.
Grande E (2000) Italian Criminal Justice: Borrowing and Resistance. *American Journal of Comparative Law* 48:227–259.
Hall DE (2009) *Criminal Law and Procedure*. Delmar, Clifton Park.
Hanley JR, Schmidt WW, Robins RK (1987) *Introduction to Criminal Evidence and Court Procedure*. McCutchan Publishing, Berkeley.
Heller R (1997) Selective Prosecution and the Federalization of Criminal Law: The Need for Meaningful Judicial Review of Prosecutorial Discretion. Comment. *University of Pennsylvania Law Review* 145:1309–1358.
Herrmann J (1974) The Rule of Compulsory Prosecution and the Scope of Prosecutorial Discretion in Germany. *University of Chicago Law Review* 41: 468–505.
Hofmański P, Śliwa J (2015) Dwugłos w sprawie nowego kształtu postępowania przygotowawczego. *Prokuratura i Prawo* 1–2:77–92.
Huber B (2008) Germany. In: Vogler R, Huber B (eds), *Criminal Procedure in Europe*. Duncker & Humblot, Berlin, pp. 269–371.
Illuminati G (2000) Italy. In Vander Beken T, Kilching M (eds) *The Role of the Public Prosecutor in the European Criminal Justice System*. Koninklijke Vlaamse Academie van België voor Wetenschappen en Kunsten, Brussels.
Illuminati G (2005) The Frustrated Turn to Adversarial Procedure in Italy (Italian Criminal Procedure Code of 1988). *Washington University Global Studies Law Review* 4:567–581.
Jackson RH (1940) The Federal Prosecutor. *Journal of Criminal Law and Criminology* 31:3–6.
Jacoby JE, Ratledge EC (2016) *The Power of the Prosecutor. Gatekeepers of the Criminal Justice System*. Praeger, Santa Barbara.
Jasiński W, Kremens K (2019) *Criminal Law in Poland*. Kluwer Law International, Alphen aan den Rijn.
Jescheck HH (1970) Principles of German Criminal Procedure. *Virginia Law Review* 56:239–253.
Juy-Birmann R (2002) The German System. Delmas-Marty M, Spencer JR (eds) *European Criminal Procedures*. Cambridge University Press, Cambridge, pp. 292–347
Kamisar Y, LaFave WR, Israel JH, King NJ, Kerr OS, Primus EB (2012) *Modern Criminal Procedure. Cases-Comments-Questions*. West, St Paul.
Kmiecik R (2011) Legalizm i konsensualizm w działalności karnoprocesowej prokuratora—między teorią i praktyką. In: Grzegorczyk T (ed) *Funkcje procesu karnego. Księga jubileuszowa Profesora Janusza Tylmana*, Wolters Kluwer, Warsaw, pp. 25–35.
Kremens K (2020) The New Wave of Penal Populism from a Polish Perspective. In: Hoven E, Kubiciel M (eds), *Zukunftsperspektiven des Strafrechts. Symposium zum 70*. Geburtstag von Thomas Weigend, Nomos, Baden Baden, pp. 123–136.
Kruszyński P (2007) The Investigative Stage of the Criminal Process in Poland. In: Cape E, Hodgson J, Pranken T, Spronken T (eds) *Suspects in Europe. Procedural Rights at the Investigative Stage of the Criminal Process in the European Union*. Intersentia, Antwerp, pp. 181–209.
Kulesza C (2014) Rola prokuratora w znowelizowanym kodeksie postępowania karnego. *Prokuratura i Prawo* 4:5–33.

Langbein J (1979) Land Without Plea Bargaining: How the Germans Do It. *Michigan Law Review* 78:204–225.

Ligeti K (2019) The Place of the Prosecutor in Common Law and Civil Law Jurisdictions. In: Brown DK, Turner JI, Weisser B (eds) *The Oxford Handbook of Criminal Process*. Oxford University Press, Oxford, pp. 139–163.

Luna E, Wade M (2010) Prosecutors as Judges. *Washington and Lee Law Review* 67:1413–1532.

Lupária L, Gialuz M (2019) Italian Criminal Procedure: Thirty Years After the Great Reform. *Roma Tre Law Review* 1:26–72.

Mangiaracina A (2019) Report on Italy. In: Quattrocolo S, Ruggeri S (eds) *Personal Participation in Criminal Proceedings*. Springer, Cham, pp. 229–278.

Marafioti L (2008) Italian Criminal Procedure: A System Caught Between Two Traditions. In: Jackson J, Langer M, Tillers P (eds) *Crime, Procedure and Evidence in a Comparative and International Context: Essays in Honour of Professor Mirjan Damaška*. Hart, London, pp. 81–98.

Murzynowski A (2005) Criminal Procedure. In: Frankowski S (ed.) *Introduction to Polish Law*. Kluwer Law International, the Netherlands.

Neubauer DW, Fradella HF (2019) *America's Courts and the Criminal Justice System*, 13th edn. Cengage, Boston.

Nowak C, Steinborn S (2013) Poland. In: Ligeti K (ed) *Toward a Prosecutor of the European Union, Volume 1: A Comparative Analysis*. Hart, London, pp. 498–509.

Panzavolta M (2004) Reforms and Counter-Reforms in the Italian Struggle for an Accusatorial Criminal Law System. *North Carolina Journal of International Law & Commercial Regulation* 30:577–624.

Perrodet A (2002) The Italian System. In: Delmas-Marty M, Spencer JR (eds) *European Criminal Procedures*. Cambridge University Press, Cambridge, pp. 348–411.

Pizzi WT, Marafioti L (1992) The New Italian Code of Criminal Procedure: The Difficulties of Building an Adversarial Trial System on a Civil Law Foundation. *Yale Journal of International Law* 17:1–40.

Podgor ES (2012) Prosecution Guidelines in the United States. In: Luna E, Wade M (eds) *The Prosecutor in Transnational Perspective*. Oxford University Press, Oxford, pp. 9–19.

Pound, R (1960) Discretion, Dispensation and Mitigation: The Problem of the Individual Special Case. *New York University Law Review* 35:925–937.

Roberts P (2007) Law and Criminal Investigation. In: Newburn T, Williamson T, Wright A (eds) *Handbook of Criminal Investigation*. Routledge, New York, pp. 92–145.

Rogacka-Rzewnicka M (2007) Oportunizm i legalizm ścigania przestępstw w świetle współczesnych przeobrażeń procesu karnego. Wolters Kluwer, Warsaw.

Roxin C, Schunemann B (2017) *Strafverfahrensrecht. Ein Studienbuch*. CH Beck, Munich.

Scheb JM, Scheb JM II (1999) *Criminal Procedure*. Wadsworth, Belmont.

Siegismund E (2003) The Public Prosecution Office in Germany: Legal Status, Function and Organization. In: Effective Administration of the Police and the Prosecution in Criminal Justice. The 120th International Senior Seminar, Visiting Experts' Papers. www.unafei.or.jp/publications/pdf/RS_No60/No60_10VE_Siegismund2.pdf. Accessed 12.07.2020, pp. 58–64

Skorupka J (2010) Uwagi o modelu postępowania przygotowawczego i sądowego. *Ius Novum* 4:31–74.

Skorupka J (2018) *Proces karny*. Wolters Kluwer, Warsaw.

Skorupka J (2019) Komentarz do art. 10 k.p.k. In: Skorupka J (ed) *Kodeks postępowania karnego*. Komentarz. 3rd ed. CH Beck, Warsaw.

Sobolewski Z (1999) Zasada legalizmu w ograniczonym zakresie. In: Nowak T (ed) *Nowe prawo karne procesowe. Zagadnienia wybrane*. Księga ku czci Profesora Wiesława Daszkiewicza, Poznań.

Stuntz WJ (2005) Bordenkircher v. Hayes: The Rise of Plea Bargaining and the Decline of the Rule of Law. *Harvard Law School Research Paper* 120. https://papers.ssrn.com/sol3/papers.cfm?abstract_id=854284. Accessed 12.07.2020.

Tomasiewicz P (2015) Double Jeopardy, Pre-Arrest Delay, Speedy Trial, and Prosecutorial Discretion. In: Schuman CJ (ed) *Connecticut Criminal Procedure*. Connecticut Law Tribune, Hartford, pp. 233–295.

Trendafilova E, Róth W (2008) Report on the Public Prosecution Service in Germany. In: Open Society Institute Sofia (ed) *Promoting Prosecutorial Accountability, Independence and Effectiveness*. Open Society Institute Sofia, Sofia, pp. 213–246.

Wade M (2008) The Januses of Justice: How Prosecutors Define the Kind of Justice Done Across Europe. *European Journal of Crime, Criminal Law and Criminal Justice* 16:595–617.

Wallace PR (2001) The Power of Charging Decision. In: *The Prosecutors Deskbook. Ethical Issue and Emerging Roles for the 21st Century Prosecutors*. American Prosecutors Research Institute, Alexandria.

Waltoś S (2008) *Proces karny. Zarys Systemu*. Lexis Nexis, Warsaw.

Weigend T (2013) Germany. In: Ligeti K (ed) *Toward a Prosecutor of the European Union, Volume 1: A Comparative Analysis*. Hart, London, pp. 264–306.

Weigend T (2015) Throw It All Out? Judicial Dealing with Procedural Faults. In: Caianiello M, Hodgson JS (eds) *Discretionary Criminal Justice in a Comparative Context*. Carolina Academic Press, Durham, pp. 185–205.

Weigend T, Salditt F (2007) The Investigative Stage of the Criminal Process in Germany. In: Cape E, Hodgson J, Pranken T, Spronken T (eds) *Suspects in Europe. Procedural Rights at the Investigative Stage of the Criminal Process in the European Union*. Intersentia, Antwerp, pp. 79–100. Worrall JL (2012) *Criminal Procedure. From First Contact to Appeal*. Pearson, Boston.

Zacharias FC (1991) Structuring the Ethics of Prosecutorial Trial Practice: Can Prosecutors Do Justice? *Vanderbilt Law Review* 44:45–114.

Zacharias FC, Green BA (2004) Prosecutorial Neutrality. *Wisconsin Law Review* 3:837–904.

Zgryzek K (2017) Bezstronność prokuratora, osoby prowadzącej postępowanie przygotowawcze oraz innego oskarżyciela publicznego—uprawnienie czy obowiązek. *Prokuratura i Prawo* 10:5–17.

Chapter 4

Powers of the Prosecutor over Initiation of Investigation

4.1 General Considerations

This chapter commences what should be considered as a core of this work. It explores the influence that the prosecutor has on the commencement of a criminal investigation in Germany, Poland, Italy, and the USA. One preliminary note should be made at this point. No additional meaning will be attached to the choice of words naming this decision or, more accurately, the phase of criminal investigation. Therefore, such words as "opening," "starting," "initiating," "commencing" or "beginning" of investigation may be and will be used interchangeably, giving them exactly the same denotation.

Each section within this chapter, devoted to four analyzed countries, will begin with determination of the level of suspicion (threshold, standard of proof) that justifies the initiation of a criminal investigation. Furthermore, the time that the criminal justice authority has to decide on the commencement of investigation will be discussed. Even if such decision is undertaken informally, the law may determine whether the decision to open investigation be undertaken immediately after the authority learns that a crime has been allegedly committed, or is there any leeway. This requires discussion of the obligation to initiate proceedings (observance of the principle of legality) and discretion regarding such decision. Thereafter the analysis considers the steps in procedure necessary to undertake the decision to initiate investigation as well as to refuse the initiation of an investigation. This links to the question of what form (if any) these decisions take and what are the formal requirements for them. The chapter ends with discussion of the authority that makes the decision to start investigation and, in particular, whether the prosecutor plays any role with regard to it. The aim is to identify, both on the normative level and through the analysis of practice, how much power is granted in each of the four countries to the prosecutor at that moment of criminal investigation. Understanding her factual influence on this preliminary decision will help to determine the actual responsibility for the conducting of a criminal investigation.

Having thus set out the stall, we ask whether it is desirable for the prosecutor to be involved in deciding whether to initiate investigation. What are the positives of a system in which the prosecutor becomes involved early in the process? And should she decide to initiate investigation by herself, or rather only supervise the police activities in this area? Moreover, does the level of involvement of the prosecutor, regarding commencement of investigation, depend on the type of crime? Do the rules regarding a decision not to initiate investigation follow the same scheme as a decision to initiate investigation? More importantly, should the decision refusing initiation of investigation be subject to any judicial scrutiny? Or should criminal justice authorities, including the prosecutor, be free to decide whether to commence investigations?

4.2 Initiating Investigation in Germany

4.2.1 Threshold for Initiating Investigation

The subordination of the German criminal process to the principle of legality (*Legalitätsprinzip*) informs the German approach to the initiation of criminal investigation. As a general rule, the prosecutor is obliged to act with regard to all prosecutable criminal offenses whenever sufficient factual indications exist that a crime has occurred.[1] The exceptions to this rule are limited and strictly prescribed by law.[2] This means that investigation should be initiated and prosecuted whenever the relevant threshold has been met.[3] Moreover, in accordance with the principle of officiality (*Offizialmaxime, Offizialprinzip*) the state is obliged to take action and conduct proceedings independently of the will and behavior of the victim.[4] This suggests that in every case, beside the most obviously unreliable notices of a crime, the investigation will be commenced.

The question therefore remains how the German system is even able to handle this enormous amount of commenced investigations, if all reliable notices of crime must result in commencement of investigation. And even if later some of those investigations may be discontinued the number of initially opened investigation must be impossible to cope with. The answer may be that there are quite a few exceptions to the legality principle, some of informal character. One is obtaining approval in cases of offenses investigated into a victim's complaint (*Antragsdelikt*). Another obtaining authorization from the relevant authority where suspects are protected by

1 § 152 (2) StPO.
2 Cf. Section 3.2.2.
3 § 160 (1) and § 170 (1) StPO.
4 § 152 (1) StPO.

immunity (*Ermächtigungsdelikten*). Also, with certain offenses only the victim is authorized to initiate prosecution (*Privatklage*).[5] This obviously limits the number of commenced investigations.

The obligation to investigate whenever the suspicion that an offense has been committed exists (*Verdacht einer Straftat Kenntnis*) is provided in § 160 (1) StPO. Besides this rather general provision the threshold to initiate investigation is also provided in § 152 (2) StPO obliging the prosecutor to take action whenever "sufficient factual grounds" (*zureichende tatsächliche Anhaltspunkte*) exist. Importantly, the investigation must be initiated regardless of whether the identity of the suspect has been determined at this point. This suggests that the notion "sufficient factual grounds" refers to the crime itself and not to the perpetrator of the crime.

But the threshold for initiating investigation is not formulated in German law in a consistent manner. German law uses the term suspicion (*Verdacht*), which is sometimes even considered a central concept in the German criminal process.[6] As a general rule, German law avoids providing levels of suspicion (standards of proof) necessary to undertake certain actions during criminal process.[7] But in case of initiation of criminal investigation such a level is provided. To commence the first stage of the criminal process, the so-called initial suspicion (*Anfangsverdacht*), understood as sufficient factual grounds as prescribed in § 152 (2) StPO is enough. The initial suspicion necessary to initiate investigation must be based on the facts of the case and is not considered as a discretionary decision, although a certain degree of free evaluation of that threshold (*Beurteilungsspielraum*) is obviously necessary.[8] The bar of the level of suspicion isn't set too high.[9] It is definitely considerably lower than the threshold necessary for filing official charges (*Anklage*) with the court.[10] The level of suspicion required in the latter case, i.e. "sufficient cause" (*genügenden Anlaß*) can be interpreted as such level of certainty in which the evidence is so strong that a conviction can reasonably be expected.[11]

The Code provides that the commencement of investigation shall take place "as soon" (*sobald*) as the public prosecution office is notified that an offense may have been committed.[12] This again suggests a limited right of the competent authority to verify whether an investigation should be

5 §§ 374–394 StPO.
6 Volk (2010), p. 31 as cited by Wiśniewski (2014), p. 387.
7 Girdwoyń (2006), p. 59.
8 See Meyer-Großner and Schmitt (2014), § 152, nb. 4 and cited case law.
9 Weigend (2013), p. 267.
10 § 170 (1) StPO.
11 Weigend (2013), p. 268.
12 § 160 (1) StPO.

initiated and provides for an almost immediate decision. Yet, this decision is never automatic. If the evidence relative to an alleged offense having been committed is weak, or if there are doubts regarding the existence of the initial suspicion necessary to commence investigation occurs, the prosecutor (or police) will conduct an informal inquiry before undertaking any decision regarding opening an investigation.[13] This form of inquiry remains unregulated by the German Code.

4.2.2 Procedure for Initiating Investigation

Most typically investigation starts when a crime has been reported to the police[14] or because the police have detected that a crime has been committed. The notice of a crime may be reported orally or in writing with the public prosecution service, police, or even with the local court.[15] The notice filed orally is then recorded in writing,[16] which means that the formal interrogation of informants takes place whenever the informant decides to report a crime in person.

Theoretically, immediately upon learning about the possible commitment of a crime the police are obliged to transfer the file to the prosecutor,[17] leaving the decision relating to commencement of investigation to the prosecution service. But this legal norm has been replaced by the custom of commencing investigation independently by the police based on § 163 (1) StPO. The practice of establishing the facts of the case by the police first and providing the prosecutor with the file afterwards has been confirmed in the analysis of the police guidelines issued in individual Lands.[18]

The existence of the initial suspicion that an offense has been committed justifies opening of the investigation.[19] However, the decision whether to initiate investigation is not taken formally by any specific decision. There is no specific document stating that the investigation has commenced. It is also unnecessary to identify the potential suspect at this point.[20] Therefore, undertaking the decision to commence the investigation is manifested by opening the file on the matter either by the police or, less often, the prosecutor.[21]

13 Weigend (2004), p. 214.
14 Huber (2008), p. 297 (The data quoted by authors suggest that between 91 and 98 percent of investigations are initiated as a result of notifications to the police by members of the public).
15 § 159 (1) StPO first sentence.
16 § 159 (1) StPO second sentence.
17 § 163 (2) StPO.
18 Elsner and Peters (2010), p. 228.
19 § 152 (2) StPO.
20 Bohlander (2012), p. 69.
21 Weigend (2013), p. 267.

But the German system also provides for specific provisions when the decision not to commence investigation has been undertaken. Generally the law provides that in all cases in which the prosecutor decides to terminate the investigation the informant is notified of the outcome of the investigation, which contains the reasons for such decision.[22] This rule is considered to apply to all cases, regardless of whether the investigation has been officially commenced and subsequently terminated or not initiated at all. If the informant is not an alleged victim, the decision not to open an investigation terminates the criminal proceedings entirely, although the informant always has a right to file a departmental complaint regarding prosecutorial action.[23] Accordingly, individuals against whom the investigation is directed have no legal remedy against the opening of an investigation, unless they can show that the continuation of an investigation is clearly arbitrary.[24] However, the situation becomes very different if the informant is the victim of a crime. First, the victim is notified not only that the investigation has not been commenced but also about her right to contest such decision and about the time limits for such appeal.[25] This is just one example of the right to information in criminal proceedings attached to victims of crime in criminal proceedings.[26]

The victim is entitled to appeal the decision of the prosecutor not to initiate an investigation[27] which is aimed at forcing the prosecutor to bring a case to trial (*Klageerzwingungsverfahren*).[28] It is impermissible in cases of misdemeanors in which noninitiation of investigation was based on the lack of public interest as well as in cases of crimes prosecuted privately.[29] This means that the *Klageerzwingungsverfahren* is limited to cases when not opening the investigation resulted from a lack of evidence and not from discretionary reasons. The procedure involves the court and concerns several steps and is identical to the one that follows the interlocutory appeal against the discontinuation of the criminal investigation.[30] The consequences of it may lead to ordering the prosecutor to resume the investigation or even force her to file an accusation. Although since the case at that point is certainly undeveloped it is unlikely that the court will decide so.

22 § 171 StPO first sentence.
23 See Frase and Weigend (1995), p. 338.
24 See Weigend (2013), p. 291 and case law quoted in fn. 263.
25 § 171 StPO second sentence.
26 Elsner and Peters (2010), p. 229; Frase and Weigend (1995), p. 350.
27 § 172 (1) StPO.
28 Frase and Weigend (1995), p. 338 and 350 (authors translate this procedure as the "mandamus action compelling prosecution").
29 § 172 (2) StPO.
30 See Section 8.2.2.

4.2.3 Authority Responsible for Initiating Investigation

On the normative level, it is clearly stated that it is the prosecutor who initiates the investigation to verify whether public charges (*öffentliche Klage*) are to be brought in a case.[31] Even if a case was originally reported to the police, they must transfer the file without delay (*ohne Verzug*) to the prosecutor[32] who will decide on commencing an investigation. In this theoretical framework this gives the prosecutor full control over all criminal investigations in Germany, regardless of the seriousness of the crime being investigated. This makes the prosecutor the "ruler of the investigative stage," being responsible legally and factually for the investigation from its very beginning.[33]

However, in practice, it is frequently the police that commence investigations.[34] This stems from a rule allowing the police to investigate criminal offenses, taking all measures that may not be deferred in order to prevent concealment of facts.[35] Generally, this should be considered as the ability to perform crime scene investigations or interrogating witnesses and suspects on the spot, but in practice again, these competencies are much broader. Habitually the police tend to ignore an obvious rule to transfer a case without a delay to the prosecutor and do so only when they believe the case has been already resolved.[36] Therefore, when a crime is reported first to police, they will start investigating, without notifying the prosecutor. As a result, the majority of criminal investigations are conducted independently by the police.[37] Surprisingly, it has not been criticized as conflicting the concept of the police being placed under the guidance of prosecutors in the process of investigating criminal cases.[38]

Obviously, the prosecutor cannot control and supervise decisions regarding initiation of investigation made by the police in cases that she is not even aware of.[39] This means that in the majority of cases the crucial first stages of the criminal process are carried out by the police, which raises concerns. In particular, it refers to cases of crimes that police detect without prior notice from the victim or another complainant. They simply disregard some criminal behavior even without notifying the prosecutor in a form of "so-called factual opportunity."[40]

31 § 160 (1) StPO.
32 § 163 (2) StPO.
33 Elsner and Peters (2010), p. 227.
34 Weigend (2013), p. 291.
35 § 163 (1) StPO.
36 Weigend (2013), p. 291 and literature quoted in fn. 260.
37 Frase and Weigend (1995), p. 323 (with exception of homicide and economic crimes).
38 Jörg-Albrecht (2000), p. 255.
39 Gilliéron (2014), p. 267.
40 Elsner and Peters (2010), p. 224.

To sum up, in theory as well as on the normative level it is the prosecutor who is obliged to commence all investigations and take control over them from the moment a crime is reported. The police to that matter is subordinated to prosecution service and is assigned only a supporting role. But practice proves otherwise. In fact, the police informally filter the cases that are passed to the prosecutor, and they initiate the majority of investigations without any prosecutorial involvement or control. This varies depending on how serious the crime is. The prosecutor has more control over most serious cases and cases that are reported first with the prosecutor instead of police. Also when the case demands from its beginning prosecutorial involvement e.g. by filing motion for pretrial detention, the prosecutor will be obviously notified earlier. But for the overwhelming majority of investigations conducted in cases of less serious crimes, the police have assumed the role of the initiator of investigation.

4.3 Initiating Investigation in Poland

4.3.1 Threshold for Initiating Investigation

According to the general rule criminal investigation in Poland is initiated in every case when reasonable suspicion (*uzasadnione podejrzenie*) that an offense has been committed exists.[41] Theoretically, this would leave no discretion to the decision maker, with regard to initiating investigation, since the existence of reasonable suspicion obligates the competent authority to commence an investigation in compliance with the legality principle.[42] Accordingly, establishing that reasonable suspicion does not exist results in issuing decision not to commence an investigation.

The threshold for commencing an investigation remains the same regardless of the form in which the investigation is being conducted.[43] But the law does not explain how this ground is to be understood. It is argued that "reasonable suspicion" presents a higher level of certainty than mere suspicion since it must be justified in some way.[44] At the same time, absolute certainty that an offense has been committed is not required. Therefore, it is understood that reasonable suspicion arises when existing, objective information about an event, in a subjective opinion of the investigative authority, indicates the possibility of an act having been committed which establishes all elements of an offense.[45]

41 Article 303 k.p.k.
42 Article 10 § 1 k.p.k. Cf. Section 3.3.2.
43 Article 325a § 2 k.p.k. See Section 3.3.1 on forms in which investigation can be conducted.
44 Brodzisz (2018), p. 714.
45 Nowak and Steinborn (2013), p. 500. See more in Cora (2016), pp. 592–595.

As previously stated, a decision not to commence investigation into an alleged offense may be justified on grounds of lack of reasonable suspicion.[46] It may happen, however, that reasonable suspicion that an offense has been committed exists, but the criminal justice authority must refuse to commence the investigation. The law provides for a long list of such situations naming them negative grounds for the conduct of criminal proceedings (*negatywne przesłanki procesowe*). Among them the law identifies the immunity of defendant, lack of official complaint of the victim in case of investigations prosecuted upon complaint, lack of jurisdiction or expiry of the statute of limitations, or insufficiency of evidence that the suspect was involved in the crime.[47] The existence of any of these negative conditions results in the immediate termination of criminal proceedings at every stage of the criminal process. And if such circumstance is known before the decision to initiate investigation was issued the decision to refuse opening the investigation shall be undertaken.

Polish law provides for a detailed time frame for undertaking the decision to commence or not to commence investigation. The general rule states that the decision must be issued immediately after commitment of an offense has been reported.[48] This means on the same or following day on which the incident was reported. Nevertheless, the law provides for two exceptions here: the preliminary examination[49] and so-called immediate procedures.[50]

The preliminary examination (*czynności sprawdzające*) is carried out with the aim of verifying the information that an offense has been committed, regardless of the source of this information. The scope of investigatory actions that can be undertaken during this time is very limited. The authority cannot conduct any evidentiary procedures that require being recorded in written form, e.g. searches, crime scene investigations, interrogations.[51] The only possible actions that may take place during preliminary examination are limited to taking of statements from witnesses who have reported an offense, or from victims filing official complaints in case of offenses prosecuted upon complaint. But the police may also undertake unofficial actions to substantiate the information. The preliminary examination may last up to 30 days only, after which time a decision whether to commence investigation must be issued.[52] Even though this procedure should be treated as an exception, in

46 Article 303 k.p.k.
47 Article 17 § 1 k.p.k. Cf. Section 8.3.1.
48 Article 305 § 1 k.p.k.
49 Article 307 k.p.k.
50 Article 308 k.p.k.
51 See Article 143 k.p.k. for the list of evidentiary procedures that require being recorded in writing.
52 If the person that reports an offense has not been informed within six weeks of either the commencement of investigation or of the refusal to initiate investigation, that person has

practice, the criminal justice authorities use it on a daily basis in almost every case in order to gain more time before investigation officially commences. This makes a difference, since the investigation has its time limits and must be prolonged every time it expires.[53] The additional 30 days give considerable freedom to criminal justice authorities to undertake informal investigatory measures outside of the prosecutorial supervision.[54]

The immediate procedures (*czynności w niezbędnym zakresie*) allow for the preliminary proceedings not to commence immediately, even where there is reasonable suspicion that an offense has been committed. It may happen when immediate issuing of a formal decision is considered a waste of time in cases when the situation demands securing of forensic traces and the gathering of evidence that will otherwise be lost or destroyed, e.g. the necessity to conduct an urgent crime scene inspection. The evidentiary procedures that can be conducted as part of these proceedings are not limited in their scope. Thus, all evidentiary procedures requiring a written record may also be conducted which includes crime scene inspections, searches interrogations, etc. The immediate procedures may last only five days and they are considered part of the investigation from the moment the first evidentiary action is undertaken.[55]

Eventually, in every case, after examining received information, the competent authority must issue an official and written decision whether investigation was initiated.

4.3.2 Procedure for Initiating Investigation

Polish law determines that anyone possessing information on the possible commitment of a crime should report it.[56] Generally, there is no legal obligation to do so as it is seen more as a moral than a legal duty with the exception of a few very grave felonies[57] in which case reporting the crime is mandatory. Additionally, state and local government institutions that learn of an offense having been committed are obliged to report it immediately.[58] In a typical case the source of information that such reasonable suspicion exists is irrelevant. Reporting crime can be done by phone, letter, or by attending a police station, etc. Also, the criminal justice authorities can use their own methods to uncover an offense that has been committed.

the right to an interlocutory appeal against the inaction of the criminal justice authorities (Article 306 § 3 k.p.k.).

53 Cf. Section 5.3.

54 Jasiński and Kremens (2019), p. 216.

55 Jasiński and Kremens (2019), p. 216.

56 Article 304 § 1 k.p.k.

57 E.g. espionage, murder, as listed in Article 240 k.k.

58 Article 304 § 2 k.p.k.

Upon reception of an information on the possible commitment of a crime the criminal justice authority must issue a decision to initiate investigation or not. However, if the information was obtained by police from their own sources issuing decision refusing commencement of investigation is unnecessary.[59] Still, some scholars argue that if information regarding an offense comes from internal police sources, but the victim is identified, the decision should be issued to sustain her procedural guarantees to appeal the refusal.[60]

The initiation of investigation as well as the refusal to initiate investigation is always undertaken in the written form of a decision (*postanowienie*), regardless of whether the investigation is conducted in a form of inquiry or inspection.[61] The elements that every such decision must contain are precisely provided for. These are: the identification of the issuing authority as well the office where that official works, the date, the case identification, and the matter that the decision concerns.[62] The decision always also contain the description of an offense allegedly committed, and its legal qualification, i.e. relevant provisions as provided in substantive criminal law.[63] In this decision the information on the suspected offender is never provided even if he or she is already established. Only upon issuing an initially charging decision[64] is the name of the suspect revealed.

General rules on decisions issued in Polish criminal proceedings provide that every decision must be reasoned which means that it should contain a written explanation on the justification behind the decision. This is true for decisions undertaken in cases of investigations conducted in the form of an inspection which concern major crimes. But in cases of inquiries neither the decision to initiate or to refuse initiation of proceedings must provide the written reasons.[65] This exception is justified by the nature of less complicated cases subjected to inquiry. But considering the percentage of inquiries conducted in Poland (approximately 85 percent of all investigations) this is certainly the majority of cases. The lack of notification on the reasons for refusal to initiate an investigation is disturbing, since it makes the possibility for appeal against such a decision more difficult not knowing the arguments behind such decision.[66] As a form of remedy, upon request, the authority issuing the decision must provide the reasons orally for the decision.[67]

59 Grzegorczyk (2004), p. 770.
60 Zagrodnik (2020), p. 530.
61 In cases of inquiry, it is however possible to include the decision in the official record of the interrogation of the informant (Article 325e § 1 k.p.k.).
62 Article 94 § 1 k.p.k.
63 Article 303 k.p.k.
64 See on the notion of "initial charge" in Section 6.3.1.
65 Article 325e § 1 k.p.k.
66 Stanisław Stachowiak, "Odmowa wszczęcia śledztwa lub dochodzenia," 7–8 *Prokuratura i Prawo* 2006 p. 31.
67 Article 325e § 1 k.p.k.

The decision refusing initiation of investigation is subject to interlocutory appeal.[68] The right to appeal is granted to the identified victim, the state, local government, or social institution that reported an offense and the person that reported an offense if that offense resulted in the violation of the rights of this person, even if she is not a victim.[69] Those that are entitled to submit an interlocutory appeal must receive a copy of the decision,[70] and they are given access to the materials of the case, gathered up to that point in time. Those individuals that reported an offense but have no right to interlocutory appeal need only be informed that a decision has been issued.[71]

The entitled person files the interlocutory appeal with the court that holds a hearing. If the court does not see the reasons to initiate investigation, the case will remain closed. But if the court accepts the view of the appellant, it may revoke the decision refusing the initiation of an investigation, stating the reasons, and pointing out what kind of investigative measures should be undertaken.[72] Those indications shall be binding on the criminal justice authorities that will continue carrying on the investigation. This usually means that the investigation will be initiated.[73] Theoretically, it is possible that the prosecutor or police will not commence investigation and issue an adequate decision for the second time.[74] In such cases the victim will have a right to file a second interlocutory appeal, but just with the prosecutor who supervises the prosecutor responsible for the case. If the supervising prosecutor confirms the decision refusing initiation of investigation the victim has a right to file a subsidiary indictment[75] against the accused and prosecute the case by herself.[76] The truth is, however, that at such an early stage of the criminal process it is very unlikely that the victim will possess enough evidence to pursue a subsidiary prosecution (*oskarżenie subsydiarne*). Therefore, in practice, such prosecutions as a result of the reaction to the decision refusing commencement of investigation, are very rare.

There is no right to interlocutory appeal against a decision to commence investigation in either of the forms, since this decision is not targeted at anyone. However, the person that has reported an offense, as well as the identified victim, must be notified that such decision has been issued.[77] If

68 Article 459 § 1 k.p.k.
69 306 § 1 k.p.k.
70 See Article 306 § 1 in connection with Article 305 § 4 k.p.k.
71 Article 305 § 4 k.p.k.
72 Article 330 § 1 k.p.k.
73 Nowak and Steinborn (2013), p. 524.
74 Article 330 § 2 k.p.k.
75 Cf. Section 8.3.2.
76 Article 55 § 1 k.p.k.
77 Article 305 § 4 k.p.k.

the person that reports an offense has not been informed within six weeks of either the commencement of investigation or of the refusal to initiate it, that person has the right to file a complaint against the inaction of the criminal justice authorities.[78] This complaint is not filed with the court but directed to the prosecutor who would normally supervise the investigation conducted by police or, in cases of investigations conducted by the prosecutor, to her supervisor. It is so regardless of whether the prosecutor has been already notified by the police that the information of possible commitment of a crime has been received.

4.3.3 Authority Responsible for Initiating Investigation

The determination of who may initiate the investigation depends on the form in which criminal investigation is conducted which relates to the seriousness of an offense. In cases of more serious crimes when an investigation is conducted in the form of inspection only the prosecutor maintains the exclusive power to initiate it.[79] There are no exceptions to this rule. If a report received by the police concerns an offense for which an inspection is mandatory,[80] the police is obliged to submit the file immediately to the prosecutor who undertakes the adequate decision.[81] One the other hand, a decision refusing initiation of inspection can be issued either by the prosecutor or the police.[82] In such cases, however, the decision on the refusal of commencement of investigation must always be confirmed by the prosecutor. This means that with the most serious offenses the prosecutor will always oversee police decisions, leaving no room for uncontrolled initiative.[83]

The commencement of investigation in the form of inquiry (*dochodzenie*) provides for more options. Since the inquiry concerns less serious offenses, the decision to initiate and to refuse initiation of inquiry is primarily issued by the police.[84] On rare occasions, though, the prosecutor issues it upon her own initiative. The decision to initiate inquiry undertaken by the police, does not require prosecutorial confirmation, while the decision to refuse initiation of inquiry must be confirmed by the prosecutor.[85]

78 Article 306 § 3 k.p.k.
79 Article 305 § 3 k.p.k.
80 This includes all felonies (offenses punishable by imprisonment for at least three years) and some misdemeanors, e.g. those in which a suspect is judge or prosecutor (see Article 309 k.p.k.).
81 Article 304 § 3 k.p.k.
82 Article 305 § 3 k.p.k.
83 Jasiński and Kremens (2019), p. 217.
84 Article 325e § 1 k.p.k.
85 Article 325e § 2 k.p.k.

Since the decision to initiate the investigation conducted in the form of inquiry does not have to be confirmed by the prosecutor, she will most likely not be aware of the majority of initiated and ongoing inquiries. In practice, until the time comes for the extension an inquiry,[86] proceedings are conducted by the police without prosecutorial supervision. This is the most typical scenario unless the crime was first reported to the prosecutor's office. But, in theory, each and every investigation is conducted under prosecutorial supervision.[87] This suggests that the prosecutor should be aware that the inquiry has been initiated, to be able to effectively exercise her supervisory powers. But, surprisingly, no rule obliges the police to inform the prosecutor about the initiation of an investigation. This raises justified doubts regarding the effectiveness of the control over investigations conducted in the form of inquiry.[88]

Another question refers to the number of decisions regarding initiation of investigation taken annually by the prosecutor and decided by the police. According to official statistics, of 683,700 investigations launched in 2018 only 81,720 were commenced by the prosecutor: all 79,967 inspections and just 1,753 in the form of inquiry.[89] This indicates prosecutor activity in only 11.9 percent of cases. This shows that the vast majority of decisions regarding initiation of investigation) are undertaken by the police. Considering the lack of rules forcing the police to report the initiation of investigation to the prosecutor, majority of inspections remains out of the prosecutorial influence or control.

4.4 Initiating Investigation in Italy

4.4.1 Threshold for Initiating Investigation

The commencement of criminal investigation in Italy takes place when the *notitiae criminis*, i.e. information on the commission of an offense reaches the prosecutor.[90] Precisely speaking the criminal investigation is initiated when the prosecutor registers the information that allegedly the crime has been committed in the official register. However, interestingly, the start of the duration of the investigation is not related to registering the information on the

86 If there is no ground to end the inquiry after two months from its commencement the file of the case must be sent to the prosecutor with the request for extension. Cf. Section 5.3.

87 Article 326 § 1 k.p.k.

88 Jasiński and Kremens (2019), p. 211.

89 *Sprawozdanie z działalności powszechnych jednostek organizacyjnych prokuratury za rok 2019*, https://pk.gov.pl/wp-content/uploads/2020/03/PK-P1K.pdf (accessed 12.05.2020), p. 1.

90 Di Amato (2013), p. 37.

commission of an offense in the prosecutorial register, but with putting in it the name of the potential suspect.[91]

The law provides that immediately after receiving *notitiae criminis*, or acquiring them upon her own initiative, the prosecutor enters information on the possible commitment of a crime into the official register.[92] Neither this provision, nor any other, requires the standard of proof necessary to be reached by the information on the possible commitment of an offense, that would justify the commencement of investigation. This means the prosecutor commences criminal investigation (by recording the *notitia criminis* in the register) whenever she believes a crime has been committed.[93] Therefore the information on allegedly committed offense should be sufficiently detailed and specific allowing its registering. However, as it is reported, only *notitia criminis* that are considered as clearly improbable will not be recorded[94] which makes the number of initiated investigations very high

The law seems not to give much choice to the competent authority, at least in theory, whenever the information on possible commitment of a crime has reached her. This flows from the Italian Constitution's provisions stipulating that the prosecutor pursue all crimes.[95] This principle binds the authorities, not only as to when the decision to prosecute must be made, but also at the commencement of criminal investigation.[96] Even though this principle is hard to achieve, and the selection of cases reportedly exist, it has a major consequence for prosecutorial accountability. The principle of legality makes the prosecutor compelled to act and there will be no repercussions where it transpires crime unfounded. Prosecutors may therefore successfully claim that the suspicion that a crime was committed compelled them to act.[97]

The practice seems to be less idealistic and not necessarily in compliance with the rigid principle of legality. Considering the over-criminalization of the Italian system, the prosecution is simply unable to initiate investigation in every reported case.[98] Therefore, in practice prosecutors fail to register many notifications of a crime.[99] Moreover, as discussed in Section 3.4.2, the principle of legality has certain limitations: e.g. giving broad competencies to the victim with regard to offenses investigated and prosecuted upon complaint.

91 Caianiello (2016), p. 11.
92 Article 335 § 1 c.p.p.
93 Di Federico (2008), p. 302.
94 Ruggieri and Marcolini (2013), p. 392.
95 Section 3.4.2.
96 Panzavolta (2004), p. 591.
97 Di Federico (2008), p. 302.
98 Gialuz (2017), p. 24.
99 Caianiello (2012), p. 256.

The law provides that registration of *notitia criminis* take place immediately after they are received.[100] This date is crucial, since certain time limits are provided for the conducting of an investigation in Italy.[101] Formally, the law does not provide any possibility to delay the registration or to verify the trustworthiness of the information provided. However, since the *notitia criminis* may be received either by the prosecutor or police, it may take some time before they are transferred to the prosecutor's office. Even though the law provides that, upon receiving the *notitia criminis*, the police must inform the prosecutor in writing at once about an alleged offense,[102] the provision is so vague that it can be interpreted broadly. These regulations do not provide a time frame for when notification should be made to the prosecutor, so it is uncertain whether in practice this is done immediately. Moreover, the law provides that the notification to the prosecutor should contain a broad spectrum of information regarding both the crime and the potential suspect, including "activities already carried out" which assumes that some measures can be undertaken by the police to discover facts before transferring information to prosecutor. This, however, would mean that certain investigative measures take place before official registration of *notitia criminis* by the prosecutor marking the commencement of investigation. Actual control of the prosecutor over these decisions is somewhat artificial. Therefore, what takes place is a preparatory enquiry (*pre-inchiesta*) aimed at ascertaining whether criminal investigation should be initiated.[103] This happens e.g. when the so-called pseudo offenses (*pseudo notizie di reato*) are reported and, even though it lacks statutory recognition, has been legitimized by the Italian Court of Cassation.[104]

The rules are a little bit more specific in the case of carrying out activities requiring the assistance of the suspect's lawyer: these compel the police to notify the prosecutor of a crime within 48 hours.[105] For certain serious crimes—e.g. terrorism-related crimes, subversion of the constitutional system, provoking civil war[106] as well as in reasons of urgency—the law requires *notitia criminis* to be notified immediately orally, followed by written notification.[107]

100 Article 335 c.p.p.
101 But only if at the same time in the record the name of the suspect is registered (Article 405 § 2 c.p.p.).
102 Article 347 § 1 c.p.p.
103 Ruggeri (2015), p. 69–70.
104 Court of Cassation, Joint Sections, November 22, 2000, p.m. in. c ignoti.
105 Article 347 § 2bis c.p.p.
106 Full list of such crimes is enlisted in Article 407 § 2 (a) (1)–(6) c.p.p.
107 Article 347 § 3 c.p.p.

4.4.2 Procedure for Initiating Investigation

There is an obligation on both the prosecutor and police to acquire *notitia crimins* on their own initiative as well as receive those submitted to them.[108] Under Italian law there is not duty to report an offense, but there is a right to do so. However, it is mandatory for official entities to report crime while private persons are only rarely obliged to do so (in cases of some serious crimes, e.g. crimes against the state).[109]

The external sources of possible information and the way reporting should be carried on, are covered in the Code.[110] The report of a crime submitted by a private person (*denuncia*) does not have to be in any specific form.[111] It can be submitted either orally or in writing or also by a representative.[112] Generally, all reports should identify the informant and should be signed[113] while anonymous reports (*notitia criminis innominata*) should be generally disregarded[114] and only under certain circumstances considered as a basis for investigation.[115]

On the other hand, according to Article 331 § 1 c.p.p., public officials who receive information about an offense, report the crime (*denuncia*) in a prescribed form.[116] This however applies only to offenses investigated and prosecuted *ex officio* and there is no obligation to report those that demand investigation upon complaint. The other type of information on alleged crime is a medical report (*referto*) and comes from a doctor.[117] The requirement is that it must be sent immediately, or at most within 48 hours, as any delay may pose a danger; and must be submitted in prescribed form.[118]

Registration comprises information regarding the crime itself (*notizia generica*) and/or contains details of the person that committed the crime (*notizia specifica*). This information can be entered in the register simultaneously or in consecutive order. If the *notitia criminis* were obtained by the

108 Article 330 c.p.p.
109 Article 333 § 1 c.p.p.
110 See Di Amato (2013), p. 161.
111 Article 333 § 1 c.p.p.
112 Article 333 § 2 c.p.p.
113 See the case law quoted in Di Amato (2013), p. 160 (in order for a *notitia criminis* to be admissible at trial, it must be contained in a document which has an identifiable author).
114 Article 333 § 2 and 3 c.p.p.
115 See Article 230 c.p.p.
116 The contents of the denunciation include the description of the essential elements of the alleged offense, the specification of the day when the information was acquired as well as the sources of evidence which are already known to the notifying official and, if available, the personal data, address and other information that may help to identify the alleged perpetrator, the victim, and witnesses to the offense (Article 332 c.p.p.).
117 Article 334 § 1 c.p.p.
118 Article 334 § 2 c.p.p.

police and notified to the prosecutor, they must contain essential elements of the alleged offense and of the any related information available, specifying the sources of evidence, the activities carried out, and, if possible, the personal data, the address for service, and anything else that may help identify the suspected person, the victim and whoever may be able to provide relevant information.[119] If in the course of preliminary investigation, the nature of information changes the prosecutor must update them.[120]

Therefore, commencing the investigation means registering the crime. As discussed above, despite the straightforward wording of Article 335 § 1 c.p.p. it is not automatic and, in some cases, preinvestigation is conducted to verify the validity of information received before registration takes place. Moreover, the ability of the prosecutor to search independently for *notitia criminis* as granted in Article 330 c.p.p. generates certain problems. Generally, the prosecutorial right to take an independent initiative to search for crime is broadly accepted and justified by the principle of mandatory prosecution, leading to the conclusion that the prosecutor cannot be limited in her capacity to detect potential crimes and relying in that regard only on information gathered by police.[121] But the law does not specify either the context in which the investigative authorities can receive information or any limits of the investigations that can lead to such discovery.[122] Therefore, it was observed that prosecutors tend to conduct preliminary examinations prior to investigation and refrain from registering some crimes or, more likely, the name of the suspect. The reason to do so is to gain time for conducting the investigation: the clock starts ticking when the name of the suspect is registered, so the prosecutor is racing against.[123]

The prosecutor has certain obligations regarding notification of initiation of an investigation. Generally, entering the *notitia criminis* in the register results in the necessity to notify the alleged perpetrator of the offense, the victim, and the lawyers, if they so request.[124] The person is always allowed to make such query if she suspects that there is possibility that the criminal justice investigation is moving against her.[125] However, in cases of *notitia criminis* relating to serious crimes enlisted in Article 407 § 2 (a) c.p.p., the prosecutor may refrain from such notification for the sake of secrecy of criminal investigation.[126] Moreover, if there are specific needs concerning the

119 Article 347 § 1 and 2 c.p.p.
120 Article 335 § 2 c.p.p.
121 Caianiello (2016), p. 11.
122 Ruggeri (2015), p. 69.
123 See Caianiello (2016), p. 11–12.
124 Article 335 § 3 c.p.p.
125 Ruggieri and Marcolini (2013), pp. 398–399.
126 Article 335 § 3 c.p.p.

investigative activity[127] the prosecutor may order secrecy over the entering of *notitia criminis* for up to three months.[128] In any case, after six months from the date of filing the information regarding the occurrence of a crime or complaint (*querela*) the victim may ask to be informed about the state of the proceedings.[129]

Since the law provides for mandatory commencement of investigation by the prosecutor whenever the information on a crime reaches her there is no decision to decline commencement of investigation and all cases are considered as being investigated (or at least registered to be investigated). This also means that there is no need to provide a remedy for not commencing an investigation. It has been confirmed by the case law that the commencement of a criminal investigation is solely in the hands of the prosecutor, and the judge is not in a position to exercise effective control over such decision.[130] This changes when an investigation is discontinued.[131]

4.4.3 Authority Responsible for Initiating Investigation

On a normative level, separation of powers dictates that the prosecutor is vested with the power to prosecute and the police with a power to investigate.[132] Nevertheless, the power to oversee investigation rests with the prosecutor.[133] And it is entirely so regarding the commencement of investigation. Therefore, the decision to initiate an investigation remains solely with the prosecutor, since it is only the prosecutor that is in possession of the register in which *notitia criminis* are entered (Article 335 § 1 c.p.p.).

Therefore, despite the gravity of a crime, only the prosecutor is competent to register the information on possible commitment of an offense, hence to initiate the investigation. It also does not matter if the information on commitment of an offense was acquired by the prosecutor herself or by the police. If, however, a report of an alleged offense is made first to the police, it must be transferred to the prosecutor and it must be done without undue delay (Article 347 § 1 c.p.p.). In fact, even if the police obtained information on possible commitment of a crime exercising their obligation to look for the *notitia criminis* on their own initiative (Article 55 § 1 c.p.p.) they must subsequently submit such information to the prosecutor.

127 The general regulation regarding secrecy of proceedings (*segreto istruttorio*) is provided in Article 329 c.p.p.
128 Article 335 § 3bis c.p.p.
129 Article 335 § 3ter c.p.p.
130 See the case law quoted in Caianiello (2016), p. 12.
131 Cf. Section 8.5.
132 Ruggieri and Marcolini (2013), p. 369.
133 Article 326 c.p.p.

As Fabri argues, the major objectives that led to establishing in the c.p.p. the rule obliging the police to immediately pass information to the prosecutor was to curb police discretion. [134] It was also done to early involve the prosecutor in the process with an aim to improve the administration of justice.[135] Initially the relevant rule of Code 1988 provided for the fixed time of such report and the police had only 48 hours from their obtaining such information to do so. This provision backfired, as, first, it caused a backlog of cases for the prosecutors; second, and more importantly, it led the police to think that it was unnecessary to conduct investigative actions or assemble evidence prior to receiving the prosecutor's instructions (which in turn led to loss of important pieces of information that should have been collected and secured immediately following a crime).[136] This has ended in replacing the fixed 48-hour term with the vague notion of "without undue delay."

The truth is, however, that despite the strict rule forcing all notifications of a crime to be quickly transferred to the prosecutor, the judicial police can carry out, on their own initiative, investigatory actions in order to ensure the successful collection of evidence also before the transfer of the information takes place.[137] The police in particular are urged to take the steps necessary to collect evidence that may be useful for the enforcement of the criminal law (Article 348 § 1 c.p.p.). This gives a certain level of uncontrolled independence to the police in their actions, at least during this very early, though crucial stage of criminal process.[138] Therefore, in practice, in some cases the police may undertake the investigatory actions even before the prosecutor becomes aware of the existence of any *notitia criminis*.

4.5 Initiating Investigation in the United States of America

4.5.1 Threshold for Initiating Investigation

The discussion on the initiation of investigation in the USA must start with a preliminary determination on what, in the US criminal justice framework, commencing investigation actually means and at which point in time this occurs. As discussed in Section 3.5.1, the investigation in the US criminal justice system has a noticeably different character than its Continental counterpart, being less official. Lacking formality as a whole, it also does not have a defining moment. In contrast to what our discussion on initiating

134 Fabri (2008), p. 9.
135 Fabri (2008), p. 9.
136 Fabri (2008), p. 9.
137 Di Amato (2013), p. 163.
138 Caianiello (2012), p. 258.

investigation in the Continental states has shown, US law does not see any need to regulate its commencement, nor its ending. However, this does not mean that the commencing moment of a US criminal investigation cannot be pinned down. And perhaps it should be assumed that the commencement of investigation is defined by another name.

The search for the starting point of criminal investigation in literature quickly leads to the arrest.[139] One of the most famous US Supreme Court cases *Terry* v. *Ohio* identifies the arrest as the initial stage of the criminal process.[140] It seems an obvious assumption that US criminal procedure starts with the arrest. All course books begin the discussion regarding criminal procedure with arrest as a first reaction to the possible commitment of a crime. This is certainly true for felonies, but also for many misdemeanors, since arrest seems as the first choice for many police officers even if the case is of minor importance.[141]

However, even though arrests commence many criminal investigations in the USA, obviously not all of them begin with it. Investigating before the decision to detain a suspect is taken or even before the suspect is known is routine practice for US criminal justice agents when they conduct prearrest investigations. The pre-arrest investigations may be conducted in a form of reactive investigations, aimed at solving a past crime or proactive investigations aimed at placing the police in a position to respond to an unknown but anticipated ongoing or future crime.[142] This happens after the crime has been reported to police officers, which would demand some investigative actions, e.g. to identify the suspect or to gather evidence to support the application for a warrant or summons. In such cases the commencement of an investigation will take place prior to arrest being made. Second, some cases require investigations that may lead to a judge issuing either an arrest warrant or a summons in lieu of an arrest warrant, which is an order to a suspect requesting his appearance in court on a certain date to answer charges. Finally, even in situations in which the grounds for arresting a suspect at once occur, the police officer may simply issue citations, that serve a similar purpose to a summons. As a result, the initiation of some investigations will not be linked to the arrest of the suspect. In this case, the decision to initiate an investigation will be more undefined. Therefore, identifying the threshold that must be reached to commence an investigation in these cases is even more difficult.

139 Harmon (2016), p. 335 ("arrests remain the default mechanism for starting the criminal process").
140 392 US 1, 26 (1968).
141 See data gathered by Harmon (2016), p. 353 fn. 231.
142 Kamisar et al. (2015), p. 5.

Generally, the US system is perceived as rigidly defining standards of proof necessary to undertake certain decisions, such as proof of beyond reasonable doubt for conviction or reasonable suspicion in case of conducting stop and frisk. Surprisingly, the law seems silent on what kind of standard of proof is necessary to commence investigation. The absence of a need to clearly distinguish the moment when and how the investigation commences consequently prevents there being a threshold to trigger an investigation. But, certainly, some level of suspicion must be reached to commence investigation even informally. The action of criminal justice authorities must start with information that a crime has taken place, whether received from external source or obtained internally by the police. This information must be considered as reliable, at least to some extent, to begin investigative actions.

The threshold necessary to commence investigation is easiest to determine when arrest is assumed as a mechanism for initiating criminal investigation. Under the Fourth Amendment doctrine, a "police officer may arrest a person if he has probable cause to believe that person committed a crime."[143] Efforts to define this concept seem, however, to be doomed to failure in advance, even though the US Supreme Court is constantly attempting to do so.[144] In one of its judgments it was found that probable cause exists where the facts and circumstances within the officer's knowledge and of which they had reasonably trustworthy information are sufficient in themselves to warrant a man of reasonable caution in the belief that an offense has been or is being committed.[145] The right to arrest on probable cause has been recognized in a long line of cases, including when minor crimes are committed.[146] This threshold justifies all arrests regardless whether conducted with or without a warrant.[147]

The link between the initiation of investigation and arresting a suspect makes it possible to recognize that probable cause is required for the commencement of investigation, since it is necessary to arrest an individual. However, in cases in which arrest does not take place, it should be considered whether the same threshold is also necessary for a decision to initiate proceedings. Not surprisingly, the written law is silent on that issue.

But some conclusions can be drawn, for example from the Standards on Prosecutorial Investigations which provide some guidance on the matter

143 *Tennessee* v. *Garner*, 471 US 1, 7 (1985).

144 See more on interpretation of probable cause in Colb (2010), pp. 69–105.

145 *Brinegar* v. *United States*, 338 US 160, 175–176 (1949) partially citing *Carrol* v. *United States*, 267 US 132, 162 (1925).

146 *Virginia* v. *Moore*, 553 US 164, 171 (2008).

147 Kamisar et al. (2015), p. 9 ("to obtain a warrant, the police must establish, to the satisfaction of the magistrate, that there exists probable cause to believe that the prospective arrestee committed the crime for which he will be arrested").

although it should be remembered that the Standards are not legal rules or court opinions. According to Standard 26-2.1(a)(ii) SPI, "a particularized suspicion or predicate is not required prior to initiating a criminal investigation." This means that taking a decision to open an investigation does not require any specific degree of probability that a crime occurred, and certainly not a probable cause as in the case of an arrest. The Standards, nevertheless, provide some guidance as to what factors should be taken under consideration when taking a decision to investigate, placing the public interest as important,[148] and including such additional considerations as sufficiency of evidence, costs and benefits of investigations, and collateral effects of investigation on witnesses.[149]

It should be also mentioned that the US system, which by definition rejects the principle of legality and adheres to discretion, does not insist that if a threshold is satisfied, whatever it may be, the authority is under an obligation to initiate investigation. Both the police, when arresting a suspect and the prosecutor, when deciding to initiate an investigation, may make decisions as they consider appropriate. As follows from the Standards on Prosecutorial Investigations, the prosecutor should have wide discretion to select matters for investigation, having no absolute duty to investigate any particular matter, unless required by statute or policy.[150] As explained, the prosecutor has almost unlimited discretion in deciding what and whom to investigate, with what allocation of resources, and for how long.[151]

Since US law does not provide for an obligation to initiate proceedings, it follows that there's no related time frame for making such a decision. Therefore, there is no regulation on how much time can elapse between when the complainant reported on the possible commitment of a crime (or noticed by police) and the initiation of proceedings. The decision to do so remains, again, at the discretion of the prosecutor or the police.

4.5.2 Procedure for Initiating Investigation

The informality of the investigative stage in the US criminal justice system determines the lack of formal requirements for initiation of investigation.

148 Standard 26-2.1(b) SPI. The rule determines that among factors adding to lack of public interest in initiating investigation are a lack of police interest, a lack of public or political support, a lack of identifiable victims, fear or reluctance by potential or actual witnesses and unusual complex factual or legal issues or unusual complex actual or legal issues.

149 Standard 26-2.1(c) SPI

150 Standard 26-2.1(a)(i) SPI.

151 ABA Standards for Prosecutorial Investigations, Commentary to Subdivision 26-2.1(a)(i), p. 87.

Given the lack of regulations concerning both the prerequisite for initiating proceedings, the time of making such a decision and there being no formally prescribed indication of who makes such a decision, it is hard to expect that there will be many formal steps to follow. There are some relevant regulations on this matter, but these are informal.[152]

The regular procedure regarding initiation of investigation as summed up in 1962 by Barrett remains true today: a police officer decides whether to make an arrest under given circumstances, and in such a way commences an investigation.[153] What remains troublesome is the fact that if the police decide not to make an arrest, the decision is neither visible, nor in the main, reviewable.[154] And obviously how this decision is made remains an amalgam of many factors, including "his own personality and prejudices, his knowledge of police department policy, his knowledge of the type of cases in which the prosecuting officer will issue a complaint, his knowledge of judicial decisions as bear on the situation."[155]

The absence of a formal decision to initiate investigation has other consequences. First, there is no formal requirement to notify the informant that investigation has been commenced. There are no statutory regulations on this and neither the person that reported the crime, or the victim, has a legally established right to receive such information. In accordance with internal regulations, the victim might be nevertheless informed as to the outcome of the complaint. But certainly, there is no legal obligation on the authority to do so.

Accordingly, this also means that if the investigation has not been initiated there is no formal review of such a decision. The victim lacks formal instruments allowing for assessment of such decision by the judge. This means that both the person notifying about the commission of an offense as well as the victim have no legal right to influence the decision taken by the authority, regarding the initiation of investigation. Among the rights prescribed on the federal level in the US Code the law does not provide the victim with such powers.[156] Nor does such exist at the state level.[157] Only at some later time in the course of criminal proceedings, especially when the case gets to the attention of the judge, including when the arrest takes place,

152 An example might be the detailed regulation of rules 6.5–6.7 DIOG addressed to FBI agents. These provisions cover such matters as e.g. standards for opening or approving investigations and documentation record it.

153 Barrett (1962), p. 26.

154 Goldstein (1960), p. 543.

155 Barrett (1962), p. 26.

156 See what rights the victim is provided with in 18 USC § 3771. See also Gilliéron (2014), p. 20.

157 See s. 51-286e CGS.

is the victim entitled to receive such information.[158] It should be noted however that the ability of police officers to exercise the discretion resulting in noninitiation of criminal investigation has been identified and discussed a long time ago and perceived as both too broad and unfair.[159] Lack of proper control mechanisms over such police decisions makes a strong impact on the system by narrowing the scope of discretion of prosecutors as well as judges. . Not providing neither the prosecutor nor the judge, at least upon the victim's request, with ability to review the initial police decisions therefore raises justified concerns.

This does not mean that there is no possibility of influencing whether an investigation is to be commenced. The victim may always use other forms of pressure to demand that a case be initiated. This may be done by meeting with the prosecutor to request her to influence police decisions, or informing the media about the lack of police action. But the soft forms of persuasion cannot be compared with the right to proper legal verification of the decision not to initiate investigation.

4.5.3 Authority Responsible for Initiating Investigation

It is a widely recognized rule that in the USA, being a common-law system, investigations are ordinarily carried out by the police or by other law enforcement authorities autonomously, while the prosecutor steps in only at the end of the investigation to decide on bringing the charging decision.[160] Indeed, the role of the police is perceived as being to investigate and the prosecutor's as being to prosecute.[161] As a result, it should also be assumed that the competence to initiate proceedings remains in the hands of the police and other law enforcement authorities. This is particularly true for the prearrest investigations undertaken entirely by the police without any prosecutorial input.[162]

But certainly not all investigations are commenced without the prosecutorial engagement. Even the prearrest investigations are not always entirely

158 Among the notification rights that the victims possess, if he or she requested such notification and provided the state's attorney with a current address, are judicial proceedings relating to the victim's case including, e.g. the arrest of the defendant, the arraignment of the defendant, the release of the defendant pending judicial proceedings, and proceedings in the prosecution of the defendant, including the dismissal of the charges against the defendant, the entry of a *nolle prosequi* to the charges against the defendant, the entry of a plea of guilty by the defendant, and the trial and sentencing of the defendant (s. 51-286e CGS). See also on the federal level, Rule 60(a)(1) FRCP.

159 Goldstein (1960).

160 Ligeti (2019), p. 145.

161 Richman (2003), p. 751; Burnham (2011), p. 270.

162 Kamisar et al. (2015), p. 5.

conducted solely by the police.[163] Actually, the power of the prosecutor to initiate investigations is recognized straightforwardly. For one, NDAA *National Prosecution Standards* provide that the prosecutor should have a discretionary authority with regard to initiation of investigation, depending upon many factors, including, but not limited to, available resources, adequacy of law enforcement agencies' investigation in a matter, office priorities, and potential civil liability.[164] It is subsequently explained that this authority must be used where the law enforcement agency that would normally conduct the investigation has a conflict of interest; where the investigation has been handled improperly and is in need of reinvestigation; where the investigation calls for expertise that is available in the prosecutor's office; and where the law enforcement agencies do not have sufficient resources to conduct the investigation.[165]

Similarly, at the federal level, one of the provisions of the Justice Manual explicitly provides for the competence of instituting investigation at the direction of a federal prosecutor. The relevant rule provides that the US Attorney is authorized to request the appropriate federal investigative agency to investigate alleged or suspected violations of federal law.[166] It follows that the federal prosecutor herself does not initiate an investigation, but may request the relevant federal investigator, such as an FBI agent, to do so. The question remains as to what formal authority the prosecutor has in this respect and whether his or her requests are binding. Answering this, the rules confirm that federal investigators are not ordinarily subject to direct supervision by the US Attorneys. But if the US Attorney requests an investigation and does not receive a timely preliminary report, he may wish to consider requesting the assistance of the Criminal Division, i.e. to discipline the reluctant agent.[167] It is furthermore provided that in certain matters the US Attorney may wish to request the formation of a team of agents representing the agencies having investigative jurisdiction of the suspected violations. This provides for a considerably broad competencies of federal prosecutors to commence investigations on their own.

It is true that the above presented provisions are not of a binding character and function more like a guiding authority. However, as was previously discussed,[168] the recognition that guidelines enjoy makes them a good point of reference and assures that they are respected and followed. In fact, in the light of the established prosecutorial neutrality and objectivity[169] the inability

163 Kamisar et al. (2015), p. 5.
164 Standard 3-1.1 NPS
165 Commentary to Standard 3-1.1, NDAA, *National Prosecution Standards*, 3rd ed. 2009, p. 45.
166 9-2.010 JM.
167 9-2.010 JM.
168 See Section 2.5.1.
169 See Section 3.5.3.

to commence investigation by the prosecutor would infringe a responsibility granted to the prosecutor to seek justice as an independent administrator of justice. Limiting prosecutorial powers for cases selected by the police would undermine the position that the prosecution service is deemed to hold in the USA.

4.6 Summary

The initiation of investigation as the first step in the criminal process is a decision of a significant character. Regardless of whether there are any formal requirements relative to such decisions, it always opens the door to further actions in the course of criminal proceedings. Therefore, actions leading to initiation of investigation should be treated with a due attention since may result in depriving the victim of her right to trial.

The three Continental countries provide for a similar theoretical framework for initiating investigation. The rules call for either an immediate or at least a very quick reaction from the authority competent to commence investigation on being notified of an alleged offense having taken place. The more (Poland) or less formal (Germany, Italy) decision, should be always undertaken when a certain threshold has been met. This complies with the principle of legality. But, as practice shows, since the rigid application of legality is impossible, some cases, slip through the cracks in the system either by not being registered or by being declined investigations. In this regard, the US system provides the more honest approach giving criminal justice authorities the power to decide on the issue under a discretionary regime. It seems to go along with informality of the US criminal investigation.

The case studies provide for different regulations relating to the decision refusing to initiate investigation and availability of its review. While the USA does not provide the victim with a legal remedy toward such a decision, in Italy the rule demanding registration of all crimes suggests that when the prosecutor subsequently discontinues a case, a remedy will nevertheless be available. Poland and Germany provide for full judicial review at the victim's request.

Similarly, the countries differ in the authority competent to take decision on initiation of investigation. The distinction is made on the line of division between adversarial vs inquisitorial systems. The USA gives preference to the police to initiate investigation. This is based on the presumption that this is the police who are bound to investigate, while the prosecutor is generally oriented towards prosecuting. But as the analysis have shown the prosecutor is not precluded from triggering the investigation herself. It is for the most part an unregulated sphere, but in cases of severe crimes the prosecutor engages very early in the investigation. This is, however, hard to monitor since the commencement of investigation in the USA does not take any formal arrangement.

By contrast, all three Continental countries provide for the prosecutor to be the primary authority to commence investigations and take control over every single investigation. Yet, these systems in practice fail to achieve the promised standard, and are much closer to the US system than they would like to admit. However, this is not a novel observation. More than 40 years ago Goldstein and Marcus concluded that in systems working under the principle of legality "it is inevitable that the police will exercise broad discretion in deciding which cases to begin and may deprive the prosecutor . . . to monitor their decisions."[170] As discussed in the German case, in practice the prosecutor does not receive files immediately at least in minor cases. This is happening despite the existence of rigid code provisions that mandates police to submit all cases to prosecutor immediately. The Italian example is even more striking. The original provision forcing police to submit all notifications of crime to the prosecutor within 48 hours of their reception resulted in an overwhelming backlog of cases and proved that the control of the prosecutor over initiation of all investigations is utopian. Currently the Italian judicial police customarily takes its time to undertake investigative measures making prosecutor's decision to initiate investigation mere formality. The Polish case seems no different. Prosecutors are able to comply with obligation to initiate investigations but only because of the low number of serious cases conducted in the form of inspection. When they are given the choice of commencing inquiries in cases of less severe crimes, they pass this competence to the police. This shows a tendency to provide the police with freedom to informally initiate investigations without any involvement of the prosecutor.

Despite the normative regulations that aspire to the unachievable standard of prosecutors initiating investigation in all cases and maintaining control over them from the very beginning in all four states the power to initiate investigation in the majority of cases remains in the hands of authorities other than the prosecutor. There is, however, a noticeable distinction between cases concerning severity of crime. Although only in the case of Poland is this distinction pronounced clearly, which has been regulated normatively. In the other three case studies, there is a tendency to reserve for the prosecutor a greater role in initiating investigation when the case concerns serious crimes.

170 Goldstein and Marcus (1977), p. 281.

References

Barrett Jr EL (1962) Police Practices and the Law-From Arrest to Release or Charge. *California Law Review* 50:11–55.

Bohlander M (2012), *Principles of German Criminal Procedure.* Hart Publishing, London.

Brodzisz (2018) Komentarz do art. 303 k.p.k. In: Jerzy Skorupka (ed) *Kodeks postępowania karnego. Komentarz.* CH Beck, Warsaw.

Burnham W (2011) *Introduction to the Law and Legal System of the United States.* 5th edn. West, St Paul.

Caianiello M (2012) The Italian Public Prosecutor: An Inquisitorial Figure in Adversarial Proceedings. In: Luna E, Wade M (eds) *The Prosecutor in Transnational Perspective.* Oxford University Press, Oxford, pp. 250–267.

Caianiello M (2016) *Increasing Discretionary Prosecutor's Powers: The Pivotal Role of the Italian Prosecutor in the Pretrial Investigation Phase.* Oxford Handbooks Online, Oxford.

Colb SF (2010) Probabilities in Probable Cause and Beyond: Statistical Versus Concrete Harms. *Law and Contemporary Problems* 73:69–105.

Cora S (2016) Wszczęcie postępowania przygotowawczego. In: Ryszard Stefański (ed) *System Prawa Karnego Procesowego. Postępowanie przygotowawcze. Volume X.* Wolters Kluwer, Warsaw, pp. 579–662.

Di Amato A (2013) Criminal Law in Italy. Kluwer Law International, Alphen aan den Rijn.

Di Federico G (2008) Report on the Public Prosecution Service in Italy. In: Open Society Institute Sofia (ed) *Promoting Prosecutorial Accountability, Independence and Effectiveness.* Open Society Institute Sofia, Sofia, pp. 301–339.

Elsner B, Peters J (2010) The Prosecution Service Function within the German Criminal Justice System. In: Jehle J-M, Wade M (eds) *Coping with Overloaded Criminal Justice Systems. The Rise of Prosecutorial Power Across Europe.* Springer, Heidelberg, pp. 207–236.

Fabri M (2008) Criminal Procedure and Public Prosecution Reform in Italy: A Flash Back. *International Journal for Court Administration.* January:3–15.

Frase RS, Weigend T (1995) German Criminal Justice as a Guide to American Law Reform. *Boston College International and Comparative Law Review* 18:317–360.

Gialuz M (2017) The Italian Code of Criminal Procedure: A Reading Guide. In: Gialuz M, Lupária L, Scarpa F (eds) *The Italian Code of Criminal Procedure. Critical Essays and English Translation.* Cedam, Milan, pp. 17–55.

Gilliéron G (2014) *Public Prosecutors in the United States and Europe.* Springer, Cham.

Girdwoyń P (2006) *Zarys niemieckiego procesu karnego.* Temida2, Białystok.

Goldstein AS, Marcus M (1977) The Myth of Judicial Supervision in Three "Inquisitorial" Systems: France, Italy, and Germany. *Yale Law Journal* 81: 240–283.

Goldstein J (1960) Police Discretion Not to Invoke the Criminal Process: Low-Visibility Decisions in the Administration of Justice. *Yale Law Journal* 69:543–594.

Grzegorczyk T (2004) *Kodeks postępowania karnego. Komentarze Zakamycza.* Kantor Wydawniczy Zakamycze, Kraków.

Harmon RA (2016) Why Arrest? *Michigan Law Review* 115:307–364.

Huber B (2008) Germany. In: Vogler R, Huber B, *Criminal Procedure in Europe.* Duncker & Humblot, Berlin, pp. 269–371.

Jasiński W, Kremens K (2019) *Criminal Law in Poland.* Kluwer Law International, Alphen aan den Rijn.

Jörg-Albrecht H (2000) Criminal Prosecution: Developments, Trends and Open Questions in the Federal Republic of Germany. *European Journal of Crime, Criminal Law and Criminal Justice* 8(3):245–256.

Kamisar Y, LaFave WR, Israel JH, King NJ, Kerr OS, Primus EB (2015) *Modern Criminal Procedure. Cases-Comments-Questions.* West, St Paul.

Ligeti K (2019) The Place of the Prosecutor in Common Law and Civil Law Jurisdictions. In: Brown DK, Turner JI, Weisser B (eds) *The Oxford Handbook of Criminal Process.* Oxford University Press, Oxford, pp. 139–163.

Meyer-Goßner L, Schmitt B (2014) *Strafprozessordnung.* CH Beck, München.

Nowak C, Steinborn S (2013) Poland. In: Ligeti K (ed) *Toward a Prosecutor of the European Union, Volume 1: A Comparative Analysis.* Hart Publishing, London, pp. 498–509.

Panzavolta M (2004) Reforms and Counter-Reforms in the Italian Struggle for an Accusatorial Criminal Law System. *North Carolina Journal of International Law & Commercial Regulation* 30:577–624.

Richman DC (2003) Prosecutors and Their Agents. Agents and Their Prosecutors. *Columbia Law Review* 103:749–832.

Ruggeri S (2015) Investigative and Prosecutorial Discretion in Criminal Matters: The Contribution of the Italian Experience. In: Caianiello M, Hodgson JS (eds) *Discretionary Criminal Justice in a Comparative Context.* Carolina Academic Press, Durham, pp. 59–85.

Ruggieri F, Marcolini S (2013) Italy. In: Ligeti K (ed) *Toward a Prosecutor of the European Union, Volume 1: A Comparative Analysis.* Hart Publishing, London, pp. 368–404.

Stachowiak S (2006) Odmowa wszczęcia śledztwa lub dochodzenia. *Prokuratura i Prawo* 7–8:24–32.

Trendafilova E, Róth W (2008) Report on the Public Prosecution Service in Germany. In: Open Society Institute Sofia (ed) *Promoting Prosecutorial Accountability, Independence and Effectiveness.* Open Society Institute Sofia, Sofia, pp. 213–246.

Volk K (2010) *Grundkurs StPO.* CH Beck, München.

Weigend T (2013) Germany. In: Ligeti K (ed) *Toward a Prosecutor of the European Union, Volume 1: A Comparative Analysis.* Hart Publishing, London, pp. 264–306.

Weigend T (2004) The Prosecution Service in the German Administration of Criminal Justice. In: Tak PJP (ed) *Tasks and Powers of the Prosecution Services in the EU Member States.* Volume I. Wolf Legal Publishers, Nijmegen, pp. 203–222.

Wiśniewski Ł (2014) Niemiecki proces karny. Postępowanie przygotowawcze. In: Piotr Kruszyński (ed) *System Prawa Karnego Procesowego. Proces karny. Rozwiązania modelowe w ujęciu prawnoporównawczym.* Volume II. Lexis Nexis, Warsaw, pp. 365–419.

Zagrodnik J (2020) Postępowanie przygotowawcze. In: Jarosław Zagrodnik (ed) *Proces karny.* Wolters Kluwer, Warsaw.

Chapter 5

Powers of the Prosecutor over the Conduct of Investigation

5.1 General Considerations

The commencement of the criminal investigation and the involvement of the prosecutor in it has been discussed in the previous chapter. This one takes a further step on the dynamic line in the course of criminal investigation and aims at discussing the conduct and measures undertaken during this stage of the criminal process. It focuses mainly on the scope of powers shared by the prosecutor and other criminal justice authorities; in particular the police considered as the primary authority conducting criminal investigation in all countries.

For this purpose, it is necessary to begin with establishing the pure nature of the relationship between the prosecutor and the police in each analyzed country. The level of organizational and functional dependence of the police on the prosecution determines the degree to which a police officer will be obliged to follow prosecutorial orders regarding the conduct of investigation and measures to be undertaken. To achieve that it is necessary to include an analysis of the binding force of prosecutorial orders directed at the criminal justice authorities and the ability to effectively control their execution by the prosecutors.

Thereafter, the analysis will be substantially devoted to establishing the influence that the prosecutor has on the conduct of criminal investigation and investigative measures undertaken during that stage of criminal process. There are two levels of prosecutorial impact to be considered regarding this phase. First, the scope of the supervisory powers of the prosecutor over the police or any other agency entitled by law to conduct criminal investigation must be determined. Obviously, some of the measures and activities that are conducted during criminal investigation can be undertaken by the police regardless of whether or not they were ordered by the prosecutor. But it is important to determine how deeply the prosecutor should get acquainted with the course of criminal investigation when exercising her supervisory role and how much freedom both in theory and in practice is given to criminal justice agencies when undertaking decisions as to what measures should be employed.

The second level of analysis involves the exclusive powers of the prosecutor during the course of criminal investigation. Even though many investigative steps can be carried out equally by the public prosecutor or the police, this is not necessarily the case in all investigative measures.[1] Identifying the prosecutor's exclusive measures is essential to complete the picture of prosecutorial engagement at this stage of criminal proceedings.

This will be carried out with a focus on one aim. Both issues—the supervisory prosecutorial powers and the exclusive competencies of the prosecutor—have an impact on how objective the prosecutor can remain when the ultimate decision that she must eventually make will be undertaken i.e. whether or not to prosecute a case. Even when it has been established that the conduct of the investigation in all countries should be carried on against and in favor of the suspect according to the principle of objectivity,[2] the level of engagement of the prosecutor in criminal investigation may have an adverse impact on the neutrality of such decision. It can be preliminarily assumed that the more engaged the prosecutor becomes both in terms of personal activity (e.g. questioning the suspect, ordering searches, and participating in their conduct, taking a part in crime scene investigations) and as supervisor (ordering the conducting of certain investigative actions), prejudice toward the case is built up. And usually it is not that kind of bias that favors the suspect.

Moreover, the scope of criminal investigation and how much can be done during it, is heavily influenced by its expected length. Some of the researched countries have adopted interesting perspectives on how the time frame of criminal investigation should be measured and limited, including a peculiar Italian concept of the expiration of the prescribed time for criminal investigation. This provides a full perspective on the shape of criminal investigation and the powers that the prosecutor exercises over it.

At the same time, one should not forget that the powers of the prosecutor during the conduct of criminal investigation are limited in several aspects. It is strongly shaped through the position that other participants in criminal investigation, always the suspect but in some countries also the victim, are assigned at this stage of the criminal process. The amount of rights that they are granted, including a right to conduct independent private investigations as allowed in some countries, influences not only how much the prosecutor and police can and will do during investigation but also changes the position of the prosecutor from the "master of criminal investigation" to being simply a party to it.

1 Cf. Mathias (2002), p. 466.
2 Cf. Chapter 2.

Finally, the judicial involvement in conducting criminal investigation is discussed in this chapter. It is true that the court (judge) plays an important role at this stage of the criminal process, being engaged in different ways whether it is connected with interference with the rights and freedoms of the individual, or whether it adds to preserving evidentiary measures that are unique or unrepeatable. The impact that the judge (court) has on the imposition of measures infringing rights and freedoms of individual (coercive measures) is a subject of Chapter 7. This has been done with the aim of underlying the importance of these measures in the course of criminal investigation. Also, the complexity of these measures in the sphere of authority competent to employ them in practice demanded a separate discussion. Thus, this chapter focuses on less intrusive measures that can be undertaken with judicial involvement ex officio or at the request of the prosecutor, the suspect, the victim.

Another omission in this chapter is the issue of preliminary charging of the suspect. One may expect that this topic will be discussed here, since it is normally considered to be inherently connected with the conduct of criminal investigation. The initial charges are in all countries aimed at informing the suspect about the crimes that she eventually will be accused of and enabling the suspect to start preparing for her defense even during criminal investigation. This is particularly crucial in terms of the effective exercise of the right to defend oneself, especially in cases in which the decisions concerning pretrial detention are undertaken during criminal investigation. The questions regarding the responsibility for selecting these charges, their sustainability in the official charging document, the conduct and nature of this procedure as well as those people involved in will be discussed in Chapter 6. This is so because the prosecutorial control over preliminary charging is so complex that it requires separate analysis.

Additionally, it should be noted that some general considerations regarding the shape of the criminal investigation relevant for this chapter have been already discussed in Chapter 2 while comparing investigations in the four countries. This relates to aims of criminal investigation that specifically influence the scope of the measures to be undertaken. It is also a case of distinction between different forms in which criminal investigation is conducted, whether formal or not, that impacts the nature of proceedings, and the involvement of the prosecutor. The reader is therefore advised to read Chapter 2 before engaging in this chapter.

5.2 Conduct of Investigation in Germany

5.2.1 The Relationship between Prosecutor and Police

The shape of the relationship between the prosecution service and police in Germany is influenced by the federalist character of that country. Moreover, the prosecution service in Germany has no police of its own.

Therefore, assistance in conducting criminal investigation must be served by an external entity. On the federal level the Federal Criminal Police Office (*Bundeskriminalamt*), a national investigative police agency functioning under the supervision of the Federal Ministry of Internal Affairs performs certain investigative actions. But most police actions are done by the separate state police agencies within 16 German lands (*Länder*).[3] This is so, since on the constitutional level it has been decided that the organization of security and police forces is entrusted to the *Länder*[4] reserving, at the same time, some competencies regarding security to the federal government.[5]

As a result, within each *Länder* the police are organized independently, which may lead to differences within the structure of police offices and the organization of their work. The police are organizationally accountable to the Ministry of Internal Affairs of each *Länder* but at the same time functionally subordinated to the prosecution service when it comes to investigating crimes.[6] This creates institutional limits on the relationship between police and prosecution since the latter is answerable to the Ministry of Justice.

Within the police system in Germany there are no special police units devoted only to investigating crimes. Instead, the police in each *Länder* have two categories of police officers possessing distinct powers: officials who can act on behalf of the prosecutor and assist her; a second group who are restricted to carrying on those measures that are necessary at the crime scene.[7] The officers from the former group, which are a visible majority, are called "investigative officers" or more traditionally "auxiliary prosecutors" (*Ermittlungspersonen*).[8] This position is usually held by all police officers except those of the lowest and highest ranks.[9] The decision regarding which of the police officers should be entitled to this position and what criteria should be met to reach it belongs entirely to the legislative organs of each *Länder*. The federal law provides only that each *Ermittlungspersonen* must have attained the age of 21 and must have minimum of two years' work experience in the relevant position.[10] The scope of the competencies available to these officials is determined by § 152 (1) CCO which provides that they

3 Gilliéron (2014), p. 266.
4 Article 30 of German Constitution.
5 Article 87 of German Constitution.
6 Elsner and Peters (2010), p. 227.
7 Frase and Weigend (1995), p. 323.
8 Juy-Birmann (2002), p. 300 (in the past this group of officials was called *Hilfsbeamten der Staatsanwatschaft*—translated as "auxiliary prosecutors" or "assistant prosecutors." The new term *Ermittlungspersonen der Staatsanwatschaft* may be translated as "investigators of the prosecution" but the traditional term is still widely used).
9 Weigend, (2004), p. 209.
10 § 152 (2) CCO.

are obliged to follow the orders of prosecutors having jurisdiction in their district and comply with orders of their own superiors. But they also have considerable freedom in undertaking decisions on behalf of the prosecutor. In practice, however, the distinction between those who hold the position of *Ermittlungspersonen* or not is of an extremely low significance since almost all police officers carry that position.

Some concerns are raised by the issue of the subordination of the police officers not only to the prosecutor but also to their own superiors within the police offices. On one hand, they must execute orders received from the prosecutor concerning the conduct of investigation,[11] but, on the other, as members of the regular police forces, they are responsible for keeping order and preventing crime.[12] Therefore, in their daily work they are expected to engage in both spheres, which might be sometimes contradictory and even impossible to be carried out jointly. This problem was identified long ago and, as a result, in 1977 all German Ministries of Justice and Ministries of Internal Affairs decided to adopt the guidelines, under which the police function (crime prevention), in conflicting situations, must prevail over prosecutorial needs.[13] This visibly weakens the relationship between the prosecutor and the police since the police officers are allowed to prioritize responsibilities other than those that come from their duties during criminal investigation. In particular, this affects compliance with prosecutorial orders.

5.2.2 The Prosecutor's Supervisory Authority over Investigation

As previously discussed,[14] the criminal investigation in Germany serves two equally important purposes, i.e. establishing whether bringing public charges leads to conviction[15] and collecting evidence for future use during the trial.[16] This determines the scope of investigative measures to be undertaken both by the prosecutor and the police during criminal investigation as well as influencing the formality of the recording of these measures for later use.

The core provision regulating investigation is the so-called general investigation clause (*Ermittlungsgeneralclausel*) that remains a statutory basis for the prosecutorial authority to conduct investigation.[17] Accordingly, in achieving the objectives set by § 160 (1) and (3) StPO, the prosecution is entitled to

11 § 161 (1) StPO.
12 Frase and Weigend (1995), p. 323, fn. 31.
13 See details in Weigend (2004), p. 210.
14 See Section 3.2.1.
15 § 160 (1) StPO.
16 § 160 (3) StPO.
17 Siegismund (2003), p. 61.

request information from all authorities and to conduct investigations of any kind either itself or through the police, unless there are statutory provisions specifically regulating their powers.[18] This sets the strong position of the prosecutor over criminal investigation very clearly. It gets even stronger if one remembers that the police are obliged to immediately provide the prosecutor with the case file of each commenced investigation.[19] The prosecutor is regarded as having such extensive investigative and supervisory powers that some have called the prosecutor the *Herr des Ermittlungsverfahren*—"master of the investigation"[20] or the "ruler of the investigative stage."[21]

The prosecutor maintains control over the conduct of criminal investigations by giving orders to the police. As a rule, the police are legally obliged to comply with the requests and orders of the prosecutors.[22] Moreover, whenever the police execute prosecutorial orders, they are equally entitled to demand information from all authorities as if it were the prosecutor that was doing it. This suggests that the procedural competencies of German police are derived from the prosecutorial powers. Because of this the police are sometimes described as the "extended arm of the prosecution" (*verlängerter Arm der Staatsanwaltschaft*)[23] which is strengthened by the fact that police cannot decide on the outcome of any criminal investigation independently.

One should remember, however, that the duality of the system of supervision over police activity shared between the prosecution service and the Ministry of Internal Affairs creates a situation that raises important concerns. Even though the police are obliged to fulfill the tasks ordered by the prosecutor, subsequently, in cases of noncompliance, the prosecutor does not have any effective tool enabling their enforcement. The disciplinary measures are not available to prosecutors and only the Ministry of Internal Affairs may resort to them in cases of personal wrongdoing by a police officer.[24].

From the above analysis it follows that the police act only when ordered to do so by the prosecutor and their powers are derived from the prosecutorial competencies. However, the practice seems much more complex. Therefore, the question remains: how much independence do the German police have in the day-to-day conduct of criminal investigation?

First, the police, as the primary authority to respond to crime, have an enormous power to shape the future of the criminal investigation by pointing

18 § 161 (1) StPO.
19 § 163 (2) StPO. See Section 4.2.3.
20 Trendafilova and Róth (2008), p. 225.
21 Elsner and Peters (2010), p. 227.
22 § 161 (1) StPO.
23 Trendafilova and Róth (2008), p. 240.
24 Weigend (2004), p. 210.

it in a certain direction. Preference for some types of crimes and disregard for some others, allows them to shape the system. Moreover, because of their dual role as a crime prevention and a reactive agency they possess power to note the criminal behavior, verify it even informally, and to leave some acts in a gray area of unrecorded crime.[25] This is enhanced by the development of proactive investigative techniques which, as reported, eventually leads to "hidden discretion" on the police side.[26]

Second, at least during the very first phase of criminal investigation the police have powers other than those derived from the prosecutorial competencies. According to § 163 (1) StPO, the agencies and agents of the police service have to investigate criminal offenses and to give all those orders which do not bear delay, and which are necessary to prevent the obfuscation of the matter. The provision follows, that for this purpose, the police are authorized to request all public agencies to provide information and, if there is danger in delay, to demand such information. They are further authorized to undertake investigation of all kinds to the extent that other legal provisions do not specifically regulate their authority. It is uncertain what was the original aim of the drafters of this provision. Was it intended to give the police the freedom to act independently only at the very early stage of criminal investigation freedom or, to the contrary to, give them opportunity to conduct the full investigation independently ?[27]

Despite the intentions of its drafters and the current normative construct of § 163 (1) StPO, the police assume, in practice, an independent role in carrying on investigation and undertaking all measures, without resorting to the prosecutor, until a final decision is to be made.[28] If no special measures aiming at interference with the rights of individual are seen to be necessary, such as search, seizure, arrest the prosecutor might not even be informed about an investigation.[29] Note that this is done in contravention of the legal duty of police to submit the file to the prosecutor without delay.[30]

Additionally, even though the German police are seen as an investigative agency controlled by the prosecution, in practice the police are moving toward independence, and have a much stronger influence on the investigatory stage.[31] The studies prove that practice remains very different from the

25 Elsner and Peters (2010), p. 224.
26 Jörg-Albrecht (2000), p. 255.
27 Weigend (2004), p. 208.
28 Weigend (2004), p. 208.
29 Huber (2008), pp. 327–328 and 358–360 (see the discussion on the tension between police and prosecution in Germany regarding the growing powers of the police in the field of computer science used by police during the course of criminal investigation to fight organized crime that the prosecution had no access to).
30 § 163 (2) StPO. Cf. Weigend (2004), p. 209.
31 Elsner and Peters (2010), p. 224.

letter of the law and that prosecutors, in reality, are no longer responsible for less serious and mass crimes, and their role has been overtaken by the police.[32] The dynamics of the police–prosecutor relationship is, in particular, influenced by the severity of investigated crimes. While in cases where the chances of identifying a suspect are low, and the crime is less serious, the prosecutor will often remain unengaged. And at the same time the intensity of investigation as well as prosecutorial engagement increases whenever the crime is considered as more serious.[33] As a result, the prosecutor habitually engages from the very beginning in the investigations in few areas only, such as white-collar crimes and homicide.[34]

Other factors that influence the engagement of the prosecutor is the size of the prosecutor's office and the number of cases that each prosecutor within that office deals with. In bigger cities, were the backlog of cases is heavier, prosecutors are informed about the investigation at the very end, when it is "too late to intervene."[35] The prosecutor will most likely learn about the case by receiving the final police report (*Schlußbericht*) summarizing statements taken and the evidence found.[36] This causes substantial problems, since the police are not usually focused on the legal necessities of undertaken measures, but much more on finishing investigation successfully.[37] It might be different in smaller offices where the workload is lower, and prosecutors have more time to engage earlier in the course of proceedings.

Despite the practical domination of the investigation process by the police and the invisibility of the prosecutor in it, the prosecution remains ultimately responsible for the outcome of criminal investigation. This is so since the prosecutor must eventually make the final decision on whether to charge a suspect with a crime.[38] But it should be remembered that in the majority of cases this ultimate decision is made based on materials gathered solely by the police with no prosecutorial interference and therefore the perspective that the prosecutor eventually adopts is heavily influenced by what has been gathered and presented to her by the police. Therefore, Elsner and Peters are probably right in their conclusion, that the ability of police to "steer the proceedings in the direction they have chosen" allows them to "assume far more independent and important role than is provided on the normative level."[39]

32 Elsner and Peters (2010), p. 227.
33 Elsner and Peters (2010), p. 228; Trendafilova and Róth (2008), p. 240; Weigend (2004), p. 208.
34 Weigend (2004), p. 208.
35 Huber (2008), p. 298.
36 Juy-Birmann (2002), p. 313.
37 Trendafilova and Róth (2008), p. 241.
38 Weigend (2004), p. 208.
39 Elsner and Peters (2010), p. 225.

It should be finally added that the German criminal procedure does not provide for formal time limits upon which the criminal investigation must conclude as will be seen in the cases of Poland and Italy. Therefore, neither the prosecutor nor the court maintain any official control over that matter and the only barrier to conducting the criminal investigation is the expiry of the statute of limitations as set by § 78 StGB. The Code also lacks any regulations obliging the prosecutor to conduct the periodical reviews of a case. As discussed above, it is common that the prosecutor receives the file from police only when they decide that the investigation should end.[40] There is also no regulation allowing the judge for preliminary investigation to control the length of the proceedings as is done in Italy. Obviously, this does not exclude some less formal options like internal guidelines allowing e.g. the immediate superiors of the police officer conducting investigation to control the duration of investigations within her jurisdiction.

5.2.3 The Investigative Authority of the Prosecutor

As explicitly stated in § 161 (1) StPO the prosecutor may act independently as well as avail herself to the police in fulfilling the aims of criminal investigation. As discussed above, in practice, the prosecutor most commonly does not engage in the process, until she receives the final report, then she decides how the investigation should end. Rarely, does the prosecutor resort to the police ordering the conduct of certain investigative measures, save for in more serious cases.

There are, however, certain situations when the prosecutor is obliged by law to take an action and cannot order the police to act on her behalf,. The line between the competencies of the prosecutor that she must execute personally and those that can be done by the police is not that easy to distinguish. Therefore, the competencies of the actors conducting criminal investigation do vary and can be divided into three groups.

First, the most limited scope of powers is possessed by all police officers regardless of their status, which extends to those without the *Ermittlungspersonen* status. They have the right and the duty "to make the first move" (*erster Zugriff*) by launching an investigation.[41] Their powers are quite restricted narrowed down to those most urgent measures that, if not undertaken, might result in losing the evidence. That means that they can e.g. arrest a suspect in exigent circumstances[42] or undertake measures necessary to identify the suspect,[43]

40 Juy-Birmann (2002), p. 313.
41 Huber (2008), p. 325.
42 § 127 (2) StPO.
43 § 163b (1) StPO.

including through photographs and fingerprints.[44] They also have the power to interrogate a witness, expert witness, and even the suspect; however, this can be done only if they are willing to testify voluntarily, as they cannot be summoned by police.[45]

The second group are police officers who have the status of *Ermittlungspersonen*. Their competencies are extremely broad and comparable to those possessed by the prosecutor. Acknowledging that the majority of police officers are granted this special status makes the competencies of prosecutor less unique and exclusive. The list of measures that this group of police officers can conduct includes e.g. physical examination of the suspect,[46] physical examination of persons other than the suspect,[47] seizure,[48] DNA analysis,[49] DNA profiling,[50] searching the suspect and her premises,[51] and setting a checkpoint at public places.[52] The powers of the *Ermittlungspersonen* is constantly expanding such that they are able to conduct criminal investigations with a growing independence from the prosecutors.[53] This trend is not extending to all situations. It should be noted that the listed measures can be undertaken by *Ermittlungspersonen* only when the circumstances are considered as exigent. In a regular situation when the necessity to conduct such measures can be foreseen in advance, the decision must be undertaken by the judicial authority and it will be the prosecutor requesting the judge to intervene, not a police officer of any category.[54]

Finally, the last group of competencies is reserved for the prosecutors. Based on the general clause provided in § 161 (1) StPO, the prosecutor may carry out all measures that police of both groups may undertake. In some respects, they are not so wide, since the rules constraining the exercise of coercive measures are similar to those possessed by the auxiliary prosecutors, and they may be carried on by the prosecutors only in exigent circumstances. But there are certain measures and decisions that only the prosecutor can undertake, and which are not transferrable to police officers, even those of higher ranks. Among such measures are the seizure of postal items i.e. mail or telegrams,[55] interception of distinct forms of communication as described

44 § 81b StPO.
45 § 161a (1) StPO *a contrario*.
46 § 81a (2) StPO.
47 § 81c (5) StPO.
48 § 98 (1) StPO.
49 § 81f StPO.
50 § 81g (3) StPO.
51 § 105 (1) StPO.
52 § 111 (2) StPO.
53 Huber (2008), p. 325 (enlisting only six such measures in 2008).
54 Cf. Section 7.2.3.
55 § 99 StPO.

in § 100a–100c,[56] interception of traffic data as described in § 100g StPO[57] and seizure of real estate.[58] It is also only the prosecutor who may summon witnesses and suspects for interrogation.[59] Moreover, the police must always resort to the prosecutor when there is a need to obtain a judicial warrant for arrest, search, seizure, or surveillance. In nonexigent circumstances, there is a rule that these measures are conducted upon a judicial warrant since the request for a warrant may be issued only by the prosecutor.[60] Only in urgent situations, when the prosecutor is unavailable may the judge act without prosecutorial request,[61] but in such a case, it is still the prosecutor that afterwards gives further directions.[62]

Therefore, some criminal investigations demand the active participation of the prosecutor, and not only her supervision. This, in particular, concerns investigations during which the resorting to coercive measures is necessary and foreseen in advance.

5.2.4 The Role of the Parties in the Conduct of Investigation

As discussed above, the investigation is conducted by the police and the prosecutor who, despite the growing independence of police is still considered as leading this stage of process. Moreover, since the criminal investigation must be conducted in an objective and neutral manner, gathering the evidence for and against the suspect[63] may be perceived as sufficiently safeguarding the rights of the suspect to search for exonerating evidence. Nevertheless, the German criminal procedure allows the conduct of independent private investigation to the defense although there is no power of compulsion available on their side.[64] Even though this right has not been established on the normative level, it can be derived from the right to a fair trial, the principle of equality of arms, and the position of the defense counsel as the "organ of the criminal justice system."[65] The scope of rights available for the suspect and her defense counsel include the right to seek evidence, to interview witnesses, obtain expert evidence, and hire private

56 § 100e (1) StPO.
57 § 101a (1) StPO.
58 § 111o (1) StPO.
59 § 161a (1) StPO and § 163a (3) StPO.
60 § 162 (1) StPO.
61 § 165 StPO.
62 § 167 StPO.
63 § 160 (2) StPO.
64 Frase and Weigend (1995), p. 341.
65 Brodowski et al. (2010), p. 294 fn. 244.

investigators.[66] It is, nevertheless, reported that in practice, the use of private investigations is rare, in particular due to the mistrust toward this form of gathering of evidence.[67] This in particular concerns reluctance to carry out witness interrogations which are never considered as equal to those carried out by the police or the prosecutor.

The law also provides that the suspect has a right to demand investigative measures to be undertaken on her behalf by the prosecutor (*Beweisantragsrecht*). Suspects are notified of this right when first interrogated.[68] Complying with the suspect's request is never automatic and is always subject to the prosecutorial discretion. It is up to the prosecutor to decide whether the evidence requested by the suspect to be revealed is relevant enough to be carried out.[69] In practice, these requests are infrequent, since they are considered to be easily denied.[70] And since the decision of the prosecutor is not subject to judicial review this seems as a weak way to force the prosecutor to undertake the investigative measures that the suspect wishes to be carried out.

On the other hand, neither the suspect nor her lawyer, has the right to participate in questioning conducted by the police or prosecutor.[71] Surprisingly, this right is not even granted to the suspect and his representative when the witness is questioned at the defense counsel's request.[72] The lack of such right has been a subject of valid criticism, since it poses a risk for the prosecutor to make the final decision on the outcome of criminal investigation based only on one version of events.[73]

5.2.5 The Judicial Involvement in the Conduct of Investigation

As noted before,[74] the significant role during the course of criminal investigation is played by the judge for the investigation (*Ermittlungsrichter*). This figure is barely a successor of the famous investigating judge (*Untersuchungsrichter*) with the unique power to conduct her own investigations. Instead, the judge of the investigation has a dual function.[75] Primarily, she controls the measures that interfere with the rights and freedoms of individual during

66 Brodowski et al. (2010), p. 294 and text accompanying fnn. 248–251.
67 Brodowski et al. (2010), p. 295.
68 § 136 (1) StPO.
69 § 163a (2) StPO.
70 Weigend (2013), p. 301.
71 Vogel (2019), p. 130.
72 Weigend (2013), p. 301.
73 Huber (2008), p. 357.
74 See Section 3.2.1.
75 Weigend (2013), p. 267.

criminal investigation[76] and, secondly, she is competent to undertake certain investigative measures, at the prosecutor's request.[77] This includes requests to conduct an inspection or to interrogate a witness. The judge does not have any discretion in that regard. since she reviews only the legality of the requested measure and if it is not illegal, the judge must conduct it.[78] Importantly the outcome of the investigatory actions undertaken by the judge for the investigation are admissible during the trial despite the general rule precluding replacement of the witness testimonies by the recordings of pretrial interrogations.[79]

Note too that, as a rule, when the interrogation of a witness or an expert is being conducted by a judge of the investigation, a suspect and her defense counsel have the right to participate and are allowed to ask questions and comment on witness statements.[80] This is different to what can be seen in cases of prosecutorial and police interrogations discussed above. There are, nevertheless, certain restrictions regarding the presence of the suspect who is detained and the excused absence does not prevent the hearing.[81] Moreover, the judge may exclude a suspect from being present at the hearing if her presence would jeopardize the purpose of the investigation, e.g. when it is feared that a witness will not tell the truth in the presence of the accused.[82] Also, when a suspect is interrogated by a judge for an investigation, she has the right to request additional investigative measures to be undertaken in her favor.[83] The taking of evidence in such a case is evaluated upon its importance, the fear of losing the evidence, and if the taking of the evidence may justify the release of the suspect. The suspect and her defense counsel have the right to participate in judicial inspections and in such cases have a significant influence on expert witnesses called to participate in inspection.[84]

In sum, this makes the judge of the investigation not a proactive investigatory official as has been the case before her establishment in 1975 but rather the safeguard of the credibility of the investigative measures undertaken upon her approval and in her presence.[85]

76 This is extensively discussed in Section 7.2.
77 § 162 (1) StPO.
78 § 162 (2) StPO.
79 § 251 (2), § 254 StPO. Cf. Frase and Weigend (1995), pp. 317–360, p. 326 and comments accompanying fn. 52.
80 § 168c (2) StPO.
81 § 168c (4)(5) StPO.
82 § 168c (3) StPO.
83 § 166 (1) StPO.
84 § 168d (1)(2) StPO.
85 Note that only the judge can place a person under oath during the investigation (§ 161a (1) StPO). Cf. Huber (2008), p. 299.

5.3 Conduct of Investigation in Poland

5.3.1 The Relationship between Prosecutor and Police

The conduct of criminal investigation in the Polish system is strongly determined, at least on the normative level, by the form in which the criminal investigation may be conducted: inspection (*śledztwo*) and inquiry (*dochodzenie*).[86] It should be underlined again, that this distinction determines the authority responsible for the conduct of investigation, scope of offenses that can be subject of either form of investigation, acceptable length of proceedings, and the degree of its formality. And even though the differences between these two forms are not as visible in practice as in theory, certainly the role of the prosecutor is more exposed during inspections, as she must undertake some decisions personally during its conduct, e.g. meet with the suspect to preliminarily charge her with a crime and interrogate that person. In practice, as we will see, the distinction is not as significant as the law provides, and the inspection and inquiry are very often conducted in an almost indistinguishable manner.

As data shows, only 11 percent of investigations are conducted in the form of inspection,[87] making it a visible minority. The selection of cases to be conducted in the form of inspection or inquiry is a complicated amalgam of unclear factors based on the provisions of Articles 309 and 325b k.p.k. The basic rule provides that inspection (*śledztwo*) is generally suited to be conducted in cases regarding more complicated crimes.[88] These are cases within the regional courts' jurisdiction (*sąd okręgowy*) which are selected upon their severity.[89] Additionally, in case of misdemeanors committed by judges, prosecutors, police officers, and officers of other governmental agencies investigation must be also conducted in that form. It is always a right of the prosecutor to decide that the investigation that normally should be conducted in the form of inquiry will be conducted in the form of inspection. However, this is an almost nonexistent situation.

In the most general terms, the prosecutor is fully responsible for every criminal investigation in Poland. The prosecutor must either conduct the investigation herself or, in all other cases, supervise it.[90] Theoretically, this allows the prosecutor to retain full control over every single criminal investigation in the country. However, it is clear that prosecutors are not able to

86 See Section 3.3.1.

87 *Sprawozdanie z działalności powszechnych jednostek organizacyjnych prokuratury za rok 2019*, https://pk.gov.pl/wp-content/uploads/2020/03/PK-P1K.pdf. Accessed July 12, 2020, p. 1.

88 Article 309 k.p.k.

89 Article 25 § 1 k.p.k.

90 Article 298 § 1 and 326 § 1 k.p.k.

achieve that expectation alone and they need support. Thus, the law provides for a broad array of criminal justice agencies that are empowered to support the prosecutor during criminal investigation.

The police[91] are considered the primary authority to conduct criminal investigation.[92] This is a uniformed and armed agency serving the public, intended to protect the security of people as well as to maintain public safety and order.[93] But the criminal investigation can be also conducted by other authorities, such as the Border Guard (*Straż Graniczna*), Internal Security Agency (*Agencja Bezpieczeństwa Wewnętrznego*), National Revenue Administration (*Krajowa Administracja Skarbowa*), Central Anticorruption Bureau (*Centralne Biuro Antykorupcyjne*), Military Gendarmerie (*Żandarmeria Wojskowa*), and Customs Office (*urząd celny*).[94] The competence of these authorities during the criminal investigation is strictly limited to specific matters linked to the scope of their jurisdictions. They all have their own legislative acts regulating their organization, jurisdiction, and powers entrusted to them, which in the context of criminal investigation sometimes overlap with provisions of k.p.k.

The level of engagement of the prosecutor in criminal investigation is determined by the form in which investigation is conducted. In cases of inspections the prosecutor, by rule, is responsible for conducting the investigation,[95] while in the case of inquiries she maintains in most cases the supervisory role over the police or any other criminal justice authority empowered to conduct the inquiry.[96] But in all cases the prosecutor retains the power to take over the conduct of inspection upon her wish, although in practice it happens very rarely.

Therefore, it might be assumed that inspections are conducted by the prosecutor personally, while inquiries are left for the police to conduct it. However, the prosecutor also maintains the power to fully or partially transfer the inspection to police. The only exception is when the case concerns a suspect who is a judge, prosecutor, police officer, etc.[97] But, even in such cases, the prosecutor can transfer to the police any specified investigative measure remaining within the scope of inspection, e.g. by ordering interrogation of a witness. Despite the rule that obliges the prosecutor to conduct inspections personally, 89 percent of inspections are fully entrusted

91 See on the police structure in Bulenda et al. (2010), p. 273.
92 Article 298 § 1 k.p.k.
93 Article 1 (1) of the Law of 6 April 1990 on Police (consolidated text Dz. U. 2019, poz. 161 as amended).
94 Article 312 k.p.k.
95 Article 311 § 1 k.p.k.
96 Article 325a § 1 k.p.k.
97 Article 311 § 2 k.p.k.

to police.[98] Considering that inspections account for only 11 percent of criminal investigations, this data clearly shows that the personal prosecutorial leadership over criminal investigations in Poland is a myth.

In the light of the above, if the majority of investigations are, in practice, conducted by the police and other criminal justice authorities, the real question refers to the balance of powers between them and the prosecutor. Generally, the Polish police force remains independent from the prosecution service and there are no judicial police at the prosecutor's disposal, which also applies to all other agencies conducting criminal investigation under the prosecutorial supervision. And since the police and these agencies are obliged to obey orders from the prosecutor[99] Therefore, the Polish prosecutor maintains broad supervisory powers over police actions to ensure the proper and effective course of the entire criminal investigation.[100] The nature of these powers will be discussed below.

5.3.2 The Prosecutor's Supervisory Authority over Investigation

Despite the straightforward provisions allowing prosecutor to give orders to police, their binding force may be questioned. This is so since the police do not answer directly to prosecutor. Therefore, if a police officer fails to comply with the prosecutorial order or any other decision issued by the prosecutor, the prosecutor has no tools to directly discipline said police officer. The compliance with prosecutorial orders is enforced differently by giving the prosecutor the power to demand, from the superior of that person, the initiation of internal procedures concerning such disobedience.[101] The results of such disciplinary proceedings instituted against a police officer must be reported to the prosecutor. But even though this provision provides for the mandatory initiation of disciplinary proceedings against those who do not carry out the prosecutorial orders[102] the practice does not support the effectiveness of this procedure.

The prosecutorial supervisory authority over criminal investigation, as set in Article 326 § 3 k.p.k., is quite extensive.[103] The law reserves for the

98 Among 79,918 inspections initiated in 2019 as many as 71,329 were fully transferred to the police upon prosecutorial decision—*Sprawozdanie z działalności powszechnych jednostek organizacyjnych prokuratury za rok 2019*, https://pk.gov.pl/wp-content/uploads/2020/03/PK-P1K.pdf. Accessed July 12, 2020, p. 1.
99 Article 15 § 1 k.p.k. and Article 326 § 3 (4) k.p.k.
100 Article 326 § 2 k.p.k.
101 Article 326 § 4 k.p.k.
102 Rogalski (2016), pp. 1078–1079.
103 Cf. Bulenda et al. (2010), pp. 275–276.

prosecutor, the power to receive information regarding the investigation, to review the case file, to indicate the direction that the proceedings should take, and to issue orders relevant in this regard. The prosecutor may also issue decisions, as well as change or even revoke those issued by the police officer conducting investigation.[104] Moreover, the prosecutor may personally take part in the conduct of investigative measures during investigation as well as take them over if they deem necessary. This concerns all types of investigative measures including line-ups, show-ups, interrogations, and searches.

The scope of these supervisory powers builds a picture of the prosecutor who, if she wishes so, may have a strong direct impact on every criminal investigation shaping its course and deciding on its outcome. It applies in full to all inspections, since the decision to initiate same can be undertaken only by the prosecutor, but in case of inquiries it has a somewhat limited effect since the prosecutor may not be aware that the inspection is being conducted until it has become necessary to prolong the duration of inquiry. This is so, since the police, from 2003, have no legal obligation to notify the prosecutor on the initiation of an inquiry.[105] In such a case the prosecutor will most likely learn about the ongoing inspection within two months from the date when the decision on the initiation of the inquiry has been made by the police.[106] To make up for this considerable freedom at the early stage of criminal investigation, the expectations toward the prosecutorial supervision over such cases are set extremely high.[107] When the prosecutor comes to consider a case, after the two-month period she must assess the correctness of the proceedings[108] and evaluate *18* distinct factors including, e.g. whether the case has been conducted in an appropriate and timely manner, whether the measures undertaken have been recorded properly, whether the circumstances of the case have been examined thoroughly, and whether the procedural rights of the participants to the proceedings have been observed.[109] But, in practice, despite these provisions, the prosecutorial supervision in the majority of cases remains a fiction and the police conduct investigations without any help or mentoring from the prosecutor.[110]

104 This is subject to certain limitations concerning the decisions already announced to those to whom it is addressed.
105 See Lach (2004), p. 603. Cf. Section 4.3.3.
106 In a normative framework the only exception to the rule that the prosecutor always conducts or supervises criminal investigation is the case of inquiries concerning groups of minor crimes that at the first sight will remain unsolved (Article 325f k.p.k.)—cf. Section 8.3.3.
107 Waltoś (1968), pp. 335–336 (author notes that the prosecutorial control to be effective must be permanent yet too frequent control can hinder the course of proceedings).
108 § 239 Regulations 2016.
109 § 240 Regulations 2016.
110 Jasiński and Kremens (2019), p. 211.

The actual relationship between the police and prosecutor is, nevertheless, a result of factors other than what is prescribed normatively. It depends upon levels of police training, technical equipment available to them, and the number of cases that the police and prosecutor are burdened with.[111] Some prosecution service units organize regular meetings with the police to discuss problems in investigations, explain changes to the law, find ways of better cooperation, and so forth.[112] But, in other cases, the prosecutor's offices will simply resort to the exchange of documents and files between the prosecutor and the police and refrain from setting the guidelines, even of customary character, not to mention coordinating the interaction. Therefore, the relationship between prosecutor and police during criminal investigation will rely on the dynamics between the individual prosecutors and police officers working together. But it will be also depend on unformal strategies set for units cooperating in the course of the criminal process by their leaders. Both factors are very hard to grasp and measure.

The supervisory authority of the prosecutor over investigation is visible in her role in controlling the length of the proceedings. The prosecutor bears the responsibility to observe the principle of speedy trial at this stage of criminal process[113] Here also the form in which criminal investigation is conducted determines the differences in its duration. In the case of inspection, the proceedings must be concluded within three months from the date of issuing the decision to initiate investigation,[114] while in the case of inquiry the proceedings should end within two months.[115] In both cases, the prosecutor with no judicial involvement can extend the time limit. This can be done for up to one year in "justified cases" and for an additional time that is not limited in any way in "particularly justified cases."[116] Similarly, in the case of inquiry, an extension can be granted—up to three months without a cause and in "particularly justified cases" for an additional time indicated by the prosecutor. Each decision extending the length of inquiry or inspection must contain the determined time limit within which the proceedings should end. In each case, the authority conducting investigation needs to file a motion requesting extension, setting out the reasons justifying such request.[117]

111 Kruszyński (2007), p. 183.
112 Lach (2004), p. 605.
113 Article 2 § 1 (4) k.p.k.
114 Article 310 § 1 k.p.k.
115 Article 325i § 1 k.p.k.
116 Article 310 § 2 k.p.k. The decision to prolong the investigation up to one year is issued by the prosecutor supervising the investigation or by the prosecutor directly superior (*prokurator bezpośrednio przełożony*) to the prosecutor conducting the investigation and above one year—by the prosecutor of a higher level (*prokurator nadrzędny*) to the prosecutor conducting the investigation or supervising it.
117 § 130 Regulation 2016.

Theoretically an inspection or inquiry can last almost infinitely, and the only end date arises from the statute of limitation of the investigated offense. Therefore, despite the existence of general rules calling for the expeditious conducting of criminal proceedings, there is no mechanism creating effective pressure on the prosecutor and other criminal justice authorities to close investigation in a timely manner.[118] The rules shaped in this way seem to secure the prosecutor's rights related to periodical control of investigations conducted under her supervision, which may be considered as beneficial, rather than effectively limiting the duration of proceedings.

5.3.3 The Investigative Authority of the Prosecutor

The other factor limiting powers of the police and their freedom in conducting the criminal investigation is the number of decisions and measures that the prosecutor is burdened with and which cannot be transferred to police. The law reserves certain activities solely for the prosecutor and forbids any other authority conducting criminal investigation from undertaking them. Polish law, due to its specificity in establishing two forms of criminal investigation, divides such measures into those that must be undertaken only by the prosecutor, regardless of the form in which investigation is being conducted, and those that the prosecutor must undertake during inspection, while during inquiry the police can carry them out. The most significant example from the latter group is the decision to initially charge a person with a crime and to subsequently interrogate such person.[119] Moreover, only the prosecutor may change this decision and modify the preliminary charges, as well as decide to close the inspection.[120]

The second group concerning decisions that can be taken only by the prosecutor regardless of the form in which investigation is being conducted, is quite extensive.[121] First, it contains decisions that involve the interference with rights and freedoms of the individual. According to Polish law decisions as a rule (warrants) regarding seizure of objects,[122] interception of mail,[123] search,[124]

118 But see the remedy available under the Act of June 17, 2004, on the complaint against a breach of a party's right to have a case examined in preliminary proceedings, conducted or supervised by a prosecutor and court proceedings, without undue delay (Dz.U. 2004, Ne 179, poz. 1843 as amended). However, this mechanism is not commonly used and, even if employed, cannot necessarily be considered as effective.

119 Article 311 § 3 k.p.k. Note that it is done in the Polish system in a very formal way. See broadly Section 6.3.

120 Article 311 § 3 k.p.k. *in fine*.

121 Lach (2004), p. 604.

122 Article 217 k.p.k.

123 Article 218 k.p.k.

124 Article 219 k.p.k.

and arrests[125] are issued by the prosecutor and not by the judge. Obviously, in exigent circumstances, the police may undertake them without prior prosecutorial approval. But in such cases the prosecutor will, nevertheless, be notified and called to confirm them *post factum*.[126] Decisions normally decided by the court in exigent circumstances can be taken provisionally by the prosecutor and subsequently confirmed by the court, e.g. interception of communication.[127]

Moreover, in each case when the measures aimed at securing the presence of the suspect in criminal proceedings must be undertaken, such as pretrial detention, imposing bail, or ordering police supervision the prosecutor gets involved. This is so since the imposition of all such measures on the suspect remains in prosecutorial hands,[128] other than pretrial detention which can be imposed only by the court. But also, in the latter case the prosecutor is involved since only the prosecutor may request the court to impose pretrial detention.[129]

Finally, the prosecutor may issue some other decisions that no one else is empowered to undertake. In some cases, issuing such decisions or taking part in the investigative measure is even mandatory. For example, the prosecutor must take part in each crime scene investigation involving a suspicious death[130] as well as to participate in every autopsy resulting from such a death.[131] Only the prosecutor is authorized to appoint expert witnesses to form a psychiatric opinion regarding a suspect's sanity,[132] order confidentiality measures resulting in the concealment of the identity of a witness,[133] and order preparation of the individual assessment of a suspect.[134]

The list of actions and measures that must be personally undertaken by the prosecutor during criminal investigation as provided in the Code was subsequently expanded by provisions of the 2016 Regulations. According to its provisions, in case of investigation conducted in the form of inspection the prosecutor is obliged to personally interrogate: the only witness of a crime, every witness whose sanity is being questioned, victims of certain crimes (depriving a person of liberty, robbery, violent theft, etc.), expert

125 Article 247 k.p.k.
126 See Section 8.3.
127 Article 237 k.p.k.
128 Article 249 § 3 k.p.k.
129 Article 250 § 1 and 2 k.p.k.
130 Article 209 § 2 k.p.k.
131 Article 209 § 4 k.p.k. These rules have been criticized for engaging the time and attention of prosecutors too much since the law does not provide for any exceptions from this rule and since the "suspicious death" is considered to be a very broad threshold—see Kremens (2019b), pp. 5201–5210.
132 Article 202 k.p.k.
133 Article 184 k.p.k.
134 Article 214 k.p.k.

witnesses, a suspect against whom the request for pretrial detention has been filed.[135] Also, whenever a child under the age of 15 is being interrogated by the court, either as a witness or a victim of crimes involving domestic violence or sexual abuse,[136] the prosecutor not only participates in such an interrogation but is the authority that requests the court to conduct such a hearing.[137]

Thus, the prosecutorial engagement in criminal investigation must be considered as extensive. Even if the inspection has been fully transferred to the police or the inquiry is being conducted outside of the prosecutorial knowledge, the prosecutor might be anyway engaged in investigation when the above presented decisions and measures are to take place. Obviously, there are some cases in which the prosecutor will not be involved until the final decision on the outcome of the investigation must be taken. Numerous investigations will demand prosecutorial reaction, engagement, and activity. This means that the prosecutor will take a part in all cases in which arrest, search, or seizure has taken place or all cases concerning investigation of death as well as demanding verification of the sanity of a suspect.

5.3.4 The Role of the Parties in the Conduct of Investigation

The criminal investigation is conducted *ex officio*, which means that the investigative measures are conducted regardless of the will of other participants to the criminal process, including the suspect or the victim.[138] Because the leading role in conducting investigations has been vested in the prosecutor and the police,[139] it is their responsibility to achieve the primary aims as prescribed for that stage of criminal process, i.e. determining whether a criminal offense has been committed and to identify its perpetrator.[140]

Generally, the law provides for taking the evidence ex officio as well as upon the request of the.[141] This applies to both stages of criminal process. Certainly during the trial, the primary responsibility to introduce new evidence belongs to parties while during the investigation it will be done generally by the prosecutor and police. Yet, during investigation the parties possess the same power as at the trial. This does not mean that either the suspect or the victim has the power to undertake any evidentiary measures on their own or to conduct

135 § 170 (1) Regulations 2016.
136 Article 185a and 185c k.p.k. See Section 5.3.5.
137 § 171 Regulations 2016.
138 Article 9 § 1 k.p.k.
139 Article 298 § 1 k.p.k.
140 Article 297 § 1 (1) and (2) k.p.k.
141 Article 167 k.p.k.

independent investigation.[142] But they both retain the right to request the authority conducting the investigation to take the evidentiary measures, e.g. by interrogating a witness or searching premises.[143] As a rule, all motions should be granted unless one of the grounds for denial as provided in Article 170 § 1 k.p.k., which include the undertaking of the evidence is inadmissible or impossible, the evidence itself is irrelevant or immaterial, etc.[144] However the motion for evidence must not be rejected only because previously undertaken evidence has proven the opposite of the fact which the moving party now intends to prove.[145]

But, most importantly, at this stage of the criminal process the decision whether the motion will be granted remains with the authority that conducts investigation, which means that such decision will be taken by the prosecutor. This means that despite the potential activity of the suspect and the victim, the shape of criminal investigation and evidentiary measures undertaken during its conduct, remains the responsibility of the prosecutor (or any other authority that conducts criminal investigation). Even when the parties may try to influence the investigation, requesting certain measures to be undertaken, if the prosecutor denies the motion this cannot be challenged.[146]

The prosecutor has additional ways of limiting the rights of the suspect and victim to participate in measures undertaken during criminal investigation. The general rule provides that parties and their representatives may take part in the investigation when the evidentiary measures are being undertaken, e.g. when the witness is being questioned. Generally, the party who has submitted an evidentiary motion, as well as their lawyers, cannot be denied the right to participate in the examination of such evidence if they so demand.[147] However, a suspect who remains in custody may not be allowed to participate in the examination of such evidence if it would cause serious difficulties, e.g. by transporting the suspect from a detention facility.[148] The parties may be also denied the right to participate in other evidentiary measures based on the protection of the interest of investigation.[149]

142 De Vocht (2010), p. 465. Note, however, that since 2015, private documents, i.e. those created outside of the criminal process, are admissible even if they were created directly for the purpose of criminal process, which is particularly important in case of so-called private expert opinions (see Article 393 § 3 k.p.k.).

143 Article 315 § 1 k.p.k. Cf. Judgment of the Supreme Court of June 22, 2004, V KK 54/04, Lex no. 109522.

144 See more in Jasiński and Kremens (2019), p. 306.

145 Article 170 § 2 k.p.k.

146 Note that the rejection of a motion for evidence does not preclude later admission of evidence, even if no new circumstances are disclosed (Article 170 § 4 k.p.k.)

147 Articles 315 § 2 and 317 § 1 k.p.k.

148 Article 315 § 2 k.p.k. in accordance with Article 318 k.p.k. second sentence.

149 Article 317 § 1 and 2 k.p.k.

Since these grounds are based on a discretionary decision by the prosecutor, her powers over the conducting of investigation are not heavily affected by the rules granting parties the right to actively influence the criminal investigation.

5.3.5 The Judicial Involvement in the Conduct of Investigation

Polish criminal procedure does not recognize the traditional feature of the inquisitorial system—the investigative judge.[150] The system also lacks a separate judicial figure such as the German *Ermittlungsrichter* or Italian *giudice per le indagini preliminari* devoted to judicial activities during criminal investigation. Instead, Polish law provides for certain general powers for the court during criminal investigation that are exercised by judges that also regularly sit on trials.[151] This means that the judge that has exercised his role during criminal investigation, e.g. setting the bail and deciding on pretrial detention may subsequently hear that case on the trial since there is no rule forbidding such situation.

The role of the court during investigation is restricted to deciding on matters prescribed by law relating to protection of the rights of a suspect, e.g. on pretrial detention or participating in actions that cannot be repeated, e.g. interrogation of a dying witness, as well as—in some cases provided by law—deciding on interlocutory appeals filed against decisions taken by the prosecutor or police, e.g. discontinuation of criminal investigation.[152] Importantly, the law does not assign a judge with one criminal investigation. Instead, decisions concerning the same investigation may be undertaken by different judges learning each time about the circumstances of the case from scratch.

In any case, the investigative powers of the court are very limited and triggered only upon the request of the prosecutor or party to criminal investigation (victim or suspect) which means that the court at this stage of the criminal process never acts *ex officio*.[153] Generally, involvement of the court during investigation concerns questioning of a witness if there is a risk that it will be impossible to examine her during the trial, e.g. due to the likely death of a witness.[154] The court is allowed to refuse such request only if the

150 Cf. Section 3.3.1. See briefly the history of the investigative judge in Poland by Jasiński and Kremens (2019), pp. 44–45. In recent years the discussion on pros and cons of introducing the investigative judge back into the Polish system has been present in the literature—see e.g. Kulesza (1991); Grzegorczyk (2010).

151 Article 298 § 2 k.p.k.

152 Section 8.3.

153 Nowak and Steinborn (2013), p. 508.

154 Article 316 § 3 k.p.k.

court is convinced that no risk exists but not on the ground that the interrogation is unjustified since such evaluation belongs solely to the authority conducting criminal investigation.[155]

The interrogation of vulnerable victims and witnesses form a special category of evidence that is undertaken in the presence of the court. This concerns children under the age of 15 who are victims or witnesses of sexual offenses or offenses against the family and all victims of rape or other sexual offenses regardless of the age of the victim.[156] In these cases, the court engages in the examination of a witness at this early stage of the criminal process so the witness will not have to testify again during the trial in order to protect the witness from further traumatization and victimization.[157] To enhance the comfort of the witness some additional measures are also employed, i.e. the presence of psychologist and exclusion of the suspect from the interrogation.

5.4 Conduct of Investigation in Italy

5.4.1 The Relationship between Prosecutor and Police

The conduct of the criminal investigation in Italy remains heavily influenced by the 1988 reform. The reform set a clear distinction between the investigation and the trial phase making the pretrial findings generally inadmissible as evidence at trial.[158] It established that the examination of evidence takes place orally during the trial, as the best environment for proving the facts and discovering the truth.[159] This in turn impacted the way in which criminal investigations are conducted. Since the objective of the criminal investigation was no longer to prepare evidence with a view to its use at trial, but to allow prosecutor to decide whether to prosecute or not, the scope and volume of measures to be conducted during investigation had to change.

The other factor impacting the shape of criminal investigation in Italy is the establishment of a unique relationship between the prosecution and the police, built upon the subordination of the latter to the former. This was done even earlier, with the aim to reduce the investigative autonomy that the police had under the 1930 Code.[160] Therefore, the principle of subordination of the judicial police (*polizia giudiziaria*)[161] to the prosecution

155 Brodzisz (2015), p. 762
156 Articles 185a-185c k.p.k.
157 Jasiński and Kremens (2019), p. 213.
158 Illuminati and Caianiello (2007), p. 129.
159 Caianiello (2012), p. 253.
160 Gialuz (2017), p. 25–26.
161 Note that in some works *polizia giudiziaria* is translated as "criminal police" which seems to accentuate that this police force is not to be at the judges' disposal only, as it might

service has been raised to the constitutional level. And even though Article 109 of the Italian Constitution refers to the "judicial authority" as the organ having control over the police, since prosecutors come within that definition,[162] the prosecutors may avail themselves of the police during criminal investigation. This was confirmed by adopting provisions obliging judicial police to carry out investigation and activity as ordered or delegated by the judicial authority,[163] and under its supervision and direction.[164] The rules also forced the Prosecutor General at the Court of Appeal to ensure that the direct availability of the judicial police by the judicial authorities is respected (Article 83 of Judicial Regulations). Adopting them made it possible to keep the judicial police independent of the Ministry of Justice and preserved the autonomy of the judiciary from the executive.[165]

Therefore, Italy established a special agency—the judicial police (*polizia giudiziaria*)—solely responsible for the conducting of criminal investigation.[166] The structure of this formation is complicated, since this is not a distinct type of police formation, but rather a combination of police officers from distinct agencies dedicated to criminal investigation. Such a mechanism allows drawing a line between two typical police functions, public security, and judicial police activity, placing the latter under prosecutorial control.[167] Therefore, the judicial police include members from three principal police forces, each of which reports to a different ministry.[168] The State Police (*Polizia di Stato*) remains under the Ministry of Internal Affairs, the *Carabinieri*, being a component of the military, is a part of the Ministry of Defense and the *Guardia di Finanza* is within the structure of the Ministry of Finance. This does not exhaust the list of agencies that can participate in criminal investigations as it includes many specialized police forces less frequently engaged in these activities.[169]

The organization of the judicial police has been provided in the c.p.p. in a way that guarantees the strongest functional dependence of the police on the prosecutor.[170] The judicial police have been divided into three groups: units (*servizi*), departments (*sezioni*), and other bodies required by law to carry

seem from the direct and most common translation ("judicial police"), but predominantly works with the prosecutor—Gialuz et al. (2017), p. 572.

162 Cf. Section 2.4.2.

163 Article 55 (2) c.p.p.

164 Article 56 (1) c.p.p.

165 Di Amato (2013), p. 35.

166 Article 55–59 c.p.p. See Di Amato (2013), p. 158.

167 Caianiello (2016), p. 9.

168 Perrodet (2002), p. 353.

169 See such list in Ruggieri and Marcolini (2013), p. 369

170 Illuminati (2004), p. 308.

out investigations.[171] From those three organizational structures, the second (departments) are established at each Office of the Public Prosecutor of the Republic and its officers are exclusively assigned to investigative tasks only. Each prosecution office has, therefore, such a police department at their disposal, while the Office of the General Public Prosecutor attached to the Court of Appeal can make the use of all the departments that are established in its district.[172] The officers within the department can be promoted or removed from their duty only with the approval of the chief prosecutor of the office in which they work.[173]

Moreover, the dismemberment of police agencies represented within the judicial police under the distinct Ministries has been also designed to preserve the dependence of the judicial police on the prosecution service. But the Italian Constitutional Court has confirmed that their relationship is only of functional character.[174] This means that the police are functionally (*dipendenza funzionale*) but not organizationally (*dipendenza organizzativa*) dependent on the prosecution.[175] The prosecution service has at its disposal a unique structure of judicial police attached to each prosecutor's office, fully and exclusively devoted to conducting criminal investigation, yet with no organizational link between them.

The situation becomes even more complex when the prosecutor wishes to conduct investigation involving officers from units not subordinated to them, which often happens when investigations becomes more complicated, concerning many suspects or when there are difficult investigatory measures to be carried out.[176] The relationship that the prosecution service maintains with units is of a noticeably different character than with departments, and prosecutorial ability to issue direct orders that must be obeyed and executed is very much limited. Yet, the necessity to resort to these units might be inevitable, since they possess more resources and are frequently able to bring a higher quality to investigations, as they are more specialized, e.g. in the field of organized crimes.[177] This seems to be the important factor restricting the impact of effective prosecutorial supervision over investigations.

171 Article 56 (1) c.p.p.
172 Article 58 (1) c.p.p.
173 Di Amato (2013), p. 35.
174 Corte cost., decision no. 94 of June 18, 1963 [1963] Giur. cost. 782 as quoted in Perrodet (2002), p. 353.
175 Montana (2009), p. 317 ("Functional dependence means that superiors have the right to determine what subordinates do. Organizational dependence means that superiors have the right to manage the organization (e.g. career, promotions, transfers, allocation of resources) of their subordinates").
176 Montana (2009), p. 318.
177 Montana (2009), p. 318.

5.4.2 The Prosecutor's Supervisory Authority over Investigation

The law provides for the role of the prosecutor as leader of criminal investigation. The prosecutors possess, not only a wide discretion to define the strategy for each particular case, but also the ability to decide what measures should be used to achieve the result.[178] As per Article 327 (1) c.p.p., the prosecutor manages the criminal investigation and the criminal police are at her disposal. Even though, in recent years, the role of the police has been enhanced, the prosecution remains uncontested dominus of the investigation.[179] At least from the normative perspective this allows the prosecutor to maintain full control over criminal investigation from its very beginning. When the prosecutor assumes such control, she has a duty to take all steps necessary to determine whether a crime has been committed, as well as whether there is enough evidence to prosecute the crime.[180]

The prosecutor cannot of course conduct every investigation personally. She can however call on the police to undertake certain measures in her name. These instructions might be either of a specific or a general character.[181] In the first case the prosecutor orders the conducting of specific measures, e.g. pointing out that there is a need to conduct a search or question a witness, while in the latter case the instructions are more general, yet not so general as to become applicable in all cases.[182]

Some of the measures that the prosecutor orders police to undertake remain within the competencies of the police even without the prosecutorial requests. But some other may be conducted by the police only if delegated by the prosecutor.[183] In the latter case they must be transferred to them through delegated authority of the prosecutor (*delega*),[184] according to provisions of Article 370 (1) and 348 (3) c.p.p. However, the prosecutor cannot delegate measures that are unique to her (e.g. interrogations of persons kept in custody or confrontations that will be discussed within the next section). The prosecutor will be able to delegate all other measures such as other types of interrogations, searches, seizures.

Despite these broadly given competencies of the prosecutor, there are two situations when her competencies are limited, and the police will be able to act entirely independently, even without the prosecutor's knowledge.

178 Ruggeri (2015), p. 70.
179 Caianiello (2012), p. 258; Illuminati (2004), p. 309.
180 Caianiello (2012), p. 256.
181 Illuminati (2004), p. 310.
182 Illuminati (2004), p. 310.
183 Mathias (2002), p. 463.
184 Montana (2009), p. 316.

First, the police can carry out investigative acts independently from the moment they receive the notification that the crime has been committed until this information reaches the prosecutor. It is so despite the fact that the prosecutor must be informed without undue delay about the commitment of a crime.[185] The obvious aim of this is to secure the factual prosecutorial supervisory powers over criminal investigation. Initially, prosecutorial supervision over police activities was strengthened by setting a 48-hour deadline for police to pass on the information to the prosecutor. But since it resulted in an enormous backlog of cases the rule was removed.[186] As a result, in this early stage of investigation, the police gained freedom and independence to make any decision regarding the conduct of criminal investigation. Until the case is reported to the prosecutor and until the police receive the guidelines from her, they may carry on the investigation in order to gather evidence and identify suspects and witnesses.[187] This potentially creates a situation in which the police have the right to determine the initial strategy and direction of the investigation.[188] So, when the prosecutor takes over a case, its direction has already been determined by the police.

Second, even though the judicial police work under prosecutorial supervision and must obey and execute prosecutorial orders and follow her guidelines, they can conduct investigatory measures on their own initiative. The police can continue the investigation independently, although the measures carried out have to be aimed at reaching the same targets as those laid down by the prosecutor.[189] As provided, even after the information on the commitment of a crime has been notified to the prosecutor, the judicial police can continue the functions referred to in Article 55 c.p.p., by collecting any element which may be useful for the reconstruction of the criminal act and for the informal identification of offenders.[190] This indeed gives a broad spectrum of measures, since Article 55 c.p.p. mentions "any measures necessary to ensure sources of evidence and collect any other material which may be needed for the application of criminal law." It is, furthermore, clarified that the judicial police can search for objects and traces, search for witnesses as well as conduct many other activities as provided in Title IV ("Activities upon Initiative of Judicial Police") of the Code.[191]

185 Article 347 (1) c.p.p. In case of investigations which require the assistance of defense counsel as well as when the investigation concerns serious crimes, the prosecutor must be informed as early as within 24 hours.
186 See Section 4.4.1.
187 Illuminati (2004), p. 310.
188 Giostra (1994), p. 180 as quoted in Montana (2009), p. 318.
189 Illuminati (2004), p. 310.
190 Article 348 (1) c.p.p.
191 Article 348 (2) c.p.p.

As a result, the scope of investigative measures that are available to the police without prosecutorial control, allows for shaping the criminal investigation by the police independently and permits an assumption that the actual influence of the prosecutor on criminal investigation, at least in cases concerning minor offenses, may be narrower than initially expected. As Caianiello confirms,

> a prosecutor ordinarily provides limited supervision during the course of an investigation, leaving it to the police to set the agenda and ask for prosecutorial orders as needed. Only in serious cases does a prosecutor exercise any real control over the work of the police through hands-on direction of the investigation.[192]

Importantly, Italian criminal procedure provides for the time limits of the criminal investigation. However, the power to prolong investigation, distinctively to what has been presented in case of Poland, does not belong to the prosecutor but to the judge for the investigation and should be rather seen as a form of constraint imposed on the prosecutor than a form of her supervisory powers. Thus, this issue will be explored further below.[193]

5.4.3 The Investigative Authority of the Prosecutor

The most general rule provides that the prosecutor may conduct personally, any investigative activity.[194] There are no limitations to prosecutorial competencies with regard to that, which means that theoretically, if the prosecutor wishes so, the whole criminal investigation can be carried on exclusively by her, especially since the law encourages the prosecutor to do everything to decide whether a case is to be prosecuted.[195] Moreover, unlike as was the case under the 1930 Code, the investigative measures falling within the competencies of the prosecutor are unlimited.[196] Despite these provisions, in practice in almost all cases the prosecutor avails her of the judicial police, exercising her right, as discussed above, to issue orders and delegate investigative measures.[197] This gives the police the power to conduct many investigative measures, although not those that can be undertaken only by the

192 Caianiello (2012), p. 258.
193 Section 5.4.5.
194 Article 370 (1) c.p.p. first sentence.
195 Article 358 c.p.p.
196 Ruggeri (2015), p. 70.
197 Article 370 (1) c.p.p. second sentence.

prosecutor. This is so, because the Code reserves certain competencies solely to the prosecutor.

The list of activities that may be conducted by the prosecutor includes many investigative measures which have been provided within the provisions contained in the Title V of the Code ("Activities of the Public Prosecutor").[198] The prosecutor also retains competence to conduct an almost indefinite number of investigative actions acceptable by law. For example, the prosecutor can interrogate a person under investigation[199] as well as one accused in joint proceedings on criminal acts being prosecuted,[200] and gather information from persons who may be able to provide information that is useful for investigative purposes (i.e. *informazioni*).[201]

However, the Italian criminal procedure provides for some powers during criminal investigation that can be conducted exclusively by the prosecutor. A good example of measures from this group is the power to compel attendance of witnesses[202] and suspects,[203] conduct confrontations,[204] or question a detained person.[205] While carrying out her functions, the prosecutor maintains coercive powers including a power to require the intervention of the judicial police, and, if necessary, national enforcement authorities, directing the implementation of all necessary measures to ensure a safe and orderly performance of the actions they are in charge of.[206]

This all makes the position of the prosecutor, during criminal investigation, particularly special and irreplaceable. Her position cannot be limited only to a supervisory role aimed at directing the activities of the judicial police. Since interrogation and confrontation of the suspect who is deprived of their liberty cannot be conducted by anyone other than the prosecutor,[207] the prosecutor is inevitable as an active figure at least in those investigations were the suspect has been detained.

198 Note however that not all that what is contained within this part of the c.p.p. relates only to prosecutorial activities and might be applied also by the police when they conduct criminal investigation on their own.
199 Article 364 (1) c.p.p.
200 Article 363 (1) c.p.p.
201 Article 362 (1) c.p.p.
202 Article 377 c.p.p.
203 Article 375 c.p.p.
204 Article 370 (1) c.p.p. The confrontation shall be understood as a form of interrogation conducted between the suspect and witness or two witnesses that having been already examined or questioned, where they are in disagreement over important facts and circumstances (Article 211 c.p.p.).
205 Article 388 c.p.p. Cf. Mathias (2002), p. 466.
206 Article 378 c.p.p.
207 Article 370 (1) c.p.p.

5.4.4 The Role of the Parties in the Conduct of Investigation

As reported, one of the main challenges of the 1988 Code was to enhance the role of all the parties in the taking of evidence.[208] This applies notably to the trial stage of the criminal process where participatory roles of the defendant and defense counsel have been significantly increased but has a strong influence also on the investigatory stage. As of 2000, a system of parallel investigations conducted by the prosecution and the defense has been introduced.[209]

The right to actively conduct private investigation granted to both the accused and the victim are provided explicitly and in detail in Title VI-bis of the c.p.p.[210] Under Article 327bis c.p.p. the suspect's and victim's lawyers have the power to conduct investigations with the aim of gathering evidence in favor of their clients. It can be carried out by defense counsel before criminal investigation has officially commenced since the prerequisite to start private investigation remains in the scope of the power of attorney.[211] The power of counsel to conduct a private investigation does not depend on the nature of charges or whether the accused is detained.[212] The investigatory activities can also be carried by authorized private investigators and technical consultants,[213] which allows this right to be used very broadly. But the practical problems arising from the existence of the availability of such institution are mainly caused by the cost of private investigation. As reported, even though they are covered to some extent by the legal aid program, such cost is prohibitive to allow conducting an effective investigation.[214]

The scope of investigative measures to be undertaken by the counsel in the course of private investigation is theoretically no different from what is done during the regular investigation by the police. For example, private expert opinions may be obtained, the parties may have access to premises both public and private,[215] or public administration documents.[216] Counsel can interview witnesses, record such interviews on a special form provided for that purpose and use it in the court on the same basis as witness statements obtained by the prosecutor.[217] The law also sets detailed rules on how the

208 Ruggeri (2017), p. 80.
209 Grande (2016), p. 370.
210 This has been introduced to Italian law by the Legge no. 397, December 7, 2000.
211 Di Amato (2013), p. 163.
212 Caianiello (2010), p. 407.
213 Article 327bis (3) c.p.p.
214 Caianiello (2010), p. 407.
215 Article 391sexies and 391septies c.p.p.
216 Article 391quarter c.p.p.
217 Article 391ter c.p.p.

interview should look and, in particular, what information is given to the interviewee, including notification on the right to refuse to answer.[218]

It becomes much more problematic when the witness that counsel wants to question refuses to cooperate. In such a case, coercion is necessary, and the intervention of the prosecutor is required who, upon the request of a lawyer should set the examination of the person within seven days from the request.[219] Alternatively, the lawyer that requests the examination of a witness can file a request with the court that will allow for an evidentiary hearing.[220]

5.4.5 The Judicial Involvement in the Conduct of Investigation

With the reform of criminal process of 1988, the very broad investigative powers of the judge were seriously modified. As noted,[221] the inquisitorial judge (*giudice istruttore*) heavily involved in the investigation directing it, performing searches and seizures, summoning and questioning witnesses has replaced with full prosecutorial control over the conduct of criminal investigation.[222] Yet, the new Code acknowledged that the influence of the judicial authority in the criminal investigation is indispensable, and created the new actor within the course of criminal investigation—the judge for preliminary investigation (*giudice per le indagini preliminari*, GIP).[223] The position of the GIP is undoubtedly weaker than the role previously played by the investigating judge. Primarily this is so since the GIP intervenes only upon the request of the parties and makes a decision on the basis of the information given by them.[224] Therefore, the GIP cannot act *ex officio* and to that extent is no different than the German *Ermittlungsrichter.*

The new GIP has been primarily vested with a power to initiate and control measures that interfere with fundamental rights of freedom, privacy, and property during investigation.[225] The GIP also has power to control the length of criminal investigation and to confirm decisions to discontinue investigation. Initially, the GIP presided over the preliminary hearing aimed at evaluation whether the prosecution of a case should be allowed, but in

218 Article 391bis (3) c.p.p. Cf. Amato (2013), pp. 163–164.
219 Article 391bis (10) c.p.p.
220 Article 391bis (11) c.p.p. See Mangiaracina (2019), p. 244.
221 Cf. Section 3.4.1.
222 Illuminati (2005), p. 567.
223 The *guidice per le indagini preliminary* is sometimes also translated as "judge of freedom" (Ruggieri and Marcolini (2013), p. 369).
224 Gialuz (2017), p. 23 (the author calls the GIP an "unarmed judge" without a file).
225 Ruggieri and Marcolini (2013), p. 369. Cf. Section 8.4.

1998 these powers were transferred to a different authority—the judge for the preliminary hearing (*giudice dell'udienza preliminare*, GUP).[226] The GIP also plays a significant role in relation to taking evidence.

It is true that the GIP maintains no control over investigations, which remain fully with the prosecutor.[227] Therefore, the GIP acts only upon the request of the parties, usually the prosecutor. The forum for the judicial action is the *incidente probatorio* sometimes called the "special evidentiary hearing"[228] or "probatory hearing."[229] Its main feature is that the evidence collected during the *incidente probatorio* is admissible and can be used in court during the trial. The hearing introduced in 1988 initially was created with an aim to allow gathering of such evidence during investigation that could not be obtained in an open court.[230] But in the course of time it has transferred into a tool for the prosecutor that allows to examine the evidence during the criminal investigation. It is for the prosecutor to decide whether the evidence will be taken during the *incidente probatorio* or autonomously.[231]

The prosecutorial powers in conducting criminal investigation are furthermore constrained by unique provisions restricting the time frame of that phase of the criminal process. The most general rule provides that the prosecutor must conclude the investigation within six months from the moment when the case has been disclosed in the prosecutorial register.[232] However, acknowledging that in many cases it might not be enough, it is provided that under certain circumstances a case may be extended. The maximum time limits are set as 18 months for regular crimes[233] and two years for very serious crimes which are listed in the Code.[234] There is, however, the possibility to extend any investigation beyond 18 months even in cases concerning less serious crimes when the prosecutor or the suspect request the conducting of *incidente probatorio* which could not be requested beforehand.[235] In any case the ultimate time limit to conduct criminal investigation is, therefore, two years. The investigative actions carried out after the expiry of the time limit are not used.[236]

The procedure for extension of criminal investigation provides that if the prosecutor is unable to close the investigation at the time of its expiry by

226 Perrodet (2002), p. 355.
227 Illuminati and Caianiello (2007), p. 133 (This is the reason why this judge received the name "judge without a file").
228 See the discussion provided in Gialuz et al. (2017), p. 504.
229 Di Amato (2013), p. 164. Cf. Panzavolta (2004), p. 588, fn. 73.
230 Ruggeri (2017), p. 83.
231 Stefano Ruggeri (2015), p. 70
232 Article 405 (2) c.p.p.
233 Article 407 (1) c.p.p.
234 Article 407 (2) c.p.p.
235 Article 393 (4) c.p.p.
236 Article 407 (3) c.p.p.

filing a case with court or dismissing it, she may request an extension of a further six months from the GIP, providing justification for such request.[237] Further extensions can be granted only if the investigation is particularly complex or if it is impossible to conclude them within the extended time limit.[238] The GIP undertakes an order regarding granting the extension in chambers, notifying the suspect and the victim that a request for extension has been filed with the court.[239] If the extension is denied, the prosecutor has ten days to close the investigation, either by dismissing the case or filing it with the court.[240]

This allows to draw a conclusion that the Italian law aims at limiting the prosecutor in her capacity to conduct lengthy investigations. It seems like a serious restriction that cannot be overcome, since the time limits are stringent, giving no discretion to the prosecutor. However, the practice found a way to circumvent the rigid rules. According to Article 405 (2) c.p.p. the time limit of investigation starts when the name of the suspect is entered into the register, not the reported crime alone. Until the suspect is identified the investigation is conducted against an unknown person (*notita criminis generica*) and if the prosecutor records only the crime committed, claiming that the author of the crime is still unknown, the clock does not start.[241] In such a case, within six months of the date of registration of the crime, the prosecutor submits to the GIP a request to either drop the case or continue investigation.[242] And if the GIP rules that the investigation conducted against an unknown person should be continued there is no time limit for it. In theory, it can last until the statute of limitation has expired.

The way the prosecutors address these apparently rigid rules in practice seems to give back to the prosecutors full control over the length of criminal investigation making judicial oversight of it "ineffective" and "useless."[243] While the GIP has been additionally given a power to compel the prosecutor to enter name of the suspect on register[244]the prosecutor can try to bypass it. This is so since the prosecutor is seamlessly in charge of the file presented to the GIP that may contain only such information that will not lead to identification of a suspect.

237 Article 406 (1) and (2-bis) c.p.p.
238 Article 406 (2) c.p.p. In case of certain crimes, the duration of the investigation may be prolonged only once—Article 406 (2-ter) c.p.p..
239 Article 406 (3)–(4) c.p.p.
240 Article 406 (7) c.p.p.
241 Caianiello (2016), p. 11.
242 Article 415 (1) c.p.p.
243 Caianiello (2016), p. 11.
244 Article 415 (2) c.p.p.

5.5 Conduct of Investigation in the United States of America

5.5.1 The Relationship between Prosecutor and Police

The shape of US police forces responsible for conducting criminal investigation is determined by two important factors. First, there is no separate police body in the USA devoted to the investigation of crimes. Therefore, the investigative function of the law enforcement authorities is usually combined in their daily work, with the powers aimed at prevention of crime. Second, for obvious reasons connected with the federalist structure of the country, law enforcement remains separately organized on the federal, state, and local levels. In the federal system, as well as in each state, there is a great variety of agencies, concerning distinct spheres of criminal behavior, who build a relationship with the prosecution service independently from each other. This makes the picture of the crime investigation in the US particularly complicated.

On the federal level, the primary agency empowered to investigate violations of criminal law is the Federal Bureau of Investigation (FBI). The FBI is perceived as the most powerful of the federal law enforcement agencies, using the most sophisticated methods in crime prevention and investigation.[245] Interestingly, even though the FBI is located in the Department of Justice, as are the US Attorneys, which makes them both a part of the executive, they remain independent of each other.[246]

Besides the FBI, there are several other federal agencies established to act when specific categories of criminal behavior are at stake. These, among others, are: the Bureau of Alcohol, Tobacco, Firearms and Explosives (ATF), the Drug Enforcement Administration (DEA), the Customs Service, the Internal Revenue Service, and the Immigration and Customs Enforcement (ICE). Not all of these are a part of the Department of Justice. Some are organized under the Department of Homeland Security, such as ICE, and some under the Department of Treasury, such as the Internal Revenue Service. But even those agencies that function within the Department of Justice are not subordinated to the US Attorneys with whom they work, and only to some extent to the Attorney General and the Deputy Attorney General.[247]

On the state level, the variety of law enforcement agencies grows further. In each state there is a state police force as well as other state agencies responsible for enforcing the law in its specific areas, such as e.g. gambling or agricultural importation.[248] Many states also have counterparts to the

245 Scheb and Scheb (1999), p. 20.
246 Gilliéron (2014), p. 73.
247 Richman (2003), p. 756.
248 Scheb and Scheb (1999), p. 20.

FBI exercising similar functions.[249] Additionally, in each state separate police forces on a local level (town and county) are established. In some of them, on a county level, the law enforcement powers are exercised by elected sheriffs and in others by the state or municipal police forces.[250] As of 2008, there were 17,985 state and local law enforcement agencies including the local police departments (12,501), sheriffs' offices (3,063), primary state law enforcement agencies (50), special jurisdiction agencies (1,733), and other agencies such as county constable offices in Texas (638).[251] All of them work independently of each other, operating only in their own geographic and political spheres.[252] Partially due to this diversity, but also because of the already discussed remarkable decentralization of the US prosecution service, there is no one scheme on which the police–prosecutor relationship can rely.

Nevertheless, some efforts have been undertaken to regulate that. The guidelines addressed at prosecutors have played an important role in shaping the relationship. According to the ABA Prosecutorial Investigations Standards, the prosecutor should respect the investigative role of the police and other law enforcement agents, by working cooperatively with them to develop investigative policies and providing legal advice regarding their investigative decisions.[253] The prosecutor is also expected to promote compliance with law, take into account the experience, skills, and professional abilities of law enforcement agents, assist in their training, and promote the timely communication concerning developments in investigations.[254] It is also recommended that in cases of complex and nonroutine investigations, in every phase of it the prosecutor should work with the police and other participating agencies and experts, to develop the investigative plan concerning, among others, potential investigative techniques and the legal issues likely to arise during investigation.[255]

In a similar way the NDAA's National Prosecution Standards regulate the prosecutorial relations with the law enforcement. The building of communication between the prosecution office and law enforcement agencies is encouraged[256] as well as the need to provide the police with information regarding the outcome of cases[257] and the assistance in training of law enforcement officers.[258] The prosecutor should advise the police on the legal

249 Hall (2009), p. 287.
250 Scheb and Scheb (1999), p. 21.
251 Reaves (2008), p. 2.
252 Harris (2012), p. 55.
253 26-1.3 (a) SPI.
254 26-1.3 (b)–(d), (f) SPI.
255 26-1.3 (e) SPI.
256 2–5.1 NPS.
257 2–5.2 NPS.
258 2–5.3 and 2–5.4 NPS.

aspects of criminal investigation, but this advisory function pertains only to criminal matters and should not be confused with the function of police in-house counsel.[259]

This gives some guidance in answering the main question concerning the functional and organizational relation that the enormous group of law enforcement agencies existing on local, state, and federal levels maintains with prosecutors. The powers of the prosecutor are weak and mostly of an advisory character. Generally, prosecutors do not have supervisory authority over police departments.[260] This system of cooperation was long ago famously described by Damaška, as a "coordinate model of organization" where the alignment of coordination is more of a horizontal character and authorities have a more equal than a subordinate status.[261] Or, as Richman called it, a "bilateral monopoly."[262] As a result, the prosecutor is incapable of giving orders to police officers and has no functional control over them.[263] Therefore, this relationship can be described as a constant struggle between "independence" and "mutual dependence."[264] However, the lack of formal dependency and forced cooperation established on the normative level between both groups has not precluded them from creating coordinating initiatives of distinct forms including training and enhanced forms of communication.[265]

5.5.2 The Prosecutor's Supervisory Authority over Investigation

The unpronounced normatively most general assumption concerning the authority responsible for the conducting of criminal investigation in US provides that the US police handles the investigative stage of the criminal process with almost complete autonomy.[266] Indeed, it is true that the police are a major player in conducting investigation and this stage does not grab prosecutorial attention until the moment the charging document is issued. But, as in case of all generalizations, this is not the whole truth.

259 Commentary to Standard 2–5, NDAA, National Prosecution Standards, 3rd ed. 2009, https://ndaa.org/wp-content/uploads/NDAA-NPS-3rd-Ed.-w-Revised-Commentary.pdf. Accessed July 12, 2020, p. 23.
260 Gramckow (2008), p. 417.
261 Damaška (1986), p. 44.
262 Richman (2003), p. 758.
263 Brown (2012), p. 201.
264 Harris (2012), p. 556. This has been also repeated by Gilliéron (2014), pp. 73–75.
265 Gramckow (2008), p. 419.
266 Richman (2003), p. 751 ("The police or (in the federal system) 'agents' decide whom to arrest or investigate, and prosecutors decide whom to charge. Each enforcement actor is treated as making an independent discretionary decision, supreme within his realm. If anyone has the upper hand, it is the prosecutor, because she has the last word").

As Langbein stated in his famous article on the origins of public prosecution in common-law systems, in the Anglo-American criminal procedure, public prosecutors perform two primary functions: the "investigatory" role, which is focused on evidence gathering and the "prosecutorial" role, aimed at presenting the evidence to the trier of fact.[267] From his article one could assume that this is a well-known fact. Yet, in 1999 Little had to shout in her article "SURPRISE! Prosecutors investigate,"[268] as this was a revelation. The truth is that US prosecutors indeed do investigate. It is also the truth that they may do it less often than their European counterparts. There are at least three prima facie reasons that create an impression that US prosecutors are absent from criminal investigation. First, they are engaged and visible during the trial when they actively argue the case, as well as in plea bargaining of cases. This role of the prosecutor is so profound that it almost seems as the only sphere of her activity during criminal proceedings. Second, the lack of assigned, on the normative level, supervisory powers over police activity, paired with broad competencies given to the police, results in perceiving prosecutors as unnecessary participants of investigations. Finally, and perhaps most importantly, the charging process happening early in the course of the criminal process, which moves a case quickly to the pretrial, blurs the boundaries of criminal investigation and prosecution, effectively making unclear the role of the prosecutor in the former. This demands some further explanation.

Because of the wide use of arrests frequently taking place very early in the course of investigations and causing a necessity to present the suspect immediately to the court through the initial appearance scheme, the involvement of the prosecutor in the criminal process is triggered soon after a crime has been discovered. This is so, because it is the prosecutor who argues in this adversarial environment before a judge whether the suspect should be released on bail. And from the moment a case hits the court proceedings and appears on the docket, the prosecutor assumes control over it. Therefore, if the case must be pushed further through the system toward trial, it will be the prosecutor deciding what evidence should be gathered along the way. As a result, the active participation of the prosecutor in criminal investigation happens a lot more often than books tend to admit if we consider post-charging events as a part of criminal investigation.

Another element of this complicated puzzle of dependencies is the customary rule, that while for the police the case ends whenever the suspect is arrested, for the prosecutors, information gathered up to that point by the police enabling the arrest remains far from being sufficient to win in

267 Langbein (1973), p. 313.
268 Little (1999), p. 724.

court. Thus, it happens that the prosecutors often receive incomplete and inadequate reports considered as sufficient by the police. The practical studies show that these reports often lack names and addresses of victims and witnesses, full details of how the crime was committed, and laboratory reports.[269] This makes the quality of police reporting the primary factor affecting prosecution.[270] As a result, the prosecutors, learning about a case for the first time during the initial appearance, are often faced with two options. One to drop the charges due to insufficiency of evidence, as prosecutors may do exercising their broad discretionary powers. And second, to carry on with the case being aware that further investigation is necessary to prove the case beyond reasonable doubt.[271] In the common situation when the prosecutor has received the police report and is willing to go to trial, she must carry on investigation herself. This is usually done with the help of investigators (inspectors) hired within each prosecutor's office, or by resorting to the police.

In order to illustrate this mechanism, we consider the example of the State of Connecticut. Within each of the thirteen state's attorney offices, their chiefs may appoint inspectors required to conduct investigations concerning criminal offenses and to assist in all investigations and other matters pertaining to the criminal business of the office, or the judicial district, and in procuring evidence for the state in any criminal matter.[272] Importantly, inspectors have the same powers as officers of the state police, including the power of arrest within the state.[273] This means that after the case reaches the docket and comes to the prosecutor's attention, she may resort to the inspectors for help in the conducting of investigation necessary for successful preparation for the trial. That doesn't mean that, in such an arrangement, the police cannot be called to support the prosecution. On the contrary, the law imposes an obligation on the police to provide all assistance to the state's attorney office in carrying out investigations.[274] This regulation is not in any way atypical to the rules and practice as applied in other states.[275] As a result, prosecutors throughout the USA, while conducting post-arrest investigations, make use

269 The study by Nugent and McEwen conducted in 1983 quoted in Neubauer and Fradella (2019), p. 191.
270 Jacoby and Ratledge (2016), p. 35.
271 There is also another possibility that, unfortunately, is not that uncommon. Despite the lack of evidentiary grounds prosecutors often decide to bargain the plea counting on the terrified accused to accept the offer and end the case. See more in Turner (2012), pp. 102–115.
272 § 51–286 (a) CGS.
273 § 51–286 (b) CGS.
274 § 51–286 (d) CGS.
275 The same mechanism is also available on the federal level. See on investigative units within US Attorneys' Offices in Richman (2003), p. 825.

of investigators (inspectors) and the police to help in gathering evidence. It is also acknowledged by the ABA guidelines regarding prosecution function that funds should be available to the prosecutor's office to employ professional investigators.[276]

The prosecutor can act at earlier, even prearrest. Generally, the conduct of criminal investigation in the USA is highly dependent on the nature of the crime being investigated. Even though US criminal procedure does not provide a formally distinctive scheme of procedures relating to the seriousness of the crime,[277] the type of a crime nevertheless influences the level of engagement of the prosecutor in investigation. In more complex cases, where investigations, sometimes taking years, precede arrest and charging, not only the prosecutor, but also other institutions, become substantially involved even at a very early stage in investigations.[278] In many of those cases the prosecutor will participate actively through grand jury proceedings, gaining enormous investigatory powers.[279] But even without resorting to the grand jury mechanism, the US prosecutors are engaged in crime investigation on a daily basis. This fact has been recognized on numerous occasions in literature and in case law. This is particularly true for the federal prosecutors to carry on pretrial investigations[280] but also on the state level, in rural areas especially, the prosecutor may be the primary investigating officer and some state legislatures have given the prosecutor the chief responsibility for detection, arrest, and conviction of criminals in her county.[281] Certainly, some states provide for greater powers in that area than some others. One of the examples of a more generous jurisdiction is the State of Florida, where the prosecutor is even empowered to summon witnesses,[282] which was famously confirmed in *Imparato* v. *Spicola*, where the District Court of Appeal of Florida stated that indeed the prosecutor is

> the investigatory and accusatory arm of our judicial system of government, subject only to the limitations imposed by the Constitution, the common law, and the statutes, for the protection of individual rights and to safeguard against possible abuses of the far-reaching powers so confided.[283]

276 Standard 3-2.3 PFS.
277 See more in Section 3.5.1.
278 Miller and Wright (2007), p. 725.
279 See Section 5.5.3.
280 Singband (2001), p. 1967–68.
281 Sigler (1979), p. 61.
282 § 27.04 Florida Statutes.
283 238 So. 2d 503 (Fla. Dist. Ct. App. 1970),

The power of the prosecutors to actively participate in investigations is broadly acknowledged, e.g. by the ABA Standards on Prosecutorial Investigation. In its Preamble it is recognized that "a prosecutor's investigative role, responsibilities and potential liability are different from the prosecutor's role and responsibilities as a courtroom advocate" although conceding that "Standards may not be applicable to a prosecutor serving in a minor supporting role to an investigation undertaken and directed by law enforcement agents."[284] The Standards than contain a long list of suggestions regarding measures to be undertaken during investigations. They regulate the use of many other measures available during investigation, such as arrests, subpoenas, secret surveillance, undercover operations, and, in particular, provide guidance on what factors should be taken under consideration by the prosecutor when recommending the use of such measures during criminal investigation. For example they provide that, in cases when the prosecutor is involved in an investigation, the prosecutor should review applications for search warrants prior to their submission to a judicial officer, and in all other cases, the prosecutor should encourage police and law enforcement agents to seek prosecutorial review and approval of search warrants prior to their submission.[285]

The measures available to prosecutors are broad. But the practice regarding the level of engagement of the prosecutors in criminal investigations varies, not only depending on the type of a crime and its gravity, but also upon the practice adopted in the particular prosecutor's office. In one interesting study from 2018 concerning conduct of investigations relating to violent crimes, it was found that, e.g. prosecutors in Kansas City remain on the regular two-week long crime scene duties and take part in all homicide crime scenes, while prosecutors from Little Rock or Milwaukee almost never attend crime scenes.[286] The practice varies also regarding interrogations. While prosecutors in the Bronx following arrest conduct a videotaped interview with the suspect and obtain a summary statement, those in Kansas City observe the custodial interrogations and provide advice to law enforcement officers that conduct it.[287]

284 American Bar Association, *Standards on Prosecutorial Investigations* (3d ed. 2014), p. 7.

285 Standard 26-2.8 (d) SPI.

286 *Investigating Violent Crime: The Prosecutor's Role: Lessons Learned from the Field*, National Resource & Technical Assistance Center, June 2018. https://crimegunintelcenters.org/wp-content/uploads/2018/09/Investigating-Violent-Crime-The-Prosecutors-Role-Lessons-Learned-from-the-Field-NRTAC-June-2018.pdf. Accessed July 12, 2020, p. 5.

287 *Investigating Violent Crime: The Prosecutor's Role. Lessons Learned From the Field*, National Resource & Technical Assistance Center, June 2018. https://crimegunintelcenters.org/wp-content/uploads/2018/09/Investigating-Violent-Crime-The-Prosecutors-Role-Lessons-Learned-from-the-Field-NRTAC-June-2018.pdf. Accessed July 12, 2020, p. 7.

But also in such situations when the supervisory prosecutorial powers are not formally demanded, some prosecution offices, in cooperation with the police, set the computer-messaging systems to exchange documents and establish frequent phone and personal consultations and in some cases even conduct daily briefings.[288] These strategies have been successfully adopted with the aim of improving coordination and cooperation between offices to enhance the quality of criminal investigations.

US criminal law does not provide for straightforward limitations of the duration of criminal investigation. Nor does it burden the prosecutor with the responsibility for the length of this stage of criminal process. But there are certainly boundaries to the length of the criminal process as a whole, that also have an impact on criminal investigation.

Generally, all criminal defendants have a right to a speedy trial as per the Sixth Amendment.[289] This applies to all criminal processes on the federal level and has been extended to states by the Fourteenth Amendment to the Constitution. But the US Constitution does not specify a time limit by which a case is deemed to be no longer valid. Therefore, the US Supreme Court in the landmark decision *Barker* v. *Wingo* provided some guidance, stating that four factors must be taken into consideration: the length of delay, the reason for the delay, whether the defendant has asserted the right to a speedy trial, and how seriously the defendant was prejudiced.[290]

Despite efforts to narrow down the vagueness of "unnecessary delay," the federal and state legislatures felt the need to specify it in a more straightforward way. The Speedy Trial Act[291] enacted in 1974, provides that the time from arrest to indictment cannot exceed 30 days, from indictment to the trial 70 days.[292] However, certain time periods are to be excluded, such as examination of the mental competency or physical capacity of the defendant or pretrial motions.[293] Similar provisions are set on the state level.[294] For example, in the State of Connecticut, the trial should start within 12 months from filing the indictment or information with the court or from the date of the arrest, whichever is later, unless the defendant is incarcerated, in which case the trial commences within eight months.[295] Accordingly, the excludable times are provided in the state law including delays resulting from other

288 Neubauer and Fradella (2019), p. 191.
289 "In all criminal prosecutions, the accused shall enjoy the right to a speedy and public trial."
290 *Barker* v. *Wingo*, 407 US 514, 530 (1972).
291 Speedy Trial Act, 88 Stat. 2080, 18 USC §§ 3161–3174.
292 18 USC § 3161 (b) and (c)(1).
293 18 USC § 3161(h)(1)(A) and (D).
294 Neubauer and Fradella (2019), p. 159.
295 § 54-82m CGS.

proceedings against the same defendant, as well as the defendant's mental incompetence or physical inability to stand a trial.[296] However, the right to a speedy trial may be waived by the defendant.[297] This is unfortunately her common decision which results in nonobservance of regulations prescribed in this place.

Everything what has been discussed above regarding the right to a speedy trial applies from the moment the defendant is arrested or formally charged. Taking into account that a significant amount of investigatory measures are undertaken after arrest, the applicability of right to a speedy trial to that part of investigation is obvious. However, does this right extend also to the prearrest stage of criminal process? The answer to this question was given in *United States* v. *Marion*, where the Supreme Court argued that "the Sixth Amendment's guarantee of a speedy trial is applicable only after a person has been 'accused' of a crime," since the text of the Amendment refers to "criminal prosecutions."[298] There is, nevertheless, some hope. The court has also suggested that the violation of due process would exist "if it were shown at trial that the pre-indictment delay . . . caused substantial prejudice to rights to a fair trial and that the delay was an intentional device to gain tactical advantage over the accused."[299] But taking into account the considerably small number of long precharging investigations, which happen in high-profile cases often involving grand jury, this is rather of marginal character.

5.5.3 The Investigative Authority of the Prosecutor

It is believed that US prosecutors do not normally possess any specific powers, exclusive to them, during the criminal investigation. This is not entirely true. Although in some states they do not interfere even when warrants are issued, in some others and in the federal system, prosecutors are very much engaged in that process.[300] Moreover, in some jurisdictions the prosecutor just reviews applications prepared by police officers, while in some others she may be obliged to prepare the application for a warrant herself.[301]

The prosecutorial engagement in conducting other investigative measures may be even more visible. A good example is the interception of communications. To obtain a wiretap warrant on the federal level, the

296 § 43-40 CPB.
297 § 43-43 CPB. See more in Tomasiewicz (2015), pp. 288–289.
298 *United States* v. *Marion* 404 US 307, 313–320 (1971).
299 *United States* v. *Marion* 404 US 307, 324 (1971). See Dressler and Thomas (2017), p. 1023.
300 See on the search warrant applications in federal law by government attorneys—Rule 41 (b) FRCP, and in case of Connecticut by state attorneys—Sec. 54-33a CGS.
301 Neubauer and Fradella (2019), p. 331.

prosecutor must either apply for it or authorize such application.[302] Therefore, it is fair to say that US prosecutors do have investigative authority, or at least their participation in certain criminal investigations is inevitable.

Moreover, prosecutorial powers tremendously increase when one considers the unique position that the prosecutor plays in grand jury proceedings. The grand jury is an extraordinary organ, composed of laypeople, primarily granted with a power to decide whether or not to accuse a person with a crime. This is a so-called shield power preventing mistaken or vindictive prosecution, available in federal criminal law and in most states, at least for some felonies.[303] But from the perspective of conducting criminal investigations, even more interesting are the investigative powers that a grand jury possesses. These are considered as "sword" powers enabling a grand jury to actively combat crime and uncover evidence unavailable during criminal investigation.[304] And because the most important role during grand jury proceedings is played by the prosecutor, the investigative authority of a grand jury becomes the power that in reality belong to the prosecutor.

How the extensive coercive competencies of a grand jury are so easily transferrable to the prosecutor can be answered through the structure of this organ and its relationship with the prosecutor. A grand jury is composed of 16 to 23 laypeople[305] on a similar basis as the regular juries deciding cases in criminal trials. However, they are empaneled for a set period: ten days up to 24 months depending on the state.[306] This allows them to build much stronger ties with the criminal justice system than is the case for regular jurors.

What is the most striking is the organization of the daily work of a grand jury. To put it simply, grand jury proceedings are "orchestrated" by the prosecutor.[307] The main feature of these proceedings is the unrestricted control that the prosecutor possesses over the activities undertaken by a grand jury. Usually they remain passive and all actions during hearings are initiated by the prosecutors whose actions a grand jury only observes. Commentators also point out that there is no legal provision that allows jurors to obtain any additional assistance in the proceedings and they rely solely on the prosecutor for this purpose.[308] Besides the prosecutor, a grand jury only contacts

302 18 USC § 2518. Similar regulation can be found in state systems. See e.g. in case of Connecticut § 54-41b CGS.
303 Kamisar et al. (2012), p. 747.
304 Kamisar et al. (2012), p. 747.
305 This is so on the federal level (Rule 6(a)(1) FRCP). It might be much different in case of state systems.
306 Neubauer and Fradella (2019), p. 302.
307 Vorenberg (1981), pp. 1537–1538.
308 Schiappa (1993), p. 332.

the judge, who swears them in, gives them instructions on the nature of their duties, and assists them when they decide to call witnesses to give evidence, but is not involved in the proceedings herself.[309] It is the prosecutor who convenes a grand jury, directs proceedings, takes evidence, questions called, witnesses, and drafts the indictment.[310] Although nothing stands in the way of the jury taking an active part in these activities, it is rare. The dominance of the prosecutor's office over the proceedings seems to be obvious, also because of the lack of legal knowledge and experience that the jury should have.

One of the characteristics of a grand jury that creates an environment contributing to full prosecutorial control over its actions is the secrecy of the proceedings conducted before grand jury.[311] Only prosecutors, witnesses, interpreters (if necessary), and reporters are allowed to participate in such proceedings.[312] Moreover, the minutes of the proceedings of the jury as well as the orders and summonses issued by a grand jury are never disclosed.[313] The main reason for establishing the full secrecy of proceedings is the need to ensure the protection of the person against whom proceedings are brought.[314] If a grand jury decides not to prosecute, there is no stigma for the individual. Theoretically, the effect of a grand jury's activity is that the charge is brought before a court, but in practice it is a recognition that the prosecution has gathered enough evidence to convict the accused; it is therefore an act that can ruin his or her career and reputation. The secrecy of the proceedings is also designed to protect the jurors from attacks by the public, as is sometimes the case with members of an ordinary jury who pass unpopular convictions or acquittals, or even possible retaliation by others interested in the outcome of the proceedings.

Despite these arguments, the secrecy of proceedings allows the prosecutors to keep control over the jurors and softly force on them what the prosecutors expect. This is particularly helpful when the prosecutor wants to use a grand jury in its investigative function, to obtain evidence that she cannot gather by regular means. Among the mechanisms that can be used by a grand jury is its power to formally summon witnesses to testify (*subpoena ad testificandum*). A grand jury may also force witnesses to provide documents (*subpoena duces tecum*), although this power is a bit more controversial.[315]

309 Miller and Wright (2007), p. 725.
310 Dressler and Thomas (2003), p. 824.
311 Rule 6(e)(2) FRCP.
312 Rule 6(d)(1) FRCP.
313 Rule 6(e)(6) FRCP.
314 See *United States* v. *Procter & Gamble Co.*, 356 US 677 (1958) for the complex analysis on the aims of secrecy of grand jury proceedings.
315 Kamisar et al. (2012), p. 750.

Failure to appear before a grand jury to testify or give evidence is considered as criminal contempt that can result in imprisonment. A grand jury may also use other coercive measures, e.g. in the *United States* v. *Dionisio* case, the grand jury's right to require 20 witnesses to submit samples of their votes in order to carry out comparative tests with material obtained on the basis of an interview control ordered by the court was confirmed.[316]

A grand jury's power to summon witnesses is the only way to receive coerced information from the witness at this stage of the criminal process. Neither the police, nor the prosecutor has the power to issue subpoenas or otherwise compel unwilling witnesses or victims to give statements, or even talk to them.[317] And the court subpoenas are only permitted to compel witness attendance at trials or other hearings. Giving such a power to the authority conducting the investigation is perceived as detrimental to the freedom of the individual and, as such, should be protected.[318] Therefore, at the investigative stage, the law enforcement agencies may interview a witness only with her consent, either where the witness is encountered or by inviting her to the police station. In the latter case the presence of the witness is voluntary and the conversation with her, even if recorded, may be interrupted by the witness at any time. Any forcible appearance of the witness at the police station means that she has been detained and therefore should be informed of the famous *Miranda* rights,[319] gaining certain protection. Such a system obviously limits the evidentiary capacity of law enforcement agencies, as not all potential witnesses will be willing to share their knowledge voluntarily. Therefore, the only way prosecutors can compel a witness to come forward is if a grand jury conducts the investigation and issues a subpoena.

From the efficiency of the investigation standpoint, the proceedings before a grand jury and the powers that it possesses may therefore appear to be extremely advantageous. This is also a direct reason for its popularity as an instrument available to prosecutors. Interestingly, the literature points out that hearings before a grand jury exerts a particular kind of psychological pressure on the witnesses, which makes them particularly eager to give their testimony, even if they were silent beforehand.[320] This is supposed to result from a sense of moral compulsion to be honest, in a situation in which the disclosure of information held is to take place not toward law enforcement authorities, but toward citizens of "equals."[321]

316 410 US 1, 93 (1973).
317 Burnham (2011), pp. 270–271.
318 Kremens (2019a), p. 251.
319 *Miranda* v. *Arizona*, 384 US 436 (1966).
320 Kamisar et al. (2012), p. 751.
321 Keeney and Walsh (1978), p. 579.

The prosecutor also may use further mechanisms such as less restricted rules on the admissibility of evidence. As decided in the landmark case *Costello* v. *United States*[322] many of the evidentiary rules that apply at the trial stage are not applicable to proceedings before a grand jury. In particular, the relaxation of rules concerning hearsay evidence and rights derived from the Fourth and the Fifth Amendment, although this causes a considerable amount of controversy and the practice among states varies.[323]

In this context, the scope of evidence presented to a grand jury becomes a fundamental issue. Proceedings before a grand jury are not adversarial and it is not a "small trial" similar to that of an ordinary jury. It is based solely on evidence presented by the prosecutor, and the suspect as well as her defense counsel have neither the right to participate in it nor to present their evidence during the proceedings.[324] And as a rule, the prosecutor is not obliged to disclose evidence in favor of the accused, as discussed in *United States v. Williams*, that the imposition of such a duty on the prosecutor would be contrary to the role of a grand jury in the US criminal trial system.[325] On the other hand, various codes of ethics and instructions to prosecutors require them to disclose evidence in favor of the accused, including in proceedings involving a grand jury.[326]

The criticism directed at the grand jury focuses mostly on the instrumentalization of this institution by prosecutors. The fact that the grand jury does not necessarily perform its functions in the best possible way can be seen from one of the most frequently cited statements evaluating this institution, which indicates that "a grand jury would indict a ham sandwich if the prosecutor asked it to."[327] Speaking somewhat less vividly, the US Supreme Court in the *United States* v. *Dionisio* also expressed the belief that "[t]he grand jury may not always serve its historic role as a protective bulwark standing solidly between the ordinary citizen and an overzealous prosecutor."[328] Stronger is the voice of Justice Douglas, dissenting and pointing out that the grand jury, instead of fulfilling its actual function, had become "a tool of the Executive" over time.[329]

322 350 US 359, 76 S.Ct. 406, 100 L.Ed. 397 (1956).
323 Kremens (2019a), p. 252.
324 Scheb and Scheb (1999), p. 134.
325 *United States v. Williams*, 504 U.S. 36, 112 S.Ct. 1735, 118 L.Ed. 2d 352 (1992)
326 § 9–11.233 JM. A similar regulation is contained in Rule 3–3.6 (b) of the American Bar Association Standards for Criminal Justice, Prosecution Function Standards.
327 This has been quoted among others by Cassidy (2000), p. 361 and Bibas (2001), p. 1171, fn. 403.
328 410 US 1, 17 (1973).
329 410 US 19, 23 (1973).

Statistically speaking, a grand jury very rarely makes decisions incompatible with the prosecutor's intentions. According to official data, prosecutors obtain indictments in 99.6 percent of cases in which they initiated grand jury proceedings.[330] The literature mainly cites examples of cases in which a grand jury filed an indictment with the court whenever the prosecutor has requested it. But a grand jury usually makes decisions in accordance with the prosecutor's intentions, also where the prosecutor does not wish to prosecute the case.[331] This happens when the prosecutor wants to use the grand jury as a protection from accusations from the victim and the public when she wishes not to charge a person with a crime. Instead of simply dismissing the case, the prosecutor may initiate grand jury proceedings and hide behind this authority without having to explain the reasons for such decision. Sometimes prosecutors also even decide to use this institution in cases of a political nature, so that the responsibility for deciding to file an indictment with the court is blurred between themselves and the jury.[332]

The State of Connecticut is an atypical example of a grand jury system. It is referred to as a "one-man investigatory grand jury,"[333] since the responsibility of conducting investigation is vested in hands of a single judge and not a group of laypeople. This can be seen as contradictory to what had been historically available in the common-law system. But the investigative grand jury in Connecticut remains a creation of statutes[334] and only because of the function it serves—investigating cases—does it bear the same name.[335]

Unlike many states, Connecticut does not have regularly sitting grand juries.[336] Instead an investigatory grand jury may only be appointed by a grand jury panel[337] upon the written application by a judge, the Chief State's Attorney, or a State's Attorney.[338] When making an application, the applicant must have a reasonable belief that the administration of justice requires an investigation to determine whether there is probable cause that a crime has been committed.[339] Moreover, the power to conduct an investigation

330 Dressler and Thomas (2017), p. 918.

331 Dressler and Thomas (2017), p. 919 (the authors cite as an example the proceedings in which the prosecutor referred to the grand jury a case in which a 30-year-old woman was suspected of living with a 16-year-old student with his consent).

332 Miller and Wright (2007), p. 216.

333 *Connelly* v. *Doe*, 213 Conn. 66, 70 (1989)

334 §§ 54-47b through 54-47h CGS.

335 See *State* v. *Menillo*, 159 Conn. 264, 273 (1970).

336 Gailor (2015), p. 135.

337 The "grand jury panel" is a panel of three Superior Court judges designated by the Chief Justice of the Supreme Court from time to time to receive applications for investigations into the commission of crimes, one of whom may be the Chief Court Administrator (§ 54-47b (4) CGS).

338 § 54-47c CGS.

339 § 54-47c (a) CGS.

involving the one-man grand jury is limited to certain types of crimes, which include crimes involving corruption in the state or local government, organized crime or racketeering activity, violation of state elections laws, or any felony punishable by more than five years' imprisonment for which Chief State's Attorney or a State's Attorney is able to show that there is no other means of obtaining enough information as to whether a crime has been committed or the identity of the person who committed it.[340] In the application, if it's made by the Chief State's Attorney or a State's Attorney, it must also include information regarding other "normal investigative procedures" used which have failed or reasons why they were not tried.[341]

How often is the investigative grand jury used in the State of Connecticut? The available data speaks for itself: very rarely. According to a 2016 official study, between 1985 and 2015 only 43 applications for a grand jury were made, of which only in 27 was an investigatory grand jury appointed.[342] This gives less than one so case investigated every year of the 30-year period. The reason for such a low number is the complicated and time-consuming process of appointing the judge as a grand jury[343] as well as the strictly limited number of cases that can be investigated by it.

5.5.4 The Role of the Parties in the Conduct of Investigation

The adversarial nature of the US criminal process has its straightforward implications, of which equality of arms paired with belief in revealing the truth are perhaps most significant. As a consequence of making a prosecutor a party to the criminal process, the system created a necessity to provide the defendant with a right to counsel, one of the most fundamental rights guaranteed in a criminal process. One of the obligations of defense counsel is the duty to investigate. This is so because the "adversarial balance cannot take place without investigation by both the prosecution and the defense."[344]

The duty to investigate is not stated in legal norms in any way. It is, however, pronounced by the US Supreme Court in the landmark case *Strickland*

340 See for full list of crimes for which an investigatory grand jury may be used § 54-47b (2) CGS.

341 § 54-47c (c) CGS.

342 See Kirby (2016).

343 Gailor (2015), p. 135.

344 Roberts (2004), p. 1105. The author supports her view by quoting the *United States v. Nixon*, 418 US 683, 709 (1974) ("The ends of criminal justice would be defeated if judgments were to be founded on a partial or speculative presentation of the facts. The very integrity of the judicial system and public confidence in the system depend on full disclosure of all the facts, within the framework of the rules of evidence").

v. *Washington*[345] addressing the issue of the effective assistance of counsel. As a result, defendants are entitled to be represented by counsel, regardless of whether appointed or retained, with a right to be represented, not only during the trial stage, but to be provided with effective assistance that should be understood broadly. The defense counsel "has a duty to make reasonable investigations or to make reasonable decision that makes particular investigation unnecessary."[346] What this duty encompasses and how the "ineffective assistance of counsel" should be interpreted in general is one of the most frequently addressed issues in appellate opinions.[347]

Ever since *Strickland* ruling, the duty to investigate has been evaluated through the lens of the trial. This was partially a result of perspective adopted in it where it was explicitly stated that "[c]ounsel also has a duty to bring to bear such skill and knowledge as will render the trial a reliable adversarial testing process."[348] It was not until *Missouri* v. *Frye*[349] and *Lafler v. Cooper*[350] when the Supreme Court rejected the trial-centered conception of the right to counsel. And since the trial is no more the essential element in the criminal process, the obligation to investigate should apply also during earlier stages in the criminal process, e.g. with plea-bargained decisions.[351]

Defense counsel is therefore burdened with the duty to conduct adequate investigation into facts and witnesses, but whether this extends to expert witnesses is debatable.[352] Some guidance here is provided in the ABA Criminal Justice Standards—The Defense Function.[353] They have become an important instruction, although the Supreme Court has warned on numerous occasions including in *Strickland* that

> they are only guides. No particular set of detailed rules for counsel's conduct can satisfactorily take account of the variety of circumstances faced by defense counsel or the range of legitimate decisions regarding how best to represent a criminal defendant.[354]

345 466 US 668 (1984).
346 *Strickland* v. *Washington* 466 US 668, 691 (1984).
347 Kamisar et al. (2012), p. 143.
348 *Strickland* v. *Washington* 466 US 668, 688 (1984).
349 566 US 134 (2012).
350 566 US 156 (2012).
351 Marceau (2012), p. 1162.
352 See Saltzburg (2018) discussing possibility to conduct an effective defense investigation without the assistance of expert testimony.
353 *ABA Criminal Justice Standards for the Defense Function*, 4th ed. Washington: American Bar Association 2017 (hereafter: DFS).
354 *Strickland* v. *Washington* 466 US 668, 688–689 (1984).

The most general rule confirms that defense counsel has a duty to investigate in all cases, and to determine whether there is a sufficient factual basis for criminal charges.[355] This duty should commence promptly and should not be affected by the force of the prosecution's arguments or the defendant's desire to plead guilty.[356] The defense counsel should seek to secure relevant information in the possession of the prosecution, law enforcement authorities, and others, as well as conduct independent investigation.[357] This extends to engaging fact investigators, forensic, accounting, or other experts, or other professional witnesses such as sentencing specialists or social workers.[358] Moreover, it is the responsibility of counsel to seek resources from the court, the government, or donors if the client lacks sufficient resources to pay for necessary investigation.[359] Further regulations relate to distinct forms of evidence such as witnesses, expert witnesses, and physical evidence, providing detailed ways in which they should be handled.[360] The bottom line in the investigative actions undertaken is that defense counsel should not use illegal or unethical means to obtain evidence or information, or employ, instruct, or encourage others to do so.[361]

5.5.5 The Judicial Involvement in the Conduct of Investigation

The judge plays the most significant role during the course of criminal investigation when intervening in the infringement of the rights and freedoms of individuals e.g. issuing arrest and search warrants. Her role in that regard is clear and unquestionable even though practice shows that the preauthorized searches and arrests are a minority when compared to those conducted without a warrant. This will be further discussed later in this book.[362]

This section focuses on the role of the judge during the criminal investigation in terms of taking evidence. In all three Continental countries such powers of the court upon the request of the prosecutor or other parties exist. Although these powers should not be confused with the broad investigatory powers that "investigative judge" once had in these states. We have seen that in the USA similar powers are invested in the judge in the State

355 4–4.1(a) DFS.
356 4–4.1(b) DFS.
357 4–4.1(c) DFS.
358 4–4.1(d) DFS.
359 4–4.1(e) DFS.
360 4–4.3 – 4.4.7 DFS.
361 4–4.2 DFS.
362 See Section 7.5.

of Connecticut, employed in her "one-man grand jury" capacity.[363] But this should be considered as an extraordinary tool than the effective system widely used among US states.

Another mechanism has been, however, identified as recalling the evidentiary powers of European courts participating in evidence-taking during criminal investigation: the deposition.[364] A deposition is oral testimony recorded out of court for future use in court proceedings.[365] While this procedure is widely used in civil proceedings for various purposes it is much more restricted in criminal cases being permitted only to preserve the testimony of a witness who might not be available at trial (due to age, infirmity, etc.).[366] Under federal law the court may order deposition upon a party's request in order to preserve testimony for a trial "because of exceptional circumstances and in the interest of justice."[367] The scope of the court's order may also include document, recordings, or data, etc.

As reported, the practice among states varies with regard to the level of judicial involvement in making depositions.[368] In Connecticut it has been recognized that there is a common-law rule that the party had no right to depose a prospective witness, even upon proof that the witness was not likely to be available at trial.[369] But this has been replaced by the rules allowing for depositions in criminal cases in four circumstances: (1) where physical infirmity prevents the witness from testifying, (2) where the witness's presence cannot be compelled by an out-of-state subpoena, (3) where the witness is otherwise unavailable, and (4) where an expert witness has not filed a report.[370] The party that requested deposition should notify other parties about taking depositions who make take part including the right of the defendant to be present and represented by counsel.[371] The role of the court is limited to ordering the deposition and deciding on its organization. But the deposition may be taken before any officer authorized to administer oaths even though the examination of a witness during deposition is the same in its scope as during trial including the cross-examination.[372] Despite detailed provisions, the case law regarding depositions is considered as sparse and the use of deposition "extremely rare."[373]

363 See Section 5.5.3.
364 Del Duca (1991), p. 83.
365 Hall (2009), p. 458.
366 Kamisar et al. (2015), p. 1129.
367 Rule 15 (a) FRCP.
368 Kamisar et al. (2015), p. 1130.
369 *State* v. *Zaporta*, 237 Conn. 58, 64 (1996).
370 § 40–44 CPB.
371 §§ 40–47 and 40–54 CPB.
372 § 40–50 CPB.
373 Kirschbaum (2017), p. 375.

5.6 Summary

The relationship between the prosecutor and the police and other law enforcement agencies in the four examined countries provides for distinct approaches towards the shape of investigation. Their relationship is however predetermined by the adopted system of state authority. While in the case of Poland and Italy the national agencies have been created with a clear hierarchical structure and systems of dependency, the federalist states of the USA and Germany offer a decentralized structure. The US system is particularly fragmented, where state, city, and county police offices are organized independently of each other, even within one state.

But when it comes to the organizational and functional relation of the prosecution service and the police some more interesting features can be observed. In all four countries there is no dependence on the prosecution service on the part of the police. Even in states that openly declare the proximity of the prosecution to the executive (the USA, Poland through the recent merger of Minister of Justice with Attorney General, and to some extent Germany) of which the police are a part, there is no organizational link between the two. This results from proximity of the prosecution service to the Ministry of Justice that puts distance between prosecution and the police, usually subordinated to the Ministry of Internal Affairs. This makes it more difficult to oversee and supervise the police actions and demand execution of prosecutorial instructions and orders when available within the system.

On the functional side, the power of the prosecutor to give orders to the police is clearly articulated in the three European states. The law provides for a power to demand certain investigative actions and the police are obliged to answer to the prosecutor regarding the conduct of investigation. The system has its flaws, since for instance both in Poland and Germany police agents are not answerable directly to the prosecutor who must resort to their "real" supervisors in matters of discipline. Moreover, in Germany the police are officially allowed to prioritize crime prevention over prosecutorial needs. Only in the case of Italy can we even speak about subordination, since the judicial police in that country are located within the prosecutor's office and closely cooperate with the prosecutor in criminal investigations.

In the USA, the independence of the police from the prosecutor is strongly underlined and the prosecutor is expected to respect the investigative role of the police and engage rather as a consultant or a trainer and not the supervisor. Yet, as discussed above, when the case reaches the charging stage the prosecutors assume control over investigation, which does not cease at that point. Prosecutors have at their disposal investigators (inspectors) exercising a policing function throughout the investigation if necessary. Also, the prosecutors maintain competence to demand certain investigatory actions to be undertaken by various agencies at their request, even if based more on a mutual cooperation mechanism than a rigid normative rule. The effect might be similar to the one achieved in the Continental system, since the European prosecutors are also described as having no effective instruments to enforce their orders. Therefore, in all cases the relationship seems to be rather built on trust and personal competencies and communication skills than being an effect of normative prescriptions.

The normatively established relationship between police and prosecution impacts the supervisory role of the prosecutor during criminal investigation. The power of the prosecutor to issue orders to the police during criminal investigation in Continental countries is closely bound with the supervisory role of the prosecutor over that phase of the criminal process. In each of these countries, in theory, the prosecutor maintains control over the whole criminal investigation from its very beginning until the very end. But as discussed in Chapter 4, the immediate embracement of investigation by the prosecutor, even though in some states demanded by law *expressis verbis*, does not always happen in practice and the police retain considerable freedom in that regard. So, the broad supervisory powers of the prosecutor over criminal investigation as prescribed in Germany, Poland, and Italy remain just a theory. Additionally, in each of these countries the police possess their own competence to undertake investigative measures at least early in the criminal investigation before the case file is submitted to the prosecutor and also in the course of proceedings when exigent circumstances demand action. Moreover, each European country provides for the separate powers of the police that can be exercised by them without the awareness of the prosecutor exercising control over such investigation. In the case of Poland this is possible in all types of crimes if the prosecutor delegates such investigation to the police. Similarly, in Italy these powers are based on the delegated authority of the prosecutor.

It should, however, be noted that Germany, Italy, and Poland provide for very wide lists of separate measures that can be undertaken only by the prosecutor. This includes measures such as suspect interrogations and undertaking coercive measures during investigation. However, this should not mean that the prosecutors engage in investigation every time they are empowered to do so. Rather they restrict themselves to decision-making, becoming "judges before the judges" which on the other hand allows the police to engage in practice in independently carrying out the task of crime investigation.[374]

374 Jörg-Albrecht (2000), p. 255.

The US case seems quite different; prosecutors having no direct powers to issue orders to the police and no clearly prescribed competence to supervise criminal investigation. In practice, though, the role of the prosecutor during investigation is recognized also in the US criminal process, contrary to the popular belief that she is entirely absent from it. In particular, the prosecutor gets involved in investigation when the case concerns more severe crimes in which prosecutors are actively engaged from the very beginning, even before the arrest takes place. But prosecutors also regularly take active control over those investigations that directly aim at preparing evidence for the trial when the case passes the arrest stage and the accused has not pleaded guilty. Therefore, while not every US criminal investigation involves a prosecutor, some do. One interesting observation comes from the role of the US prosecutor defined in that system as not authorize to directly interfere with the rights and freedoms of the individual. Even though the engagement of the prosecutor in investigation is formally and normatively lower than in case of her European counterparts, which would prompt the assumption that her objectivity is considerably larger than German, Polish, and Italian prosecutors, the US system firmly excludes the prosecutor from the group of authorities empowered to do so. This issue will be further explored in Chapter Seven.

But there is no doubt that the investigatory authority of the US prosecutor is much weaker than her counterparts from Europe and she cannot, for instance, summon the witness and the suspect for interrogation. The US prosecutor is without the superpowers that their German, Italian, and Polish colleagues have that manifestly enhance the effectiveness of criminal investigation. This stems from the philosophy standing behind the purpose that is served by investigation in these states. If the evidence gathered during investigation is perceived as having the same probative value as the evidence taken during the trial it is expected that the prosecutor will have similar powers as the judge. This approach enables prosecutor to call and question witnesses during investigation in a similar way as is done during the trial by the judge. To the contrary, if the investigation is not focused on gathering and preserving all relevant evidence for the future trial, there is no need to equip the prosecutor with the same powers. Consequently, also the police in such system cannot resort to such measures during investigation and any coercion used should be imposed with judicial approval, at least in theory. There is, however, one interesting exception to that rule. As discussed, the prosecutor may resort in certain cases to a grand jury, if the law provides for its existence, to employ the investigatory functions normally unavailable during investigation, that allow for compulsory interrogations of witnesses and suspects and summoning documents.

The dynamics between the prosecution service and the police when it comes to powers over conducting criminal investigations is not affected by the role that the court and the parties play during criminal investigation in taking evidence. In all four countries the judicial authority is called on to decide on the measures that relate to infringement of rights, but also to take part in preserving evidence for trial. Despite distinct circumstances under which this can be done, each country provides for mechanisms that, upon the prosecutor's request, allow for interrogating unavailable witnesses. Thus, the scope of the judicial powers in that regard is so weak that she is rather just "subordinate to the prosecutor's wishes."[375]

The systems differ as to how the parties engage in criminal investigation. While in Poland the suspect and the victim, by law may only request evidentiary actions to be performed by the prosecutor and the police, and are forbidden to undertake any investigative actions themselves, all other countries allow for independent defense investigations. This does not preclude the parties in Germany from filing with the prosecutor similar requests as is done in the Polish case. This might be also why in Germany the power to independently conduct investigation by the defense is rarely used. The division between the approaches stems from the adopted system models. While the adversariality of the Italian and US systems calls for allowing the parties to collect evidence independently, and based on it advance their arguments during trial, Poland and Germany rely on the premise of the objective prosecutor able to gather evidence against, as well as for, the accused. In the latter case, conducting the investigation in an official way makes the independent investigation unneeded.

Two important conclusions can be drawn here. First, the law deviates from practice to a significant extent. The reasons for this have been aptly summarized by Mathias, who identified two factors that, in his opinion, made a shift in powers between the police and the prosecutor allowing the former to dominate criminal investigation; the failure of the police in their duty to inform the public prosecutor about committed crimes and the passivity of the prosecutor during the investigations.[376] It is true that on the normative level in some of the researched states (Germany, Poland, and Italy) the supervisory powers of the prosecutor have a mandatory character and should commence almost immediately after information that a crime has been committed reaches the prosecutor, while in the US case the supervisory powers are never required by law and only triggered when the prosecutor so wishes. But all countries, even those that provide for the mandatory supervision of prosecutors, report that they refrain from observing such rules in full.

375 Weigend (2012), p. 379.
376 Mathias (2002), p. 472.

The cause is obvious and simply results from the overwhelming number of cases that are investigated in all countries, which makes it simply impossible to keep all cases under the careful and conscious control of the prosecutor.

Therefore, in practice, prosecutors do not supervise the case unless the crime is sufficiently serious or there are other circumstances that force her to actively engage in proceedings. And even if they report that they do, such supervision has an illusionary character. And even though the prosecutorial function on the European Continent indeed includes oversight of police investigations to guarantee accuracy and compliance with the individual rights,[377] this standard in all cases is simply unachievable, as the European examples show.

This leads to the second conclusion that the relationship between prosecution and police in the conduct of criminal investigation is not homogeneous in nature and is shaped to a great extent by the type of offense the investigation concerns. There is, indeed, a virtual consensus in Europe, even if it goes against the letter of law, that the prosecutors should be personally involved in the investigation of serious crimes.[378] Therefore, one can observe a tendency toward greater involvement of the prosecutor in proceedings relating to more serious crimes while the participation of the prosecutor in investigations involving minor offenses is reduced or even eliminated, in contravention of rules. In cases of some major offenses, especially those demanding the use of coercive measures, since the prosecutor also plays a role in their imposition, the presence of the prosecutor will be even more visible.

In sum, with minor offenses, it is observed that regardless of the criminal justice system discussed, the police play a crucial role when it comes to limiting the powers possessed by the prosecutor during the criminal investigation by deciding which cases to investigate and which to hand over to the prosecution. Even in those states which on the normative level force the police to report crimes to the prosecutor without delay, in practice this rule is not strictly respected. As reported, in all these states either this legal obligation is not observed by delaying the transfer of the report beyond the prescribed time frame, or the police circumvent the law by not transferring information to the prosecutor at all until the end of the investigation. The prosecutor is therefore at the mercy of the police, especially since the hidden discretion can be easily employed by the police. As discussed in Chapter 4, even the rigid rules forcing the police to bring to the prosecutor information about *every* crime are rarely employed.

The reasons for the practice of excluding the prosecutor from criminal investigation have been recently rehearsed by Weigend, who suggested that

377 Luna and Wade (2010), p. 1482.
378 Luna and Wade (2010), p. 1482.

they result from the manpower and expertise on the side of the police.[379] The failure to supervise investigations effectively may open the door to extensive and uncontrolled police powers that, accordingly, can undermine both the rights of the suspect as well as those of the victim.[380] But should the answer to this problem be the strengthening of the prosecutor's role during criminal investigation? I return to this crucial question in Chapter 9.

References

Bibas S (2001) Judicial Fact-Finding and Sentence Enhancements in a World of Guilty Pleas. *Yale Law Journal* 110:1097–1185.

Brodowski D, Burchard C, Kotzurek N, Rauber J, Vogel J (2010) Germany. In: Cape E, Namoradze Z, Smith R, Spronken T (eds) *Effective Criminal Defence in Europe*. Intersentia, Antwerp, pp. 253–319.

Brodzisz (2015) Komentarz do art. 316 k.p.k. In: Jerzy Skorupka (ed) *Kodeks postępowania karnego*. Komentarz. CH Beck, Warsaw.

Brown DK (2012) American Prosecutors' Powers and Obligations in the Era of Plea Bargaining. In: Luna E, Wade M (eds) *The Prosecutor in Transnational Perspective*. Oxford University Press, Oxford, pp. 200–213.

Bulenda T, Gruszczyńska B, Kremplewski A, Sobota P (2010) The Prosecution Service Function within the Polish Criminal Justice System. In: Jehle J-M, Wade M (eds) *Coping with Overloaded Criminal Justice Systems. The Rise of Prosecutorial Power Across Europe*. Springer, Heidelberg, pp. 257–284.

Burnham W (2011) *Introduction to the Law and Legal System of the United States*. 5th edn. West, St Paul.

Caianiello M (2010) Italy. In: Cape E, Namoradze Z, Smith R, Spronken T (eds) *Effective Criminal Defence in Europe*. Intersentia, Antwerp, pp. 373–423.

Caianiello M (2012) The Italian Public Prosecutor: An Inquisitorial Figure in Adversarial Proceedings. In: Luna E, Wade M (eds) *The Prosecutor in Transnational Perspective*. Oxford University Press, Oxford, pp. 250–267.

Caianiello M (2016) *Increasing Discretionary Prosecutor's Powers: The Pivotal Role of the Italian Prosecutor in the Pretrial Investigation Phase*. Oxford Handbooks Online, Oxford.

Cassidy RM (2000) Toward a More Independent Grand Jury. Recasting and Enforcing the Prosecutor's Duty to Disclose Exculpatory Evidence. *Georgetown Journal of Legal Ethics* 13:361–403.

Damaška MR (1986) *The Faces of Justice and State Authority*. Yale University Press, New Haven and London.

De Vocht D (2010) Poland. In: Cape E, Namoradze Z, Smith R, Spronken T (eds) *Effective Criminal Defence in Europe*. Intersentia, Antwerp, pp. 425–488.

379 Weigend (2012), p. 379.
380 Montana (2009), p. 310.

Del Duca LF (1991) An Historic Convergence of Civil and Common Law Systems – Italy's New "Adversarial" Criminal Procedure System. *Dickinson Journal of International Law* 10:73–92.

Di Amato A (2013) *Criminal Law in Italy*. Kluwer Law International, Alphen aan den Rijn.

Dressler J, Thomas GC (2017) *Criminal Procedure. Principles, Policies and Perspectives*. West Academic Publishing, St. Paul.

Elsner B, Peters J (2010) The Prosecution Service Function within the German Criminal Justice System. In: Jehle J-M, Wade M (eds) *Coping with Overloaded Criminal Justice Systems. The Rise of Prosecutorial Power Across Europe*. Springer, Heidelberg, pp. 207–236.

Frase RS, Weigend T (1995) German Criminal Justice as a Guide to American Law Reform. *Boston College International and Comparative Law Review* 18:317–360.

Gailor MA (2015) Grand Jury, Arraignment, Transfers from Juvenile Court, Bail and Probable Cause Hearings. In: Schuman CJ (ed) *Connecticut Criminal Procedure*. Connecticut Law Tribune, Hartford, pp. 141–232.

Gialuz M (2017) The Italian Code of Criminal Procedure: A Reading Guide. In: Gialuz M, Lupária L, Scarpa F (eds) *The Italian Code of Criminal Procedure. Critical Essays and English Translation*. Cedam, Milan, pp. 17–55.

Gialuz M, Lupária L, Scarpa F (eds) (2017) *The Italian Code of Criminal Procedure. Critical Essays and English Translation*. Cedam, Milan.

Gilliéron G (2004) *Public Prosecutors in the United States and Europe*. Springer, Cham.

Giostra G (1994) Pubblico ministero e polizia giudiziaria nel processo di parti. In: *Centro Nazionale di Prevenzione e Difesa Sociale, Problemi attuali di diritto e procedra penale*. Il pubblico ministero oggi, Milan.

Gramckow H (2008) Prosecutor Organization and Operations in the United States. In: In: Open Society Institute Sofia (ed) *Promoting Prosecutorial Accountability, Independence and Effectiveness*. Open Society Institute Sofia, Sofia, pp. 385–432.

Grande E (2000) Italian Criminal Justice: Borrowing and Resistance. *American Journal of Comparative Law* 48:227–259.

Grzegorczyk T (2010) Kilka refleksji na temat sugestii wprowadzenia instytucji sędziego śledczego. In: Hofmański P (ed) *Węzłowe problemy procesu karnego*. Oficyna a Wolters Kluwer, Warsaw, pp. 105–114.

Hall DE (2009) *Criminal Law and Procedure*. Delmar, Clifton Park.

Harris DA (2012) The Interaction and Relationship Between Prosecutors and Police Officers in the United States and How This Affects Police Reform Efforts. In: Luna E, Wade M (eds) *The Prosecutor in Transnational Perspective*. Oxford University Press, Oxford, pp. 54–66.

Huber B (2008) Germany. In: Vogler R, Huber B, *Criminal Procedure in Europe*. Duncker & Humblot, Berlin, pp. 269–371.

Illuminati G (2004) The Role of the Public Prosecutor in the Italian System In: Tak PJP (ed) *Tasks and Powers of the Prosecution Services in the EU Member States*. Volume I. Wolf Legal Publishers, Nijmegen, pp. 303–332.

Illuminati G (2005) The Frustrated Turn to Adversarial Procedure in Italy (Italian Criminal Procedure Code of 1988). *Washington University Global Studies Law Review* 4:567–581.

Illuminati G, Caianiello M (2007) The Investigative Stage of the Criminal Process in Italy. In: Cape E, Hodgson J, Pranken T, Spronken T (eds) *Suspects in Europe. Procedural Rights at the Investigative Stage of the Criminal Process in the European Union*. Intersentia, Antwerp, pp. 129–154.

Jacoby JE, Ratledge EC (2016) *The Power of the Prosecutor. Gatekeepers of the Criminal Justice System*. Praeger, Santa Barbara.

Jasiński W, Kremens K (2019) *Criminal Law in Poland*. Kluwer Law International, Alphen aan den Rijn.

Jörg-Albrecht H (2000) Criminal Prosecution: Developments, Trends and Open Questions in the Federal Republic of Germany. *European Journal of Crime, Criminal Law and Criminal Justice* 8(3):245–256.

Juy-Birmann R (2002) The German System. Delmas-Marty M, Spencer JR (eds) *European Criminal Procedures*. Cambridge University Press, Cambridge, pp. 292–347.

Kamisar Y, LaFave WR, Israel JH, King NJ, Kerr OS, Primus EB (2015) *Modern Criminal Procedure. Cases-Comments-Questions*. West, St. Paul.

Keeney J, Walsh P (1978) The American Bar Association's Grand Jury Principles: A Critique from a Federal Criminal Justice Perspective. *Idaho Law Review* 14:545–590.

Kirby M (2016) Connecticut's Investigatory Grand Jury, Office of Legislative Research (2016-R-210). www.cga.ct.gov/2016/rpt/pdf/2016-R-0210.pdf. Accessed 12 July 2020.

Kirschbaum DAR (2017) Discovery and Depositions. In: Schuman CJ (ed) *Connecticut Criminal Procedure*. The Connecticut Law Tribune, Hartford, pp. 333–382.

Kremens K (2019a) Grand Jury and Involvement of Citizens in Criminal Proceedings in the Light of U.S. v. P. Manafort and R. Gates. *Ius Novum* 13:241–264.

Kremens K (2019b) Oględziny zwłok, sekcja zwłok, ekshumacja. In: Skorupka J (ed) *System Prawa Karnego Procesowego, Dowody*. Volume VIII. Wolters Kluwer, Warsaw, pp. 5155–5218.

Kruszyński P (2007) The Investigative Stage of the Criminal Process in Poland. In: Cape E, Hodgson J, Pranken T, Spronken T (eds) *Suspects in Europe. Procedural Rights at the Investigative Stage of the Criminal Process in the European Union*. Intersentia, Antwerp, pp. 181–209.

Kulesza C (1991) *Sędzia śledczy w modelu postępowania przygotowawczego na tle prawnoporównawczym*. Dział Wydawnictw Filii UW w Białymstoku, Białystok.

Lach A (2005) The Prosecution Service of Poland. In: Tak PJP (ed) *Tasks and Powers of the Prosecution Services in the EU Member States*. Volume 2. Wolf Legal Publishers, Nijmegen, pp. 597–616.

Langbein JH (1973) The Origins of Public Prosecution at Common Law. *American Journal of Legal History* 17: 313–335.

Little R (1999) Proportionality as an Ethical Percept for Prosecutors in Their Investigative Role. *Fordham Law Review* 68:723–770.

Luna E, Wade M (2010) Prosecutors as Judges. *Washington and Lee Law Review* 67:1413–1532.

Mangiaracina A (2019) Report on Italy. In: Quattrocolo S, Ruggeri S (eds) *Personal Participation in Criminal Proceedings*. Springer, Cham, pp. 229–278.

Marceau JF (2012) Embracing a New Era of Ineffective Assistance of Counsel. *University of Pennsylvania Journal of Constitutional Law* 14:1161–1218.

Mathias E (2002) The Balance of Power between the Police and the Public Prosecutor. In: Delmas-Marty M, Spencer JR (eds) *European Criminal Procedures*. Cambridge University Press, Cambridge, pp. 459–487.

Miller ML, Wright RF (2007) *Criminal Procedures: The Police*. Aspen Publishers, New York.

Montana R (2009) Paradigms of Judicial Supervision and Co-ordination between Police and Prosecutors: The Italian Case in a Comparative Perspective. *European Journal of Crime, Criminal Law and Criminal Justice* 17:309–333.

Neubauer DW, Fradella HF (2019) *America's Courts and the Criminal Justice System, 13th edn*. Cengage, Boston.

Nowak C, Steinborn S (2013) Poland. In: Ligeti K (ed) *Toward a Prosecutor of the European Union, Volume 1: A Comparative Analysis*. Hart Publishing, London, pp. 498–509.

Panzavolta M (2004) Reforms and Counter-Reforms in the Italian Struggle for an Accusatorial Criminal Law System. *North Carolina Journal of International Law & Commercial Regulation* 30:577–624.

Perrodet A (2002) The Italian System. In: Delmas-Marty M, Spencer JR (eds) *European Criminal Procedures*. Cambridge University Press, Cambridge, pp. 348–411.

Reaves BD (2008) *Bureau of Justice Statistics, Census of State and Local Law Enforcement Agencies*. U.S. Department of Justice, Washington.

Richman DC (2003) Prosecutors and Their Agents. Agents and Their Prosecutors. *Columbia Law Review* 103:749–832.

Roberts J (2004) Too Little, Too Late: Ineffective Assistance of Counsel, the Duty to Investigate, and Pretrial Discovery in Criminal Cases. *Fordham Urban Law Journal* 31:1097–1155.

Rogalski M (2016) Nadzór prokuratora nad postępowaniem przygotowawczym. In: Ryszard Stefański (ed) *System Prawa Karnego Procesowego. Postępowanie przygotowawcze*. Volume X. Wolters Kluwer, Warsaw, pp. 1050–1135.

Ruggeri S (2015) Investigative and Prosecutorial Discretion in Criminal Matters: The Contribution of the Italian Experience. In: Caianiello M, Hodgson JS (eds) *Discretionary Criminal Justice in a Comparative Context*. Carolina Academic Press, Durham, pp. 59–85.

Ruggeri S (2017) *Audi Alteram Partem in Criminal Proceedings*. Springer, Cham.

Ruggieri F, Marcolini S (2013) Italy. In: Ligeti K (ed) *Toward a Prosecutor of the European Union, Volume 1: A Comparative Analysis*. Hart Publishing, London, pp. 368–404.

Saltzburg SA (2018) The Duty to Investigate and the Availability of Expert Witnesses. *Fordham Law Review* 86:1709–1726.

Scheb JM, Scheb JM II (1999) *Criminal Procedure*. Wadsworth, Belmont.

Schiappa SM (1993) Preserving the Autonomy and Function of the Grand Jury. *Catholic University Law Review* 43:311–350.

Siegismund E (2003) The Public Prosecution Office in Germany: Legal Status, Function and Organization. In: Effective Administration of the Police and the

Prosecution in Criminal Justice. The 120th International Senior Seminar, Visiting Experts' Papers www.unafei.or.jp/publications/pdf/RS_No60/No60_10VE_Siegismund2.pdf. Accessed 12 July 2020, pp. 58–64.

Sigler JA (1979) The Prosecutor: A Comparative Functional Analysis. In: McDonald WF (ed) *The Prosecutor*. Sage, Beverly Hills, pp. 53–74.

Singband LR (2001) The Hyde Amendment and Prosecutorial Investigation: The Promise of Protection for Criminal Defendants. *Fordham Urban Law Journal* 28:1967–2003.

Tomasiewicz P (2015) Double Jeopardy, Pre-Arrest Delay, Speedy Trial, and Prosecutorial Discretion. In: Schuman CJ (ed) *Connecticut Criminal Procedure*. Connecticut Law Tribune, Hartford, pp. 233–295.

Trendafilova E, Róth W (2008) Report on the Public Prosecution Service in Germany. In: Open Society Institute Sofia (ed) *Promoting Prosecutorial Accountability, Independence and Effectiveness*. Open Society Institute Sofia, Sofia, pp. 213–246.

Turner JI (2012) Prosecutors and Bargaining in Weak Cases: A Comparative View. In: Luna E, Wade M (eds) *The Prosecutor in Transnational Perspective*. Oxford University Press, Oxford, pp. 102–115.

Vogel B (2019) Report on Germany. In: Quattrocolo S, Ruggeri S (eds) *Personal Participation in Criminal Proceedings*. Springer, Cham, pp. 123–164.

Vorenberg J (1981) Decent Restraint of Prosecutorial Power. *Harvard Law Review* 94:1521–1573.

Waltoś S (1968) *Model postępowania przygotowawczego na tle porównawczym*. PWN, Warsaw.

Weigend T (2004) The Prosecution Service in the German Administration of Criminal Justice. In: Tak PJP (ed) *Tasks and Powers of the Prosecution Services in the EU Member States*. Wolf Legal Publishers, Nijmegen, pp. 203–222.

Weigend T (2012) A Judge By Any Other Name? Comparative Perspectives on the Role of the Public Prosecutor. In: Luna E, Wade M (eds) *The Prosecutor in Transnational Perspective*. Oxford University Press, Oxford, pp. 377–391.

Weigend T (2013) Germany. In: Ligeti K (ed) *Toward a Prosecutor of the European Union, Volume 1: A Comparative Analysis*. Hart Publishing, London, pp. 264–306.

Chapter 6

Powers of the Prosecutor over the Preliminary Charging

6.1 General Considerations

Much has been written on the power that has been vested in the prosecutor to charge an individual. This decision is considered as one of the most important and consequential of those made by the public officials notwithstanding the differences that exist between legal systems. The discussion on the charging powers of the prosecutor focuses so frequently on the scope of her discretion, that it seems that the topic has been almost exhausted. Such questions as who the prosecutor may charge, what charge should she impose and, most importantly, what are the influences and constraints to making this decision, are all of interest to scholars. When combined with the growing powers of the prosecutor concerning engagement in negotiated settlements, this topic becomes arguably the most heated debate in the criminal process discourse as discussed in Chapter 1.

But at the same time the earlier stage of the criminal process when the preliminary determination regarding charges is being made, and where the suspect is identified as a target of criminal investigation, attracts far less attention, while this in fact seems to be that moment which is just as pivotal, if not more. Therefore, this chapter will be devoted to analysis of sometimes hard-to-grasp procedure, in which an individual learns that she became a suspect in criminal proceedings. The difficulty in capturing how this happens stems from the diversity of ways in which the attachment of the status of suspect is being carried on not only in distinct legal systems but even within each of them. Nonetheless, the importance of the preliminary charging is determined by two factors.

The first lies with the criminal justice authorities. Establishing the identity of suspect is their ultimate goal, as without this no charges can be brought. Obviously, lots can be said about failures to effectively search for suspects, but in general the criminal justice authorities are geared towards fighting crime and devoted to doing their job, even if some of their attempts cannot be called successful. Moreover, the determination of a suspect allows the police and other agencies to focus their actions on a designated individual and to gather even more evidence to eventually convince the trier of facts of her guilt. Finally, in some countries, imposition of investigative measures of coercive character is allowed only against the person with a status of a suspect. Therefore, if the criminal justice authorities want to detain it might be possible only when she has been preliminary charged first.

The second reason lies with the suspect herself, which concerns gaining by her a unique status with which a certain amount of protection is provided. Among these, is the right to be informed about scope of accusations. This right as available at the early stage of the criminal process needs to be distinguished from the defendant's right to learn about the prosecution evidence before trial.[1] The prerequisite for conducting a useful defense is a right to know the nature and cause of accusation as stated in one of the ECtHR judgments.[2] For the defense to commence early in the course of criminal investigation, the individual should have a right to know what she is suspected. And it should be known to her as soon as the criminal proceedings are starting to be aimed against her. Only then can the suspect begin preparing her defense, with possibly support from an attorney, among others. Some authors even argue that an individual's right to be informed that she is under investigation is crucial, since it affects the applicability of all other rights.[3]

Two types of consequences flow from the initial charging decision. On one hand, as mentioned before, when an individual becomes a suspect, she gains certain rights and may start to effectively defend herself. It is crucial that it is done in time to prepare a proper defense before the trial starts. This also allows the suspect and her attorney to actively participate in investigation. They may try to convince the prosecutor and police that the suspect was not involved in the allegedly committed crime, which even in some situations may help to avoid of wrongful accusations. But the initial charging decision has also an adverse effect. Regardless of the presumption of innocence, there are those who adhere to the adage no smoke without fire, so when charges are brought some will feel tainted. Especially where someone has been detained they may suffer; other people can be impacted in different ways, including in their professional lives. Therefore, the label of the suspect might upset an individual in the most harmful ways.

Since the preliminary charging is so consequential, how the term is used in this chapter and throughout the whole work demands explanation. It should be understood as the procedure aimed at identifying and designating

1 Weigend (2017), p. 939.
2 *Pelissier and Sassi* v. *France*, March 25, 1999, 25444/94, § 54.
3 Caianiello (2010), p. 390.

an individual as a suspect which attaches certain rights to provide her with sufficient protection during the course of criminal investigation.[4] The "preliminary charging" can be also understood as the procedure of "initially charging a person with a crime" and both expressions will be used interchangeably within this work.

It must be admitted, however, that the phrases "preliminary charging" or "initially charging" are rarely used and not clearly distinguishable from the term *charging*, due to their ambiguity, vagueness, and the overlap in their meaning. However, this is not just the result of distinct approaches towards the charging decision as is expected to appear in between Continental and common-law countries. This is also a problematic issue even within the boundaries of the European states. Despite of the use of *criminal charge* in Article 6 § 1, 2, and 3 ECHR, which could suggest that there is one common understanding of this term, it does not resolve the problem at all. To the contrary, the ECtHR has noted on several occasions that the concept of criminal charge as used in Article 6 has an autonomous meaning[5] which means that the Court's interpretation of it is made solely for the purpose of the Convention and its understanding is not binding on other occasions. However, of some guidance may be that the approach taken by the ECtHR on that concept is more of "substantive" rather than "formal" character.[6] In some decisions the Court has confirmed that such acts as the arrest[7] and questioning the suspect about the involvement in a crime,[8] despite the formal treatment of the individual as a witness, could be all regarded as equal to being charged with a criminal offense. From this perspective, the relation between the term *accusation* and *charging* should not be understood as being obvious and may also be a subject of misunderstandings leading to treating them separately, at least in light of the ECtHR case law.[9] However, for the purpose of this work the term *preliminary charging* will maintain the meaning similar to the one proposed by the ECtHR while *accusation* and *charging* will be used interchangeably as synonyms, both meaning accusing someone formally of having committed an offense by filing a case with the court denoting the decision to prosecute.

For the sake of clarity, it should be also noted that the term *suspect* will be reserved for those who were preliminarily but not formally charged with a crime while the term *accused* will be reserved for a person who has already

4 See also a similar approach undertaken in Ruggeri (2015), p. 70.
5 *Blokhin* v. *Russia*, no. 47152/06, March 23, 2016 (Grand Chamber), § 179; *Adolf* v. *Austria*, no. 8269/78, March 26, 1982, § 30.
6 *Deewer* v. *Belgium*, no. 6903/75, February 2,71980, § 44.
7 *Heaney and McGuiness* v. *Ireland*, no. 34720/97, December 21, 2000, § 44.
8 *Yankov and Others* v. *Bulgaria*, no. 39084/97, December 11, 2003, § 23.
9 See discussion in Scarpa et al. (2017), p. 75.

gone through a formal charging procedure that accused her of crime which is connected with e.g. filing an indictment with the court.[10] Explanations of the problems that the adoption of such terminology causes in each of the researched systems are given below for each of the four case studies.[11] Moreover, in some of the researched countries, the preliminary charging procedure encompasses the "interrogation" of the suspect. It has been decided that the term "interrogation" will be used throughout this work regardless of the authority carrying on this measure i.e. prosecutor, police, or, in some cases, even the judge. Therefore, this term will be used interchangeably with such words as "questioning" or "interview" despite some distinctions in the meaning that may be associated with these terms.[12]

Finally, it should also be explained that the purpose of this work is not to describe the rights of the suspect in detail. This has been successfully achieved by various authors.[13] This is not to say that the topic is unimportant or does not need further research. Definitely the scope of rights, when they attach, and what they truly mean, remains an important issue and should be continuously researched, in particular in the light of the recent activity of the EU legislation aimed at setting a common standard regarding the rights of the individual with an aim to enhance the suspect's protection. But it is not the aim of this work to focus on the rights as such, but to identify under what circumstances, by what means, and— most importantly—by whose decision, they attach to the individual during the course of criminal investigation.

6.2 Preliminary Charging in Germany

6.2.1 General Considerations concerning Charging Decisions

The decision to charge a person with an offense in Germany is the final act of the investigation. It takes the form of filing an indictment (*Anklageschrift*) with the court.[14] This provision, in very general terms, establishes not only a threshold that allows for such a decision (*genügenden Anlaß zur Erhebung der öffentlichen Klage*) but also confirms that the power to file an indictment with the court remains exclusively with the prosecutor. According to the principle of accusation (*der Anklagegrundsatz*), as provided in § 151 StPO, without the formal accusation of the prosecutor, no court will be able to

10 The similar approach has been undertaken in e.g. Thaman (2001), p. 589 fn. 61.

11 See Sections 6.2.1, 6.3.1, 6.4.1, and 6.5.1.

12 Some authors argue that the term "interview" has a more friendly and non-inquisitorial connotation than "interrogation" (Malsch and De Boer (2019), p. 319).

13 See e.g. Cape et al. (2010); Cape et al. (2007) and partially also Ligeti (2013).

14 § 170 (1) StPO.

hear a case.[15] The law also provides for other forms of charging instruments i.e. the request for imposition of a penal order,[16] which is also considered as fulfilling the accusation principle.

Therefore, the formal charging of a person with an offense always takes a written form. The contents of the indictment are provided in § 200 StPO and include detailed information concerning accused, the crime she is accused of, and a note of the evidence supporting the indictment. This document is accompanied by the full dossier of the materials gathered during investigation and sent to the court.[17] The procedure of submitting an accusation does not entail the presence of the accused and she is not expected to appear before the court until the court proceedings commences. The accused may take representation and present her position on the admission of indictment[18] but this is just a right and not an obligation and it is never presented orally. As a result, the first personal encounter of the accused with the court will take place upon the commencement of the court proceedings sometime after the indictment has been admitted which might be the beginning of a trial.

But before the formal accusation is filed with the court, the future accused retains certain powers allowing her to actively participate in criminal investigation and prepare for the future trial. This is based on the view that she is an autonomous actor in the criminal process, being a party in the proceedings and not a mere object in the process.[19] This applies fully to the investigative stage, at least from a certain moment in time when the investigation starts to focus on a specified person. Yet, German law does not provide for any formal act designating a person to become the suspect.[20] This raises a vital question regarding the status of an individual who is not yet officially charged with a crime and, in particular, whether this individual is guaranteed certain rights in the course of criminal investigation and, most importantly, when exactly these rights attach to her. According to Weigend and Salditt the person becomes a suspect rather through a totality of circumstances that enforces the change of status and not at any particular moment in the course of investigation.[21]

In this context terminology describing the individual against whom proceedings are conducted becomes particularly problematic, since it varies

15 Kühne (1993), p. 146; see also Bohlander (2012), pp. 24–25.
16 § 407 StPO.
17 § 199 (2) StPO.
18 § 201 (1) StPO.
19 Weigend (2017), p. 938.
20 Weigend (2013), p. 270.
21 Weigend and Salditt (2007), p. 89.

according to the stage of criminal proceedings.[22] A person suspected of a crime is referred to as a *beschuldigter*—"suspect," after the filing of an accusation with the court she becomes *Angeschuldigte*—"accused," and after the acceptance of the accusation *Angeklagter*—"defendant."[23] It shall be noted, however, that some other sources provide distinct interpretations of these notions e.g. associating the term "accused" with *Beschuldigter.*[24] This is not without reason, since an individual prior to obtaining the status of *Beschuldigter* has the status of *Tatverdächtiger*, an individual against whom some suspicion exists but not enough to become the suspect, which makes it difficult to find an adequate translation for the latter term if the former is translated as a suspect. But for the purpose of this work, based on the resolutions adopted for other states,[25] the *Beschuldigter* will be consequently translated as a "suspect" while the *Tatverdächtiger* will be translated as a "suspected person."

And it is precisely the distinction between the terms "suspect" and "suspected person" which is particularly significant, since only the status of a suspect brings certain rights to a person during criminal investigation and presumably leaves a suspected person with no protection. Therefore, since there is no specified preliminary charging decision that would allow for such clear distinction, it is possible to identify two separate ways by which a person acquires the status of a suspect. First of all, every individual that the prosecutor wishes to indict is examined, at the latest, prior to the conclusion of the investigations.[26] Therefore, it will be exactly during the interrogation that the suspect will learn about her status as such, as well as about the offenses that she is charged with.[27] But, a person may also become a suspect when the police decides to undertake such an investigative measure from which it becomes clear that the criminal investigation is conducted against her.[28] For example, when an application for the arrest warrant against individual is filed with the court, it becomes clear that the police considers such person as a suspect.[29]

In the literature, a third method of becoming a suspect is also mentioned, i.e. when the law enforcement agency has objectively collected sufficient factual indications that the person concerned has committed a crime but

22 Juy-Birmann (2002), p. 303.

23 See Weigend (2013), p. 270; Juy-Birmann (2002), p. 303; Bohlander (2012), pp. 16–17. See also an interesting discussion on the issue in Polish literature, by Girdwoyń (2006), pp. 232–235.

24 See e.g. Huber (2008), p. 300 and Brodowski et al. (2010), p. 259.

25 See, in particular the explanation of the translation adopted for Poland in Section 6.3.1.

26 § 163a (1) StPO. Note that the interrogation is not mandatory if the prosecutor plans to end criminal investigation with dismissal.

27 § 163a (3) StPO.

28 BGH Beschl. 28.02.1997, StB14/1996, NJW 1997, 1591.

29 Brodowski et al. (2010), p. 259–260.

did not decide to initiate formal proceedings and interviewed such person as a witness and not a suspect.[30] Even though the authors agree that the latter scenario is illegal, and the courts have the power to determine during the trial whether a defendant while interrogated as a witness should have been treated as a suspect, it is hard to accept that this is "a way to become a suspect." This is rather a failure to attach the rights to an individual even if corrected in some way during the court proceedings. But despite that, it is true that it is tempting for the criminal justice authorities to avoid attaching the status of a suspect and proceed against a witness (suspected person) who possesses no comparable rights. It happens in practice that regardless of availability of the evidence that the suspect should be interrogated as such, the prosecutor and police withhold the suspect's interrogation as well as the information about the charges until the very end of the investigation.[31] It leads not only to a serious restriction of the suspect's defense rights but precludes the authorities from the possibility to obtain the suspect's cooperation in searching for a compromise resolution of the case which might make a trial unnecessary.[32]

When it comes to the consequences of not properly informing the suspect of charges, there is no straightforward answer in German law or practice. Remedies for failures to inform of some other rights are much clearer. For example, withholding the information on the right to counsel results in the exclusion of evidence.[33] But, at the same time, a violation of the caution about the right to remain silent may not result in exclusion if e.g. it can be proven that the right was already known to the suspect.[34] It is believed that in a case of withholding from the suspect, information on her charges, the court would rather apply a balancing test than automatic exclusionary rule, calling evidence inadmissible only when the accused's interest in effective defense outweighs the social interests of a fair and effective prosecution.[35] However, if the statements that the accused has made results from "deception" (*Täuschung*) the law provides for their immediate exclusion even if the accused agrees to their use.[36] Misleading the accused by saying that the investigated crime against the accused is minor compared to the one really investigated, can add up to "deception" and therefore in such a case the subsequent statements of the accused may be excluded based on their

30 Brodowski et al. (2010), p. 260.
31 Weigend (2017), p. 944.
32 Weigend (2017), p. 944 (fnn. omitted).
33 Brodowski et al. (2010), p. 270.
34 See broader explanation in Bohlander (2012), pp. 96–97.
35 Brodowski et al. (2010), p. 270. See also Meyer-Grossner and Schmitt (2018), § 136, nb 21.
36 See § 136a (1) and (3) c.p.p.

inadmissibility.[37] But there are voices that the rules on admissibility of such statements should be equated, resulting in their exclusion.[38]

6.2.2 Threshold for Preliminary Charging

Since the German system does not provide for any formal act or decision that would attach the status of a suspect to a certain person, there is no separate decision released by officials initially charging a person with an offense. As discussed above, most commonly the suspect will acquire her status by initiation of a formal investigation against her through the interrogation with preliminary charges being presented prior to questioning. Such interrogation is required for each suspect before the end of investigation unless the proceedings result in termination.[39] But the law remains silent both on when exactly such an interrogation should take place and on the threshold that should exist to employ such measure.

In establishing these circumstances, other thresholds that must exist when certain actions during criminal investigation are to be undertaken are helpful. The public prosecution is obliged to take action in relation to all prosecutable criminal offenses, provided there are *zureichende tatsächliche Anhaltspunkte*—sufficient factual indications.[40] This rule provides for mandatory prosecution, but should be understood more broadly, also covering the investigative stage. Therefore, this is not only an obligation to prosecute but also an obligation to investigate (if sufficient factual indications exist) and should be understood as such. It should also be borne in mind that the principle of legality (*Legalitätsprinzip*), despite some exceptions, remains a founding premise of the German criminal process that forces the authorities to act.[41] The law is nevertheless silent on whether from this principle one can also derive an obligation to interrogate the suspect as soon as the criminal justice authorities realize that this is the individual against whom the suspicion is of such a kind that the indictment is inevitable.

Probably the most helpful is the threshold required for filing an accusation with the court. Since it is mandatory to interrogate a future defendant as a suspect, at least once before the end of investigation it can be assumed that the threshold provided for filing an accusation is also a necessary prerequisite for the interrogation. As § 170 (1) StPO provides, the prosecutor must file charges if the investigation offers "sufficient suspicion" (*genügenden Anlaß*) to

37 Weigend (2017), p. 952 (see case law cited in fnn. 58 and 59).

38 Weigend (2017), p. 952 (the author gives leeway for exception in cases when there was no impact on the effectiveness of the defense).

39 § 163a (1) StPO.

40 § 152 (2) StPO.

41 Cf. Section 3.2.2.

prosecute.[42] The "sufficient suspicion" is not defined, and it can be understood as the belief that the suspect will be convicted in a court of law.[43]

But since the prosecutor and the police are the ones who must establish when the time has come to question the suspect, they possess enormous power to manipulate the time of stripping the suspect of her rights. The Federal Court of Justice has tried to prevent delaying the notification to the suspect of her status, by pointing out that when the suspicion becomes solid (*verdichtet*) the criminal justice authorities are obliged to treat such a person as a suspect and advise her of her rights.[44] But in practice, despite the possible problems with revealing the status of a suspect to individuals, the delays in interrogating suspects do not happen frequently.[45] This might be a result of the preference of German police officers and prosecutors to conducting investigation in an open style and not hiding the information that the investigation has been directed against certain individual.[46] Thus, even though the StPO does not oblige the prosecutor and the police to notify at any given time someone that they have become a suspect, the criminal justice authorities seem not to misuse their powers. The lack of proper regulations on the matter should not be however considered as satisfactory.

The discussion on the threshold that triggers the obligation to interrogate the suspect becomes less problematic when considering a second scenario for preliminary charging which is the undertaking of the investigative measure against the suspect. As soon as e.g. judicial orders to arrest a person are issued or when the police undertake such a measure without the warrant, the individual immediately becomes the suspect. In such a case it is not the level of suspicion which is used for the evaluation of the status of an accused but more objective criteria by which the prosecutorial acts are measured.[47]

6.2.3 Procedure for Preliminary Charging

The two ways of designating an individual as a suspect provide for distinct procedures that must be undertaken to preliminarily charge a person with

42 Note that the notion *genügenden Anlaß zur Erhebung der öffentlichen Klage* is translated into English in various ways. The official translation of StPO provides for "sufficient reason to prefer public charges" (www.gesetze-im-internet.de/englisch_stpo/englisch_stpo.html#p1542 – accessed 04. 17.2020). In other sources the "sufficient evidence" (Gilliéron (2014), p. 276) or "sufficient cause" (Weigend (2013), p. 268) can be found.

43 Bohlander (2012), p. 103 and the case law quoted in fn. 13.

44 37 BGHSt 48, 51–52 (1990); 53 BGHSt 112, 114 (2008) as cited by Weigend (2013), p. 271.

45 Weigend (2017), p. 944.

46 Weigend (2017), p. 944.

47 Huber (2008), p. 301 and case law quoted in fn. 107.

a crime. In the first situation, when the investigative measure, i.e. arrest is employed the suspect learns about her status as soon as she is arrested and is immediately given a copy of the judicial warrant[48] that must indicate, among other things, the details of the offense[49] in connection with which she has been arrested.[50] The same rules are applicable in cases of arrests conducted in exigent circumstances without a warrant.[51] Moreover, each arrested individual (suspect at this point) is informed of her rights, including the right to remain silent and the right to consult with a defense counsel.[52] This raises no concerns as to the proper notification of the suspect on the scope of rights that are attached to her at this point.

But the second scenario of informing a person about her status, which happens during the interrogation, is more problematic. Since the law provides for the mandatory interrogation before the end of investigation, the suspect is obliged to take a part in it. This gives a prosecutor the power to summon a suspect to appear for the purpose of interrogation.[53] Since § 133 (1) StPO regarding judicial interrogations, apply *mutatis mutandis* to the prosecutorial interrogations,[54] the suspect must obey such a summons and may be forcibly brought before the prosecutor in the case of noncompliance.[55] This is true regardless of the gravity of the crime[56] as well as even if the suspect has clearly indicated that she will make use of her right to remain silent.[57] The summons must be made in writing and must contain the name of the suspect as well as the description of the criminal offense that the suspect has been charged with.[58]

At the commencement of the interrogation, the suspect must be informed by the prosecutor of the offense that she is charged with and of the applicable

48 § 114a StPO.

49 The warrant includes the offense of which the arrestee is strongly suspected, the time and place of its commission, the statutory elements of the offense and the penal provisions to be applied.

50 § 114 (2) StPO.

51 See § 127 (4) StPO.

52 § 114b (2) StPO.

53 § 163a (3) StPO first sentence.

54 § 163a (3) StPO second sentence.

55 Note, however, that only the judge may order the suspect to be forcibly brought to the prosecutor's office for interrogation (§ 134 StPO). The suspect must be warned about this when the summons is served on her (§ 133 (2) StPO).

56 But see below for a simplified written procedure in lieu of interrogation, applicable in cases of minor offenses.

57 See Bohlander (2012), p. 93, fn. 120, citing case law supporting that approach, as well as dissenting decisions on the latter issue.

58 § 133 (1) and (2) StPO in conjunction with § 163a (3) StPO second sentence. Cf. Brodowski et al. (2010), p. 268, fn. 57 and literature cited there.

legal provision, as well as of the rights of the suspect.[59] However, the scope of the preliminary charges as presented to the suspect is disputable. It is clear that, since the information about the charge must enable the suspect to conduct an effective defense, it should be clear and precise. But the law does not provide how detailed this information should be, which leaves room for interpretation. Some scholars argue that it is permissible to inform the suspect about one offense out of a few that are under investigation and to introduce other later in the course of investigation, while others claim that all factual allegations have to be disclosed immediately.[60] The interrogation of the suspect must be recorded in a written form[61] and the record must reflect the charges that are presented to the suspect during interrogation and the views of the suspect, since she has a right to be heard. Although there is no obligation to provide the suspect with the letter of rights and just to inform about them orally,[62] in practice the standard forms that are used provide some rights of the suspect in writing.[63]

The interrogation by the police is regulated slightly differently, which substantially influences the nature of the preliminary charges presented to the suspect and subsequently changes her situation during proceedings. First of all, the police cannot compel anyone, including the suspect, to talk to them. There is no provision similar to § 163a (3) StPO first sentence, which gives only to a prosecutor a power to summon the suspect for interrogation.[64] Therefore, the suspect may simply not appear for the interrogation after receiving the police summons. The suspect is also not obliged to talk to the police, even if she chooses to appear. But in such a case, the police will, most likely, transfer the file to the prosecutor[65] and the suspect will be summoned by the prosecutor according to the procedure as outlined above. Moreover, the police summons tends to create an impression that they must be complied with.[66] Therefore, in practice, suspects respond to police summonses and show up for the police interrogations, being under the impression that they are obliged to do so.

59 These include among others, the right to be heard, the right to remain silent, the right to consult with defense counsel and the right to demand from investigative authorities gathering of additional evidence (see § 136 (1) CCP).

60 Weigend (2017), p. 948 quoting contradictory positions in fn. 41.

61 § 168-168b StPO.

62 The exception relates to the case when the suspect is arrested when she must receive a letter of rights in a written form.

63 Brodowski et al. (2010), p. 270.

64 Also § 133 StPO does not apply to police interrogations. Note, that § 163a (4) StPO provides for mutatis mutandis application only of § 136a (1) StPO (and not even fully!) and § 136a StPO.

65 § 163 (3) StPO.

66 Weigend and Salditt (2007), p. 83.

Second, the scope of information released to the suspect by the police, regarding charges, is somewhat limited when compared with the scope of the preliminary charges presented to the suspect by the prosecutor. It is striking that the first sentence of § 136 (1) StPO, providing the obligation to inform the suspect of the "offense with which she is charged and of the applicable legal provisions," does not apply to police interrogations.[67] Instead the police have a duty to inform the suspect of the "offense with which she is charged"[68] as the notification does not have to contain an applicable legal provision from the StGB. It is justified by the fact that police are not legally trained, and therefore the interrogating officer is unable to accurately assess what legal provision would apply.[69] In such a case the police might be obliged to refer the suspect to the prosecutor or ask the prosecutor's office for such information.[70] The lack of full information is seen as being partially compensated by the fact that the suspect must follow only the order to appear before the prosecution or pretrial judge and not before the police.[71] But in any case, the information on preliminary charges given to the suspect by the police must be precise enough to dispel the reasons for suspicion against her and to assert the facts, which are in her favor.[72]

Third, there is no straightforward provision that demands recording of the police interrogation. Unlike in cases of judicial interrogations[73] and prosecutorial interrogations,[74] nothing within the StPO obliges the police to do so. Nevertheless, the police record the interrogation, although the records need not contain any verbal description of the course of questioning and it is sufficient that the content and the results of the examination are recorded.[75] This means that the prosecutor will receive a report of the interrogation from the police, that contains less accurate information than other records would contain and encompassing impressions and prejudice expressed in it by the police officer which may tremendously influence the prosecutor when undertaking a final charging decision. This is so since, despite the notable criticism of the incompleteness of the police records and the manner in which they are taken, they are perceived in practice as having a high probative value.[76]

67 It is so since § 163a (4) StPO regulating police interrogations does not set applicability of this particular sentence. Yet, sentences from two to four of § 136 (1) StPO do apply.
68 § 163a (4) StPO first sentence.
69 Weigend (2017), p. 943.
70 Weigend (2017), p. 950.
71 Brodowski et al. (2010), p. 268.
72 § 136 (2) StPO.
73 § 168–168a StPO.
74 § 168b StPO. Although the regulation on prosecutorial records are less extensive than the ones that judicial interrogations must comply with.
75 Huber (2008), p. 302.
76 Huber (2008), p. 302.

Finally, it should be noted that the law provides for only one mandatory interrogation of the suspect during criminal investigation. The interrogation may happen early after the commencement of investigation or just before filing the accusation with the court. And no strict rules regulate when it should be done, while the practice shows both. It raises serious concerns regarding the necessity to notify the suspect on charges if they have been amended or changed during the course of criminal interrogation. Since the facts of the case may be seen from a different perspective due to evidence gathered after the interrogation or even due to information given by the suspect herself while questioned, it is not rare that the charges will be significantly modified. Moreover, since the police are not necessarily qualified enough to adjust legal provision to criminal behavior of the suspect, it may happen that when the prosecutor receives the file (§ 163 (1) StPO), the prosecutor will decide that the final charge should differ from the preliminary charges during police interrogation. This raises an important question, whether it calls for subsequent interrogation of the suspect. Unfortunately, German law does not give a straightforward answer to it, although some scholars argue that the fact that the investigation leads to new results does not oblige the police or prosecutor to interrogate the suspect again.[77] This raises some valid concerns about the ability of the suspect to engage in effective defense during investigation under such circumstances.

6.2.4 Authority Responsible for Preliminary Charging

Having analyzed the preliminary charging procedure as ordinarily made during the interrogation of a suspect, we can now move to the discussion on who is responsible for conducting such interrogation and providing the suspect with information on initial charges as put against her. In the most general terms, the power to interrogate the suspect during investigation rests mainly with the prosecutor and the police as well as with the judge of the investigation (*Ermittlungsrichter*). The latter happens rarely but, since the law provides for it, this procedure should not be overlooked.

The power to interrogate the suspect seems to rest primarily with the prosecutor.[78] From how the rules are constructed the impression remains that it is mainly the duty of the prosecutor to conduct such interrogation in every case. But in practice the interrogation is generally done by the police while the prosecutor engages herself in that procedure if she so wishes.[79] Therefore, the interrogation is done most frequently by the police when

77 Meyer-Goßner and Schmitt (2018), § 136 nb 6; Bohlander (2012), p. 68.
78 § 163a (3) StPO.
79 Huber (2008), p. 300; Bohlander (20142), p. 93.

they apprehend the person while conducting investigation without prosecutorial knowledge. This usually happens in two situations. First, when the suspect is caught at the crime scene or in the aftermath of a criminal offense, when he might be interrogated on the spot. Second, when police conduct the investigation and summon the accused to appear according to § 163a (4) StPO.

In the first situation there will be obviously no previous contact between the police and the prosecutor regarding the scope of investigation and charges. Catching the suspect on remand and interrogating him immediately, usually happens too quickly for such exchange of views. In such a case, by the time the prosecutor learns about the commitment of a crime, preliminary charges are already set by the police. But also, in the second scenario, it might happen that the prosecutor will have no impact on the scope of preliminary charges. Technically, the prosecutor is well equipped with powers to give instructions to the police on how to handle a specific case and order specific investigative actions.[80] But in practice, the case will come to the attention of the prosecutor only when the police terminate their own investigation and submit it to the prosecutor for further instructions. Moreover, since the police habitually disregard their legal duty to submit the file without delay to the prosecutor, and they do not inform the prosecutor about pending investigation unless they consider it useful, the prosecutor might learn about the existence of the case when it may be too late to give any orders or instructions to the police regarding the scope of charges that police should present to the suspect during interrogation.

Therefore, the impact of the prosecutor on how preliminary charges are constructed is limited or even nonexistent. It is particularly troublesome since, as explained above, there is a duty to interrogate the suspect only once and no obligation to amend preliminary charges exists. And since it depends only on police whether the preliminary charges will be consulted with the prosecutor or not, the formal charges, as submitted in the indictment, may be substantially different from the preliminary charges presented to the suspect during interrogation. So, the prosecutorial powers at this stage of proceedings are completely dependent on police actions and decisions.

The third, and most rarely engaged, actor in presenting the preliminary charges to the suspect is the judge of the investigation. According to § 162 (1) StPO the judge may be requested by the prosecutor to perform certain investigative acts, such as e.g. interrogation of the suspect or witness. This happens, most often, in order to make evidence more reliable, i.e. when it is expected that the suspect might not be available during the trial.[81] The advantage of this

80 § 161 (1) StPO second sentence.
81 Cf. Section 5.2.5.

measure being undertaken by the judge is that recordings of such interrogation can be later read out during the trial[82] which is not possible in case of records of the prosecutorial or police interrogations. In cases of judicial interrogations, the influence of the prosecutor on the shape of preliminary charges with which the suspect will be presented seems substantial, since it is the prosecutor that triggers such actions of the judge of the investigation. If asked by the prosecutor to interrogate the suspect, the judge must carry out the interrogation, unless she establishes that it is not permitted by law.[83] The judge does not act in her judicial capacity, but only exercises administrative powers and is not entitled to undertake her own investigative actions by adding or amending the charges.

6.3 Preliminary Charging in Poland

6.3.1 General Considerations concerning Charging Decisions

In Poland, the indictment is known as *akt oskarżenia*. Charing a person is considered to be one of the most important decisions, determining the scope of criminal liability of the accused and initiating the criminal trial.[84] Although the indictment should be considered a primary charging instrument, the law provides for a few more options, including a motion to convict a defendant without a trial[85] and the motion for the conditional discontinuation of the proceedings.[86] The power to charge a person is conferred almost exclusively on the prosecutor[87] although an indictment—but not other charging instruments—can be filed in some circumstances by another authority.[88]

Importantly, the described procedure of charging a person with a crime is conducted in a written form that involves transferring the charging instrument together with a whole case file (dossier) to the court. Filing an accusation with a court also does not involve the appearance of the accused before the court.[89] Obviously, the accused has a right to participate in the

82 § 254 (1) StPO.
83 § 162 (3) StPO.
84 Waltoś (1963), p. 5.
85 Article 335 § 1 k.p.k.
86 Article 324 k.p.k. The variety of charging instruments in Poland is a result of adoption of the broad understanding of accusatorial principle in criminal process – see Kulesza (2019), p. 604.
87 Article 45 § 1 k.p.k.
88 The charging instrument can also be brought to court by other authorities such as Border Guard or Customs Office in cases remaining in the scope of their jurisdiction although never by the police. See Nowak and Steinborn (2013), p. 527.
89 However, the accused is notified about the content of the indictment (Article 338 § 1 k.p.k.) and has a right to file a response to it in a written form (Article 338 § 2 k.p.k.).

court proceedings conducted against her, both when it comes to the hearing concerning the procedure akin to plea-bargaining as well as attendance at the trial stage but there is no separate procedure involving her presence when the charging document is filed with the court.

Before the indictment or other charging instrument is drafted and filed with the court, the very formal and mandatory decision initially charging a person with a crime (*przedstawienie zarzutów*) must be issued. This decision is effective only when the suspect has been notified in person about its contents and interrogated with regard to them.[90] The significance of the preliminary charging decision has been continuously underlined in Polish legal literature.[91] It is considered as drawing the line between the first phase of criminal investigation conducted *in rem*, i.e. when the case is still developing and its second stage conducted *ad personam*, i.e. against the identified person.[92] The Polish Supreme Court has even stated on one occasion that the preliminary charging decision should be understood as "the formal act of bringing a person to criminal liability"[93] although this does not seem accurate when relating it to the formal charging decision. The importance attached to this procedure is also demonstrated through provisions that allow for imposing pretrial detention, or a financial surety only, against a person that has been presented with preliminary charges in their written form.[94] But most importantly, because of the above discussed written nature of the procedure, the preliminary charging might be the only time the suspect encounters the criminal justice system in the course of criminal proceedings. Frequently this is also the only moment for her to answer questions regarding the plea since there is generally no legal obligation to show up at court at any later time.

The very formal procedure in which the person is preliminarily charged with a crime was incorporated in the course of investigation, primarily to provide that person with information about the content of the charges as adopted by the investigating authority.[95] Unfortunately, the creation of such a mechanism resulted in formally setting the point in time when the rights that the suspect is guaranteed actually do attach to her. As a result, only a person presented with preliminary charges during criminal investigation is granted the status of a suspect (*podejrzany*), and therefore provided with rights associated with that status including the right to access a defense counsel, the right to remain silent, the right to legal aid. There are also other

90 Article 313 § 1 k.p.k.
91 See the literature quoted by Stefański (2013b), pp. 5–6, fn. 2.
92 Waltoś (2013), p. 494.
93 Judgment of the Supreme Court of 10 June 2009, II KK 1/09, Lex No. 519595.
94 Article 249 § 2 k.p.k.
95 Tylman and Grzegorczyk (2014), p. 669.

consequences of preliminarily charging a suspect with an offense besides those that have a strictly procedural effect. Sometimes they are detached from the investigation itself but cause greater harm to the suspect than those associated with the criminal process.[96]

In the discussion on preliminary charging the definition of suspect becomes crucially important. This is, in particular, due to the fact that, as a result of formal presentation of preliminary charges, a strict distinction is made between the status of a so-called suspected person (*osoba podejrzana*) and a suspect (*podejrzany*).[97] While the latter term has been normatively defined as a person, with regard to whom a decision initially charging a person with a crime has been issued, or who, without the issuance of such a decision, has been informed about charges in connection with the initiation of the person's interrogation in the capacity of a suspect,[98] the former term has no legal definition which, on the other hand, does not preclude the Code from directly referring to it on several occasions.[99] The suspected person can be nevertheless defined as a person on whom the attention of criminal justice authorities focuses due to suspicion that she has committed a crime, but who has not yet been initially charged with an offense through the procedure provided in Article 313 k.p.k.[100] It is crucial to understand, though, that according to a formalistic view of the Polish Code of Criminal Procedure, the suspected person, because of the lack of formal preliminary charging procedure launched against her, remains unprotected by the rights that are normally attached to the suspect.

Indeed, none of the rights that are applicable to the suspect belong to the suspected person.[101] As a consequence, such an individual does not have to be informed about the existence of any right even if approached by the criminal justice authorities.[102] On the other hand, many investigative measures are allowed against the suspected person, which triggers certain rights that are attached to the conduct of such a measure. A good example is

96 This concerns e.g. the notification of the employer of the charged individual, suspension of the statute of limitations or the confiscation of legally possessed guns – see Kosonoga (2016), p. 809.

97 De Vocht (2010), p. 435; Jasiński and Kremens (2019), p. 221.

98 Article 71 § 1 k.p.k. The difference between these two ways of charging a person initially with crimes will be discussed later.

99 The Code uses the term "suspected person" when e.g. the scope of identification measures to be conducted against a person such as taking blood, hair, or saliva samples is being determined (Article 74 § 3 k.p.k.) or regulating arrest of such individual (Article 244 § 1 k.p.k.).

100 Jasiński and Kremens (2019), p. 202.

101 Compare with the rights of the suspect as provided in Article 300 § 1 k.p.k. – see below for discussion. De Vocht (2010), p. 436.

102 Kruszyński (2007), p. 184.

the arrest. The suspected person may be arrested and detained by the police for up to 48 hours.[103] At the time of the arrest the suspected person is immediately notified, among other things, about the reasons for such detention, the right to be assisted by a lawyer,[104] the right to first aid, etc.[105] Moreover, when a suspected person is subjected to e.g. search or inspection of the body, fingerprinting, or taking blood samples the law does not provide for any right that should attach to her while they are conducted. This means that the rights that the suspected person possesses until the preliminary charging takes place, are a consequence of the investigative measure involving her, and only if such measure provides for it. .

As one might expect, the lack of adequate protection of the individual before the preliminary charging takes place, has been criticized by Polish scholars in the past,[106] as well as more recently.[107] Interestingly, the Polish Constitution confer the right to defend oneself to anyone against whom the criminal proceedings are conducted,[108] which should also include a person before her formal designation as a suspect, e.g. when arrested.[109] As a result, the formalistic approach as applied in the Code of Criminal Procedure appears not to comply with the constitutional standard.[110]

The problem has recently returned with a vengeance when a need to implement EU directives focused on the rights of the suspect and accused. All directives use the term "suspect" which has been translated into Polish as *podejrzany*. This causes misunderstanding and misinterpretation as to whether directives are properly and fully implemented or not. Such interpretation allowed the Polish government to claim that the Polish criminal procedure remains in compliance with the EU directive since *podejrzany* in the Polish legal system is

103 Article 244 § 1 and 248 § 1 k.p.k.
104 Note that this is not the "defense counsel" but a "lawyer" which makes a difference concerning the nature of the relationship between the lawyer and a client which is different to the relationship of defense counsel with a suspect/accused.
105 Article 244 § 3 k.p.k.
106 See especially the famous dispute between leading Polish scholars of their times: Prusak (1971); Murzynowski (1971). In this discussion Andrzej Murzynowski presented a very progressive view for the time, expressly stating that "a person suspected of having committed a criminal offense and in respect of whom procedural steps have been taken, such as interrogation, search, detention, temporary seizure of movable property, inspection, is placed in the legal position of the suspect, exceptionally before the decision to bring preliminary charges against her has been made" and that such person "enjoys all rights provided in the Code for the suspect" (p. 43).
107 See e.g. Steinborn (2012), p. 1781; Stefański (2013c), pp. 305–307 and Sakowicz (2019), pp. 236–253.
108 Article 42 (2) of the Polish Constitution.
109 See Wróbel (2010), p. 225.
110 See also analysis regarding the applicability of the right to remain silent to a suspected person during arrest in De Vocht (2010), pp. 436–437.

indeed guaranteed most of the rights provided for the *suspect*, which obviously remains inconsistent with the concept of a *suspect* as used in EU directives. The truth is that Polish law does not remain in compliance with EU directives since *osoba podejrzana* (suspected person) is not entitled to the same protection that is given to *podejrzany* (suspect). In order to assume that the EU directives are properly and fully implemented in Poland the guarantees provided for the *suspect* should be extended also to those individuals who acquired the status of a suspected person through measures aimed at them such as arrest or taking samples, and are not yet preliminarily charged with a crime.

6.3.2 Threshold for Preliminary Charging

The standard that has to be met for preliminary charging an individual with a crime is described as a "sufficiently reasonable suspicion" (*dostatecznie uzasadnione podejrzenie*) that the offense was committed by a specified individual.[111] It is understood in the literature as being not only a subjective conviction of the criminal justice authority that the person has committed a crime, but it must be also objectively based on verified facts.[112] However, the threshold is considered as very weak since the evaluation of its existence remains fully discretionary.[113] And, in fact, it is even debatable what the notion "verified facts" means. As some argue, the decision may be based only on the legitimate evidentiary findings admitted properly during the course of criminal investigation according to general rules provided in Article 170 § 1 k.p.k.[114] This would preclude relying on internally obtained secret information that cannot be presented later in the courtroom.

The issuance of the preliminary charging decision whenever the grounds to do so exist is not an option but an obligation of the criminal justice authority. This obligation can also be derived from the principle of legality as strictly applicable in Polish criminal process as well as during the course of criminal investigation.[115] Despite the fact that Article 10 k.p.k. regulating that principle focuses on the obligation to initiate the investigation and to commence prosecution, it also affects the preliminary charging procedure. Since, according to that rule, the prosecutor is obliged to file an accusation with a court and to prosecute a case, and the indictment cannot be filed

111 Article 313 § 1 k.p.k.
112 Kosonoga (2016), p. 745.
113 Stefański (2013a), p. 22.
114 Note that information gathered during criminal investigation is considered as evidence and referred to as such and the general rules on admissibility of evidence do apply to them also at this stage of criminal process – see Jasiński and Kremens (2019), pp. 305–307.
115 Cf. Section 2.3.2.

without the preliminary charging procedure being employed first, it seems that this mechanism, at least indirectly, results from the principle of legality. Moreover, it can be assumed that the preliminary charging is directly an element of the obligation to "initiate and conduct criminal investigation" provided in Article 10 k.p.k., forcing the prosecutor and criminal justice authorities to conduct investigation, not only when they search for the alleged perpetrator, but also against the targeted suspect.

Regardless of whether or not this obligation can be derived from the principle of legality, there is no doubt that the individual must be presented with preliminary charges as soon as the sufficiently reasonable suspicion that the person has committed an offense exists.[116] This puts a burden on the authorities to conduct the preliminary charging procedure in a timely manner. It also raises some concerns, since the criminal justice authorities have a tendency to make a tactical choice not to issue a preliminary charging decision despite the existence of sufficiently reasonable grounds and question a person as a witness first. As discussed, the failure to press charges prevents the individual from exercising her rights, including the right to defend oneself and, especially, the right to remain silent.[117] In consequence, interrogating a person as a witness, despite the existence of grounds for the preliminary charge, must be regarded as a tactical move which manifestly breaches the standard of a fair trial and constitutes a severe infringement of Article 313 k.p.k.[118] And even though the records of such interrogation are inadmissible in court forcing the suspected person to appear as a witness and answer questions, despite the protection as provided in Article 183 § 1 k.p.k., should be considered as depriving the individual from the full application of the right not to incriminate oneself.

The Polish Supreme Court took a strong position stating that a person who has been questioned as a witness in violation of Article 313 § 1 k.p.k., instead of being presented with preliminary charges and questioned as a suspect, shall not be held criminally liable for false testimony.[119] This is so, since the decision to preliminarily charge a person with a crime

> is not a matter left to the discretion of the law enforcement authority and does not boil down to an insignificant violation of the law. Modern procedural solutions—not without good reasons—no longer accept the

116 Brodzisz (2015a), p. 754.

117 Nowak and Steinborn (2013), p. 502. The suspected person testifying as a witness has only a limited protection to refrain from answering questions when she perceives that the answer might be incriminating (Article 183 § 1 k.p.k.). This does not include the right to deny the whole interrogation.

118 Kosonoga (2016), p. 750.

119 Judgment of the Supreme Court of April 26, 2007, I KZP 4/07, OSNKW 2007/6/45.

subjective approach of a law enforcement authority as a criterion for initiating proceedings *in personam*.[120]

Therefore, questioning a suspected person as a witness, when there is sufficient evidence to preliminarily charge that person , shall be treated as a flagrant violation of the rules of criminal procedure.[121]

Therefore, the proper moment for employing the preliminary charging procedure against the suspect should be accurately assessed by the criminal justice authority conducting criminal investigation. As it is argued, the determination of this moment is neither a matter of discretion nor of intuition of the criminal justice authority.[122] It will depend on the nature of the crime as well as on the circumstances of the case. In some of them, the identification of the alleged perpetrator will take place immediately after initiating the investigation, while in some others the police will have to work harder.

6.3.3 Procedure for Preliminary Charging

The procedure for preliminary charging a person with a crime in the Polish criminal process has comparably an extremely formal character. In order to present the charges, it is necessary to perform three actions indicated in the provision of Article 313 k.p.k. that is: (1) issue a decision for preliminary charging person with a crime; (2) immediately announce it to the suspect; (3) interrogate the suspect. The Polish Supreme Court stated that, in order for the preliminary charging to be considered as legally effective, all three conditions must be met cumulatively and issuing a decision is not considered enough.[123] But, at the same time, if it is found impossible to announce the charge to a suspect and to interrogate her, the issuance of the decision is considered as sufficient which may happen when e.g. a person is at large.[124]

In the light of the above considerations, the suspect is obliged to participate in a preliminary charging procedure in person. It stems directly from the provision of Article 75 § 1 k.p.k., obliging the suspect to respect the summons from the criminal justice authorities. But this is also a natural consequence of the obligation to preliminary charge a person before formally filing with the court the final charge contained in the indictment. The suspect may be even arrested and forcibly brought before the criminal justice

120 Judgment of the Supreme Court of April 26, 2007, I KZP 4/07, OSNKW 2007/6/45.
121 Nowak and Steinborn (2013), p. 502.
122 Kosonoga (2016), p. 750.
123 See decision of the Supreme Court of April 24, 2007, IV KK 31/07, Lex No. 262649.
124 See Article 279 § 2 k.p.k. See judgment of the Supreme Court of June 24, 2013, V KK 453/12, Lex No. 1341289. See also decision of the Supreme Court of June 13, 2012, II KK 302/11, Lex No. 1212890.

authority on the prosecutorial arrest warrant if there is a justified concern that she will not answer the summons.[125] This assumes a visible amount of coercion directed at the suspect. These rules are nevertheless perceived as not standing against the right of the suspect to remain silent. As will be discussed below, the suspect will not be forced to answer any questions during the interrogation and the coercion is just to secure her presence to make sure that she becomes acquainted with the preliminary charge.

Therefore, the first step in the procedure of preliminarily charging a person with an offense is issuing the relevant decision. The law regulates in detail what such decision should consist of, including the identification of a suspect, the precise description of the act she is suspected of, and the alleged crime committed.[126] The decision does not have to be justified, but the suspect has a right, of which she should be informed, to demand the justification.[127] In such case the reasons are first delivered orally during interrogation and subsequently, within 14 days from submitting the request, in a written form.[128] In any case the justification must contain information on the facts and evidence that supported the preliminary charging decision.[129]

The precise description of the act that the person is suspected of is of particular importance in the decision. It is aimed at providing efficient protection for the suspect, since it allows the suspect to take up an effective defense. If to defend oneself also means countering the accusation, its effectiveness, and the general ability to react is determined by the degree to which it is made specific.[130] Moreover, only what the suspect has been charged with in the preliminary charging decision can constitute the basis for the indictment.[131] The Supreme Court has confirmed on several occasions that if both documents do not refer to the same act, the indictment has a formal defect that needs to be supplemented by the prosecutor.[132]

To ensure that the act that the suspect was charged with in the preliminary charging decision is identical to the charge presented in the indictment, the law provides for the possibility to amend or change the preliminary charging decision.[133] If, in the course of investigation, it transpires that the suspect

125 Article 247 § 1 (1) k.p.k. Cf. Section 7.3.
126 Article 313 § 2 k.p.k.
127 Article 313 § 3 k.p.k.
128 De Vocht (2010), p. 437 and text accompanying fn. 62 (the author invokes the views of practitioners according to which the written reasons are of low value due to their laconic, general, and misleading nature).
129 Article 313 § 4 k.p.k.
130 Kosonoga (2016), pp. 753–754.
131 Brodzisz (2015b), p. 823.
132 See judgment of the Supreme Court of February 9, 2011, II KK 228/10, Lex No. 784521, and judgment of the Supreme Court of October 4, 2013, III KK 158/13, OSNKW 2014/3/19.
133 Jasiński and Kremens (2019), p. 222.

should be charged with an offense not included in the preliminary charging decision that has been already issued, or with an offense in a significantly changed form, or that the offense should be classified under a provision that sets out a more severe penalty, a new decision should be issued immediately and the suspect should be notified.[134] This rule is also aimed at guaranteeing the suspect the right to defend herself efficiently since the charge in the indictment will not be coming as a surprise. Moreover, the procedure to amend or to change charges includes interrogating the suspect so, if the suspect wishes, she may counter the charges immediately. The suspect is also allowed at this point to file request to have certain investigatory measures conducted in her favor.[135]

The second step in the preliminary charging process is the announcement of the preliminary charging decision to the suspect. Article 313 § 1 k.p.k. states that the announcement must be done "immediately" (*niezwłocznie*) which has been interpreted by the Supreme Court as "the obligation to immediately announce the order is thus incumbent on the authority and only for practical reasons (the suspect being at large or not available in the country) can be delayed in this respect."[136] The term "announcement" assumes that the criminal justice authority will read out the content of the preliminary charging decisions, but this does not preclude a suspect from being personally acquainted with its content by reading it in person or further explaining it to the suspect by the authority, which may be relevant for exercising the suspect's right to defend herself.[137]

The final step constituting the effective preliminary charging procedure is the interrogation of the suspect. It is the essential element of the procedure of preliminarily charging a person with an offense which means that the interrogation is mandatory, save for in exceptional circumstances. The interrogation of a suspect is recorded officially and offers the suspect the opportunity to refute the charges brought against her.[138] Prior to the interview, the suspect must be informed about all of her rights. The letter of rights is given to the suspect and its receipt must be confirmed by the suspect's signature.[139] Among those rights are the right to remain silent and the right to be represented by defense counsel during interrogation. Additionally upon the request of the suspect, defense

134 Article 314 k.p.k.

135 See more on the right of the suspect to request the conducting of evidentiary measures during criminal investigation in Section 5.3.4.

136 Judgment of the Supreme Court of January 16, 2009, IV KK 256/08, OSNwSK 2009/1/124.

137 Tarnowska (2013), p. 56.

138 Kruszyński (2007), p. 185.

139 Article 300 § 1 k.p.k. Regarding the scope of the right of the suspect, see extensively in English literature De Vocht (2010), pp. 435–471 and Nowak and Steinborn (2013), pp. 530–539.

counsel must be present during interrogation. In theory, the suspect may refrain from answering any question until her counsel appears.[140] However, in practice, most suspects, even when notified of this right, do not make use of it.[141]

The conducting of the interrogation of the suspect is almost identical to the one that takes place during the trial.[142] The nature of the criminal process in Poland, allowing for the reading out in court of the records of the suspect's testimony given during interrogation,[143] forces the criminal justice authorities to respect the same rules of conduct as applicable to the examination of the accused during the trial.[144] Therefore, the suspect must be primarily asked whether or not she pleads guilty to the preliminary charges and whether she wants to make use of her right to remain silent or to provide explanations.[145] Subsequently, if the suspect wishes to talk, she can refer to charges in a narrative way and is subjected to questions asked by the interrogating authority as well as her own defense counsel if present.[146] During interrogation, a suspect has the right to change her mind and to subsequently refuse to answer questions.

It should be highlighted that this interrogation might be the only experience of the suspect (and future accused) with the criminal justice authorities throughout the whole of the criminal proceedings. This is also one of the reasons why the guilty plea has to be entered at this point. This happens, in particular, when it comes to cases that end without a trial upon some forms of negotiated justice in accordance with Article 335 k.p.k. But also when the trial takes place, the presence of the accused is not mandatory, unless the court decides otherwise.[147] Although the plea might be changed later in the course of further interrogations, if they happen during investigation as well as during a trial, the significance of the first interrogation, and the admission of guilt at

140 Brodzisz (2015a), p. 723.

141 Note that the Supreme Court has stated "[t]he absence of a lawyer during the first hearing of the suspect in the pre-trial proceedings does not constitute in itself . . . obstacles to the use of his or her explanations at the trial under such conditions, unless there is an objectively existing vulnerability of the suspect to harm" (decision of the Supreme Court of February 6, 2013, V KK 314/12, Lex No. 1289070). See also Kruszyński (2007), p. 195.

142 There is however one significant difference since during criminal investigation the suspect may also provide her testimonies in a written form (Article 176 k.p.k.).

143 Article 389 k.p.k.

144 Jasiński and Kremens (2019), pp. 308–309.

145 Note that due to the interpretation of the right to remain silent in Poland which precludes the suspect from being interrogated under oath or notified on the obligation to testify according to the truth, she is not giving "testimonies" as a witness but "explanations" (*wyjaśnienia*).

146 The law also provides that the victim, and her legal adviser are able to participate during interrogation and can ask questions (Article 171 § 2 k.p.k. and Article 317 k.p.k.). In practice it happens quite rarely.

147 Article 374 § 1 k.p.k.

that point, cannot be underestimated. Therefore, in the majority of cases, the entering of a plea takes place before the police officer, since this is the authority entitled to conduct the preliminary charging procedure against a suspect in case of all inquiries. But the fact that in the case of inspections it is the prosecutor that initially charges the suspect and therefore receives the plea enhances the quality of the procedure only to a limited extent since she is also not the judge.

The procedure to preliminarily charge a person with a crime does not encompass the arrest. Interestingly, when the suspected person is arrested, she is notified of the right to give or not to give a statement,[148] which should not be confused with the right to remain silent. Giving a statement in such a situation is not a part of any interrogation and cannot be used in court as evidence. But the statement, if given, will nevertheless be taken in the records of the arrest and be available in the case file to all that in the future will interrogate the suspect, even for the court during the trial.[149] This is particularly problematic in cases where a person confesses, which in practice happens quite frequently.

In addition to the rigid rules regulating the preliminary charging procedure, the law provides for the possibility to achieve the same goal more informally. This option is available only in cases of investigations conducted in a form of inquiry[150] or when the case is dealt with in "immediate procedures."[151] In these two situations, the authorities may orally present the suspect with the preliminary charges at the beginning of her interrogation, without handing over a written decision, although it is necessary to precisely formulate the preliminary charge in the written records of interrogation.[152] However, this relaxed procedure is not applicable if the suspect is under pre-trial detention.[153] In practice, the criminal justice authorities rarely resort to this option due to the habit of issuing the decision.

6.3.4 Authority Responsible for Preliminary Charging

As with all criminal investigation activities in Poland, the authority that is empowered to issue the initial charging decision is determined by the form of investigation. In the case of inspection, only the prosecutor can present the preliminary charges, even if the investigation has been entrusted to the police,[154] while in case of inquiry, this procedure may be employed by both

148 Article 244 § 2 k.p.k.
149 See the discussion by De Vocht (2010), pp. 436–437.
150 Article 325g § 2 k.p.k.
151 Article 308 § 2 k.p.k.
152 Stefański (2013b), p. 25.
153 Cf. Article 325g § 1 k.p.k. *in fine* and Article 249 § 2 k.p.k.
154 Article 311 § 3 k.p.k.

the prosecutor and the police. This means that the full control over the preliminary charging process in cases of grave crimes remains solely in the hands of the prosecutor. Importantly, in such cases, all essential elements of the preliminary charging procedure, including the interrogation of a suspect, must be conducted by the prosecutor.

This distinction has a long-standing tradition. But for a short period of time, when the criminal procedure was working under the amended Code (July 2015–April 2016) that has brought the process closer to an adversarial regime, the law provided for a right for police to conduct the preliminary charging procedure, regardless of the type of offense, without prosecutorial supervision.[155] This change was justified by the need to relieve the prosecutor from extensive obligations during investigation, since she was expected to intensify the activity during a new adversarial trial.[156] It was rather inconsistent with the remaining obligations of the prosecutor, since she was still obliged to participate in autopsies and crime scene investigations, which are far less significant than the issuance of preliminary charges. This also raised concerns from the point of view of protecting the rights of the suspect.[157] Not surprisingly, as a result of the reversal of the change of the system in 2016, the right to preliminarily charge a suspect during inspection, has again become the exclusive competence of the prosecutor.

In the light of the normative regulations in cases of more serious crimes, the prosecutor remains the only authority responsible for shaping the content of the charge and identifying the crime that's allegedly been committed. Moreover, even in case of less serious crimes when the decision is undertaken by the police, the prosecutor, who is empowered to supervise the proceedings, may modify the preliminary charging decision if it is not properly constructed[158] (Article 326 § 1 and 3 k.p.k.). In fact, she is obliged to do so, if the alleged crime does not match the one committed, since the preliminary charge and the final charge in the indictment must be identical. This confirms the power that the prosecutor maintains over every preliminary charging procedure.

However, it is important to take into account the importance of the content of the dossier for the prosecutor's reception of the case. Although not legally trained, police officers, on a daily basis and very early in the course of proceedings, make the legal qualification of the criminal act. And the approach that the police will therefore carry out the investigation in the direction they consider appropriate and which will not necessarily correspond

155 Jasiński and Kremens (2019), p. 222.
156 Kremens (2015), p. 79.
157 Kiełtyk (2016), p. 548.
158 Article 326 §§ 1 and 3 k.p.k.

to the crime that has actually been committed. As a result, the police will collect evidence in connection with the crime they have assumed has happened. This, in many cases, becomes prejudicial to the prosecutorial decision with what offense a person should be preliminarily charged.

6.4 Preliminary Charging in Italy

6.4.1 General Considerations concerning Charging Decisions

The charging of a person in the Italian criminal process may take different forms. At the end of criminal investigation the prosecutor, who possesses an exclusive power with regard to that, must formulate a final charge which, according to Article 60 (1) c.c.p. may take the form of a request for committal to trial (*richiesta di rinvio a giudizio*), immediate trial (*giudizio immediate*), proceedings by penal decree (*decreto penale di condanna*), application of punishment at the request of the parties (*applicazione della pena su richiesta delle parti*), decree of direct summons for trial (*decreto di citazione diretta*), and direct trial (*giudizio direttissimo*). Each of these forms of charging instruments should be considered as the accusation (*imputazione*) that makes an individual an accused (*imputato*).[159]

All forms of charging instruments should clearly identify the accused person and the charges filed against her. For instance, the request for committal to trial should contain, among other things, the details of the accused person, the clear and precise description of the criminal act together with aggravating circumstances and those that may result in the application of precautionary measures, with indication of the relevant legal provisions describing the alleged crime and an indication of the gathered sources of evidence.[160] Moreover, together with the request, the prosecutor forwards the dossier of the case containing carefully selected materials of the case according to the double-dossier (*doppio fascicolo*) system.[161] Similar requirements, although with some derogations, accompany all forms of accusation. In all cases the accusation procedure is of a fully written character and until the preliminary hearing commences, the suspect is not called to appear before the court.

The accusation is not the first document in which the criminal justice authorities name the accused. Before the final charge against the accused is filed with the court, she must be identified as a person against whom proceedings are carried on. This is done through the registration in the

159 See also Scarpa et al. (2017), p. 76.
160 Article 417 c.p.p.
161 Article 416 (2) c.p.p. See the discussion on the double-dossier system in Panzavolta (2004), pp. 586–587.

prosecutorial register of the name of such person and the crime she is initially charged with.[162] The identification of the suspect in the registry has consequences for the conduct of criminal investigation, since the expiration date for the investigation commences exactly at that very moment.[163]

It should also be noted that the Italian criminal procedure provides for the enforcement of the preliminary charges on the prosecutor by the judge. Even if the prosecutor believes that the suspect is unknown and does not record the name of such person in the prosecutorial registry, the GIP (*giudice per le indagini prelimiari*, the judge for preliminary investigation) has powers to order entering the name of such suspect, and decides on the initial charge of the individual. This may be done in accordance with Article 415 (1)–(2) c.p.p., that obligates the prosecutor who has been conducting the investigation against an unknown person for six months, to submit a request to discontinue or to prolong the investigation. If the judge, after examining the file, holds that the author of the offense is a person that has already been identified, he has the power to enforce such individual's name to be entered in the register.

Nevertheless, from the fact that the name of the suspect has been registered, should not result that such person will be notified about it immediately or even within a reasonable time. Actually, there is nothing that obliges the prosecutor to inform the suspect about her status until the very end of criminal investigation when the suspect must be mandatorily acquainted with the whole materials gathered during the course of proceedings.[164] This, however, happens only in cases that do not require any form of the suspect's participation in the process. Otherwise the law provides that the prosecutor must notify the suspect about her status whenever she wishes to perform an act at which the defense counsel has the right to be present.[165]

Accordingly, there are two common situations when the suspect will learn about her status. First, where the suspect is subject to the investigative measure that is directed against this individual, such as search or arrest, from which it is obvious that the person has become a suspect. Second, a suspect must be notified about her status and rights whenever she is questioned.[166] This may happen when the prosecutor or the police interrogates a suspect or when a suspect herself becomes aware of an investigation being carried out against her, demands such interrogation. It should be noted that this does not cancel the obligation to subsequently inform the suspect about the

162 Article 335 (1) c.p.p.
163 Ruggeri (2015), p. 70. See also Section 5.3.
164 Article 415-bis c.p.p.
165 Article 364 c.p.p.
166 Article 65 (1) c.p.p.

charges at the conclusion of the criminal investigation (Article 415bis c.p.p.). And whenever the legal definition of the criminal act changes or turns out to be differently circumstantiated, the prosecutor updates the entry in the registry.[167] This means that at the conclusion of the investigation, the most current version of the charges, as reflected later in the indictment or any other accusatory instrument, will be notified to the suspect.

One should wonder what kind of consequences the law attaches to the noncompliance with an obligation to provide the suspect with the notification on her status whenever the law demands it. Primarily, the failure to comply with the obligation to acquaint the suspect with the preliminary charges at the conclusion of investigation results with declaration of the indictment void,[168] since the discovery at the end of investigative stage is of compulsory character. As a result, the case is returned to the prosecutor who must meet the requirements of Article 415-bis c.p.p. before filing a case again with the court.[169] Severe consequences accompany receiving statements during the investigation from the suspect whose rights were not respected. The failure to give the proper notification of her rights results in statements being nulled.[170]

Finally, a note on terminology. In the Italian Code of Criminal Procedure, distinct terms are used to describe a passive party to the criminal process: *persona sottoposta alle indagini preliminari* or *indagato* and *imputato*. The term *persona sottoposta alle indagini preliminari* or *indagato* as used in Article 61 (1) c.p.p. describes the person under investigation conducted by the prosecutor while the term *imputato* as used in Article 60 (1) c.p.p. refers to the person being prosecuted and committed to trial.[171] These may be translated tentatively as suspect (*indagato*) and accused (*imputato*).[172] Notwithstanding he adoption of different terms, both the suspect and the accused are equipped with the same rights. Moreover, it is understood as these rights are to be particularly protected during the investigation when the police and prosecutor use measures interfering with rights and freedoms.[173] Therefore, at the early stage of the criminal

167 Article 335 (2) c.p.p.
168 Article 416 (1) c.p.p.
169 Caianiello (2010), p. 391.
170 Article 369bis c.p.p.
171 Ruggieri and Marcolini (2013), p. 396.
172 Scarpa et al. (2017), p. 74. Note that authors use the term "suspected person" as a translation of the term *indagato* based on the terminology used in EU Directive 2010/64. However, for the consistency of this work, since the Polish system differentiates between the terms "suspect" and "suspected person" attaching significantly different statuses to individuals holding these names – see Section 6.3.1 – it has been decided that the term *indagato* will be translate as a "suspect."
173 Ruggieri and Marcolini (2013), p. 396.

process the suspect has among others the right to information, counsel and to remain silent.[174]

6.4.2 Threshold for Preliminary Charging

In the discussion on the threshold necessary to initially charge a person with a crime in the Italian system, one should differentiate between the moment when the prosecutor identifies the suspect as such and the moment when a suspect should be notified about her status.

The first situation is carefully regulated in the Code and provides for the immediate reaction of the prosecutor when the identity of the suspect is known to her, by entering the suspect's name on a register in the prosecutor's office, together with a note of the related alleged crime.[175] The Code does not provide for any particular standard of proof to register the suspect, although it appears in the light of the legality principle and wording of Article 335 (1) c.p.p. that the prosecutor is compelled to register the suspect's details where she believes that such person has committed a crime. Yet, the same concerns raised with regard to the failure to register crimes are also valid at this point.[176] Moreover, because certain benefits apply when the suspect remains unregistered, since the terms of maximum duration of the investigation do not commence, the prosecutors might be interested in not registering the name of the suspect as soon as it appears.[177] Therefore, the rule is not as rigid as one might expect.

Even more importantly, there is no formal obligation on either the prosecutor or the police to inform a suspect that she is under investigation.[178] This means that the individual may have the status of a suspect as provided in the prosecutor's registry without being aware of it. Yet, the right to be notified on proceedings being aimed against oneself is of a crucial character, since it affects the applicability of all other rights available in criminal proceedings. Therefore, the duty to notify the suspect that investigation is being conducted against her is considered to be implied.[179] This should be balanced against the confidentiality of investigation (*segreto istruttorio*) as provided in Article 329 c.p.p. that allows the police and the prosecutor to conduct investigative measures in secrecy.

174 See the comprehensive discussion on the scope of the right of the suspect in Italy in Caianiello (2010), pp. 390–412.
175 Article 335 (1) c.p.p.
176 See Section 4.3.1.
177 Caianiello, (2016), p. 11. See also Section 5.4.5.
178 Corso (1993), p. 230.
179 Caianiello (2010), p. 390.

Thus, there is no general threshold that would oblige the prosecutor and police to notify the suspect about her status. The suspect will be notified if there is a need to undertake a certain investigative measure targeted against her in which the lawyer has the right to be present. This concerns all acts such as questioning, inspections, line-ups, searches. Therefore, if the grounds justifying such a measure exist, the person must be served with a letter of rights. On the other hand, the rules on questioning the suspect do not provide for any particular threshold.[180] The triggering mechanism to notify the suspect about her status and her rights in that case is just the will of the suspect and the fact that she has been preliminarily charged with a crime by registering her name.

6.4.3 Procedure for Preliminary Charging

From the moment when the person appears in the registry identified through her name and the crime she has allegedly committed she sustains her position as a suspect. During investigation, if there is a change in the nature of the charges, the prosecutor will update the register entries, but recording any new *notitia criminis* is not necessary.[181]

Neither the prosecutor nor the police have an obligation to interrogate the suspect during the course of criminal investigation, which could be considered as the most obvious way to notify the suspect about the preliminary charges. Moreover, since there is no obligation to do so the prosecutor may not be tempted to share such information, hiding behind the secrecy of proceedings, until the very end of investigation. There are a variety of ways in which the suspect may be notified of her status, allegedly committed offenses as well as the rights that she has.

When the prosecutor intends to charge a suspect, she must inform the latter that the investigation has come to an end (*avviso di conclusione delle indagini preliminari*) and that the suspect has been the subject of said investigation. In such a case the suspect receives a notice which contains, among other things, a brief description of the criminal act she has been suspected of committing and the legal provisions allegedly violated.[182] This gives the suspect a chance to get unlimited access to the prosecutor's file, as well as to produce evidence and request that the prosecutor conduct certain investigative actions.[183] This is also an opportunity for the suspect to introduce defensive arguments, in an attempt to convince the prosecutor to request the

180 Article 374 c.p.p.
181 Article 335 § 2 c.p.p.
182 Article 415bis (2) c.p.p.
183 Article 415bis (3)–(5) c.p.p. See broadly on the access to dossiers in the Italian system at the conclusion of criminal investigation, Caianiello (2019), p. 573.

judge to dismiss the case.[184] An indictment will be declared void in the event that such notice is not served.[185]

The second way of notifying a suspect about preliminary charges formulated against her takes place when the prosecutor intends to carry out an act to which the defense counsel has a right to attend: "guaranteed acts" (*atti garantini*).[186] These are, among others, questioning of the suspect, inspections, line-ups, or searches. The organization of such a measure is carefully regulated as demanding from the prosecutor sending a letter of rights (*informazione di garanzia*) that contain the legal provisions which have allegedly been violated, as well as the date and place in which the criminal act was committed, along with a request to exercise the right of appointing a retained lawyer.[187] This also includes a very detailed notice to the suspect on the right to have a defense lawyer.[188] The consequence of carrying out the investigative measures without such notifications is the nullity of these acts.[189]

Among these investigative actions, a particular kind of a measure is the interrogation of the suspect by the police or the prosecutor. The prosecutor has the power to summon a suspect to appear for interrogation and even forcibly bring the suspect in.[190] The requirements of what the summons should contain are very broad and they include notification of the rights of the suspect, including the right to remain silent in the first place, as well as all details of the preliminary charge and evidence gathered against her.[191] But in practice it rarely happens that the prosecutor, while sending out the summons, informs the suspect of the evidentiary findings.[192] Thus, questioning a suspect as a witness is forbidden. The law is clear that if the person should have been heard as an accused or a suspect, her statements given as a witness shall not be used.[193] But if the witness has been questioned as such, and it became clear that she gives self-incriminating information, the interrogation must be stopped and the person shall receive notification of the rights while her former statement cannot be used.[194] This provision even led some scholars to believe that the scope of the right to remain silent, is "the most radical protection for criminal suspects when confronted with interrogation."[195]

184 Di Amato (2013), p. 166.
185 Caianiello (2010), p. 391.
186 Ruggieri and Marcolini (2013), p. 398.
187 Article 369 c.p.p.
188 Article 369bis c.p.p. See broadly in Caianiello (2010), p. 391.
189 Article 369bis (1) c.p.p.
190 Note that these rules apply not only to interrogations but to all measures that require the presence of the suspect (Article 375 (1) c.p.p.).
191 Article 64 c.p.p. and Article 65 (1) c.p.p.
192 Caianiello (2010), p. 392.
193 Article 63 (2) c.p.p.
194 Article 63 (1) c.p.p.
195 Thaman (2001), p. 592.

There is a significant difference between interrogations depending on which authority is asking the questions. If the investigation takes place before the prosecutor, the defense lawyer must be informed in advance, but her presence is not mandatory; police interrogations can only take place in the presence of counsel.[196] The scope of the information that is received by the suspect depends on the interrogating authority. When the suspect is questioned by the prosecutor, all facts for which the person is involved in the proceedings must be communicated to the suspect, while in cases of police interrogations just the juridical qualification of the charge must be provided, but not the facts.[197] Interestingly, the police also have limited rights in terms of questioning a suspect, which can be done only under the condition that she is not in custody.[198] This means that when a suspect is detained, only the prosecutor will be able to conduct the interrogation. The use of spontaneous testimonies of the suspect at the crime scene or immediately after the offense has occurred is strongly restricted, not allowing them to be admissible during trial.[199]

In rare circumstances, the suspect may be identified as such, due to the urgent need to conduct investigative measures involving her. It frequently happens that the police approach the person before her name has been registered or even before the *notitia criminis* has reached the prosecutor. This takes place when the police decide to arrest a person in exigent circumstances immediately after the discovery of the crime without any time to inform the prosecutor. In such a case the arrestee should be informed about the nature of his arrest and receive the letter of rights (*informazione di garanzia*) and the police should also inform the prosecutor that the arrest has occurred.[200] Therefore, despite the lack of registration of the suspect, this will allow the arrestee to gain the desired status.

Finally, the law provides for the considerably extraordinary mode of making a suspect acquainted with preliminary charges, when a person somehow learns that the prosecutor conducts investigation against her.[201] The suspect, upon her request, has the right to be informed on what has been registered against her in the prosecutorial registry, and only under specific circumstances may the prosecutor not reveal such information.[202] This concerns certain crimes as provided in Article 407 (2) (a) c.p.p. relating, among others, to organized crime and "specific needs concerning the investigative activity" occur. In the

196 Article 350 (3) c.p.p.
197 Illuminati and Caianiello (2007), p. 138 fn. 35.
198 Illuminati (2004), p. 310.
199 Article 350 (7) c.p.p. See Ryan (2014), pp. 196–197.
200 Ruggieri and Marcolini (2013), p. 386.
201 Ruggieri and Marcolini (2013), p. 399.
202 Article 335 (3) c.p.p.

latter scenario the prosecutor may not want to compromise the investigation by revealing this information too early and is allowed to keep this information confidential for up to three months. The Code guarantees that a person that has learned about being a suspect is entitled to appear before the prosecutor and make a statement.[203] Such appearance is considered as questioning if the person is initially charged with a crime and therefore all rules regarding interrogations of a suspect apply, including notification of her rights, in particular concerning the assistance of a lawyer and details of the preliminary charge as provided in Article 374 (2) c.p.p.

6.4.4 Authority Responsible for Preliminary Charging

The most basic rule provides that the prosecutor has an exclusive power to preliminarily charge a person with a crime. Bound by the legality principle, she must immediately enter the name of the alleged perpetrator of the offense on the register. The register is retained in the office of the prosecutor and the police have no power to enter either the offense or the name of the suspect on such registry.

Yet, in a very obvious way, the police actions will impact what exactly the prosecutor will put on that record. Since in many cases the prosecutor does not engage in the conduct of investigative actions unless the coercive measures are employed,[204] the decision as to what offense should be registered and who allegedly is responsible for commitment of such act will rely on the materials transferred to the prosecutor by the police. As a result, the prosecutorial decision regarding whom to preliminarily charge is, very indirectly, influenced by the investigative actions undertaken by the police. There is nothing to prevent the prosecutor from influencing the direction in which the investigation is carried on by the police. She may change the juridical qualification of an offense suggested by the police and refuse to register the name of the suspect. However, taking into account the number of cases prosecutor is ordinarily faced with it is very unlikely she will find enough time to verify each file. It is more plausible when prosecutor engages actively in the investigation.

The judge for the investigation also has certain powers with regard to entering the name of the suspect in the registry. As will be discussed below, the GIP, in cases when the prosecutor requests discontinuation of criminal investigation against an unknown person,[205] has the authority to register the identified individual into the prosecutorial registry and therefore

203 Article 374 (1) c.p.p.
204 Section 5.4.
205 Section 8.4.

conclusively decide on the shape of the initial charge of the suspect. This procedure is, however, very much an exception to the rule.

On the other hand, when it comes to the authority responsible for the notification of the suspect on her status, the law provides for a variety of choices. From the normative regulation it can be assumed that the primary authority is the prosecutor, who is obliged to do so at the conclusion of the investigation but also can summon the suspect for interrogation and in this way reveal to her all information about the charges and the attached rights. Moreover, absent exigent circumstances, the prosecutor plays an important role in ordering and conducting investigative measures concerning a suspect who demands the presence of her defense counsel, and therefore the prosecutor will determine the need to conduct such measure and through that notify the suspect about her status.

However, in the majority of cases the engagement of the prosecutor in criminal investigation is considerably low, especially when there is no need to impose coercive measures on the suspect. Therefore, in many cases the necessity to interrogate the suspect will be assessed solely by the police conducting the proceedings. It seems that the law foresees the threat that comes with such allocation of powers and sets a higher standard for the questioning of the suspect by enforcing the presence of the defense counsel, which is only optional in cases of prosecutorial interrogations. Moreover, the police can question the suspect only when she is not detained, which also substantially limits their powers.

Thus, on the normative level the engagement of police in preliminary charging seems minor. However, since the actions undertaken by the police in a very obvious way influence the shape of criminal investigation, their actual impact on the initial charging process might be much higher yet concealed. In the lack of prosecutorial involvement in the majority of cases, the police possess very broad powers to bring evidence in support of certain charges. And due to the overload of cases, the prosecutor might not even have the time or will to verify their accuracy. This makes the position of police very influential not only in terms of the conduct of investigation but also with regard to preliminary charging.

6.5 Preliminary Charging in the United States of America

6.5.1 General Considerations regarding Charging Decisions

Paradoxically, the discussion on the charging decisions in the USA is the most challenging within this chapter, and perhaps also throughout this whole work. This might be surprising, since the legal scholarship regarding the issue of charging a person with a crime in the USA is vast. However, taking into account the structural outlook adopted for this work, that demands separate discussions on preliminary charging, this issue appears to be not completely covered. This results from the very short and informal precharging investigation in the US system,[206] which does not provide for the clear separation of stages and which causes the overlap of such decisions as the initiation of investigation, the preliminary charging decision, and the decision formally charging an individual with a crime. Moreover, formal charging in the USA typically occurs much earlier in the course of proceedings than in its European counterparts, which resembles and to some extent replaces the procedure of preliminary charging a person with a crime.[207] Therefore, it is important to carefully delimit what can be understood as the formal charging decision and what can be considered as the preliminary charging that allows for the attachment of rights to the alleged perpetrator.

Generally, the prosecutor's charging powers are considered in the USA as the most important decisions made in the criminal justice system.[208] They are understood as decisions commencing criminal proceedings that can lead to criminal trial sanctions, including incarceration.[209] Indeed, the charging embodies the decision "to prosecute" even if at a later stage such decision might be changed so the case may be discontinued.

But there is no agreement what exactly constitutes the charging decision. Generally speaking, the formal charging decision takes one of two forms: the information and the indictment. These charging instruments differ, at least at first sight, in the authority that files them with the court. While the indictment is issued by the grand jury,[210] the information is filed by the prosecutor. The power of the grand jury to issue indictments is provided by the Fifth Amendment to the US Constitution which states that "[n]o person shall be held to answer for a capital, or otherwise infamous crime, unless on a presentment or indictment of a Grand Jury." But today only 18 states make a grand jury indictment mandatory for the prosecution of all felonies and four more in cases of capital offenses.[211] The trend to depart from this medieval mechanism of accusation started in 1859, when Michigan was the first state that decided to move away from the compulsory prosecution by the grand jury indictment. The practice, eventually confirmed by the Supreme Court,[212] has let many states[213] gradually adopt prosecution by information

206 Cf. Section 3.5.1.
207 Turner (2016), 1 p. 14, fn. 66.
208 Jacoby and Ratledge (2016), p. 61.
209 Neubauer and Fradella (2017), p. 289.
210 Cf. Section 5.5.3.
211 Kamisar et al. (2015), p. 975.
212 *Hurtado* v. *California* 110 US 516 (1884).
213 Since in the State of Connecticut the grand jury indictments were abolished by referendum held in 1982 a criminal prosecution may be instituted only by complaint or information (§ 39-11 CPB). See generally Spinella (1985), p. 392.

only also in felony cases.[214] But even in the federal system and those states that decided to keep up to date the grand jury indictments, the original role of the grand jury, that is to protect the individual from the prosecutor's wrongful accusations, has been for the most part instrumentalized. As a result, the prosecutor retains almost exclusive control over the grand jury decisions which makes her the ultimate decision maker when it comes to the charging decision in the US criminal justice system.

Therefore, from this perspective, the formal charging decision, whether it is indictment or information, belongs to the prosecutor. One of the most interesting features of this mechanism is that filing the charging document with the court does not necessarily make the shape of the charge final. Theoretically, after the formal charge has been filed, the arraignment takes place, which is a hearing to which the defendant is brought before court to hear the charges and to enter a plea.[215] But even though it has a significant influence on the further outcome of the proceedings, this is not the last chance for an individual to plead guilty, causing termination of proceedings outside of trial. This is due to the fact that the filing of a charge which technically leads to trial, is never a promise that a trial will take place. Since a long time can pass between arraignment and trial, the prosecutor is allowed to change the scope of charges that she wishes to prosecute. Actually, the charges that the defendant ultimately faces are ordinarily the result of prosecutor–defense negotiations. As it comes from the very nature of the US system, all actors are strongly encouraged to reach agreement and resolve the issue out of court. At arraignment, the prosecutor usually has little information about the defendant and the offense she is accused of and this decision is commonly premature, and therefore subject to changes. The prosecutor retains the broad power to change the charges, add additional counts, substitute the charges with others, and even dismiss some of them. Therefore, even if we talk about the decision to charge as a significant moment in arraignment, this is not the entire truth. As aptly stated by Frank W. Miller in his classic work on the prosecution and the charging powers of the prosecutor,

> the decision to charge, unlike the decision to arrest is not a unitary decision made at a readily identifiable time by a specified individual. It is, instead, a process consisting of a series of interrelated decisions, and the steps in the process do not always occur in the same sequence.[216]

It is also true that there are more than just two charging decisions. Some scholars describe four types of charging instruments i.e. arrest warrant,

214 See the discussion on indictment states vs. information states in Kamisar et al. (2015), pp. 950–951.
215 Hall (2009), p. 455.
216 Miller (1969), p. 11.

complaint, information, and indictment.[217] While the arrest warrant is the decision issued by the judicial officer preauthorizing the arrest of the person, the complaint should be understood as a brief document signed by the complainant (usually victim or police officer) produced in support of the request for a warrant or a charging document when the person was arrested without a warrant.[218] While in some jurisdictions the complaint may be replaced by the information or indictment,[219] in some others it can be used as the only charging instrument to prosecute misdemeanor offenses or city ordinance violations.[220] These markedly distinct approaches are an obvious result of the variations that appear in state legislations and even between court practices within one state.[221]

Probably the best way to answer the question of what can be considered as the formal charge is to link it to the determination of when the criminal process moves to the "prosecution" phase.[222] This is significant, since only after the prosecution commences, does the individual become covered by the provisions of the Sixth Amendment, which directly provides for the complex attachment of all rights that guarantees an individual a fair trial, including the right "to be informed of the nature and cause of the accusation" and "to have the assistance of counsel for her defense."[223] This has been addressed by the US Supreme Court on several occasions. The beginning of the criminal prosecution has been interpreted as the "initiation of adversary judicial criminal proceedings" which can take the form of the formal charge, preliminary hearing, indictment, information, or arraignment.[224] When it happens the accused transfers from being a suspect to a defendant[225] and the rights as provided in the Sixth Amendment attach to her in full. This is so, since when the judicial criminal proceedings commence "the adverse

217 Neubauer and Fradella (2017), pp. 288–289.
218 Hall (2009), p. 441.
219 Kamisar et al. (2015), p. 14.
220 For instance, in the State of Connecticut all felonies shall be prosecuted by information, but all misdemeanors, violations, and infractions shall be prosecuted by information or complaint (§ 36-11 CPB). However, in all jury cases, and in all other cases on written requests of the defendant, the prosecuting authority shall issue information in place of the complaint (§ 36-11 CPB). In practice, the information is issued by the prosecutor while the complaint by the police officer – see Spinella (1985), p. 394.
221 Del Carmen (2004), p. 311.
222 Although it should be recalled that entering the prosecution phase does not close the investigation in the US system, since they can smoothly coexist – see Section 3.5 for more on the boundaries of criminal investigation in the USA.
223 Similar provisions apply also at the state level – Cf. Article I § 8 of the Connecticut Constitution.
224 See *Kirby* v. *Illinois*, 406 US 682 (1972), 689. See also *Gilbert* v. *California*, 388 US 263 (1967) and *United States* v. *Wade*, 388 US 218 (1967).
225 Gottfredson and Gottfredson (1988), p. 115. Cf. Bradley (2007), p. 537

positions of the government and the defendant have solidified [, and] … a defendant finds himself faced with the prosecutorial forces of organized society, and immersed in the intricacies of substantive and procedural criminal law."[226]

Thus, we are now faced with the crucial question of whether during the criminal process but even before the "initiation of judicial criminal proceedings" the individual gets any protection. This can be narrowed down to the question of what can be called an initial charging decision under the adopted definition, i.e. the procedure aimed at identifying and designating an individual as a suspect, which attaches certain rights to provide her with sufficient protection during the course of criminal investigation.

First, resorting to the definition of the suspect in US legal scholarship is not particularly helpful. The US system, not very fond of categorizations and not eager to pay attention to precise definitions, lacks the determination of when exactly the individual becomes a suspect. Preoccupied with the attachment of certain rights under the Fourth, Fifth, and Sixth Amendments, the legal scholars almost overlook the need to classify this notion as the Continental lawyer would expect them to do. Yet, following the undertaken approach focused on the rights of the targeted individual and the moment when they become attached to that person, it is feasible to draw some conclusions.

Three terms are used in the US literature describing the passive party to the criminal process: "suspect," "accused," and "defendant" although they are used for most of the time without attaching to them a definite meaning. It is considerably easier to define the two latter terms. The term accused is explained by some legal dictionaries simply as a "person charged with the commission of a crime"[227] while in some others, as "a person who has been arrested and brought before a magistrate or who has been formally charged with a crime (as by indictment or information)."[228] The defendant can be understood more broadly as "a person accused in criminal proceeding or sued in a civil proceeding."[229] Therefore, for the purpose of this work, it is assumed that the accused or defendant (the latter in the criminal law context) are terms to be used interchangeably, meaning an individual formally charged with a crime, i.e. against whom the judicial criminal proceedings has been initiated and to whom the rights as provided in the Sixth Amendment are attached. The suspect is defined in dictionaries as "a

226 *Kirby* v. *Illinois*, 406 US 682, 689 (1972). See also *State* v. *Pierre*, 277 Conn. 42, 92–93 *cert. denied*, 547 US 1197 (2006) as quoted by Danaher (2017), p. 438.

227 See e.g. *Law Dictionary* (1997), p. 5.

228 See e.g. Garner (2000), p. 9. Cf. *Law Dictionary* (1997), p. 78 ("The person accused in a criminal case or sued in a civil action").

229 Garner (2000), p. 187.

person believed to have committed a crime or offense"[230] or "one who is suspected of committing crime"[231] which says nothing of when exactly such belief or suspicion obtains. As a result, the only certain part of the definition of the term suspect is the moment when the person loses such status and becomes the defendant i.e. the initiation of the adversary judicial criminal proceedings.

But it is more than clear that even before the person becomes formally charged, the law also provides protection to an individual who can be described as a suspect. This protection, however, does not stem from the Sixth Amendment but from the right against self-incrimination as proclaimed in the Fifth Amendment, which particularly concerns the right to counsel. These rights are triggered when the "custodial interrogation" takes place as famously decided in *Miranda* v. *Arizona*,[232] but they are most commonly a consequence of the arrest conducted by the police. Therefore, the most accurate answer to the question of what constitutes the preliminary charging decision is an arrest. The frequency with which the arrest takes place makes it the most common method of notifying an individual that she is the subject of a criminal investigation.[233]

It should be noted, however, that in those jurisdictions that acknowledge the arrest warrant as the formal charging instrument, the arrest conducted under the warrant loses its "initial" character as a preliminary charging measure. But, as discussed, drawing a firm line between the initial charging and formal charging is almost impossible. Therefore, for the purpose of this work, the arrest, regardless of whether preauthorized by the judicial authority or conducted without a warrant, will be considered as the preliminary charging decision. The vague nature of the arrest comes from the fact that, while being a part of the charging process, it also contributes to the investigation.[234]

Finally, much has been written about the severe consequences that a formal decision to charge a person with a crime brings to the defendant, but also to victims and the public. It is perceived as a decision that can change the life of a defendant exposing her to the threat of trial, most often accompanied by the pretrial detention stigma as well as social and financial consequences.[235] It also impacts the victim, who has limited legal tools to challenge the prosecutor's decision when charges are modified and especially when they are waived.[236] Moreover, it defines the workload of courts and

230 Garner (2000), p. 657.
231 Law Dictionary (1997), p. 325.
232 *Miranda* v. *Arizona*, 384 US 436 (1966).
233 Cf. Section 4.5.1.
234 Kamisar et al. (2015), p. 9.
235 Miller (1969), p. 3.
236 Gilliéron (2014), p. 77 and the literature cited in fn. 99.

defense counsels, determines the types of cases that the probation officers will handle, and partially determines the population of detention facilities.[237]

However, the significance of the preliminary charge is not that much different, even if it is not followed by the formal charging. As Miller points out, the decision to arrest involves many of the same considerations that are important in making charging decisions, including evaluation of the probability of guilt as well as whether it would be in the community interest to do so.[238] But the arrest may have even more severe consequences than the formal charging. As the Supreme Court has stated,

> [a]rrest is a public act that may seriously interfere with the defendant's liberty, whether he is free on bail or not, and that may disrupt his employment, drain his financial resources, curtail his associations, subject him to public obloquy, and create anxiety in him, his family and his friends.[239]

Taking into account the frequency with which arrests occur despite the severity of the crime, the inevitable consequences of the preliminary charge made in the form of arrest are unquestionable.

6.5.2 Threshold for Preliminary Charging

US law broadly discusses standards of proof that need to be reached at each stage of the criminal process that allows the authority to act. Probable cause is the standard necessary for arrest. Importantly, it is exactly the same standard of proof that must be met when the formal charging takes place. In the latter, the existence of probable cause is checked when the prosecutor files an information with a court and the preliminary examination takes place, which in some jurisdictions for that reason is known as the probable cause hearing. The hearing is designed to prevent malicious and wrongful prosecutions, providing a screening of the decision to charge by a neutral judicial body.[240] The same purpose is served by the grand jury, when operating in its capacity as a "shield" concerning the charging by indictment.[241]

The probable cause requirement for conducting an arrest stems from the Fourth Amendment to the US Constitution that protects an individual against arbitrary search and seizure.[242] This also means that the same

237 Jacoby and Ratledge (2016), p. 63.
238 Miller (1969), p. 3.
239 *United States* v. *Marion*, 404 US 307, 320 (1971).
240 Kamisar et al. (2015), p. 13.
241 Kamisar et al. (2015), p. 747. See also Alexander (1974), p. 998.
242 "The right of the people to be secure in their persons, houses, papers, and effects, against unreasonable searches and seizures, shall not be violated, and no Warrants shall issue, but

standard of proof is required for the search and seizure of property and of persons (arrest). Moreover, establishing the existence of it is necessary regardless of whether the measure results from the warrant or is conducted without preauthorization. In the former, it will be done before the person is arrested, while in the latter, the verification, if the police and the prosecutor decide not to release a suspect, will take place afterwards. But the attempts to define such an ambiguous term as probable cause always bear risk of misunderstanding. In *Brinegar* v. *United States*, it was explained that probable cause means "more than bare suspicion" and it "exists where the facts and circumstances within their [the officer's] knowledge and of which they had reasonably trustworthy information [are] sufficient in themselves to warrant a man of reasonable caution in the belief that an offense has been or is being committed."[243]

This is perceived as not being sufficiently useful for the police officers who are expected to react in exigent circumstances on the spot when making a rapid decision to arrest or not.[244] Therefore, in *Illinois* v. *Gates* the Supreme Court admitted that "probable cause is a fluid concept—turning on the assessment of probabilities in particular factual context—not readily, or even usefully, reduced to a neat set of legal rules."[245] Moreover, the phrase used by the Court in the *Brinegar* judgment suggested that the "man of reasonable caution" should be understood as the average person and not one with any related training who under the same circumstances would come up with the same conclusion that the probable cause exists. The Supreme Court eventually reached the conclusion that the evaluation of the behavior of such person must also take into account the experience of the police officer.[246] The Court has also focused on the issue of how reliable the source of information should be and in a series of judgments[247] tried to clarify it, ultimately reaching the conclusion that probable cause should be valued in the light of the totality of circumstances.[248]

In the discussion regarding the threshold necessary to arrest a person as a form of charging her preliminarily, it is necessary to briefly also mention

upon probable cause, supported by Oath or affirmation, and particularly describing the place to be searched, and the persons or things to be seized."

243 *Brinegar* v. *United States*, 338 US 160, 175 (1949).

244 Worrall (2012), p. 88.

245 *Illinois* v. *Gates*, 462 US 213, 232 (1983).

246 See *United States* v. *Ortiz*, 422 US 891, 897 (1975).

247 See in particular *Aguilar* v. *Texas*, 378 US 108 (1964) and *Spinelli* v. *United States*, 393 US 410 (1969). Note that the two-prong test for assessing the credibility of the information as well as informant being a basis for the arrest took the name *Aguillar–Spinelli* test after these judgments.

248 See *Illinois* v. *Gates*, 462 US 213, 233 (1983).

a second standard that is provided for other police activity quite similar to arrest i.e. stop—which is called "reasonable suspicion." This is

> a less demanding standard than probable cause not only in the sense that reasonable suspicion can be established with information that is different in quantity or content than that required to establish probable cause, but also in the sense that reasonable suspicion can arise from information that is less reliable than that required to show probable cause.[249]

This lower standard has been recognized by the Supreme Court in response to the needs of police to briefly deprive a person of liberty at the scene and conduct a pat-down of her clothing. This has been called stop and frisk or a *Terry* stop, after *Terry* v. *Ohio* which allowed for this different, much lower level of suspicion.[250]

It should be remembered, however, that even if probable cause exists the police officer has no duty to act and to arrest a suspect. In fact, the decision-making in that regard is similar to the one undertaken by the prosecutor in the case of charging. It is true that factors impacting the prosecutorial discretion at the time of deciding whether to charge and with what, are different than those that influence the police officer arrest decisions made on the spot. This results from the dynamics of the situation that the police officer is usually faced with. While the prosecutor should take into consideration such elements as sufficiency of evidence, the victim's reluctance to testify, lack of public interest, to name just a few, the police officer usually has no time to evaluate all circumstances and must react quite quickly. But despite the differences, the discretionary authority of the police officer is not limited by the principle of legality in a similar way as attaches to prosecutor and the police officer is free to decide whether and how to react.[251] Therefore, it may happen that despite the existence of probable cause, the police officer decides not to arrest an individual or even not to react at all.

6.5.3 Procedure for Preliminary Charging

The arrest has different definitions for various purposes. As defined in some works, it is "the act of taking a person into custody for the purpose of charging him with a crime"[252] or "taking of a person into custody for

249 *Alabama* v. *White*, 496 US 325, 330 (1990).
250 See *Terry* v. *Ohio*, 392 US 1 (1968).
251 Note however that there are certain circumstances that might force the reaction of the police officer. An interesting example of binding an officer with an obligation to arrest are domestic violence laws. See more broadly e.g. Hirschel et al. (2007), p. 255.
252 Kamisar et al. (2015), p. 8.

the commission of an offense as the prelude to prosecuting him or her for that offense."[253] It is also provided that besides this "full custody" version of arrest, it may be also understood as brief detention that results with release upon summons to appear in court on a given date.[254] Note that the latter understanding of "arrest" does not change much in the perception of the individual being the subject of a criminal investigation. Therefore, the individual receiving summons usually understands her position as a suspect since the summons contains the information on what offenses she has allegedly committed.

On the other hand, when the full custody arrest takes place, it is followed by taking the arrestee to the police station for the so-called booking, which is a procedure of making an entry in the police blotter or arrest book which indicates the suspect's name, the time of arrest and, most importantly, the preliminarily defined offense involved.[255] At the police station a higher-ranking police officer will usually informally review the sufficiency of the evidence to determine whether to sustain the preliminary charge. This may result in releasing a suspect without a charge as reportedly happens in 10 to 15 percent of arrests concerning misdemeanors.[256] The arrestee is usually also searched, fingerprinted, and photographed and allowed to make a call.[257]

As a follow-up procedure, if the suspect is to remain in custody, she must be taken for the initial appearance (or presentment as it is called in some states) before the competent authority (judge or magistrate). This must be done promptly and without delay.[258] During this judicial proceeding, the suspect will be informed about the reasons of the detention i.e. the offenses that she has been charged with and her rights, including the protection against self-incrimination and the right to counsel.[259] As discussed before, the initial appearance is considered as moving a case to the "judicial criminal proceedings," and therefore the rights as covered by the Sixth Amendment attach and the suspect becomes the accused. At this point we can no longer talk about the suspect and preliminary charges.

In the light of the above, the key importance should be attached to the interrogation that the suspect might go through before the initial appearance takes place. This is closely linked to the scope of the protection that, during such interrogation, is attached to the suspect as derived from the Fifth Amendment's privilege against self-incrimination. The scope of these rights—famously known as

253 Neubauer and Fradella (2017), p. 285.
254 Kamisar et al. (2015), p. 8.
255 Del Carmen (2004), p. 36.
256 Burnham (2011), p. 270.
257 Hall (2009), p. 441.
258 See *Gerstein* v. *Pugh*, 420 US 103 (1975).
259 Worrall (2012), p. 306.

the *Miranda* rights has been the subject of concern at the US Supreme Court.[260] To provide sufficient safeguards for the vulnerable suspect, who had not yet been formally charged with a crime, and therefore to whom the protection under the Sixth Amendment does not yet apply, it was held that before interrogating the suspect who is in custody, the police must, among other things, advise her of her right to remain silent and the right to have a counsel present during questioning.

The critical issue in triggering the rights of the suspect is the fact that she is exposed to the "custodial interrogation." In the decisions preceding the *Miranda* ruling the Court suggested that there is a visible difference between "general inquiry" and the moment when investigation begins to focus on a particular suspect which should activate the suspect's full protection but abstained to clarify when this happens.[261] This was resolved in the *Miranda* judgment, as the Supreme Court did not refrain from explicitly stating that the standard applies "when a person has been taken into custody or otherwise deprived of his freedom of action in any significant way."[262] This concerns most typically an arrest but also other forms of depriving a person of liberty, yet, when a person "voluntarily comes to the police station, and is allowed to leave unhindered by police after a brief interview,"[263] the custodial requirement is considered as not present. Moreover, for the person to be afforded Fifth Amendment protections, the interrogation must take place. The Court tried to narrow down the notion of interrogation by explaining that this means "questioning initiated by law enforcement officers"[264] but there is no easy answer to it.[265] Interestingly, when the custodial interrogation takes place the suspect must be earlier informed about her rights[266] among which there is no obligation to notify the suspect of the nature of offenses that she is initially alleged committing. Therefore, despite the attachment of the right to counsel and the right not to incriminate oneself, the effectiveness

260 See also cases preceding the Miranda judgment that have paved the way to this groundbreaking decision: *Brown* v. *Mississippi*, 297 US 278 (1936), *Chambers* v. *Florida*, 309 US 227 (1940), *Spano* v. *New York*, 360 US 315 (1959).

261 See e.g. *Escobedo* v. *Illinois*, 378 US 748 (1964).

262 *Miranda* v. *Arizona*, 384 US 436, 444 (1966).

263 *California* v. *Beheler*, 463 US 1121, 1121 (1983).

264 *Miranda* v. *Arizona*, 384 US 436, 444 (1966).

265 See e.g. *Rhode Island* v. *Innis*, 446 US 291 (1980) where the Supreme Court held that the discussion between two officers to which no response was from the suspect was invited or expected while driving him in the car does not equal interrogation.

266 *Miranda* v. *Arizona*, 384 US 436, 479 (1966) ("He must be warned prior to any questioning that he has the right to remain silent, that anything he says can be used against him in a court of law, that he has the right to the presence of an attorney, and that, if he cannot afford an attorney one will be appointed for him prior to any questioning if he so desires").

of protection can be queried if the information on the scope of preliminary charges under which the suspect is being questioned are not revealed to her.

One should note that if neither the custodial interrogation nor the arrest takes place, the individual might not be notified about her status as a suspect. This, however, should not be considered as particularly problematic by the nature of the US criminal justice system practices. First, the system unfortunately provides for the very strong preference for the arrest and almost mandatory imposition of this measure in serious cases, which leaves nonarrested suspects in a striking minority. Second, since the formal charging decision is undertaken so early in the course of criminal proceedings that it can be assumed that no harm is done to the suspect in terms of exercising the rights that should already belong to her at that point. The time from the formal charges until the first day of trial allow for preparation of defense with the help of counsel. The problems that may arise with the effectiveness of such a defense are not a result of delayed notification of the status of suspect. Although it certainly can be detrimental to the suspect in such cases as when the prosecutor seeks the grand jury indictment and does not attempt to arrest an individual first. Then, secret proceedings with no judicial involvement are conducted, providing no protection for the individual who may be summoned and questioned in front of the grand jury along the lines desired by the prosecutor. From this perspective, it should be admitted that the exceptional protection belonging to the suspect could guarantee better protection of her procedural rights.

6.5.4 Authority Responsible for Preliminary Charging

The most commonly pronounced perspective on the formal charging decision in the USA is that it belongs solely to the prosecutor.[267] The prosecutors alone determine whether or not to charge someone with a crime and, moreover, they alone determine the course of the prosecution. But the exclusiveness of the prosecutorial powers in that regard, might not be as absolute as we would like to think if the preliminary charging decision remains outside of the scope of their powers. As Miller stated more than 50 years ago, "a problem of central significance in current criminal justice administration is who should have responsibility for making the initial charging decision."[268] This phrase has never lost its value.

In the large majority of cases the initial decision to charge a suspect with a crime is made when a police officer makes a warrantless arrest of a suspect.

267 See e.g. Jacoby and Ratledge (2016), p. 61; Anderson (2001), p. 3; Kamisar et al. (2015), pp. 10–11.

268 Miller (1969), p. 9.

Certainly, these preliminary charges on which the suspect was arrested are recorded during booking and might be changed, or even waived, at this point and the prosecutor can decide immediately afterwards to decline the case even against the will of the police.[269] But the importance of the police impact cannot be underestimated. In most cases, no person can be charged with anything by the prosecutor if the police do not undertake some preliminary decision. They are the first on the line and the first decision whether to arrest belongs to them. Some would like to wish that the police are just "doing their job" and have no discretion whether to screen a case in any sense, but in reality, it is done on a daily basis. As aptly concluded by one former prosecutor, the truth is that "the most important factors in determining who gets prosecuted for what are the decisions of supervisory and line personnel in police departments or investigative agencies."[270]

Despite the prosecutorial power to refrain from charging a person contrary the police officer's view, in the majority of cases the suspect comes to attention of the prosecutor only because the police officer arrested a suspect. This gives the police a very real power over the initial decision to charge a person with a crime. Throughout the whole arrest and booking process, the prosecutor remains uninvolved and when later formally charging a suspect, she must base her knowledge regarding the case on the police report and what the police officer has decided to reveal in it. Moreover, "where the police decide not to invoke the criminal process, effective methods of review and control are largely lacking, and this issue of the proper scope and function of police discretion is of great, current importance and difficulty."[271] This makes an important observation regarding the scrutiny of the police arrests that do not subsequently transfer into formal proceedings against the suspect.

It is therefore true that, although the prosecutor has the legal authority to charge a suspect with a crime, the police influences the prosecutor's decision. This is so since the initial decision to charge a person with a crime remains almost exclusively in the hands of police. The impact that the initial charging has on building the formal charges, especially in minor cases which are a visible majority, should not be underestimated in discussing the scope of prosecutorial powers during criminal investigation.

269 Although some prosecutors allow police input into the charging decision, the study shows that the number of police arrests that results in no criminal charges being filed varies between 20 and 50 percent – see research cited by Neubauer and Fradella (2017), p. 292.

270 Richman (1997), p. 957.

271 Miller and Remington (1962), p. 115.

6.6 Summary

The states differ tremendously regarding the ways in which a suspect is preliminarily charged with a crime. The differences result from the inherent models of criminal procedure and are obviously predetermined by the way in which the formal charges occur—in the case of the USA, early in the process moving the case immediately to a judicial stage, and in the Continental system—after a long and thoroughly conducted investigation aimed at gathering all evidence for the purpose of a future trial. However, the diversity of choices cannot be simply justified by the regular distinctions that exist between systems, but should be considered rather as the proof that systems have no straightforward answer as to how this issue should be resolved. They are torn between the formal determination of the status of a suspect as early as the criminal investigation is directed against the person, and on the other hand attaching the status only when certain measures are performed preserving the secrecy of the criminal investigation and information about the gathered evidence until its very end.

Accordingly, preliminary charging in Poland takes a very formal shape and seems to protect the suspect in the best way. From the decision, officially issued by the authority conducting criminal investigation, that must contain the specified crime that the person is charged with, the suspect can learn all that is necessary to be able to undertake an effective defense. There is also no way in which the suspect may overlook such information since the law provides that she must be present in person for the presentment of charges, notified about her rights, and interrogated. Additionally, building the strong connection between the preliminary charging decision and final charges as appearing in the indictment and forcing the authorities to notify the suspect in the same form whenever the preliminary charges are amended, prevents the suspect from being ambushed with new, previously unseen, charges at the end of criminal investigation and allows her to prepare the defense in advance.

But the system has its very obvious flaws. Nothing in the discussed procedure prevents the authority responsible for presenting the charges from hiding from the suspect information about her status and interrogating her primarily as a witness. The threshold is construed in such vague terms that allow for a considerable level of discretion as to when to summon the suspect and interrogate her as such. This is not to say that construing the appropriate threshold applicable to all situations is even possible, but nor does this lead to the admission that the formality of the prescribed procedure safeguards the rights of individual in a sufficient way. Second, since the presentment of preliminary charges has a mandatory character, this forces the unnecessary coercion on the suspect even if she is not interested in giving testimony at that moment in the course of criminal process. She must appear before the interrogating authority, under threat of being forcibly brought before the prosecutor or the police, to hear the preliminary charges and be interrogated with regard to them. Even if there are no grounds to arrest the suspect and no coercive measures are objectively applicable, if she refrains from showing up at the time and place to where she was summoned she will be arrested and by force brought to face charges and be subsequently interrogated. Particularly striking, and resembling the darkest communist times, is the police power to freely and unquestionably summon the suspect to subject her to the procedure of presentment of preliminary charges. And even though only the prosecutor in such a case has the authority to decide on forcibly bringing the suspect noncomplying with the police summons, this mechanism definitely gives too much power to police officers conducting criminal investigations. Finally, because during the preliminary charging procedure the suspect is presented with initial charges that must be presumably identical to those that will become the basis for the final formal charges as contained in the indictment, there is a temptation to receive the plea from her at that time. This temptation has been confirmed normatively, providing for the same procedure regarding interrogation at that point and during a trial which means that the suspect is forced to decide on the plea. As discussed above, this is often the only moment in the course of criminal process that the suspect interacts with the criminal justice system. If she pleads guilty and accepts the penalty as proposed by the prosecutor, the law does not demand the subsequent presence of the defendant at the hearing when the judge confirms the agreement reached reflected in the records of interrogation. This raises serious concerns regarding the actual voluntariness of the guilty plea, since most frequently it is filed without defense counsel being present.

The German case is just one step down from the Polish system. The law provides for the mandatory interrogation of a suspect before filing a case with the court, during which the suspect learns about the initial charges in more or less exhaustive terms, depending on the authority that conducts the interrogation. The person is compelled to appear before the authority for that procedure although, again depending on the authority, this might indeed be compulsory when the prosecutor summons, or just appear as such when it is done by the police. Also, in this case, the law only assumes that the notification will be done as soon as sufficient evidence is gathered, establishing who is the suspect, but the practice seems to be more problematic. Therefore, nothing forbids the German criminal justice authorities from presenting the suspect with initial charges late in criminal investigation, which can be considered as depriving her of her rights to effectively defend herself and prepare for defense as well as to rebut gathered evidence and convince the prosecutor to refrain from filing charges.

The Italian system provides a less intrusive approach. Until the very end of criminal investigation, the suspect is not called for interrogation to be notified about her status. Even though the identity of the suspect is revealed quite early in a very formal way by entering her name in the prosecutor's registry, the suspect might not learn about it for a long time. In the event that a suspect becomes aware that she is the subject of a criminal investigation, then she can request the interrogation herself. . As in all other countries, on concluding an investigation, the prosecutor is forced to notify the suspect about her status and allow her to acquaint herself with the materials gathered before the trial.

The US system does not provide for any compulsory mechanism to notify the suspect of initial charges unless a certain coercive measure is employed, usually the arrest. As discussed extensively, the early formal charging process by indictment, information, or by other means does not trigger such necessity. Moreover, since even the formal charging document is subjected to changes being a result of ongoing negotiations, it is no wonder that the initial charging process attracts less attention.

But the USA, Germany, and Italy all provide for mechanisms through which the individual immediately becomes the suspect. This happens when the suspect becomes the subject of a criminal investigation. In all three countries, when the investigation turns against the individual as manifested by the arrest of that person, she gains the status of a suspect and most importantly she is notified about all her rights applicable at that moment, including the right to a lawyer, and to remain silent. The rule might be even broader, considering not only pure arrest but custodial interrogations as in the USA, or when a search is carried out in Italy or Germany. Surprisingly, this mechanism is not available in the Polish system, which can be considered as depriving the arrested individual of her rights as should be applicable under the relevant EU directives.[272]

In those countries where the preliminary charging also takes the form of arrest, the authority to make the decision rests entirely with the police. But also in those cases where the preliminary charging takes the form of interrogation of a suspect, the police are engaged in doing so. Only in Poland are there rigid rules excluding the police from doing so in cases of investigations conducted in the form of inspection concerning severe

272 Cf. Directive 2012/13/EU of the European Parliament and of the Council of May 22, 2012 on the right to information in criminal proceedings, OJ L 142, 1.6.2012 and Directive 2013/48/EU of the European Parliament and of the Council of 22 October 2013 on the right of access to a lawyer in criminal proceedings and in European arrest warrant proceedings, and on the right to have a third party informed upon deprivation of liberty and to communicate with third persons and with consular authorities while deprived of liberty, OJ L 294, 6.11.2013.

crimes. But in all other cases the police are a primary authority to conduct the measure by which the suspect learns about her status, rights, and crimes she is preliminarily charged with. This has its obvious flaws. In the majority of cases the police actions are of a reactive character and take place in exigent circumstances. Moreover, the police are not trained legally, which in many cases make the initial charge, as presented to the suspect at the time when the measure is being undertaken, quite shaky and imprecise if not inappropriate. This means that there may be a considerable discrepancy between the final charge filed with court by the prosecutor and its preliminary version drafted by police. This calls into question the ability to prepare an effective defense against the charge that eventually will be proceeded in court.

Certainly, the prosecutor in each system possesses the unquestioned power to decide on whether to prosecute the suspect or not. Even where the formal charges by law must be identical to the initial charges (Poland), the prosecutor may correct them by presenting the amended charges to the suspect and subsequently filing them with the court. Yet, the position of the prosecutor on what should be the shape of the ultimate charge relies heavily on the police reports and files and the direction in which investigation is aimed through the initial charging decisions. There is no doubt that the preliminary charges will have an impact on the final charges as presented in the indictment. And since it is usually not the prosecutor who arrests and conducts an early interrogation of the suspect, the impact of the police on the final formal charges should not be underestimated.

To restrain police powers and limit the imposition of the police perspective in that regard, the law is tempted to provide for the insight of the prosecutor in the criminal investigation, encouraging or even enforcing mechanisms that engage the prosecutor earlier than at the time when the decision to prosecute is undertaken. Some countries even empower the prosecutor to initially charge a suspect and interrogate her, especially when serious crimes are at stake. Such authority is provided either directly, like in Poland where the prosecutor is obliged to initially charge a suspect in the case of all felonies and some misdemeanors, or encouraged as in Germany by limiting the police competencies to summon the suspect for the mandatory interrogation. Whether this is a desirable approach, especially in the context of the prosecutorial ability to effectively evaluate the outcome of investigation, will be discussed further in Chapter 9.

References

Alexander RP, Portman S (1974) Grand Jury Indictment Versus Prosecution by Information – An Equal Protection-Due Process Issue. *Hastings Law Journal* 25:998.

Anderson S (2001) The Changing Role of the Prosecutor. In: *The Prosecutors Deskbook. Ethical Issue and Emerging Roles for the 21st Century Prosecutors.* American Prosecutors Research Institute, Alexandria, pp. 3–23.
Bohlander M (2012) *Principles of German Criminal Procedure.* Hart Publishing, London.
Bradley CM (2007) United States. In: Bradley CM (ed) *Criminal Procedure. A Worldwide Study.* Carolina Academic Press, Durham, pp. 519–548.
Brodowski D, Burchard C, Kotzurek N, Rauber J, Vogel J (2010) Germany. In: Cape E, Namoradze Z, Smith R, Spronken T (eds) *Effective Criminal Defence in Europe.* Intersentia, Antwerp–Oxford–Portland, pp. 253–319.
Brodzisz (2015a) Komentarz do art. 313 k.p.k. In: Jerzy Skorupka (ed) *Kodeks postępowania karnego.* Komentarz. CH Beck, Warsaw.
Brodzisz (2015b) Komentarz do art. 332 k.p.k. In: Jerzy Skorupka (ed) *Kodeks postępowania karnego.* Komentarz. CH Beck, Warsaw.
Burnham W (2011) *Introduction to the Law and Legal System of the United States.* 5th edn. West, St Paul.
Caianiello M (2010) Italy. In: Cape E, Namoradze Z, Smith R, Spronken T (eds) *Effective Criminal Defence in Europe.* Intersentia, Antwerp–Oxford–Portland, pp. 373–423.
Caianiello M (2016) *Increasing Discretionary Prosecutor's Powers: The Pivotal Role of the Italian Prosecutor in the Pretrial Investigation Phase.* Oxford Handbooks Online, Oxford.
Caianiello M (2019) Access to and Limits on Evidence Dossiers in Civil Law Systems. In: Brown DK, Turner JI, Weisser B (eds) *The Oxford Handbook of Criminal Process.* Oxford University Press, Oxford, pp. 563–585.
Cape E, Hodgson J, Pranken T, Spronken T (eds) (2007) *Suspects in Europe. Procedural Rights at the Investigative Stage of the Criminal Process in the European Union.* Intersentia, Antwerp.
Cape E, Namoradze Z, Smith R, Spronken T (eds) (2010) *Effective Criminal Defence in Europe.* Intersentia, Antwerp.
Corso P (1993) Italy. In: Van Den Wyngaert C (ed) *Criminal Procedure Systems in the European Community.* Butterworths, London, pp. 223–260.
Danaher III JA (2017) Right to Counsel. In: Schuman CJ (ed) *Connecticut Criminal Procedure.* Connecticut Law Tribune, Hartford, pp. 435–467.
De Vocht D (2010) Poland. In: Cape E, Namoradze Z, Smith R, Spronken T (eds) *Effective Criminal Defence in Europe.* Intersentia, Antwerp–Oxford–Portland, pp. 425–488.
Del Carmen RV (2004) *Criminal Procedure. Law and Practice.* Thomson, Belmont.
Di Amato A (2013) Criminal Law in Italy. Kluwer Law International, Alphen aan den Rijn.
Garner BA (2000) *A Dictionary of Criminal Law Terms.* West Group, St. Paul.
Gilliéron G (2004) *Public Prosecutors in the United States and Europe.* Springer, Cham.
Girdwoyń P (2006) *Zarys niemieckiego procesu karnego.* Temida2, Białystok.
Gottfredson MR, Gottfredson DM (1988) *Decision Making in Criminal Justice. Toward the Rational Exercise of Discretion.* 2nd edn. Plenum Press, New York.
Hall DE (2009) *Criminal Law and Procedure.* Delmar, Clifton Park.

Hirschel D, Buzawa E, Pattavina A, Faggiani D (2007) Domestic Violence and Mandatory Arrest Laws: To What Extent Do They Influence Police Arrest Decisions? *Journal of Criminal Law and Criminology* 98:255.
Huber B (2008) Germany. In: Vogler R, Huber B, *Criminal Procedure in Europe*. Duncker & Humblot, Berlin, pp. 269–371.
Illuminati G (2004) The Role of the Public Prosecutor in the Italian System In: Tak PJP (ed) *Tasks and Powers of the Prosecution Services in the EU Member States. Volume I*. Wolf Legal Publishers, Nijmegen, pp. 303–332.
Illuminati G, Caianiello M (2007) The Investigative Stage of the Criminal Process in Italy. In: Cape E, Hodgson J, Pranken T, Spronken T (eds) *Suspects in Europe. Procedural Rights at the Investigative Stage of the Criminal Process in the European Union*. Intersentia, Antwerp, pp. 129–154.
Jacoby JE, Ratledge EC (2016) *The Power of the Prosecutor. Gatekeepers of the Criminal Justice System*. Praeger, Santa Barbara.
Jasiński W, Kremens K (2019) *Criminal Law in Poland*. Kluwer Law International, Alphen aan den Rijn.
Juy-Birmann R (2002) The German System. Delmas-Marty M, Spencer JR (eds) *European Criminal Procedures*. Cambridge University Press, Cambridge, pp. 292–347.
Kamisar Y, LaFave WR, Israel JH, King NJ, Kerr OS, Primus EB (2015) *Modern Criminal Procedure. Cases-Comments-Questions*. West, St Paul.
Kiełtyka A (2016) Formy postępowania przygotowawczego. In: Ryszard Stefański (ed) *System Prawa Karnego Procesowego. Postępowanie przygotowawcze. Volume X*. Wolters Kluwer, Warsaw, pp. 400–578.
Kosonoga J (2016) Przedstawienie zarzutów. In: Ryszard Stefański (ed) *System Prawa Karnego Procesowego. Postępowanie przygotowawcze*. Volume X. Wolters Kluwer, Warsaw, pp. 725–820.
Kremens K (2015) Śledztwo po 1 lipca 2015 r. z perspektywy obrońcy i pełnomocnika. In: Wiliński P (ed) *Obrońca i pełnomocnik w procesie karnym po 1 lipca 2015 r. Przewodnik po zmianach*. Wolters Kluwer, Warsaw, pp. 70–87.
Kruszyński P (2007) The Investigative Stage of the Criminal Process in Poland. In: Cape E, Hodgson J, Pranken T, Spronken T (eds) *Suspects in Europe. Procedural Rights at the Investigative Stage of the Criminal Process in the European Union*. Intersentia, Antwerp, pp. 181–209.
Kühne H-H (1993) Germany. In: Van Den Wyngaert C (ed) *Criminal Procedure Systems in the European Community*, Butterworths, London, pp. 137–162.
Kulesza C (2019) Zasada skargowości w polskim procesie karnym. In: Wiliński P (ed) *System Prawa Karnego Procesowego. Zasady Procesu Karnego*. Volume III. Part I. Wolters Kluwer, Warsaw, pp. 546–634.
Law Dictionary (1997) *Gilbert Law Summaries*, Orlando.
Ligeti K (ed) (2013) *Toward a Prosecutor of the European Union, Volume 1: A Comparative Analysis*. Hart Publishing, London.
Malsch M, De Boer MM (2019) Interview of Suspects of Crime. Law and Practice in European Countries. In: Brown DK, Turner JI, Weisser B (eds) *The Oxford Handbook of Criminal Process*. Oxford University Press, Oxford, pp. 317–340.

Meyer-Großner L, Schmitt B (2018) *Strafprozessordnung mit GVG und Nebengesetzen*. CH Beck, München.
Miller FW (1969) *Prosecution. The Decision to Charge a Suspect with a Crime*. Little, Brown and Company, Boston.
Murzynowski A (1971) Faktyczny podejrzany w postępowaniu przygotowawczym. *Palestra* 10:36–43.
Neubauer DW, Fradella HF (2019) *America's Courts and the Criminal Justice System*, 13th edn. Cengage, Boston.
Nowak C, Steinborn S (2013) Poland. In: Ligeti K (ed) *Toward a Prosecutor of the European Union, Volume 1: A Comparative Analysis*. Hart Publishing, London, pp. 498–509.
Panzavolta M (2004) Reforms and Counter-reforms in the Italian Struggle for an Accusatorial Criminal Law System. *North Carolina Journal of International Law & Commercial Regulation* 30:577–624.
Prusak F (1971) Faktycznie podejrzany w procesie karnym. *Palestra* 3:32–47.
Richman DC (1997) Old Chief v. United States: Stipulating Away Prosecutorial Accountability? *Virginia Law Review* 89:939–990.
Ruggeri S (2015) Investigative and Prosecutorial Discretion in Criminal Matters: The Contribution of the Italian Experience. In: Caianiello M, Hodgson JS (eds) *Discretionary Criminal Justice in a Comparative Context*. Carolina Academic Press, Durham, pp. 59–85.
Ruggieri F, Marcolini S (2013) Italy. In: Ligeti K (ed) *Toward a Prosecutor of the European Union, Volume 1: A Comparative Analysis*. Hart Publishing, London, pp. 368–404.
Ryan A (2014) *Towards a System of European Criminal Justice*. Routledge, New York.
Sakowicz A (2019) *Prawo do milczenia w polskim procesie karnym*. Temida2, Białystok.
Scarpa F, Peruzzo K, Pontrandolfo G (2014) Methodological, Terminological and Phraseological Challenges in the Translation into English of the Italian Code of Criminal Procedure: What's New in the Second Edition. In: Gialuz M, Lupária L, Scarpa F (eds) *The Italian Code of Criminal Procedure. Critical Essays and English Translation*. Cedam, Milan, pp. 57–95
Spinella AP (1985) *Connecticut Criminal Procedure*. The Atlantic Law Book Company, West Hartford.
Stefański RA (2013a) Czynności przedstawienia zarzutów. *Prokuratura i Prawo* 7–8:20–48.
Stefański RA (2013b) Skuteczność przedstawienia zarzutów. *Prokuratura i Prawo* 6 5–32.
Stefański RA (2013c) Prawo do obrony osoby podejrzanej. In: Grzegorczyk T, Izydorczyk J, Olszewski R (eds) *Z problematyki funkcji procesu karnego*. Wolters Kluwer, Warsaw.
Steinborn S (2012) Status osoby podejrzanej w procesie karnym z perspektywy Konstytucji RP (uwagi de lege lata i de lege ferenda). In: Kardas P, Sroka T, Wróbel W (eds) *Państwo prawa i prawo karne. Księga jubileuszowa Profesora Andrzeja Zolla*. Wolters Kluwer, Warsaw, pp. 1781–1802.
Tarnowska D (2013) *Instytucja przedstawienia zarzutów w polskim procesie karnym*. Wydawnictwo Naukowe Uniwersytetu Szczecińskiego, Szczecin.

Thaman S (2001) Miranda in Comparative Law. *St. Louis Law Journal* 45:581–624.
Turner JI (2016) Plea Bargaining and Disclosure in Germany and the United States: Comparative Lessons. *William & Mary Law Review* 57:1–49.
Tylman J, Grzegorczyk T (2014) *Postępowanie karne*. Lexis Nexis, Warsaw.
Waltoś S (1963) *Akt oskarżenia w procesie karnym*. Wydawnictwo Prawnicze, Warsaw.
Waltoś S (2013) *Proces karny. Zarys Systemu*. Lexis Nexis, Warsaw.
Weigend T, Salditt F (2007) The Investigative Stage of the Criminal Process in Germany. In: Cape E, Hodgson J, Pranken T, Spronken T (eds) *Suspects in Europe. Procedural Rights at the Investigative Stage of the Criminal Process in the European Union*. Intersentia, Antwerp, pp. 79–100.
Weigend T (2013) Germany. In: Ligeti K (ed) *Toward a Prosecutor of the European Union, Volume 1: A Comparative Analysis*. Hart Publishing, London, pp. 264–306.
Weigend T (2017) Learning about the Charges: The Suspect's Right to Information. In: Spinellis CD, Theodorakis N, Billis E, Papadimitrakopoulos G (eds) *Europe in Crisis: Crime, Criminal Justice and the Way Forward. Essays in Honour of Nestor Courakis*. Volume II. Ant. N. Sakkoulas LPP, Athens, pp. 937–954.
Worrall JL (2012) *Criminal Procedure. From First Contact to Appeal*. Pearson, Boston.
Wróbel W (2010) Konstytucyjne prawo do obrony w perspektywie prawa karnego materialnego. In: Konarska-Wrzosek V, Lachowski J, Wójcikiewicz J (eds) *Księga Pamiątkowa ofiarowana Profesorowi Andrzejowi Markowi*. Wolters Kluwer, Warsaw.

Chapter 7

Powers of the Prosecutor over Imposition of Coercive Measures

7.1 General Considerations

No criminal investigation can be conducted effectively without the use of measures that interfere with the rights and freedoms of individual. In the pursuit of the aims of the criminal process the compulsion is almost inevitable. Criminal justice authorities responsible for resolving a case, establishing the offense committed, and identifying its perpetrator, to achieve these goals in an effective manner often must resort to measures interfering with an individual's rights. This is because some information might be concealed whether intentionally or not, and some individuals might be eager to hinder or obstruct the proceedings. This can be overcome only through coercion. Therefore, the law provides for a broad spectrum of measures for authorities to employ to fulfill their duties to investigate the crime.

But the power to impose such measures can never be absolute. Continuous efforts are made to limit the powers of criminal justice authorities in an arbitrary application of coercion in the course of criminal proceedings, and in particular during criminal investigation. When, how, and in accordance with what procedure these measures should be employed remains a subject of vivid debate among scholars and policymakers. Moreover, issues such as the proportionality of undertaken measure is inconclusive. Finally, two important questions: Who is responsible for such decisions? Should it be by the same authority in all cases?

First, a few terminological and methodological reservations. For the purpose of this work the term "coercive measures" is used to cover all instruments available to the authorities during criminal investigation that allow for interference with the rights and freedoms of individual. While this notion is used by European scholars[1] it is not utilized at all on the American

1 See for example how this notion is used in a similar context by Delmas-Marty (2008), p. 253.

continent, where no general category is used to describe such measures. This is not to say that the word "coercion" does not appear in American legal literature[2] but it is not as common as in the European context and it is not easy to find it even in indexes of course books. One can also find in the literature attempts to define such measures by other terms as e.g. "intrusive measures"[3] but as a less popular option, this was rejected.

Certainly, there is no common ground even between the countries researched within this work as to what mechanisms can be counted as coercive measures. In Germany, search, seizure, and surveillance are grouped as investigative measures in chapter 8 of StPO while arrest, provisional arrest, and so-called measures securing criminal prosecution and enforcement of sentence are placed in chapters 9, 9a, and 9b. Similarly, in Poland even though there is a separate chapter in k.p.k. devoted to coercive measures (*środki przymusu*) which covers a variety of instruments such as arrest, provisional arrest, and issues concerning bail, the other instruments of similar kind such as search, seizure of things, and secret surveillance remain outside its scope. In Italy inspections, searches, seizures, and interception are gathered under the c.p.p. chapter on means of obtaining evidence while provisional arrest is regulated within the chapter devoted to coercive measures (*misure cautelari reali*). At the same time, issues regarding arrest are covered even further in the next parts of c.p.p. on the conduct of criminal investigation. Not unexpectedly, US law treats these topics in an even more dispersed way. On one hand the protection of liberty and the privacy of individuals are coherently protected by the Fourth Amendment but, on the other, there is no coherent regulation on that matter at either federal or state levels. This might, however, not be perceived by American lawyers as an obstacle considering the extensive jurisprudence on the matter that fills that gap; but from a Continental lawyer's perspective of systematic regulations it is a visible shortcoming.

There are also some attempts at categorization in the literature. Two examples can be given. In a classic book analyzing systems of criminal procedure in Europe,[4] the group of coercive measures has been shown in a common scheme designed for the chapters devoted to each researched state. It contains four separate types of measures: arrest and detention; search and seizure; examination of body and mind; interference with the right to

2 See for example a classic work by Hans Kelsen that discusses the coercive order as a "social order that seeks to bring about the desired behavior of individuals by the enactment of such measures of coercion" which proves that it is not a notion that is totally foreign to US scholars, although much more often invoked with reference to international legal order or theoretical deliberations. See Kelsen (2000), p. 235. See also Witt (1973), pp. 320–332.

3 See e.g. Bohlander (2012), p. 71.

4 Van Den Wyngaert (1993), p. vii.

privacy. It is interesting that the last category has been created separate from search and seizure which tend to interfere with privacy in the most obvious way.[5] In another book devoted to the rights of suspects in Europe,[6] coercive measures of investigation—or as they are called there "coercive investigative methods," are also identified. Interestingly, in this case the arrest and preliminary detention remained outside of this group as well as so-called secret investigative methods, understood as wiretaps and surveillance. This adds searches, inspections, seizures of things, and taking DNA samples to the category of coercive measures. But some of the authors writing about their own countries made their own choices. This only proves that the issue is extremely complex and does not allow providing for one ideal resolution to what is, and what is not, within the group specified as coercive measures.[7]

In a recent volume on comparative criminal procedure,[8] the editors have even decided to not dedicate a chapter on coercive measures, while one part of the book is titled "Surveillance and Investigation." In the same volume, Ligeti discussed the issue of coercive measures in the context of the need to subject them to judicial authorization[9] and identifying them as investigative measures interfering with the fundamental rights of suspects and third parties. Yet, only a few years ago she was editing another book that was in part devoted to a description of these measures[10] she restricted herself to calling them "investigative measures" and included within this group a very broad scope of measures undertaken during investigation which are not all of coercive character.

In the light of these considerations one can say that perhaps there is no need to categorize and systematize or to invent a common name for measures available to criminal justice authorities during criminal investigation. Perhaps calling such instruments investigative measures could be considered sufficient. But the shared element of all of the measures that this particular chapter is concerned with i.e. the potential breach of rights and freedoms of an individual during the criminal process that they can cause, calls for such distinction especially when we look at it from the perspective of the authority that should be allowed to order the measure and control its application. This, however, causes another obstacle.

Even if the definition of coercive measures can be narrowed down to the measures that encompass interference with the rights and freedoms of

5 The chapters referring to the protection of privacy are devoted solely to a discussion on the interception of communications.

6 Cape et al. (2007).

7 See also choices regarding the categorization of discussed measures as provided in e.g. Caianiello (2012), pp. 259–260; Quattrocolo and Ruggieri (2019); Vogler and Huber (2008).

8 Brown et al. (2019).

9 Ligeti (2019), pp. 149–150 and 159–160.

10 Ligeti (2013).

an individual during the criminal process, the number of such measures is enormous and, to make matters even worse, there is no exhaustive list of what measures should belong to it. It has been established that the variety of measures that can fall under the discussed group is so overwhelming that even a brief description of those that could belong to this category could fill several books. Therefore, to advance the arguments chosen for this volume, some limits on what will be discussed as coercive measures and what examples should be used must be set. Accordingly, this chapter focuses on two coercive measures: search; arrest. The choice can be justified primarily by the frequency with which these measures are employed. These two are the most commonly used mechanisms by the criminal justice authorities in every system of criminal process employed in the researched countries and definitely beyond them. In contrast with so-called secret investigative methods such as surveillance, wiretaps, seizure of correspondence or infiltrations to name just a few, the search and the seizure of a person are available in almost every criminal investigation. Second, even if the inclusion of certain instruments in this category is debatable, we can agree that both search and arrest encompass visible aspects of coercion. In case of search, the privacy is at stake while arresting a person deprives her of liberty in the most painful way. Finally, the decision to exclude pretrial detention here and to focus on arrest has been justified by the fact that among the states it is widely accepted that the only authority empowered to impose detention of an individual for a longer period of time than the preliminary 72–96 hours of arrest is the court (judge).[11]

Accordingly, the search and arrest will serve as appropriate examples of coercive measures employed during criminal investigation in all four researched countries. It should be repeated however that the aim of this book is not to provide a comprehensive analysis of all coercive methods available in each country. It is rather aimed at providing an answer as to how deeply and to what extent the prosecutor should be engaged in interfering with the rights of individuals during the first stage of the criminal process. From such a perspective there is an obvious potential overlap between considerations of this chapter and those of Chapter 5. The latter, however, was devoted mostly to discussion on the scope of the police–prosecutor relationship and the supervisory powers of the prosecutor over investigation; whereas this chapter discusses measures that can be employed during criminal investigation specifically interfering with rights and freedoms. This leads to the question regarding the appropriate authority to impose and control

11 Note however that in case of Germany a discussion on pretrial detention was necessary to advance the arguments on authority issuing the preauthorized order depriving individual of liberty—Cf. Section 7.2.

these measures. What should be the features and systemic guarantees of the authority that controls them? If such an authority is to be the prosecutor, then what other authority, if any, is to control the prosecutor? Finally, what should be the relationship between authorities at this stage and what role is envisaged for the court (judge) in the changing shape of the investigation? These are all questions to be addressed in this chapter.

7.2 Imposition of Coercive Measures in Germany

7.2.1 General Considerations on Search and Arrest

Search and arrest in the German system are not perceived as similar mechanisms despite the fact that they both severely interfere with the rights of the individual and that procedure of imposing these measures is quite similar, involving almost the same actors. Both the German Constitution and StPO provide for the protection of individuals from unlawful searches and arrests in separate provisions not linking them normatively together. The inviolability of a person and the right to personal integrity are provided in Article 2 (2) of the German Constitution that also makes an assurance that such rights may be interfered with only pursuant to the law. The right to the privacy of an individual is protected by Article 13 (1) of the German Constitution that provides for the inviolability of the home, while the basis for restrictions of personal freedom is provided in Article 104 of the German Constitution.

The search (*Durchsuchung*) under German law is perceived as a typical coercive measure yet must also be considered as an important investigative tool.[12] The search of a person, property, and premises including the home are allowed under § 102 StPO. The threshold to order it is quite low, i.e. the search can be conducted for the purpose of arresting the suspect, as well as in cases where it may be presumed that the search will lead to the discovery of evidence. This refers to the suspect, but upon additional prerequisites the search may also be conducted against other persons. This type of search is permissible only for the purpose of the arrest of a suspect or to follow up the traces of a criminal offense or to seize certain objects, and only if certain facts support the conclusion that the person, trace, or object sought is located on the premises to be searched.[13] It shows that the interference with the rights of persons other than the suspect demands a higher threshold than

12 Weigend (2013), p. 285.

13 § 103 (1) StPO. These restrictions do not apply to multiple rooms in a building in cases of a number of serious crimes against national security and terrorism, as long as there is well-founded reason to believe that the suspect is hiding somewhere in the building (§ 103 (1) StPO second sentence), or if the room is one in which the suspect was either apprehended or which he entered while being pursued (§ 103 (2) StPO).

in cases of a person suspected of committing of a crime. Moreover, since § 103 StPO refers only to premises, it is doubtful whether the search of a person other than the suspect is even permissible.

There is a preference for conducting searches upon a warrant issued by the judge, but it is also provided that police and prosecutor, in exigent circumstances, may conduct searches without a warrant. The exigent circumstances (*Gefahr im Verzug*) are understood as situations in which the search would become futile if the police officer would have to involve the prosecutor, who would then in turn have to apply to a judge for a search warrant. But in practice searches are reported to be frequently conducted without a judicial order due to the fact that *Gefahr im Verzug* has been interpreted quite broadly.[14] Moreover, the mistake in that regard i.e. conducting the search without a warrant when the exigent circumstances did not exist does not make the whole search illegal.[15]

When it comes to arrest, there are two separate provisions concerning arrest with and without warrant. Judge-warranted arrests are preferable to arrests conducted without a warrant. Note, that in such case the StPO talks rather about the *Untersuchungshaft* which can be translated as provisional detention[16] (§§ 112 StPO *et seq.*) and not about the arrest upon warrant. At the same time, arrest without warrant in exigent circumstances upon the decision of the prosecutor or the police is called *vorläufige Festnahme*, translated as provisional arrest.[17] Therefore, these are considered as separate measures, although both aim at interference with the liberty of the suspect and are based on similar grounds.

The threshold to arrest a suspect provisionally is complex. This is partially a result of perceiving the arrest in Germany as not the regular method of initiating the criminal process and therefore the reasons for such decisions are far more restricted than, for instance, in the USA.[18] Generally, only a person that is strongly suspected (*dringender Tatverdacht*) of having committed the offense[19] may be subjected to provisional detention ordered by the court. Additionally, certain conditions justifying detention must be satisfied i.e. danger of flight and danger of unlawful tampering with evidence.[20] Moreover, if the person is suspected of having committed one of the offenses

14 See the discussion on the case law regarding the meaning of the "danger in delay" by the German Federal Constitutional Court and attempts to narrow down its broad interpretation in Weigend and Salditt (2007), p. 85.

15 Frase and Weigend (1995), p. 331 and literature cited in fn. 85.

16 See the discussion on the terminology used with regard to provisional detention in Germany in Brodowski et al. (2010), p. 258, fn. 28.

17 § 127 StPO.

18 See on the nature and function of arrest in Germany in contrast to the US, Frase and Weigend (1995), p. 327.

19 § 112 (1) StPO.

20 § 112 (2) StPO. See on the grounds for issuing detention in Huber (2008), pp. 305–306.

prescribed as particularly severe, the person may be detained even in the absence of these grounds.[21] It is also possible to detain the suspect on preventive grounds if it is likely that the suspect might reoffend.[22] But, most importantly, in all cases the decision to detain must be made in the light of the proportionality of the measure in the context of the gravity of the crime in question and the expected penalty.[23]

The less formal way of arresting a suspect conducted without judicial preauthorization on the prosecutorial or police order is allowed similarly to warrantless searches in exigent circumstances (*Gefahr im Verzug*) if the conditions for issuance of a warrant of arrest are met.[24] It is also permissible to arrest a person caught in the act or being pursued.[25] Therefore, arrest is not just aimed for questioning a suspect, although the police may use the time when she is detained to interrogate the arrestee.[26]

7.2.2 Procedure for Imposing Coercive Measures

The important role in the imposition of coercive measures is played by the judge of investigation (*Ermittlungsrichter*).[27] As a rule, the prosecutor and the police may not resort to the use of a measure without the judicial warrant; and the prosecutor must seek permission unless the grounds for warrantless search are met. Filing a request for authorization of the search with the court is accompanied by the case file, although transferring the whole dossier to the judge does not prevent the investigation from being continued.[28] The hearing regarding the request is conducted *ex parte* not to frustrate the measure if the suspect was not made aware of it before the measure has been applied.[29]

But even though it is expected that searches will be primarily preauthorized by the judge, it is reported that the practice shows the opposite.[30] The authority capable of ordering a search in exigent circumstances is primarily the prosecutor.[31] But this power extends to a substantial group of police officers acting on behalf of the prosecutor; so-called auxiliary prosecutors

21 § 112 (3) StPO.
22 § 112a StPO.
23 § 112 (1) StPO.
24 § 127 (2) StPO.
25 § 127b (1) StPO. Note that the power to arrest a person also belongs to any private citizen in a form of *Flagranzfestnahme* under § 127 (1) StPO.
26 Weigend (2013), p. 273.
27 See Section 5.2.5.
28 Trendafilova and Róth (2008), p. 233.
29 Weigend and Salditt (2007), p. 85.
30 Kühne (1993), p. 151.
31 § 105 (1) StPO.

(*Ermittlungspersonen*).[32] The only exception from this broad mandate are searches conducted for the purpose of arresting a person strongly suspected of certain grave crimes as prescribed in § 103 (1) StPO, in which case a search of private and other premises conducted in a building in which it may be assumed that the suspect is located, may be ordered only by the prosecutor and not by the police.[33]

Searches that take place in exigent circumstances without a judicial search warrant must be subsequently confirmed by the court. Every person that such a search concerns can request subsequent judicial review of its legitimacy and must be informed of the right to do so.[34] Moreover, if at the time the measure was undertaken the person affected by the search objected against it, the request for judicial confirmation of such search must be submitted to court within three days by the official conducting a search without a warrant.[35] Importantly, the person concerned must be notified about this right. Even though this mechanism is formally prescribed only for the seizure of objects, the courts, by analogy, extended this rule to other instances of infringements of individual rights.[36]

In any case an individual affected by the search may file an interlocutory appeal (*Beschwerde*) with a court according to general rules that provide for the right to double check decisions undertaken during investigation.[37] This applies to the searches upon warrant as well as without a prejudicial authorization. The remedy is available to anyone else affected by the search and not only to the suspect.[38] The fact that the search has been confirmed *post factum* by the judge does not preclude an affected person from filing an interlocutory appeal against such decision. Therefore, German law provides not only for prior judicial scrutiny of the decision to search, but, at the request of an individual, gives an opportunity for a post-revision of the conducted measure.

When it comes to arrests, the German criminal procedure concerns the issuing of the order by the judge[39] upon the application of the prosecutor.[40] The order must identify the suspect, provide the details of the offense, grounds for the arrest, and facts supporting the commission of the offense.[41]

32 See Section 5.2.1.
33 § 105 (1) StPO second sentence.
34 § 98 (2) StPO second and fifth sentences.
35 § 98 (2) StPO first sentence.
36 Weigend and Salditt (2007), p. 86.
37 § 304 (1) StPO.
38 § 304 (2) StPO.
39 § 114 (1) StPO.
40 § 125 (1) StPO.
41 § 114 (2) StPO.

When the detention order is executed, the suspect must be informed about its contents and a copy must be handed over to her, together with full notification of the rights that attach to her; and the relatives of the arrestee must be notified on request.[42] After execution of the arrest warrant, the suspect must be brought before the court for a hearing at the latest on the day following the arrest.[43] The judge for investigation questions the suspect, who is presented with the evidence against her and who may present arguments in her favor.[44] The judge may decide to suspend the warrant or to uphold the decision to continue detention.[45]

When the police or prosecutor decide to arrest a person without a warrant under exigent circumstances, §§ 114a–114c StPO safeguarding the rights of the arrestee apply. This shows that despite the separate regulation of the arrest and pretrial detention on the normative level, these measures directed at restriction of the freedom of individual are interconnected. Following the warrantless arrest, the suspect must be presented to the judge of the investigation unless it has been decided by the authority conducting the measure to release the detainee.[46] This must be done without delay and at the latest on the day after the arrest.[47] The judge holds a hearing in the presence of the suspect in accordance with § 115 (3) StPO. If the judge does not consider the arrest justified or if it is considered that the reasons therefore no longer apply, release is ordered. If the judge concludes otherwise, the custody warrant (*Haftbefehl*) is ordered[48] to keep the suspect in custody pending investigation.

The suspect has a right to contest the decision of detention both when arrested upon a warrant[49] or without a warrant.[50] The rules regarding judicial revision are similar[51] and allow for the decision to be undertaken after an oral hearing. The arrestee should be informed about her right to appeal the decision.

7.2.3 Authority to Impose Coercive Measures

German law leaves no doubt that the only authority empowered to impose coercive measures is the judge. The German Constitution states clearly that

42 § 114a–114c StPO.
43 § 115 StPO.
44 § 115 (3) StPO.
45 § 116 StPO. For detail on the procedure, see Weigend (2013), pp. 275–277.
46 § 128 (1) StPO.
47 See the thorough analysis of the timeframe for various forms of arrest as presented by Huber (2008), pp. 306–307. See also the criticized practice of prolonging the registration of the arrest to earn extra time in Bohlander (2012), p. 73–74.
48 § 128 (2) StPO.
49 § 115 (4) StPO.
50 § 128 (2) StPO.
51 § 117–119 StPO.

both search (Article 13 (2)) and arrest (Article 104 (2)) may only be imposed by the judge with some strict exceptions in favor of the police and the prosecutor.[52] Even though the prosecutor is responsible for the conduct of investigation, she needs judicial authorization for every investigatory measure that may infringe an individual's rights as a result of a general assumption that only a judge can impose a measure that interferes with the rights and freedoms of an individual.[53]

Therefore, the imposition of any investigative measure that can be considered as coercive must be authorized by the judge, who serves as an external monitor of prosecutorial (and police) actions when rights and liberties of the individual are at stake.[54] This is done both through the preauthorization of imposition of coercive measures and by regulations demanding post factum verification of such measures employed without a warrant and also by the extensive right to appeal the conduct of the measure. The *Ermittlungsdurchsuchung* is an exceptional figure. As discussed, the judge of the investigation was established with the sole aim of protecting individuals from being oppressed by criminal justice authorities.[55] The judge is not a proactive investigatory official, but takes action only at request of the prosecutor when specific investigative measures are to be performed. Despite the practice of the extensive use of coercive measures without a warrant, the judicial impact of their use is profound due to the extensive availability of the variety of judicial revisionary mechanisms conducted *post factum*.

On the other hand, the powers of the *Ermittlungsdurchsuchung* in limiting coercion undertaken during criminal investigation should not be overestimated. As discussed in the literature, preauthorizing the measures usually is based solely on police reports as submitted for the purpose of issuing the order, and refusals are rare: only in cases when it is obvious that suspicion is groundless.[56] This led scholars to describe the judicial preauthorization powers as a "fig leaf."[57] It is found in particular in cases of applications for warrants of searches which tend to be granted more easily than arrest warrants.[58] But the mere fact that the availability of judicial scrutiny exists can work in practice at least as an effective deterrence mechanism. Even if only triggered by the request of the individual affected by the measure it allows for verification of the appropriateness and legality of the measure. Most importantly such verification takes place still during the investigation

52 Cf. Articles 13 (2) and 104 (2) of the German Constitution.
53 Weigend and Salditt (2007), p. 85.
54 Trendafilova and Roth (2008), p. 233.
55 Section 5.2.5.
56 Weigend and Salditt (2007), p. 86.
57 Brodowski et al. (2010), p. 267.
58 Trendafilova and Roth (2008), p. 234.

without a need to wait until the trial for it. Therefore, even if the case is dismissed or decided without a trial the illegality of the measure can be nevertheless determined.

The powers of the prosecutor with regard to coercive measures are limited not only by the judicial powers to impose them and control their execution, but also because the prosecutorial involvement in the process of issuing warrants is often just provisional. The police, by playing a major role during criminal investigation, not only undertakes searches and arrests without any preauthorization, but also through building up the case in a certain direction are able to justify the unauthorized coercive measures. For instance, in arrest matters it is usually the police that takes the suspect before the judge.[59] And even if the prosecutor is involved, she relies heavily on the materials gathered by the police who rarely do it in an objective way. Surprisingly, this practice does not raise too many concerns and it has been also argued that, for instance, in cases of searches there is even a further need to institute judicial emergency services with the aim of facilitating contact between police officers and the court.[60] This shows that the engagement of the prosecution in the imposition of coercive measures, at least in less severe cases, is restricted both by the judge and the police. But there are voices calling for the prosecutorial powers to be strengthened so that those of the police are thereby reduced.[61]

7.3 Imposition of Coercive Measures in Poland

7.3.1 General Considerations on Search and Arrest

Search and arrest are regulated in Polish criminal procedure as two distinct measures, despite some visible similarities both with regard to procedure and the authorities engaged in ordering and executing each of them. While arrest is covered in the chapter of Polish Code of Criminal Procedure on coercive measures, search remains outside of its scope, being regulated between other forms of taking evidence. Yet, there is no question under Polish law that the latter belongs to the group of measures that use coercion to achieve but the goals of the measure (search).

The law provides for search (*przeszukanie*) of premises and other places as well as persons and objects.[62] This is described in rather vague terms, but it should be understood very broadly as allowing for searching all places, vehicles, personal apparel, and objects belonging to the searched person,

59 Weigend (2004), p. 208
60 Siegismund (2003), p. 62.
61 Siegismund (2003), p. 72.
62 Article 219 § 1 and § 2 k.p.k.

computers and all file storage systems etc. The relevant provision exposes the aim of the search, which is the need to find, arrest, or forcibly bring the suspected person as well as discover objects which might constitute evidence in a case, or which are subject to seizure in criminal proceedings.[63] The law does not limit the scope of persons who can be searched and allows for applicability of that measure to all types of offenses. But every search should be conducted in compliance with its aims, proportionally, and with respect for the dignity of the searched person, and without unnecessary damage or inconvenience.[64] The threshold that must be met to undertake search, regardless of whether with warrant or unwarranted, is described as reasonable basis to believe (*uzasadnione podstawy do przypuszczenia*) that a suspected person or a sought object are located in the place where the search will be conducted or are in possession of a person that is about to be searched.[65] Unfortunately, case law provides no guidance on how to interpret that requirement. In particular, it is unclear whether this requirement sets a standard of prima facie obviousness.[66]

Arresting a person under Polish law (*zatrzymanie*) is generally an option and not an obligation. The arrest of an individual is authorized for the purpose of criminal investigation only if there is justified supposition[67] that he or she has committed an offense, and if simultaneously it is feared that such a person may escape or hide or hinder the evidence or when the identity of the individual is uncertain or there are reasons to carry out accelerated proceedings against someone.[68] The mere suspicion of commitment of an offense is therefore not enough for an arrest to take place since it must be accompanied by at least one other ground. The only exception to the rule that arrest is nonmandatory are cases of domestic violence when there is suspicion that an offense has been committed with a firearm, knife, or another dangerous item and there is a compelling reason to believe that the suspect might commit an offense again.[69] Arrest of this type is known as police arrest and may be targeted only against the suspected person.[70]

But there is also a separate set of rules that allow to arrest the suspected person as well as the suspect. This is done with warrant issued by the prosecutor if there is a justified fear that such a person would not appear voluntarily before the authority that needs to conduct the investigative measure

63 Nowak and Steinborn (2013), p. 519.
64 Article 227 k.p.k.
65 Article 219 § 1 k.p.k.
66 Cf. Koper (2014), p. 19.
67 On the threshold to arrest, see Kruszyński (2007), p. 184.
68 Article 244 § 1 k.p.k.
69 See Articles 244 § 1a and § 1b k.p.k. Cf. Jasiński and Kremens (2019), p. 284.
70 See on the definition of suspected person under Polish law in Section 6.3.1.

in the presence of that person, for instance to initially charge that person or to take DNA samples etc., as well when there is a justified fear that they may otherwise illegally impede the proceedings, or there is a need to immediately impose pretrial detention or other forms of protective measures.[71]

The conduct of the police arrest without a warrant and the arrest ordered by the prosecutor is identical since the same rules apply in both cases. Interestingly, the warranted arrest is not preferred over the arrest without a warrant. The police do not have to justify warrantless arrests, nor do they have to notify the prosecutor of same until the arrest occurred. This applies both to new and ongoing investigations.

7.3.2 *Procedure for Imposing Coercive Measures*

There are two distinct procedural regimes for search and arrest under Polish law. They show certain similarities, in particular in terms of the authority empowered to order these measures, but there are also differences between them when it comes to the preference of warrants and the availability of post-authorization mechanisms.

The search can be conducted by a prosecutor herself or, upon her decision, by the police.[72] Where a search is not conducted by the prosecutor, the officer willing to search a place or a person should obtain a prosecutorial search warrant prior to exercising the measure.[73] Therefore, it is only in exigent circumstances, when the search warrant could have not been issued, that the warrantless search may be justified. The power to issue a search warrant during an investigation rests ultimately with the prosecutor and the law does not consider either a judge or any other authority as being competent to issue search warrants at this stage of criminal proceedings.

The obvious need to conduct searches in exigent circumstances forced lawmakers to allow the police to conduct searches without warrant, although the term "exigent circumstances" is continuously criticized for being too unclear and imprecise.[74] Surprisingly, the case law provides no help on the matter, but in legal literature it has been accepted that they occur whenever "commencing an investigative action with a delay resulting from a time lost while obtaining prosecutorial warrant or lack of action, would result in the loss, distortion or destruction of evidence."[75] Existence of these circumstances must be evaluated in the light of the setting that occurred when the search was conducted and not from the perspective of the time

71 Article 247 § 1 and § 2 k.p.k.
72 Article 220 § 1 k.p.k.
73 Nowak and Steinborn (2013), p. 519.
74 Sakowicz (2000), p. 21.
75 Koper (2014), pp. 20–21 and the literature cited in fn. 14.

when evaluation of the need to undertake the measure is being made post factum. Nevertheless, in every case the general threshold as prescribed in Article 219 § 1 k.p.k. must be established before undertaking a search in this dynamic situation.

However, every search conducted without a warrant must be immediately confirmed by the prosecutor, which forces the police to request such post-authorization in every single case.[76] The lack of such application or the decision not to authorize a warrantless search that has been conducted have potentially grave consequences. If the search is not confirmed by the prosecutor within seven days from the day it took place, the objects seized during the search must immediately be returned to the owner.[77] This happens regardless of the request of the owner to receive such confirmation. The only exception from this rule is when the items are seized from the owner who voluntarily hands them over, which means that the search has not in fact been necessary.[78] In such case the subsequent confirmation is dependent only at the request such owner.

Arrests upon a warrant are conducted on the order of the prosecutor.[79] Just as in the case of search, the court is not authorized to decide on arresting an individual during the criminal investigation, since this power belongs solely to the prosecutor. As already noted, the warranted arrests have no priority over the unwarranted ones. Even the order of these articles in k.p.k. with police arrests preceding warranted arrests suggest otherwise. Specifically, the need to conduct warrantless arrests does not have to be justified by exigent circumstances and must meet only the threshold for police arrests. This, however, is limited only to cases which concern the arrests of "suspected persons" which, on the other hand, also means that when the person has been already initially charged with a crime the police have no possibility to arrest such individual without the knowledge of the prosecutor and the warrant issued by her against the suspect. But it does not exclude arresting a suspected person during the ongoing investigation already covered by the prosecutorial supervision if the grounds for police arrest are met.

In all cases involving arrest a detailed record of the measure undertaken must be made that should also include the statements of the arrestee who must receive a copy.[80] The arrestee should be notified of the reasons for the arrest, and of the wide range of her rights, including the right to challenge the arrest.[81]

76 Article 220 § 3 k.p.k.
77 Article 230 § 1 k.p.k.
78 Article 217 § 2 k.p.k.
79 Article 247 § 1 k.p.k.
80 Article 244 § 3 k.p.k.
81 Article 244 § 2 k.p.k. Cf. Section 6.3.1. On the scope of the rights, see De Vocht (2010), p. 436; Jasiński and Kremens (2019), pp. 284–286.

Warrantless arrests, distinct to search cases, do not demand any subsequent confirmation from the prosecutor. But the prosecutor must be informed about every arrest that takes place[82] even if the arrestee has been released by the police soon after the arrest. This obviously concerns only those arrests that are conducted for the purpose of criminal proceedings and not for other reasons.[83] The prosecutor, informed about the arrest, may decide to immediately release the arrestee, if she has not been already released, or to apply to the court for pretrial detention if the prerequisites of such measure are met.[84] The prosecutor has 48 hours to decide whether further detention is necessary, and the court has an additional 24 hours to decide whether the request is justified.[85]

A common feature of searches and arrests in the Polish criminal process is their eligibility for the judicial review, although the legal basis is distinctive. But judicial review is allowed regardless of whether the search or arrest has been conducted based on a warrant or without it. In case of search the decision pre- or post-authorizing the search as well as the conduct of the search itself is broadly granted to all persons whose rights have been infringed by the search.[86] In cases of arrests the detained person may file an interlocutory appeal to challenge the measure, questioning the existence of the ground justifying the arrest, its legality, and the way in which it has been conducted.[87] However, the prosecutor who receives the interlocutory appeal against the search, before transferring it to the court might accept it, which ceases the procedure, while in the case of the interlocutory appeal against arrest the application for verification of the measure must always reach the court, who decides on the case after the hearing.[88]

7.3.3 Authority to Impose Coercive Measures

Polish law places full responsibility for searches and arrests during criminal investigation on the prosecutor. In cases of searches she is empowered to conduct the search by herself, to issue the search warrant as well as to authorize searches conducted by the police in exigent circumstances post

82 Article 244 § 3 k.p.k.
83 For the analysis of reasons to arrest a person under Polish law outside of the scope of criminal process, see Jasiński and Kremens (2019), pp. 282–283.
84 Article 244 § 3 k.p.k. On the grounds for pretrial detention, see Jasiński and Kremens (2019), pp. 287–289; Kruszyński (2007), pp. 186–187.
85 Article 248 § 1 and § 2 k.p.k.
86 Article 236 § 1 k.p.k.
87 Article 246 § 1 k.p.k.
88 Article 246 § 2 k.p.k. This can be derived also from Article 41 (2) Polish Constitution that demands the judicial verification of arrests—cf. Skorupka (2015), p. 575.

factum. Therefore, despite the substantial number of warrantless searches the prosecutor controls all of them. Also, in the case of arrest the prosecutor maintains the power to issue arrest warrants but prosecutorial powers are also visible in these cases when the arrests are conducted without preauthorization. Despite the fact that the police do not have to resort to the prosecutor in every case and are given considerable freedom in arresting potential offenders per the provisions of Article 244 k.p.k. and that the post-confirmation of warrantless arrests is not necessary, the supervisory role of the prosecutor imposes some limits.

First, the police must inform the prosecutor about all arrests that were conducted in the context of the criminal process, even in those cases in which investigation has not been yet initiated. This allows the prosecutor to maintain full control over all arrests and immediately decide on the release of the arrestee if deemed necessary. Second, in case of ongoing investigations in which the suspect has already been identified and preliminarily charged with a crime, the police have no power to arrest such person without a prior prosecutorial authorization under exigent circumstances of any kind. This can only be executed by the prosecutor and only for the reasons directly expressed in Article 247 § 1 and § 2 k.p.k. Both Articles are consistent with the concept that the criminal investigation is always under the prosecutor's supervision, who is responsible for all actions during its course.[89]

The judicial involvement in the imposition of coercive measures becomes visible only upon the request of a person whose rights has been infringed by it, which means that there is no immediate and mandatory mechanism for judicial verification of these measures. The law provides for the right to an interlocutory appeal that will allow for judicial review of the legality of such measures. This gives the court of law the power to decide on the issue without having to wait until trial.

The consequences of the judicial review are nevertheless not obvious. Although recognition of the search being illegally conducted should result in returning the evidence on a similar basis as provided for nonconfirmation of search there is no clear answer to the question of consequences of the wrongfully conducted arrest. It is provided that if the court established that the arrest was illegal or groundless the arrestee must be released and the authority supervising the person that decided on the arrest must be informed.[90] This says nothing about the legality of evidence obtained from the arrestee. Due to the lack of regulations on the matter the statements of such a person, even if obtained as a result of unlawful arrest, will be admissible in court.

89 Cf. Section 5.3.1.
90 Article 246 § 3 and § 4 k.p.k.

The broad powers of the prosecutor toward imposition of search and arrest has been critiqued in Polish legal literature. It is true that since the Polish Constitution lacks provisions prescribing the authority competent to issue search and arrest warrants and does not demand that it should be a judicial authority, the k.p.k. does not violate any constitutional rules. However, some scholars have argued that the level of engagement of the prosecutor in criminal investigation makes her too prejudiced to make an independent evaluation of the need to conduct a search or to arrest a person.[91] Simply, the prosecutor who is always responsible of the outcome of investigation against the suspect should not be considered as the appropriate authority deciding on imposition of measures interfering with rights of such individual. The fact that the law provides for judicial review of coercive measures does not seem to be an efficient mechanism protecting the suspect against unreasonable searches and arrest. Triggering judicial review only at the request of the suspect, has its obvious limits since it only can fix a mistake that has already been made and not prevent them from occurring.

7.4 Imposition of Coercive Measures in Italy

7.4.1 General Considerations on Search and Arrest

The search and arrest have been regulated in Italy in a similar way as in other Continental countries, which is by providing slightly different procedures in each case. Yet, the protection of the individual against search and arrest[92] are regulated jointly in the Constitution of the Italian Republic as a form of interference with personal freedom (Article 13) providing clearly that the measures may be imposed only on the order of the judicial authority and only in cases and manner provided by law. Searches of the home and other premises are protected by the Constitution (Article 14) as a form of interference with privacy.

When it comes to the types of searches, the c.p.p. differentiates between the search of a person (*perquisizione personale*), search of premises (*perquisizione locale*), and search of computers and electronic systems (*perquisizione informatica*). Generally, all searches may be conducted only if there are reasonable grounds to believe (*fondato motive di ritenere*) that objects used to commit an offense or related to an offense are possessed by the person that is to be searched or are located in a place that is to be searched or when the

91 See Steinborn (2008), p. 375; Skorupka (2007), p. 52.

92 Note that the same constitutional provision provides also for the same standard of protection in case of inspections (*ispezioni*) aimed at ascertaining the traces or other effects of the crime on persons, places, and objects, including computer, and telecommunication systems—cf. Lasagni (2018), p. 393, fn. 27.

accused who should be arrested remains in such place.[93] This considerably vague prerequisite allows for conducting a search if it is reasonable to predict that the search will be fruitful, and, even if at the end of a search it turns out that this suspicion was groundless and no objects were found, it does not necessarily undermine the legality of search.[94] But the legitimacy of a procedure must be strongly linked to the probability of discovering the items that are searched for and not only to revealing the existence of any crime.[95]

It is also allowed under Italian law to conduct searches without a preauthorization and in such cases additional grounds must be met. Therefore, the police may engage in warrantless search whenever there are exigent circumstances and when they have reasonable grounds to believe that the person is hiding objects or traces related to the offense on his body that can be deleted or lost, or that such objects or traces are in a certain place or that a suspected person or an escapee is in such a place.[96] The exigent circumstances are understood as an urgent situation that happens in case of a flagrant crime or in case of an escape.[97]

The Italian c.p.p. makes the matter of depriving a person of liberty more complicated when compared to the simple words of the Constitution. Thus, two types of short-term deprivation of liberty are recognized, i.e. arrest (*arresto*) and detention (*fermo*).[98] They both serve the same goals of public safety and facilitating investigations.[99] Out of these two, the arrest plays a major role in Italian criminal investigation. This is the power of the police to arrest a person in flagrant situations (*flagranza*), which means that an individual is apprehended while committing or attempting to commit a culpable offense.[100] The threshold for *arresto* is considered as high and applicable only to the most serious crimes.[101] The law categorizes offenses according to their gravity and in some cases the police are even obliged to arrest a suspect[102] while in other cases this is at police discretion.[103] Both mandatory

93 Article 247 (1) c.p.p.
94 Caianiello (2016), p. 6.
95 See Ryan (2014), p. 192.
96 Article 352 (1) c.p.p.
97 Di Amato (2013), p. 181.
98 Note that in some works the *fermo* is translated as "detention" (e.g. Ruggieri and Marcolini (2013), p. 385) while in others as "stop" (Caianiello (2010), p. 383).
99 Caianiello (2010), p. 383.
100 Article 380 (1) c.p.p.
101 Ruggieri and Marcolini (2013), p. 385.
102 The mandatory arrest (*arresto obligatorio in flagranza*) is provided for offenses for which the law imposes a life sentence or the penalty of imprisonment for a minimum term of five years and a maximum term of 20 years (Article 380 (1) c.p.p.) and some other offenses from the catalogue of offenses as provided in Article 380 (2) c.p.p.
103 This optional arrest (*arresto facoltativo in flagranza*) refers to offenses for which the law imposes the penalty of imprisonment for a maximum term exceeding three years or a

and optional arrests are executed by the police, who do not need to ask anyone for any permission to do so. It is clear that in a case of flagrance the situation is so rapid that there is no way the police would have time to apply to another entity for the arrest order. The risk of losing evidence or the disappearance of the suspect in such a situation is too high.

The detention (*fermo*) may occur if there are specific reasons to believe that the person who is seriously suspected of committing certain offenses[104] may disappear.[105] In such a case the general power to order detention lies with the prosecutor. But the law provides that the police may detain a person also in that form upon their own initiative, when the prosecutor has not yet taken over the investigation, or when there is no time to inform the prosecutor and the risk of the suspect fleeing is high.[106]

7.4.2 Procedure for Imposing Coercive Measures

The procedure regarding imposition of coercive measures is primarily regulated by Article 13 of the Italian Constitution. Under this provision the power to impose coercive measures is given to the judicial authority upon a reasoned order (warrant). Only in exceptional cases, understood as necessity and urgency, can the police undertake the measure, subject to its subsequent validation within 96 hours of the moment when the arrest was made. But when it comes to the actual employment of certain measures the c.p.p. provides for a distinct procedure.

The law provides straightforwardly for the preference of the search order demanding that such warrant must be reasoned.[107] During investigation, the power to issue search warrants is granted to the prosecutor[108] and her reasoned order becomes the basis for a possible subsequent judicial review. The detailed rules on how a search is to be conducted with regard

nonintentional crime for which the law imposes the penalty of imprisonment for a maximum term of at least five years (Article 381 (1) c.p.p.) and some other offenses from the catalogue of offenses as provided in Article 381 (2) c.p.p. This, however, does not mean that arrest in such cases can be done in an arbitrary way. The restraint is that this type of arrest can be enforced only if it is justified by the seriousness of the criminal act or by the person's dangerousness inferred from his personality or the circumstances of the act (Article 381 (4) c.p.p.)

104 The list of such offenses includes offenses which are punishable with a life sentence or the penalty of imprisonment for a minimum term of at least two years and a maximum term exceeding six years or a crime concerning weapons of war and explosives or a crime committed for purposes of terrorism, even international, or subversion of democratic order (Article 384 (1) c.p.p.).

105 Article 384 (1) c.p.p.

106 Article 384 (2) and (3) c.p.p.

107 Article 247 (2) c.p.p.

108 See the discussion on interpretation of *l'autorità giudiciaria* in Italian system (Section 7.4.2).

to homes, premises, and persons[109] are focused on the protection of the rights of the searched individual providing for the right to information and participation in the measure. But the rule that the search should be primarily conducted upon a warrant is overshadowed by the practice of police conducting searches under exigent circumstances and making them subject to post factum prosecutorial confirmation.[110] In such cases the police have only 48 hours to inform the prosecutor that the search has been conducted and the prosecutor has an additional 48 hours to confirm it, which happens regardless of whether the search resulted in seizure or not.

All searches, whether conducted upon a prosecutorial warrant or without such authorization, are subject to judicial review. This is, however, true only for those searches that resulted in the seizure of property. The suspect, the person from whom objects have been seized, and the person who would be entitled to their restitution, may submit a request for reexamination of the seizure, which includes the grounds for search and seizure[111] in accordance with the "reexamination" procedure.[112] This means that searches ordered or confirmed by the prosecutor that resulted with no seizure simply cannot be appealed and reviewed by the judge. However, in seizure cases the criteria for the verification of the conduct of the measure provided by law are so vague that it is exceedingly difficult for the defense to show at the appeal stage that the warrant was invalid or ill founded.[113] The lack of judicial review of all searches stems from the adopted interpretation of the term *l'autorità giudiciaria* that encompasses the prosecutor. In result, the prosecutor is perceived as a pertinent authority to control searches.[114]

When it comes to the measures infringing the liberty of an individual, the law provides for the broad powers of the police to undertake *arresto* without any necessity to seek prosecutorial order and *fermo* which requires the prosecutorial preauthorization, although also in the latter case the police is empowered to engage in that measure independently with certain requirements. But with both *arresto* and *fermo* the prosecutor must afterwards seek validation from the judge for preliminary investigation (GIP).[115]

Accordingly, if the police conducted the measure independently, they must inform the prosecutor immediately, but not longer than within 24 hours, about the employment of the measure, together with submitting to her all necessary materials.[116] The arrested individual has a right to inform

109 Articles 248–250 c.p.p.
110 Article 352 c.p.p. See more broadly Caianiello (2012), pp. 258–259.
111 Article 257 (1) c.p.p.
112 Article 324 c.p.p.
113 Caianiello (2016), p. 5.
114 See Sections 2.4.2 and 7.4.3.
115 Article 390 c.p.p.
116 Article 386 (1) and (3) c.p.p.

her counsel and family as soon as possible and the duty to do so is usually observed by the police.[117] After making the suspect available to the prosecutor she has an additional 24 hours to either immediately release the suspect according to Article 389 c.p.p. or to seek validation of the measure.[118] In the latter case the prosecutor brings the suspect before the judge of the preliminary investigation who holds the hearing as soon as possible and within the next 48 hours at the latest.[119] During the hearing, the reasons standing behind the detention must be discussed in the presence of the lawyer representing the detainee. In case the prosecutor does not request the confirmation of the measure in the prescribed time, or the court does not issue the validation order, the *arresto* or *fermo* become ineffective.[120] The GIP may either rule on validating the measure or the arrested person must be immediately released. However, the prosecutor may at the same time request the judge to impose preventive detention on the suspect provided probable cause has been established and in accordance with Articles 273–274 c.p.p. Although the validation of coercive measures undertaken is an independent decision from the imposition of the pretrial custody (*custodia cautelare in carcere*).

Along with that mechanism and in accordance with Article 111 (7) of the Italian Constitution every decision regarding personal freedom can be additionally appealed to the Court of Cassation. Thus, the law provides one more check on the lawfulness of the undertaken coercive measure that infringes the personal freedom of an individual under the mechanism of judicial review.[121] This is however not available in case of searches.

7.4.3 Authority to Impose Coercive Measures

From the normative perspective it can be perceived that the powers in that regard have been vested primarily with the judge and only in exigent circumstances with other authorities i.e. the prosecutor and the police. The wording of the Italian Constitution seems to state clearly that the "judicial authority" (*l'autorità giudiciaria*) should be empowered to issue orders enabling searching, inspecting, and detaining individuals. But the interpretation of that regulation is less straightforward than one would expect and, as we will see, internally ambiguous.

The use of the phrase "judicial authority" has actually been interpreted as referring both to judge and prosecutor.[122] This might be somewhat surprising

117 Caianiello (2010), p. 383.
118 Article 390 (1) c.p.p. But see Ryan (2014), p. 194 and Perrodet (2002), p. 402.
119 Article 390 (2) c.p.p.
120 Articles 390 (3) and 391 (6) c.p.p.
121 Illuminati and Caianiello (2007), p. 135.
122 Caianiello (2016), p. 4.

since Italian criminal procedure, heavily reformed in 1988 in a direction leaning toward the adversarial system, established the judge for the preliminary investigation. This was created with the aim of controlling the work of the prosecutor, and to guarantee the rights of the person being investigated, and therefore seems perfectly well suited to decide on all coercive measures. However, since Italian prosecutors retain a judicial, or at least quasi-judicial, function which guarantees prosecutors the same level of independence as judges positioning both groups within the judicial system (*magistratura*).[123] And since they are not seen as a "mere prosecutor, but also an organ of justice that is obliged to search for all elements of evidence that are relevant for the correct verdict, including any elements in favor of the accused"[124] it is no wonder that they are allowed to rule on the rights of individual during a criminal process.

Yet, this interpretation of the position of the Italian prosecutor seems incoherent. Not only the prescribed independence of the prosecution service is contested[125] but even on the normative level it seems that there are some doubts when it comes to the full equality of judges and prosecutors. While the prosecutor is allowed to impose some coercive measures during criminal investigation, i.e. search, seizure, summoning, and questioning of witnesses, others remain outside of his competencies, i.e. detention, and interception of communication. Therefore, despite the interpretation of the Article 13 of the Italian Constitution the c.p.p. narrows the possibility of imposing measures depriving the suspect of the liberty only to the judge.[126] Only in case of *arresto* and *fermo* the validation by judge and power to file an interlocutory appeal are available. Similar form of judicial control over search is almost nonexistent. Not only is the preauthorization of the measure vested solely in prosecutorial hands, but the subsequent validation of searches is available only if they resulted in the seizure. This ambiguity of regulations referring to the mechanism of imposition of coercive measures in Italy has not yet been addressed in full. However, the ECtHR recently took an opportunity to criticize the lack of judicial scrutiny in no-seizure cases.[127] The case concerned Mr. Marco Brazzi, an Italian-German national whose Italian house was searched in 2010 on a warrant issued by the prosecutor of Mantua, in connection with an ongoing criminal investigation involving tax evasion by Brazzi. The ECtHR noted that the prosecutorial decision to search lacked any prior judicial oversight, which would not be considered as problematic if counterbalanced by subsequent judicial review

123 See Section 2.4.2.
124 Corte Costituzionale (Italian Constitutional Court), February 15, 1991, n. 88.
125 See e.g. Scaccianoce (2010), p. 6; Di Federico (1998), pp. 381–382.
126 Ruggieri and Marcolini (2013), p. 386.
127 *Brazzi* v. *Italy*, no. 57278/11, September 27, 2018.

of the lawfulness and necessity of the measure, which did not take place.[128] Since neither prior judicial oversight nor any effective post review of the impugned investigative measure were available, the ECtHR found that Italian law did not provide sufficient safeguards against the risk of abuse of power by the authorities conducting criminal investigation and stated a violation of Article 8 of the ECHR.[129]

Therefore, the mechanisms of imposition of coercive measures in Italy strongly depends on the type of measure employed. The prosecutor maintains full control over searches, in contrast to arrests. But even when it is established that the latter are subjected to judicial scrutiny, the GIP's post-factum validation, lack of preference for arrest warrants over the warrantless *arresto* and *fermo*, gives very broad control over coercive measures maintained by the prosecutor. It is nevertheless interesting that while the Italian system tends to argue that the prosecutors are independent and equal to judges which allows them to control searches, at the same time they are considered as not independent enough to decide on the deprivation of liberty.

Finally, one should not forget about the role of the police. The normative framework provides for the obstacles that they face when coercive measures must be employed. The thresholds are designed to prevent the overuse of the measures and exigent circumstances must be present when without prosecutorial or judicial preauthorization a coercive measure is about to be employed. Subsequently various forms of validation are necessary and must be observed by the police officers. Nevertheless, the police maintain wide competence to engage in various measures interfering with the rights and freedoms of the individual. And even though the post-factum verification is much needed and should be demanded, it may be effective only when the determination that the measure was wrongful and unlawful bears some visible consequences.

7.5 Imposition of Coercive Measures in the United States of America

7.5.1 General Considerations on Search and Arrest

Search and the arrest are jointly covered in the US Constitution by the Fourth Amendment which guarantees protection against unreasonable search and

128 It was argued at some point that eventually the judge for preliminary investigation did review the case confirming discontinuation of preliminary investigation which according to Article 408 c.p.p. is obligatory in each case when the prosecutor believes that the charge is groundless—see more in Section 8.4.

129 The ECtHR similarly decided in *Modestou* v. *Greece*, no. 51693/13, March 16, 2017, concerning a Cypriot national living in Greece whose house was searched on a prosecutorial order, also without prior or retrospective judicial review.

seizure of persons, places, and objects.[130] This regulation provides guidance on how the rights and freedoms of the individual should be observed in the US criminal process. Moreover, there is no doubt that it should also be perceived as referring to the use of other coercive measures during the criminal investigation.[131] Most importantly, the Fourth Amendment demonstrates a strong preference for coercive measures conducted pursuant to warrant.[132] And even though warrantless searches and arrests are a daily routine for police officers in all US states, the prior judicial oversight is considered the rule, not the exception.[133]

The threshold under which the coercive measures may be imposed is worded quite simply in the Fourth Amendment, providing the same standard in each case—only the existence of *probable cause* justifies the use of any limitations on the rights of the individual. However, the term is neither clear nor easy to interpret. Several times the Supreme Court has attempted to answer this question,[134] but there is no final consensus as to the meaning of that concept and an obvious lack of agreement on the meaning of the level of certainty that should be achieved in each case when a decision to search or seize is employed. This question has been addressed in this book, since the same threshold is needed to formally charge a person with a crime under US law,[135] and also because the arrest has also been discussed as a form in which most commonly the initiation of investigation takes place in the US system of law.[136]

The protection provided by the Fourth Amendment applies to the federal system and has been created as a form of protection for individuals from the federal government.[137] Initially, its applicability was not obvious and citizens whose rights and freedoms were interfered with by searches and arrests had to seek protection from state constitutions. It was not until 1949 with *Wolf* v. *Colorado* that the US Supreme Court stated that the protection provided by the Fourth Amendment, as well as all other constitutional norms contained

130 The Fourth Amendment to US Constitution reads:

> "The right of the people to be secure in their persons, houses, papers, and effects, against unreasonable searches and seizures, shall not be violated, and no Warrants shall issue, but upon probable cause, supported by Oath or affirmation, and particularly describing the place to be searched, and the persons or things to be seized."

131 On applicability of Fourth Amendment protection to wiretapping and electronic and mechanical eavesdropping, see *Katz* v. *United States,* 389 US 347 (1967), para. 388. See also pp. 962–693.

132 *Illinois* v. *Gates*, 462 US 213, 236 (1983).

133 See critically Gray (2016), pp. 433–436. See also historical arguments both against the warrant preference rule and the reasonableness requirement in Steinberg (2008), p. 581.

134 *Carroll* v. *United States* 267 US 132 (1925), para. 162. See also *Brinegar* v. *United States*, 338 US 160 (1949).

135 Section 6.5.2.

136 See Section 3.5.1.

137 Scheb and Scheb (1999), p. 40.

in the Bill of Rights, also applies to state governments through the due process clause as derived from the Fourteenth Amendment.[138] Currently there is no doubt that the protection against unreasonable searches and seizures covers the activity of federal as well as state officials although the states may always provide wider protection.

The question regarding the threshold that is required under US law to employ coercive measures becomes even more interesting when the discussion on warrantless searches and arrests comes into play. Distinctively to what is known from the European system, instead of providing a general threshold allowing the action of the criminal justice authorities without a warrant, the case law has developed many exceptions to the warrant requirement. It should be noted, however, that in every such case probable cause is also required. Moreover, there are certain other exceptions to the warrant requirement that do not require probable cause, which means that they cannot be considered "search" or "arrest." It is crucial to understand the difference that exists between the measures covered by the Fourth Amendment and other forms of interference with an individual's rights and freedoms, such as the procedure known as *stop and frisk*. In concise terms, a police officer may stop a person on the street and frisk her (conducting a pat down) without probable cause, if the police officer believes that the person has committed, is committing, or is about to commit a crime and has a reasonable belief that the person "may be armed and presently dangerous."[139] The standard of certainty required in such case is "reasonable suspicion" which requires a lower level of certainty than probable cause and for that reason remains outside of the Fourth Amendment's protection. And only if stop and frisk gives rise to probable cause to believe that the suspect has committed a crime, should the police be empowered to make a formal arrest and a full incident search of a person.[140] There is no doubt that stop and frisk should be considered as a coercive measure, perhaps of a lenient character, but still infringing the rights and freedoms of every individual faced with such measure.[141]

The list of exceptions from the warrant requirement is long. For instance, a warrant is not needed in cases of so-called searches incident to arrest. This was justified in *Chimel* v. *California*, where the Supreme Court stated that search without warrant is permitted "to remove any weapons that the [arrestee] might seek to use in order to resist arrest or effect his escape" and to "seize any evidence on the arrestee's person in order to prevent its

138 338 US 25 (1949). See also *Mapp* v. *Ohio*, 367 US 643 (1961).

139 *Terry* v. *Ohio*, 392 US 1, 27 (1968).

140 *Terry* v. *Ohio*, 392 US 1, 10 (1968).

141 On stop and frisk, see generally e.g. Kamisar et al. (2012), pp. 382–411; Worrall (2012), pp. 183–211.

concealment or destruction."[142] This long-standing and almost unquestionable practice of the criminal justice authorities has recently been reevaluated in the context of unwarranted searches of the cellphones of arrestees.[143]

Another exception to the warrant requirement is referred to as exigent circumstances. The allowance for the imposition of search or arrest without a warrant is justified by the nature of the situation that requires the police to act immediately where there is a danger to themselves or others, the foreseen possibility that evidence will be destroyed, or that the suspect will escape.[144] As it was held by the Supreme Court "where there are exigent circumstances in which police action literally must be 'now or never' to preserve the evidence of the crime, it is reasonable to permit action without prior judicial authorization."[145] As distinct from what is known from other systems of law discussed in this book but typical of the common-law systems, these exceptions are not a result of normative regulation but are much more fragmented and result from the extensive case law on the issue. Also, automobile searches are exempted from the warrant requirement[146] as well the so-called plain-view doctrine.[147] But the common requirement for all these is the existence of probable cause justifying the imposition of the measure.

7.5.2 Procedure for Imposing Coercive Measures

Both at the federal level and in the state systems there is a preference for the conducting of coercive measures with a warrant over warrantless searches and arrests. As discussed in the example of limitations of privacy, "searches conducted outside the judicial process, without prior approval by judge or magistrate, are *per se* unreasonable under the Fourth Amendment—subject only to a few specifically established and well delineated exceptions."[148] This is usually called the "warrant requirement" that demands imposition of coercive measures upon a warrant over action without a warrant. As strongly stated in *Dyson* v. *State* "the command of the Fourth Amendment to the American police officer and the American Prosecutor is simple: 'You always have to get a warrant—UNLESS YOU CAN'T.'"[149] The truth is, however,

142 *Chimel* v. *California*, 395 US 752, 763 (1969). See also *United States* v. *Robinson*, 414 US 218 (1973). Cf. Dressler and Thomas (2017), pp. 251–275
143 See *Riley* v. *California*, 573 US __ (2014).
144 This can be narrowed down to such exceptions as hot pursuit, likelihood of escape or danger to others absent hot pursuit and evanescent evidence as done e.g. in Worrall (2012), pp. 155–160. Cf. Kamisar (2015), pp. 304–356.
145 *Roaden* v. *Kentucky*, 413 US 496, 505 (1973).
146 See *Carrol* v. *United States*, 267 US 132 (1975).
147 *Coolidge* v. *New Hampshire*, 403 US 443 (1971).
148 *Katz* v. *United States,* 389 US 347, 357 (1967).
149 *Dyson* v. *State*, 122 Md.App. 413, 712 A.2d 573 (1998).

as Judge Scalia aptly observed, that "the 'warrant requirement' had become so riddled with exceptions that it was basically unrecognizable."[150] It should also be mentioned that in case of arrest warrants the strict approach of the warrant requirement is not present and it is even the situation that arrest in a public place without a warrant is allowed due to the time that the officer would have to request the warrant from the judge.[151]

The procedure for conducting the coercive measure upon a warrant primarily requires filing the request for such warrant by the police officer in the form of an affidavit in which the applicant officially confirms facts as provided in the document and which contains detailed information.[152] Each affidavit being a basis for issuing a warrant is considered to be reliable because it contains information given by the officer under oath.[153] The warrants have their own strict requirements. First, it is demanded that they are issued by a neutral and detached magistrate, which will be addressed in the next chapter. Second, the warrant must show probable cause. In the case of arrest warrants, it is enough to show that the person to be arrested has committed a crime, while in case of search warrants probable cause is required both for the commitment of the crime and the place from where the items are to be seized.[154] Finally, the warrants must provide information on who exactly or what exactly is to be seized or searched for. This is called the particularity that is intended to prevent general searches and seizing things other than those that are carefully prescribed in the warrant.[155]

The execution of a warrant depends on the type of coercive measure to be employed. The ways in which entry to the house should be made with respect to the knock-and-announce rule, the scope and manner of the measure, and how much force is allowed in such situations, are of major importance. These also all apply in the case of measures undertaken without a warrant. In fact, the only difference between searches with a warrant and those without is what happens after the measure has taken place.

In every case in which police officers conduct a search without a warrant, claiming exigent circumstances, they must provide evidence that they didn't have time to apply for the search warrant due to the suspicion that evidence may be hidden or destroyed.[156] But this will happen only when the prosecutor intends to introduce at trial evidence obtained during such search. It

150 *California* v. *Acevedo*, 500 US 565, 583 (1991).
151 *United States* v. *Watson*, 423 US 411 (1976). Cf. Kamisar (2015), pp. 307–309; Hall (2009), pp. 376–377.
152 Scheb and Scheb (1999), p. 50.
153 Cf. Dressler and Thomas (2017), p. 201.
154 Worrall (2012), p. 108.
155 Dressler and Thomas (2017), p. 227.
156 *Schmerber v. California*, 384 US 757 (1966).

is done in the form of a motion to suppress evidence in accordance with the exclusionary rule.[157] But, if the case, as typically happens, is disposed before trial as through the plea-bargaining procedure or the case is dismissed for some reason, there is no instrument available in the criminal process that allows for checking the grounds for the search and the nature of how this measure was conducted.[158] There is neither confirmation of a warrantless search by the adequate authority available to the person infringed by the search nor any form of interlocutory appeal questioning the legality of undertaken measure. The only mechanisms which are available remain outside the criminal process and allow the police to be sued under the tort law regime or to demand prosecution against her for unlawful behavior.[159] Neither can be considered as being sufficiently effective.

The situation is different in the case of arrests. It has been strongly confirmed by the Supreme Court that "the Fourth Amendment requires a judicial determination of probable cause as a prerequisite to extended restraint on liberty allowing arrest."[160] This means that whenever a person has been arrested, she must be promptly taken before the judge or magistrate for an initial appearance.[161] In the warrantless cases this is crucial since through the so-called *Gerstein* review the magistrate will determine the existence of probable cause in a similar way as such determination is done when an arrest warrant is being issued.[162] In both cases the initial appearance will allow confirming the suspect's identity, notify her about her rights, and inform her about the charges the prosecutor files against her. However, the initial appearance takes place only when the police are willing to present the suspect to the prosecutor for charging and the prosecutor agrees with it. This means that the judicial verification of an arrest will not be made in any way if the arrestee has been released either by the police or upon the prosecutorial order. As a result, a certain number of arrests remain unverified by the judge or magistrate, which also means that the evidence resulting from the arrest, similarly to search cases, will be subjected to judicial scrutiny only when the case reaches the trial stage. The only possible remedies will again remain outside of the scope of the criminal process.

Finally, it should be also noted that when the procedure of stop and frisk is considered, no judicial scrutiny is likewise available. Unless the stop and

157 See on the exclusionary rule *Boyd* v. *United States*, 116 US 616 (1886), *Weeks* v. *United States*, 232 US 383 (1914), *Wolf* v. *Colorado*, 338 US 25 (1949), *Rochin* v. *California*, 342 US 165 (1952); *Mapp* v. *Ohio*, 467 US 643 (1961).

158 Kremens (2020), pp. 1594-1595.

159 See e.g. on federal level 42 USC Section 1983 on the liability of state officials.

160 *Gerstein* v. *Pugh*, 420 US 103, 114 (1975).

161 See Sections 3.5.1 and 6.5.3.

162 Kamisar et al. (2015), p. 11.

frisk transfers into arrest and only if subsequently the arrestee is presented for initial appearance, the verification of the lawfulness of such measure through any form of complaint within the scope of the criminal process is not given to the person who claims that her rights has been infringed by the *Terry* stop.

7.5.3 Authority to Impose Coercive Measures

At this point it is crucial to answer who under the US law takes responsibility for undertaking the coercive measures. The US case law seems to have clear and convincing arguments with regard to that matter. US case law relating to the Fourth Amendment focuses on features of an official that would be allowed to issue warrant connecting it with a notion of a "neutral and detached magistrate." This is a requirement that was set 70 years ago, when in *Johnson* v. *United States*[163] the Supreme Court stated that:

> [t]he point of the Fourth Amendment which often is not grasped by zealous officer is not that it denies law enforcement the support of the usual inferences reasonable men draw from evidence. Its protection consists in requiring that those inferences be drawn by a neutral and detached magistrate instead of being judged by the officer engaged in the often competitive enterprise of ferreting out crime.[164]

It is based on a premise that between the citizen and law enforcement agents whose job is the detection of crime, the impartial magistrate should be interposed "so that an objective mind might weigh the need to invade that privacy in order to enforce law".[165]

Interestingly, this neutral and detached magistrate does not necessarily have to be a lawyer. What is, however, required is her neutrality and detachment from the case as well as the capability to determine the existence of probable cause for the requested arrest or search.[166] The Court also noted that the practice works in favor of magistrates without a legal degree and "even within federal system warrants were until recently widely issued by nonlawyers."[167] This, however, should be understood in a narrow way taking into account the special position that magistrates hold in US criminal proceedings.

Therefore, if it is established that only an independent authority is eligible to issue warrants that allow for the interference of an individuals' rights, another question can be asked: Can the prosecutor be deemed as sufficiently

163 333 US 10 (1948).
164 *Johnson* v. *United States*, 333 US 10, 13–14 (1948).
165 *McDonald* v. *United States*, 335 U.S.US 451, 456 (1948).
166 *Shadwick* v. *City of Tampa* 407 US 345, 350 (1972).
167 *Shadwick* v. *City of Tampa*, 407 US 345, 349 (1972).

neutral and detached? Again, US case law seems to give a simple answer to this question: no. First, it has been observed that prosecutors, being closely associated with the executive,[168] have a duty and responsibility to enforce the laws, investigate, and prosecute, and therefore, "should not be the sole judges of when to utilize constitutionally sensitive means in pursuing their tasks" since "unreviewed executive discretion may yield too readily to pressures to obtain incriminating evidence and overlook potential invasions of privacy."[169] Second, and probably even more importantly, the fact that the prosecutors are so engaged in criminal investigations excludes them from being able to impose coercive measures. This problem was addressed for instance in *Coolidge* v. *New Hampshire*[170] where the Supreme Court has confirmed that Attorney General does not encompass the level of detachment and neutrality that is demanded from authority issuing warrants. The fact, that the Attorney General of New Hampshire was formally and unquestionably authorized, under then existing law, to issue search warrants as a justice of peace, in that case raised some valid concerns. The Supreme Court pointed out that the Attorney General not only issued a warrant, but he personally took charge of all police activities relating to the murder at stake and a role of a chief prosecutor at the trial following the investigation. This made it ultimately obvious that he could not be seen as neutral enough since the relation that he built with a case and officers conducting the investigation made him too involved to be allowed to issue a search warrant.[171] The same is true in situations when the issuing authority has, for instance, a financial interest in the issuance of warrants.[172]

But the standard of a neutral and detached magistrate applies only when a warrant must be issued and eventually in cases where a warrantless arrest took place and the verification of the probable cause requirement, during a *Gerstein* review as discussed above, has been required. This leaves a vast number of other cases conducted without a warrant with no scrutiny of the authority of the required standard. It also brings back a well-founded question of the impact that the police and prosecutor have on the imposition of coercive measures since the vast majority of searches and arrests are conducted without a warrant.

168 For more on the proximity of prosecutors to executive in US system, see Section 2.5.

169 *United States* v. *United States District Court*, 407 US 297, 317 (1972).

170 *Coolidge* v. *New Hampshire*, 403 US 443 (1971).

171 In another case the Supreme Court has stated that taking part in search by a person that issued search warrant, is not acceptable as being a feature of a neutral and detached magistrate—see *Lo-Ji Sales, Inc.* v. *New York*, 442 US 319, 327 (1979).

172 *Connally* v. *Georgia*, 429 US 245 (1977) (in this case US Supreme Court held unconstitutional the statute that authorized payment of $5 to each magistrate issuing a search warrant while no money was given to those denying warrants). See also similar arguments in a case involving payment received by judges upon conviction in *Tumey* v. *Ohio*, 273 US 510 (1927).

The issuance of a warrant happens on the request of police officers or other agents, since they are primarily responsible for conducting criminal investigations with almost no involvement of prosecutors in the early stages of criminal proceedings. This could suggest that prosecutors do not play a role in imposing coercive measures. However, as stated for instance in NDAA National Prosecution Standards, it is desired that the prosecutor's office should develop and maintain a system for providing law enforcement with the opportunity for a prompt legal review of search and arrest warrant applications before the applications are submitted to a judicial officer.[173] Moreover, it is also expected that the prosecutor's office will assist in training law enforcement personnel within the prosecutor's jurisdiction on the law applicable to the issuance and execution of search and arrest warrants. The law also allows prosecutors to file requests for warrants with the judge personally if they deem it necessary[174] which usually happens when the prosecutor takes control of a criminal investigation after charges are filed with the court.

Nevertheless, the control of criminal investigation by the police[175] shows that they are also most likely to be the ultimate decision makers when it comes to coercive measures. This leads to the situation where the police retain an incredibly wide discretion to decide whom to arrest and what to search for in particular because the unauthorized measures conducted without a warrant created as the exception became the rule. With relatively little fear that their conduct will be verified unless the case goes to trial, which is not very likely, the police officers maintain real power over the imposition of coercive measures in the USA.

7.6 Summary

The impact that the use of coercive measures has on the lives of individuals cannot be exaggerated. As stated by the US Supreme Court in *Brinegar* v *US*, "[u]ncontrolled search and seizure are the first and most effective weapons in the arsenal of every arbitrary government."[176] Therefore, the question of when, and by what means, the search and arrest should be conducted,

173 3-2.1 NPS. The prosecutorial scrutiny in case of electronic surveillance is of even more strict character providing that the prosecutor's office should not only review but also approve the use of all electronic surveillance by law enforcement entities that are within the prosecutor's jurisdiction (3-2.2 NPS).

174 See for example § 54-33a (b) CGS providing that any state's attorney or assistant state's attorney or any two credible persons may file a complaint on oath to the Superior Court or judge trial referee with a purpose to obtain a search warrant.

175 Cf. Section 6.5.

176 *Brinegar* v. *US* 338 US 160, 180 (1949).

and who is responsible for the decision on their imposition, and how these measures should be subsequently controlled, remains a valid question for every government.[177]

The four researched countries show the variety of choices with regard to this issue. While some of them regulate the imposition of coercive measures jointly (the USA)[178] others showed doubt as to whether the arrest and search are intrusive to the same extent (Germany, Poland, Italy) and therefore structured them slightly differently. At the same time, while Poland and the USA did not consider it necessary to state at the constitutional level who should be responsible for the imposition of such measures, Germany partially regulated this issue, and Italy directly confirmed that it should be a power of the "judicial authority" which on the other hand, also did not resolve the problem, as it included prosecutors under this expression.

All countries, theoretically, set the preference for the employment of coercive measures upon a warrant. But not in every system the priority of warranted arrest is pronounced as clearly as in case of searches. For instance, Poland and the USA the provisions does not demand from police proof that they had no time to obtain the arrest warrant. However, this appears to be counterbalanced by the need to present the arrestee within a considerably short period of time to the judge for validation of an arrest if such validation is needed. Although, when the police are no longer willing to detain the arrestee the appearance before the judge is not required. In practice, the majority of searches and arrests happen without a warrant upon the immediate decision of a competent police officer or, in some cases, also the prosecutor. Importantly, for such cases, where the measure has been employed without a warrant, the Continental system generally provides some additional safeguards, that are not available in the common-law system, in the form of confirmation of the measure by another authority.

The question of the authority responsible for imposition of coercive measures seems to be most clearly resolved in the US system, where the only official authorized to order a search is a judge (magistrate) as confirmed in *Mapp* v. *Ohio*.[179] As discussed, this is based on the premise that only the neutral and detached magistrate may decide on limiting the rights of a person. The illegibility of the prosecutor to undertake such a decision is derived from the proximity of the prosecution service to the executive and, most of all, from the prosecutorial engagement in criminal investigation, that excludes her from being objective in evaluation of the need to conduct measures

177 Cf. Kremens (2020), pp. 1620–1621.

178 Although note that also the US system grades the level in which the rights are interfered with introducing a separate category of stop and frisk.

179 367 US 643 (1961).

of a coercive character.[180] Surprisingly, Poland and Italy provide for a considerably distinct approach since the power to impose coercive measures is split between judges and prosecutors. On the other hand, the German system perceived traditionally as associated with the inquisitorial system, remains closest to the US idea of who should retain such powers, vesting them in the hands of the judge for investigation.

Of the four, the Italian case seems the most disturbing. Even though Italy has established a special figure—the judge for investigation, to fulfill the task of protecting the individual during the course of criminal investigation, the full control over searches is maintained by the prosecutor. The arguments behind such wide powers of the prosecutor have focused on the prosecutor as part of the *magistratura* and remaining the "judicial authority" that the Italian Constitution equips with competencies to impose coercive measures. As discussed above,[181] even if we accept that education, pension, and training of both judges and prosecutors are the same and the position of Italian prosecutors during the criminal process is much stronger when it comes to internal and external independence than their counterparts from other states, it is still not equal to judges. But if the Italian system was eager to equate these two groups and assume that the Italian prosecutor is as independent and impartial as a judge, the legal norms contradict that assumption by not allowing prosecutors to play any profound role when it comes to coercive measures other than search. For example, the prosecutor lacks the same powers when it comes to the post-factum authorization of arrests. Even if it could be accepted that arrest infringes the individual's rights to a greater extent than the search, if the prosecutor is indeed equal to judge, she should be equally competent to undertake decisions in that regard. If she cannot, it means that there is indeed a difference between these two groups regardless of whether the prosecution is associated more closely with the judiciary than with the executive.

In the context of the authority imposing coercive measures in the four countries, the unique position of the police and other criminal justice agencies competent to employ such measures can be observed. Although it should be clear that the use of coercion is an inevitable part of criminal investigations and under certain requirements it should be always possible to impose coercive measures for the sake of efficiency of investigation, the impact that the police have regarding the use of search and arrest is tremendous. It is obvious in case of warrantless searches and arrests, but is also valid when the measures are imposed upon the warrant, since such decision is usually based solely on materials gathered by the police (dossier, police

180 Kremens (2020), p. 1621.
181 See Section 2.5.

reports). This is confirmed by the practice, as reported in some countries, of refusals to the requests for a warrant not being common, which makes the judicial or prosecutorial authorization of such measures illusionary and the police impact even greater.

Another issue in providing protection of rights of individually in the cases of all three examined Continental European states must be acknowledged. These countries offer a right to file a motion (revision, interlocutory appeal) to verify the lawfulness of the measure, even in cases when the conduct of a measure was preauthorized. This is seen as an immediate remedy for an individual that believes that her rights have been infringed. While Poland and Germany provide for the interlocutory appeal in all discussed cases, Italy provides it always for arrests but for searches only when they result in a seizure of objects. This instrument, even if only triggered at the request of the concerned individual, provides for a remarkable chance to immediately verify in court the legality and proportionality of the measure. It should be noted that the USA does not provide for a similar standard, and an infringed individual must await trial to verify the lawfulness of the search or arrest that may result in calling evidence obtained by such means inadmissible. Meanwhile the improper behavior of the criminal justice authorities in obtaining evidence cannot be reduced merely to an obstacle in admitting such evidence during the trial. It also strongly relates to the reception of police practice. Proper assessment of such practice can and should work as a deterrence mechanism. While awaiting trial, that might never happen, excludes the possibility of verification of the measure employed and does not allow to immediately correct the standard of police actions.

References

Bohlander M (2012) *Principles of German Criminal Procedure*. Hart, London.

Brodowski D, Burchard C, Kotzurek N, Rauber J, Vogel J (2010) Germany. In: Cape E, Namoradze Z, Smith R, Spronken T (eds) *Effective Criminal Defence in Europe*. Intersentia, Antwerp-Oxford-Portland, pp. 253–319.

Brown DK, Turner JI, Weisser B (eds) (2019) *The Oxford Handbook of Criminal Process*. Oxford University Press, Oxford.

Caianiello M (2010) Italy. In: Cape E, Namoradze Z, Smith R, Spronken T (eds) *Effective Criminal Defence in Europe*. Intersentia, Antwerp-Oxford-Portland, pp. 373–423.

Caianiello M (2012) The Italian Public Prosecutor: An Inquisitorial Figure in Adversarial Proceedings. In: Luna E, Wade M (eds) *The Prosecutor in Transnational Perspective*. Oxford University Press, Oxford, pp. 250–267.

Caianiello M (2016) *Increasing Discretionary Prosecutor's Powers: The Pivotal Role of the Italian Prosecutor in the Pretrial Investigation Phase*. Oxford Handbooks Online, Oxford.

Cape E, Hodgson J, Pranken T, Spronken T (eds) (2007) *Suspects in Europe. Procedural Rights at the Investigative Stage of the Criminal Process in the European Union.* Intersentia, Antwerp.

De Vocht D (2010) Poland. In: Cape E, Namoradze Z, Smith R, Spronken T (eds) *Effective Criminal Defence in Europe.* Intersentia, Antwerp-Oxford-Portland, pp. 425–488.

Delmas-Marty M (2008), "Reflections on the "Hybridisation" of Criminal Procedure. In: Jackson J, Langer M, Tillers P (eds), *Crime, Procedure and Evidence in a Comparative and International Context: Essays in Honour of Professor Mirjan Damaška.* Hart, London, pp. 251–260.

Di Amato A (2013) *Criminal Law in Italy.* Kluwer Law International, Alphen aan den Rijn.

Di Federico G (1998) Prosecutorial Independence and the Democratic Requirement of Accountability in Italy: Analysis of a Deviant Case in a Comparative Perspective. *British Journal of Criminology* 38:371–387.

Dressler J, Thomas GC (2017) *Criminal Procedure. Principles, Policies and Perspectives.* West Academic Publishing, St. Paul.

Frase RS, Weigend T (1995) German Criminal Justice as a Guide to American Law Reform. *Boston College International and Comparative Law Review* 18:317–360.

Gray D (2016) Fourth Amendment Remedies as Rights: The Warrant Requirement. *Boston University Law Review* 96(2):425–483.

Hall DE (2009) *Criminal Law and Procedure.* Delmar, Clifton Park.

Huber B (2008) Germany. In: Vogler R, Huber B, *Criminal Procedure in Europe.* Duncker & Humblot, Berlin, pp. 269–371.

Illuminati G, Caianiello M (2007) The Investigative Stage of the Criminal Process in Italy. In: Cape E, Hodgson J, Pranken T, Spronken T (eds), *Suspects in Europe. Procedural Rights at the Investigative Stage of the Criminal Process in the European Union.* Intersentia, Antwerp, pp. 129–154.

Jasiński W, Kremens K (2019) *Criminal Law in Poland.* Kluwer Law International, Alphen aan den Rijn.

Kamisar Y, LaFave WR, Israel JH, King NJ, Kerr OS, Primus EB (2015) *Modern Criminal Procedure. Cases-Comments-Questions.* West, St Paul.

Kelsen H (2000) *What is Justice? Justice, Law and Politics in the Mirror of Science. Collected Essays.* The Lawbook Exchange, Union.

Koper RT (2014) Przeszukanie w wypadkach niecierpiących zwłoki. *Prokuratura i Prawo* 11–12:14–31.

Kremens K (2020) The Authority to Order Search in Comparative Perspective: The Call for the Judicial Oversight. *Revista Brasileira di Direito Processual Penal* 6(3):1585–1626.

Kruszyński P (2007) The Investigative Stage of the Criminal Process in Poland. In: Cape E, Hodgson J, Pranken T, Spronken T (eds) *Suspects in Europe. Procedural Rights at the Investigative Stage of the Criminal Process in the European Union.* Intersentia, Antwerp, pp. 181–209.

Kühne H-H (1993) Germany. In: Van Den Wyngaert C (ed) *Criminal Procedure Systems in the European Community*, Butterworths, London, pp. 137–162

Lasagni G (2018) Tackling phone searches in Italy and the United States: Proposals for a technological rethinking of procedural rights and freedoms. *New Journal of European Criminal Law* 9:386–401.
Ligeti K (ed) (2013) *Toward a Prosecutor of the European Union, Volume 1: A Comparative Analysis*. Hart, London.
Ligeti K (2019) The Place of the Prosecutor in Common Law and Civil Law Jurisdictions. In: Brown DK, Turner JI, Weisser B (eds) *The Oxford Handbook of Criminal Process*. Oxford University Press, Oxford, pp. 139–163.
Nowak C, Steinborn S (2013) Poland. In: Ligeti K (ed) *Toward a Prosecutor of the European Union, Volume 1: A Comparative Analysis*. Hart, London, pp. 498–509.
Perrodet A (2002) *The Italian System. In: Delmas-Marty M, Spencer JR (eds) European Criminal Procedures*. Cambridge University Press, Cambridge, pp. 348–411.
Quattrocolo S, Ruggeri S (eds) (2019) *Personal Participation in Criminal Proceedings*. Springer, Cham.
Ruggieri F, Marcolini S (2013) Italy. In: Ligeti K (ed) *Toward a Prosecutor of the European Union, Volume 1: A Comparative Analysis*. Hart, London, pp. 368–404.
Ryan A (2014) *Towards a System of European Criminal Justice*. Routledge, New York.
Sakowicz A (2000) Poszanowanie życia prywatnego w postępowaniu karnym. *Jurysta* 6:21.
Scaccianoce C (2010) The principle of mandatory prosecution and the independence of public prosecutors in the Italian Criminal Justice System. *ReAIDP/e-RIAPL*, A-01:1–10.
Scheb JM, Scheb JM II (1999) *Criminal Procedure*. Wadsworth, Belmont.
Siegismund E (2003) The Public Prosecution Office in Germany: Legal Status, Function and Organization. In: Effective Administration of the Police and the Prosecution in Criminal Justice. The 120th International Senior Seminar, Visiting Experts' Papers www.unafei.or.jp/publications/pdf/RS_No60/No60_10VE_Siegismund2.pdf. Accessed 12.07.2020, pp. 58–64.
Skorupka J (2007) Konstytucyjne i konwencyjne granice przeszukania w postępowaniu karnym (cz. II). *Palestra* 11–12:52–63.
Skorupka J (2015) Komentarz do art. 246 k.p.k. In: Skorupka J (ed) *Kodeks postępowania karnego. Komentarz*. CH Beck, Warsaw.
Steinberg DE (2008) The Uses and Misuses of Fourth Amendment History. *Journal of Constitutional History* 10:581–606.
Steinborn S (2008) Problem organu uprawnionego do stosowania przeszukania w toku procesu karnego w świetle unormowań konstytucyjnych i prawnomiędzynarodowych. *Gdańskie Studia Prawnicze* 19.
Trendafilova E, Róth W (2008) Report on the Public Prosecution Service in Germany. In: Open Society Institute Sofia (ed) *Promoting Prosecutorial Accountability, Independence and Effectiveness*. Open Society Institute Sofia, Sofia, pp. 213–246.
Van Den Wyngaert C (ed) (1993) *Criminal Procedure Systems in the European Community*. Butterworths, London.
Vogler R, Huber B (2008) *Criminal Procedure in Europe*. Duncker & Humblot, Berlin.
Weigend T (2013) Germany. In: Ligeti K (ed) *Toward a Prosecutor of the European Union, Volume 1: A Comparative Analysis*. Hart, London, pp. 264–306.

Weigend T, Salditt F (2007) The Investigative Stage of the Criminal Process in Germany. In: Cape E, Hodgson J, Pranken T, Spronken T (eds), *Suspects in Europe. Procedural Rights at the Investigative Stage of the Criminal Process in the European Union*. Intersentia, Antwerp, pp. 79–100.

Witt JW (1973) Non-coercive Interrogation and the Administration of Criminal Justice: The Impact of Miranda on Police Effectuality. *The Journal of Criminal Law and Criminology* 64:320–332.

Worrall JL (2012) *Criminal Procedure. From First Contact to Appeal*. Pearson, Boston.

Chapter 8

Prosecutor's Powers to Discontinue Investigation

8.1 General Considerations

It is obvious to all that observe and research the evolution of the criminal process, or participate in it in various roles, that the impact that the prosecutor has on the outcome of criminal investigation is more than significant. The literature focuses on the powers of the prosecutor with regard to negotiating settlements and reaching agreements resulting in convictions or some other forms of punitive reactions. Chapter 1 looked at the scholarly writings describing that phenomenon. So, this chapter focuses on the flip side of the latter: the decision to discontinue criminal investigations. What are the forms of such decisions? How much impact does the prosecutor have in the normative framework with regard to them? How much can the decision to terminate proceedings be influenced by the police? Do the judges (courts) have anything to say, and can they review such decision? Can the victim oppose it?

First, though, the notion of what constitutes discontinuation of a criminal investigation should be discussed. It can be defined as a way in which criminal proceedings are terminated that does not answer the question of guilt or innocence. It encompasses all forms in which pending criminal proceedings are ending when the authority that controls the proceedings decides not to pursue the case further and terminates it (sometimes with accompanying conditions).

There is no consensus between scholars as to what expression should be used to describe this form of case-ending decisions. One can also find in the literature other phrases of a similar meaning e.g. "disposal of the case." This has been used for instance in the *European Criminal Procedures* volume edited by Delmas-Marty and Spencer[1] and more recently in a volume edited by Ligeti.[2] This expression is commonly used in the context of the unilateral and multilateral disposal of cases. While the former is used to describe the most

1 Delmas-Marty and Spencer (2002).
2 Ligeti (2013).

typical situation when the authority terminates the case based on formal grounds as well as the public interest (which could be considered as discontinuation of criminal investigation in the meaning adopted for this work), the multilateral disposals group also contains such situations where the case is moved for conviction. This would include among others penal orders or out-of-trial convictions resulting from negotiated justice settlements. Somewhere in between these types of disposals one can find so-called conditional dismissals, which in some cases might be decided unilaterally by the prosecutor but in others may result from negotiations and therefore be credited to the multilateral disposals group. In some jurisdictions the power to conditionally dismiss the case might be even shared between the prosecutor and the judge. In view of this, since "dispositions" includes also convictions and this chapter is planned to discuss only the opposite it has been decided not to use it here .

In other works, the terminology for case-ending decisions of the prosecutor varies and is not defined. For instance, in one of the most recent books on prosecutorial powers in a comparative perspective, Gilliéron uses such terms as "decision not to file criminal charges" and "decision not to prosecute" or, less commonly, "declinations" especially when the US system is discussed.[3] "Dismissals" (conditional and unconditional), "discontinuation," and "drop" are used when referring to Swiss,[4] German,[5] and French[6] systems. This shows not only the variety of terminological choices used within different works to describe this type of case-ending decisions,[7] but in particular highlights the specifics of the US system accentuating the termination of a criminal proceedings as the flip side of the charging decision. This is discussed in greater detail later in the chapter.

Therefore, choice of "discontinuation of criminal investigation" here must be considered as personal. The term should be understood as a decision to cease criminal proceedings (usually by the prosecutor) which does not lead to conviction of the accused. It should also be acknowledged that certain competencies to undertake such decision may be vested in both the court and the police. The main purpose of this chapter is to show the impact that these criminal process actors have on such decisions, while looking at how the process can also be influenced by the victim and the suspect. Finally, despite using the term "discontinuation" here, others such as termination

3 Gilliéron (2014), pp. 89–90.
4 Gilliéron (2014), pp. 211–225.
5 Gilliéron (2014), pp. 270–275.
6 Gilliéron (2014), pp. 298–301.
7 See also terminology proposed by Luna and Wade (2010), pp. 1442–1445, focusing on drops and disposals.

or ceasing are used interchangeably without attaching any particular weight to either.

8.2 Discontinuation of Criminal Investigation in Germany

8.2.1 Threshold to Discontinue the Investigation

The criminal investigation ends in Germany with the decision of the prosecutor to either file a case with the court in the form of an indictment (*Anklageschrift*) or to discontinue the criminal investigation in accordance with § 170 (2) StPO. Theoretically, the prosecutor in making her decision, is bound by the principle of legality,[8] which suggests that she is free in making the decision to discontinue investigation when an adequate suspicion to file the indictment with the court is found.[9] The threshold that must be reached to discontinue the criminal investigation is a reverse of the ground that allows the filing of the case with the court, i.e. "inadequate suspicion to prefer public charges."[10] As reported, the rate of discontinuations based on insufficiency of evidence is considered as the most common type of the prosecutorial decisions to discontinue the criminal investigations, reaching 28 percent of all criminal investigations discontinued in 2010.[11] But, as a country that works under the principle of mandatory prosecution, Germany provides for a surprisingly broad scope of the discretionary options given to the prosecutor when it comes to the forms in which the investigation can be ended beyond the discussed forms.

Primarily, the prosecutor has a broad competence to discontinue a case even if the evidence is sufficient to prosecute a suspect (*Einstellung wegen Geringfugigkeit*). In accordance with § 153 (1) StPO this is available for all misdemeanors,[12] when the perpetrator's guilt is considered minor in nature and if there is no public interest in carrying out the prosecution. The consent of the court is necessary unless the case is of a very minor character. Theoretically, this allows for a quite broad discretion of the prosecutor to assess the lack of public interest, since the term is rather imprecise. But the prevailing perception is that there is even a duty to discontinue the case when there is minor guilt and no public interest.[13] Moreover, the interpretation of the "public interest" in particular depends on the criteria as provided in

8 § 152 (2) StPO.
9 Cf. Section 3.2.2.
10 § 170 (1) StPO.
11 See Weigend (2013), p. 268 fn. 32.
12 So-called *Vergehen*; less serious crimes carrying a statutory minimum sentence of less than one year.
13 Gilliéron (2014), p. 271 and literature quoted in fn. 56.

guidelines issued separately for each *Länder*. This may concern the minimum damage caused by the offense in question or exclusion of certain offenses from the group of crimes eligible for this type of decision, e.g. cases of domestic violence.[14] Statistically, only 9 percent of all criminal investigations were discontinued in 2011 based on the lack of public interest.[15]

Second, pursuant to § 153a StPO, the prosecutors are also allowed to conditionally discontinue the criminal investigation (*Einstellung nach Erfullung von Auflagen*). This again involves only misdemeanors, but this time the consent of the suspect is required as well as the court's approval. The conditional discontinuation of a case can be imposed only where its result will satisfy the public interest, and the suspect's guilt is not so serious as to preclude disposing a case in this manner. The available conditions upon which the decision is based are e.g. compensating the victim, paying a fine, community service and upon their fulfillment by the suspect the case may be discontinued and becomes final. Even though this procedure is valid only in case of limited circumstances concerning what is considered as misdemeanor under German law,[16] some prosecution offices decided to implement internal guidelines restricting these provisions even further to avoid incoherence in a process of prosecutorial decision-making.[17] As reported, the number of this kind of decisions fluctuates at around 4–5 percent of all criminal investigations terminated in 2010.[18] It is reported that this form of discontinuation of proceedings is less attractive for the prosecutors since it demands some activity from them to identify the condition upon which the decision will be made and to ensure compliance with it.[19]

The law also provides for additional grounds that allow for discontinuation of investigation which are used even less frequently when compared with the mechanisms based on § 153 and § 153a StPO.[20] Among them are inappropriateness of the sentence,[21] committing an offense abroad,[22] or

14 Elsner and Peters (2010), p. 221.
15 Gilliéron (2014), p. 271. Similar rate is shown for 1993–2003 in Elsner and Peters (2010), p. 221.
16 Offenses in Germany are classified as felonies (*Verbrechen*) punishable by a minimum sentence of 1 year imprisonment (§ 12 (1) StGB) and misdemeanors (*Vergehen*) punishable by a lesser sentence of imprisonment than 1 year or fine (§ 12 (2) StGB).
17 Trendafilova and Róth (2008), p. 228 and Gilliéron (2014), p. 274.
18 Gilliéron (2014), p. 274. Cf. Elsner and Peters (2010), p. 223 (authors note that as of 2003 in around 88 percent of conditional discontinuations of investigation, the condition was the payment to charitable organization or the treasury was ordered, making it the most popular condition).
19 Elsner and Peters (2010), p. 223.
20 See § 153c–153f. See also Juy-Birmann (2002), p. 339 and Gilliéron (2014), p. 273.
21 § 153b StPO.
22 § 153c StPO.

foreseeability that the possible penalty imposed for the offense being a subject of the investigation will not be particularly significant due to other penalties already imposed on the same accused in other cases.[23] The latter is based on the ground of procedural economy—if a severe sentence is expected in one case, there is no point in holding expensive and time-consuming proceedings in a less serious case that will not increase the final penalty.[24] Therefore, even though compulsory prosecution remains as a binding principle of the German criminal process, there is a clear trend moving away from it toward more powerful and independent prosecuting institutions.[25]

8.2.2 Procedure for Discontinuation of Investigation

As far as the unconditional discontinuation of criminal investigation is concerned the procedure for undertaking it is not too complicated. If the investigation does not offer sufficient suspicion to prefer public charges, the prosecutor terminates proceedings.[26] When the prosecutor issues the decision, she must inform the suspect about it. However, the notification takes place only if the suspect was interrogated as such, if a warrant of arrest was issued against her, if she requested such notice, or if there is a particular interest in her being notified. Therefore, it appears that the right to be notified does not apply to a suspected person who is not officially a suspect.[27] When the decision to discontinue investigation is made the prosecutor notifies the person that reported the crime.[28] If the informant is the victim, she is notified of the right to lodge an interlocutory appeal against such decision and of the related time limit.[29]

Consequently, the victim is entitled to appeal the decision of the prosecutor, a right which is not granted to the suspect.[30] The interlocutory appeal filed by the victim is aimed at forcing the prosecutor to bring a case for a trial (*Klageerzw ingungsverfahren*).[31] The procedure first requires lodging the interlocutory appeal with the chief prosecutor at the State Court of Appeals within two weeks of

23 § 154 StPO.
24 Siegismund (2003), p. 63.
25 Elsner and Peters (2010), p. 234.
26 § 170 (2) StPO.
27 Section 6.2.
28 § 171 StPO first sentence.
29 § 171 StPO second sentence. Note that, in accordance with § 172 (1) StPO, if the victim has not been notified about the right to lodge an interlocutory appeal the time limit does not start.
30 Gilliéron (2014), p. 271.
31 Frase and Weigend (1995), pp. 338 and 350 (authors translate this procedure as the "mandamus action compelling prosecution").

receiving notification that the case has been discontinued.[32] After reviewing the case file, the chief prosecutor may then order the prosecutor to resume the investigation or even force her to file an accusation. It has been reported in the past that overthrowing of the prosecutor's decision by the chief prosecutor is in practice not likely, however the mere fact that such a mechanism exists, makes prosecutors more reluctant to discontinue the case if they know that the victim may be willing to oppose such decision.[33] However, if the decision of the chief prosecutor upholds the decision to discontinue the investigation, the victim may, within one month of receiving the decision of the chief prosecutor, file a further appeal against it with the State Court of Appeals.[34] This time the appeal must meet certain formal requirements, including indication of the facts and evidence supporting the alleged grounds for overturning the decision to not initiate investigation and must be signed by an attorney.[35] The proceedings may involve presenting the Court with the prosecutorial file containing the findings, providing the suspect with an opportunity to give a statement regarding the outcome of the proceedings and the Court may even decide to conduct further investigation.[36] The Court may uphold the prosecutor's decision and dismiss the interlocutory appeal if there are no sufficient grounds to prefer public charges notifying the victim, prosecutor, and suspect.[37] But in the event that the Court agrees with the victim that the evidence is so strong that a trial is warranted, it orders the prosecutor to file an accusation.[38]

This victim's right to interlocutory appeal and, in particular, the court's power to enforce the prosecution, might seem to be restricting prosecutorial powers to discontinue a case. But it has its own limits. It is impermissible in cases of misdemeanors in which investigation was discontinued for the lack of public interest, all other special and discretionary discontinuations, as well as in cases of crimes belonging to a group of crimes prosecuted privately (i.e. by the victim only).[39] This means that the *Klageerzwingungsverfahren* is limited only to such cases in which the discontinuation of investigation results solely from insufficiency of evidence.[40] This could still leave a good number of cases subject to this procedure, but the number of appeals nevertheless remains relatively small.[41] The victim's efforts to force an accusation

32 § 172 (1) StPO.
33 Herrmann (1974), p. 477.
34 § 172 (2) StPO second sentence.
35 § 172 (3) StPO.
36 § 173 (1)–(3) StPO.
37 § 174 (1) StPO.
38 § 175 StPO.
39 § 172 (2) StPO.
40 Trendafilova and Róth (2008), p. 229.
41 In 1998, in three German Lands out of 159, requests filed to trigger the prosecution enforcement procedure, only one appeal was addressed on merits and the rest were

are not often successful in practice, but the fact that the judicial review mechanism exists is perceived as a check on the arbitrariness of prosecutorial decisions to discontinue a case.[42]

Therefore, in the case of discontinuation of criminal investigation based on grounds other than insufficiency of evidence, the victim has no right to appeal such decision. This is partially compensated by the fact that in cases of these other forms of discontinuation, e.g. based on the public interest or conditional dismissals, it is necessary to obtain the court's consent. For some particularly minor offenses, though, the court's consent is not required.[43] Such forms of discontinuation of criminal investigation are also not considered as final and may be reopened by the prosecutor at any time.

8.2.3 Authority for Discontinuing Investigations

Prosecutorial powers to discontinue criminal investigations in Germany appear to be broad. Besides the most obvious and most commonly used power to terminate cases based on insufficiency of evidence, the prosecutor by law has a variety of choices when it comes to distinct procedures for terminating a case even on discretionary grounds. The law highlights the prosecutorial competence to discontinue proceedings, creating the impression that other actors of the criminal process have insubstantial impact on it. But the truth is that the role that the court and victim play during the procedure for discontinuation of investigation limits the prosecutorial powers to a certain extent. Also the freedom of independence in undertaking the decision may be considered as limited when taking into account the departmental constraints due to established guidelines as well as instructions the prosecutor might receive from her supervisors.[44]

Significant impact on the powers of the prosecutor with regard to termination of investigation is vested in the judge. This influence should be considered from various perspectives. First, at the request of the victim, the prosecutorial decision undertaken on insufficiency of evidence grounds, may be subject to a full judicial review. As a result, the court receives significant competence to force the prosecutor to file public charges with the court through the *Klageerzwingungsverfahren* procedure, by which she deprives the prosecutor of her right to independently decide on the outcome of criminal investigation. But, as the numbers show, this procedure is not frequently

regarded as either inadmissible or unfounded. The numbers for 1999 in the same Lands are similar (1:137). See Meyer-Krapp (2008), p. 101.

42 Weigend (2007), p. 262.

43 § 153 (1) StPO

44 Herrmann (1974), p. 477.

employed in practice and therefore the impact of the court in that regard can be considered as very limited. Having a considerably stronger impact are the decisions of the superior prosecutor who, after analyzing the victim's interlocutory appeal, may decide that the investigation should be continued.

Second, the court has broad competence to confirm prosecutorial decisions to terminate some investigations based on discretionary grounds. This concerns discontinuations based on public interest as well as those made upon conditions. In theory, the approval of the court is mandatory and provides for careful judicial scrutiny limiting the scope of prosecutorial discretion. But, as reported, in practice it is almost always granted, and the existence or absence of public interest is not subject to judicial review.[45] Moreover, in cases of minor crimes, approval is not required, which, surprisingly, seems in practice to raise little criticism.[46] And since the victim's interlocutory appeal cannot be lodged with the court in cases of discretionary decisions, the prosecutorial power to discontinue criminal investigation seems unthreatened, at least when it comes to less severe offenses.

Therefore, despite normative constraints, the prosecutors appear to exercise a wide power with regard to termination of criminal investigation. However, the independence in that regard is challenged, by the important role that the police play in conducting criminal investigation. It is true that the last word on whether a case is lodged with the court or discontinued remains with the prosecutor. And, as noted in the literature, in practice prosecutors consider a large percentage of cases as nonprosecutable due to the lack of sufficient evidence that could persuade the court that the suspect is guilty, even when the police are convinced that the case deserves to be heard by the court.[47] But, as discussed earlier,[48] the influence of the police on the criminal investigation seems somewhat greater than the normative regulations would suggest. In the majority of cases the prosecutor receives the file at the end of criminal investigation and, unless there is some form of coercive measure to be employed or some other prosecutor's activity demanded, she does not get involved in investigation until the final steps in the process. This, in particular, concerns most simple cases, being the majority of all that are investigated. Obviously, in the more complicated and time-consuming investigation that demands some additional measures to be involved, the prosecutor might become more engaged. However, this means that generally the prosecutor will decide on the outcome of criminal investigation based on the version as prepared by the police, who possess all powers to

45 See Weigend (2013), p. 268 fn. 36. See also Section 8.2.
46 Trendafilova and Róth (2008), p. 228; Elsner and Peters (2010), p. 220 and fn. 16.
47 Weigend (2013), p. 268.
48 See Section 5.2.

"steer the proceedings in the direction they have chosen"[49] even if the case is more severe. In result, the prosecutorial power to terminate the case should be definitely considered as limited in the first place by the extensive powers that the police possess during the conduct of criminal investigation. This, in particular, concerns minor crimes but is also not without influence in cases of more severe offenses in the conduct of which the police are commonly engaged in broad terms.

8.3 Discontinuation of Criminal Investigation in Poland

8.3.1 Threshold to Discontinue the Investigation

After all evidentiary procedures have been concluded in every criminal investigation the authority conducting investigation freely evaluates the material gathered during this phase of the criminal process, bearing in mind the presumption of innocence and the settling of doubts that have not been resolved in evidentiary proceedings exclusively in favor of the suspect.[50] Then a decision between two options must be made, i.e. whether to discontinue a case[51] or to send it to court in one of the permissible forms. The statistics provide that in 2019 the decision to discontinue criminal investigation was undertaken in 36 percent of all closed investigations whereby 30 percent of those decisions was based on the fact that the offender had not been identified.[52]

Generally, Article 322 § 1 k.p.k. provides that, if there are no grounds to file an indictment with the court, the investigation must be discontinued. This refers to a situation when the evidence collected in the course of the proceedings does not confirm the suspicion that an offense has been committed, or that a given person has not committed it, or that the law enforcement authorities failed to identify the offender, or when the offense is prosecuted by private accusation. Additionally, the law prescribes the list of grounds, the existence of which, demands immediate termination of criminal proceedings regardless of the stage of criminal process, naming them negative grounds for the conduct of criminal proceedings (*negatywne*

49 Elsner and Peters (2010), p. 225.

50 Article 5 and Article 7 k.p.k. Cf. Jasiński and Kremens (2019), p. 224.

51 Polish law uses the term *umorzenie* to describe the discontinuation of criminal proceedings. This term is used uniformly regardless of whether the discontinuation takes place during the investigation or after trial. Also, the conditional discontinuation of proceedings (*warunkowe umorzenie postępowania*) bears the same name.

52 *Sprawozdanie z działalności powszechnych jednostek organizacyjnych prokuratury za rok 2019*, https://pk.gov.pl/wp-content/uploads/2020/03/PK-P1K.pdf. Accessed July 12, 2020, p. 5.

przesłanki procesowe).[53] The comprehensive list of these grounds is provided in Article 17 § 1 k.p.k. which includes primarily, formal reasons to terminate the case, such as the death of the accused, the expiration of the statute of limitations, double jeopardy, lack of jurisdiction (diplomatic immunities), lack of relevant permissions (formal immunities of e.g. members of parliament) or lack of complaint in case of offenses prosecuted upon complaint. The law also prescribes, in great detail, such reasons as establishing that the act has not been committed or insufficiency of evidence to suspect that it has been committed, lack of elements of the offense in a committed act or the insignificance of the degree of social harm caused by the offense that justify the termination of the case under that rule. Also the law provides that the case should be discontinued if the perpetrator committed an act that cannot be understood as an offense, which concerns such cases as insanity and self-defense or if it has been established by law that the offender cannot be subject to a penalty (e.g. when a perpetrator voluntary ceases a prohibited act or prevented the consequences of the act). The list is nonexhaustive and allows for the existence of other grounds excluding the possibility of investigating a case, such as amnesty.

The ground prescribed as the lack of social harm caused by the offense is particularly interesting, since it may resemble the ground of "lack of public interest" as available in other systems. This would allow the claim that the Polish system also allows terminating the case based on discretionary grounds. However, this is more tricky, since the "social harm higher than negligible" is a part of the definition of the crime under the Polish Criminal Code.[54] As a result, the prosecutor is obliged under the legality principle, to establish whether an investigated act has caused social harm higher than negligible and, if not, to discontinue a case based on the fact that the act was not an offense since it lacked one of its required elements, that is social harm in the essential amount. Therefore, it is perceived that the prosecutor has no discretion in that regard. Despite the fact that such discussion might seem somewhat artificial, this appears to be an adopted interpretation of the law.[55] Polish law does not provide for the discontinuation of investigation based on public interest which is strongly bound to the applicability of the principle of legality in Polish criminal proceedings.[56] The only possibility

53 On the concept of negative grounds for the conducting of criminal proceedings, see Hofmański and Jeż-Ludwichowska (2015).

54 Article 2 § 1 k.k. states that "An act cannot be considered as a crime if it presents a negligible degree of social harm." Cf. Jasiński and Kremens (2019), p. 78.

55 See Rogacka-Rzewnicka (2007), pp. 313–316.

56 See Section 3.3.2. Note in particular, discussion on separate grounds for discontinuation of criminal investigation based on some discretionary measures in the Drug Abuse Prevention Act of 2005 and Juvenile Justice Act of 1982.

that the law gives to the prosecutor at the end of criminal investigation is a "simple" discontinuation of criminal proceedings based on normatively regulated grounds.[57]

It should also be mentioned that the prosecutor in Poland is not entitled to apply diversionary measures on her own or to reach settlements that would result in the case not being sent to court.[58] Even the so-called conditional discontinuation of criminal proceedings (*warunkowe umorzenie postępowania)* is not a prosecutorial decision and she may only file a motion for the court to decide so,[59] which is considered as a form of triggering court proceedings against the defendant that the motion concerns.[60] Similarly, when the prosecutor wishes to discontinue investigation and impose protective measures due to the insanity of the offender (*umorzenie postępowania i zastosowanie środków zabezpieczających*), she cannot do it on her own and must file a motion with the court.[61]

8.3.2 Procedure for Discontinuation of Investigation

The decision on the discontinuation of criminal investigation must include an exact description of the offense, its legal classification, and the ground on which the discontinuation has been based.[62] If the investigation was conducted against a person, i.e. after the suspect has been formally charged with a crime,[63] the decision on discontinuation should additionally contain the name of the suspect and, if needed, other information that enables her identification.[64]

57 But note that the law also provides for the possibility to discontinue investigation due to the absorption of an offense by conviction in other proceedings against the same accused (Article 11 k.p.k.) perceived as a straightforward exception to the principle of legality. This is an extremely rarely invoked ground for discontinuation—in 2019 out of 406,770 decisions to discontinue investigation in only 39 cases this ground had been used—*Sprawozdanie z działalności powszechnych jednostek organizacyjnych prokuratury za rok 2019*, https://pk.gov.pl/wp-content/uploads/2020/03/PK-P1K.pdf. Accessed July 12, 2020, p. 5. Between 1998 and 2008 the number of such discontinuation fluctuated around 0.024 percent (see Kołodziejczyk (2013), p. 339). Cf. Section 3.3.2.

58 Nowak and Steinborn (2013), p. 524.

59 Article 336 § 1 k.p.k.

60 Note also that the decision to conditionally discontinue proceedings may also be undertaken by the court on its own initiative, without the need to be initiated by the prosecutor (Article 339 § 1 (3) k.p.k. and Articles 341–342 k.p.k.). Therefore, in Polish cases this should rather be perceived as the court's decision with some prosecutorial influence. See also Bulenda (2010), pp. 262–263.

61 Article 324 k.p.k. Jasiński and Kremens (2019), p. 234.

62 Article 322 § 2 k.p.k.

63 See Section 6.3.1.

64 Article 322 § 3 k.p.k.

The decision is either issued by the prosecutor or confirmed by her with no influence of the court. However, in every case, regardless of the reasons for which the case was discontinued, the decision can be subject to judicial review in the form of an interlocutory appeal (*zażalenie*). The right to lodge an interlocutory appeal against the decision that precludes the possibility of delivering a judgment[65] is generally possible under Article 459 § 1 k.p.k., but is additionally strengthened by Article 306 § 1a k.p.k. The latter provision also sets out who is able to lodge the interlocutory appeal, that is the party to the criminal investigation, i.e. the suspect and the victim as well as the state, local government or social institution that reported an offense and the person that reported one of the listed offenses if that offense resulted in the violation of the rights of this person.[66] Although it should be remembered that since the decision to discontinue proceedings is undertaken in favor of the suspect (if she has been already officially identified as such) she does not hold a power to appeal it due to the general assumption that one can only dispute the decisions that violates her rights.[67] A separate rule provides that those who have a right to lodge an interlocutory appeal against the discontinuation of criminal investigation are also given the right to familiarize themselves with the dossier containing evidence gathered up to the moment when a decision has been made.[68] This allows the proper analysis of the case by the appellant and to build a basis for the interlocutory appeal since the majority of decisions to discontinue proceedings in case of investigation conducted in a form of inquiry does not have to contain the reasoning.[69]

The person entitled to lodge the interlocutory appeal files it with the court via the prosecutor that issued or confirmed the decision to discontinue criminal investigation.[70] The prosecutor, after verification of the formal requirements of the interlocutory appeal, should immediately pass it on to the court for review, but may also accept the arguments and decide to reopen the investigation.[71] This allows the authority that issued the decision to take into

65 The preclusion of the possibility to deliver a judgment has been interpreted by the Supreme Court as only such decision that is "unconditionally" closing the road to a judgment, i.e. independently of the accuracy of the court's assessments (see Decision of the Supreme Court of June 21, 1996, V KZ 16/96, OSNKW 1996, Nr 7–8, poz. 41).

66 The list is quite broad and includes such offenses as corruption (Article 228 k.k.), forgery (Article 270 k.k.) or even a simple theft (Article 278 k.k.). The allowance for filing the interlocutory appeal for such individuals has been a result of the concept of an "indirect victim," i.e. a person that is not a victim per se but whose rights has been affected by the offense. See Brodzisz (2015), pp. 734–735.

67 Article 425 § 3 k.p.k.

68 Article 306 § 1b k.p.k.

69 Stefański (2016), pp. 1467–1470. See also on the right to reasoned decision by De Vocht (2010), p. 460.

70 Article 428 § 1 k.p.k. in connection with Article 465 § 1 k.p.k.

71 Article 463 § 1 k.p.k. in connection with Article 465 § 1 k.p.k.

account the view of the appellant and agree with her on the merits without the necessity to resort to the higher instance.[72] When the case reaches the court, the hearing regarding the decision to discontinue criminal investigation is held.[73] The suspect, the victim, and their legal representatives may take part in it and present their views on the issue. If the court is not convinced that the investigation should be reopened, it issues the decision confirming discontinuation of proceedings and the case remains closed.[74] However, the court may accept the appellant's view, revoke the decision to discontinue the investigation, and reopen proceedings while stating the reasons and pointing out the investigative measures that the prosecutor and police should undertake in the ongoing investigation which are binding on the criminal justice authorities.[75]

The described procedure forces the prosecutor and police to carry on investigation further according to the suggestions of the court which may result in eventually filing a case with the court by the prosecutor. But it should not be understood as forcing the prosecutor to bring formal charges against an individual in a form of mandamus since the power to accuse is vested solely in prosecutorial hands with which the judge is not allowed to interfere, at least not directly. This means that if, after conducting the investigation, the prosecutor is still not convinced that the case should be heard in court she may again decide to discontinue.[76] In such case the victim will be allowed to file an interlocutory appeal again against the decision, but this time it will be lodged not with the court, but with another prosecutor—the one who supervises the prosecutor responsible for the case. If the supervising prosecutor sustains the decision refusing initiation of investigation, the victim in such case will have a right to file her own subsidiary indictment against the accused and prosecute the case herself.[77] To commence a subsidiary prosecution, besides obtaining two consecutive decisions on the discontinuation of proceedings, the applicant must submit an indictment which must be drafted and signed by a lawyer, within one month of receiving the second decision on the discontinuation and also pay a fixed fee.[78] If the court accepts the indictment, the dossier containing evidence gathered during investigation is sent to the court by the prosecutor and, if it is demanded by the aggrieved party, additional evidentiary procedures may be conducted by the police at the court's request.

72 Jasiński and Kremens (2019), p. 273.
73 Article 464 § 1 k.p.k.
74 Article 437 § 1 k.p.k. in connection with Article 465 § 1 k.p.k.
75 Article 330 § 1 k.p.k.
76 Article 330 § 2 k.p.k.
77 Article 55 § 1 k.p.k. Note that almost identical procedure is available to the victim in case of decision refusing initiation of investigation—Cf. Section 4.3.2.
78 Jasiński and Kremens (2019), p. 238.

8.3.3 Authority for Discontinuing Investigations

The power to discontinue investigation in Poland is vested solely in the prosecutor. This is entirely true when it comes to the inspection but also for the most part in case of an inquiry.[79] Therefore, the prosecutor may personally undertake the decision to discontinue every criminal investigation. But it is also provided that such decision may be issued by the police, although it becomes valid only upon the confirmation by the prosecutor.[80]

The only exception to that rule is the decision to discontinue the inquiry when the suspect remains unknown and there is literally no foreseeable hope of her being identified.[81] This category of discontinuations are customarily called the "recorded discontinuation of investigation" (*umorzenie rejestrowe*) since the data regarding the commitment of an offense and the circumstances of it are recorded in a special police registry. The aim is to keep it separately from other cases to easily so you can pull the case again when and if the new information allowing for identification of a perpetrator will be someday discovered. But leaving the power to decide on discontinuation of criminal investigation only in the hands of police concerns only relatively small group of less serious offenses. While the case remains closed the police are continuously obliged to conduct activities directed at revealing the perpetrator[82] although in practice this is just a theoretical obligation, and in case that she is identified the inquiry may be reopened.[83] The prosecutor has no power to reopen such case also because she is simply not aware that such case exist . But if the victim of such crime, disappointed with the outcome of the short investigation disagrees with that decision, the prosecutor will also be notified since in such case the interlocutory appeal will be directed to her. [84]

Besides the cases of the recorded discontinuations of investigation, which concerns minor crimes in considerably rare circumstances, the prosecutor maintains full control over the decision to discontinue a case. This also results from the general rule that the police are subordinate to the prosecutor who makes decisions and gives orders regarding criminal investigation.[85] This gives the prosecutor the power to not confirm the decision to discontinue

79 See on the distinction between inspection and inquiry in Section 3.3.1.

80 Article 305 § 2 k.p.k. and Article 325e § 2 k.p.k. Stefański (2016), pp. 1460–1461.

81 Article 325f k.p.k.

82 Article 325f § 2 k.p.k.

83 Article 325f § 3 k.p.k. Cf. Jasiński and Kremens (2019), p. 237.

84 As an exception to the general rule that provides for lodging an interlocutory appeal with the court in case of the recorded discontinuation of the investigation the interlocutory appeal is filed against the decision with the prosecutor and only when she does not wish to reopen a case passes it on to the court (Article 325e § 4 k.p.k.). See also Article 465 § 3 k.p.k.

85 Article 326 k.p.k. Cf. Section 5.3.2. See also Kruszyński (2007), p. 183

criminal investigation when preliminarily issued by the police and order further investigatory measures to be conducted, or even immediately file a case with the court. But one should also note that in the overwhelming majority of cases the prosecutor receives the preliminary decision to discontinue investigation together with the dossier prepared by the police which in an obvious way influences the prosecutor's perspective on the case. In theory this should not be of decisive character, but, in practice, prosecutors leave the majority of investigations under the sole control of the police, which in particular concerns the investigations conducted in a form of inquiry.[86] From this perspective, the confirmation of the discontinuation of criminal investigation by the prosecutor seems a mere formality.

On the other hand, the prosecutorial power to discontinue criminal investigation is limited by the impact that the court has on this decision. However, the judicial review of the decision is triggered only at the victim's request and the court has no *ex officio* powers to supervise the decision-making in that regard and is not even notified about the discontinuation of the investigation. The statistical data provides that out of 406,770 investigations discontinued in 2019, interlocutory appeals were filed against such decisions in only 18 percent of all discontinued cases.[87] And in only 28 percent of those cases that were appealed, either the court or the prosecutor herself, conducting the preliminary verification of the victim's request, agreed with the complainant and ordered continuation of investigation. This gives a low success rate for the victim's complaint, although the existence of the possibility to appeal by the victim might still work as a deterrence mechanism for reckless or hasty decisions.

8.4 Discontinuation of the Criminal Investigation in Italy

8.4.1 Threshold to Discontinue the Investigation

At the end of the criminal investigation in Italy, as in all other states, the prosecutor has a choice of whether to prosecute a case by filing an accusation with the court against the suspect[88] or to discontinue (*archiviazione*)[89] a

86 See Section 5.3.1.

87 *Sprawozdanie z działalności powszechnych jednostek organizacyjnych prokuratury za rok 2019*, https://pk.gov.pl/wp-content/uploads/2020/03/PK-P1K.pdf. Accessed July 12, 2020, pp. 4–5.

88 See Section 6.4.1 for the variety of choices that the prosecutor has.

89 The Italian c.p.p. uses the term *archiviazione* to describe the discontinuation of the criminal investigation by the GIP while the term *proscioglimento* that may be translated as "dismissal" is reserved for the decision made by the trial judge. In some works, the former term is translated as "dropping the case" (see Gialuz et al. (2017), pp. 567 and 573). Also,

case.[90] In fact, it is not her choice at all since the prosecutor must proceed with criminal prosecution when a case is not to be discontinued.[91] This implies that unless grounds to discontinue the case exist the prosecutor is obliged to move a case further.[92] This appears to remain in compliance with the legality principle as applicable in the Italian criminal process.[93]

The law provides for a variety of reasons under which the prosecutor may request discontinuation of a criminal investigation. First, the case may be dismissed, according to Article 408 CCP, when the notice of the crime is groundless (*la infondatezza della notizia di reato*). This means that during the preliminary investigation not enough evidence has been collected to support a charge.[94] The lack of grounds supporting a charge may mean that the reported offense recorded in the prosecutorial registry actually did not occur, or did occur but does not constitute a crime or did occur, does constitute a crime but the suspect did not commit it.[95] In fact, the prosecutor can ask the judge for preliminary investigation (GIP) to discontinue a case only if she deems the case too weak to lead to a conviction at trial.[96] This ground has been perceived as being too broad, allowing for too much prosecutorial discretion and as a result the Constitutional Court decided to narrow it down by obliging the prosecutor to carry out "complete" investigations.[97] This considerably enhanced the action of the prosecutors in weak cases but did not rule out the prosecutorial discretion since the prosecutor can still claim that the case is groundless, despite the efforts undertaken.[98]

The list of other grounds upon which the criminal investigation may be discontinued is provided in Article 411 (1) c.p.p. For instance, it must be done when the requirement of the prosecution is missing, which means that the police and the prosecutor did not receive a complaint (*querela*) from the victim or authorization of the competent authority in case of immunity of the offender. Another reason to discontinue a case concerns the expiry of the time for criminal investigation and should be considered as a mere

when the dismissal takes place during the preliminary hearing (*udienza preliminare*) such decision holds the name of "judgment of no grounds to proceeds" (*sentenza di non luogo a procedere*) and has a different character than the regular discontinuation upon the prosecutorial request. See also the explanation of term "dismissal" in Pizzi and Marafioti (1992), p. 39.

90 Article 405 c.p.p.

91 Article 50 (1) c.p.p.

92 Di Federico (2008), p. 305.

93 See Section 3.4.2, on the applicability of the legality principle in Italy.

94 Di Amato (2013), p. 168.

95 Ruggieri and Marcolini (2013), p. 392.

96 Grande (2000), p. 233.

97 Constitutional Court, judgment 88, January 28, 1991, quoting Caianiello (2016), p. 12.

98 Caianiello (2016), p. 13.

formality.[99] It is also provided that the investigation will be discontinued if the act is not deemed an offense in law. The case may also be dismissed if the perpetrator of the offense is unknown.[100]

Finally, not so long ago, the Italian criminal procedure recognized a separate ground for discontinuation of criminal investigation based on the "triviality of the offense" (*tenuità del fatto*) which can be understood as a form of lack of public interest.[101] This ground was introduced in 2015[102] despite the apparent existence of the principle of legality in the Italian criminal procedure. The criteria for evaluation of whether an offense can be considered trivial are set in Article 131-bis c.p.p. According to that provision, discontinuation based on this ground is possible only in cases of offenses punishable with up to five years of imprisonment, taking into account among other things, the manner of the conduct of the offense, the extent of the damage or danger caused by the offense, the conduct of the offender (who cannot be a habitual offender). As a result, the case may be discontinued even if the suspect is guilty, but her conduct does not appear serious enough to justify a trial.[103] If the prosecutor requests the discontinuation of the investigation based on this ground, the suspect and the victim must be informed and they both can raise opposition, which will result in holding a hearing.[104] In any case the final decision on the discontinuance of the criminal investigation rests with the GIP. It should be noted that the introduction of this new ground for discontinuation of criminal investigation as a strong exception to the principle of mandatory prosecution, has provoked academic discussion.[105]

8.4.2 Procedure for Discontinuation of Investigation

The procedure for discontinuation of investigation is triggered at the request of the prosecutor filed with the judge for investigation. The request is sent together with the dossier containing the *notitiae criminis*, the records of the investigation that has been carried out and the records of the actions carried

99 See Section 5.4.5 for more on the duration of the criminal investigation in Italy. See also Section 8.4.2. on the allocation of power over the decision to discontinue a case when the investigation has expired.
100 Article 415 (1) c.p.p.
101 Article 411 (1) c.p.p.
102 Decreto-legge n. 28, March 16, 2015.
103 Caianiello (2016), p. 13.
104 Article 411 (1bis) c.p.p.
105 See the review of the recent case law by Simone Marani, *Particolare tenuità del fatto*, Altalex, www.altalex.com/documents/altalexpedia/2020/02/27/particolare-tenuita-del-fatto (accessed April 26, 2020).

out before the GIP.[106] The court and not the prosecutor then decides on the discontinuation of criminal investigation.

The law provides for certain rights of the victim regarding discontinuation of investigation.[107] If the victim, while reporting a crime or at any point in the course of criminal investigation, demanded to be notified that the prosecutor plans to discontinue a case she should receive such notice, together with information that within 20 days, she may raise opposition to the prosecutorial request.[108] In cases of certain crimes, for instance committed with violence against the person as provided in Article 624bis c.p.p, the victim will be notified regardless of whether she requested such notice. In such cases the time for raising opposition against the prosecutorial request is prolonged to 30 days.[109] The victim's opposition to the prosecutorial request (*opposizione all'archiviazione*) is aimed at quashing the request and demanding continuing investigation.[110] In order to decide whether to raise an opposition, the victim and her legal representative are allowed to investigate and copy the dossier in a similar way as when the prosecutor wishes to file an accusation with the court.[111] This enables the victim to provide in her opposing motion the purpose of further investigation and the related elements of evidence as required by law, under the penalty of inadmissibility of opposition.[112]

Once the GIP receives the prosecutorial request for discontinuation of a case, she makes the decision primarily based on the materials provided by the prosecutor. There are two distinct ways in which the GIP can handle the case, depending on the involvement of the victim in the process and on the decision that the GIP plans to issue. Basically, in cases when the victim is not opposing a prosecutorial request and when the GIP foresees the possibility to grant the request to discontinue a case, she issues a reasoned decree and returns the case file to the prosecutor.[113] In such case, the suspect shall be notified if she has been subjected during investigation to precautionary detention. The scope of materials forwarded to the GIP along with the prosecutorial request, allows the GIP to undertake the decision regarding dismissal in the light of all available materials and is not based on an oral presentation of facts during the hearing, which in this case does not even have to be held.

106 Article 408 (1) c.p.p.
107 See more on the involvement of the victim and the suspect in the decision to terminate criminal investigation in Ruggeri (2017), pp. 34–39.
108 Article 408 (2) c.p.p.
109 Article 408 (3bis) c.p.p.
110 Article 410 (1) c.p.p.
111 Ruggieri and Marcolini (2013), pp. 392–393.
112 Article 410 (1) c.p.p.
113 Article 409 (1) c.p.p.

However, in a second scenario, if the victim has submitted the opposition or when the GIP wants to reject the request, she must conduct the hearing within three months, and the suspect as well as the victim must be notified of same.[114] The hearing takes place in chambers (Article 127 c.p.p.) and the parties have a chance to be heard if they appear. After the hearing the judge has three possibilities: to discontinue a case, to order the conduct of further investigation or, even, to force bringing a charge against the suspect.[115] If the GIP believes that the further investigation is necessary, she should set the time limit for completing the investigation. The GIP's decision to discontinue the case does not prevent the investigation being reopened at prosecutorial request filed in future with the GIP,[116] which may be a result of the effective persuasion of the prosecutor by the victim.[117] Additionally, in cases of prosecutorial requests seeking discontinuation based on the lack of identification of the suspect, the GIP may also order the registration of the name of the suspect in the prosecutorial registry if the GIP believes that such suspect has been identified.[118]

The most interesting of the above decisions is the judicial order obliging the prosecutor to bring an accusation against the suspect.[119] This possibility is reportedly borrowed from the German *Klageerzwingungsverfahren* procedure.[120] If the GIP, convinced by the victim's arguments, believes that, contrary to position of the prosecutor, the case should be prosecuted, she orders the prosecutor to file an accusation with the court within ten days.[121] Within two days of filing the formal accusation, the GIP sets the preliminary hearing. This is perceived as waiving the principle of judge impartiality but at the same time beneficial to guaranteeing the proper exercise of the principle of legality.[122]

To sum up, the powers of the GIP over the discontinuation of criminal investigation is broad and triggered not only by the victim's request. The judge is obliged to verify all cases that the prosecutor wishes to discontinue and issue a decision based on the pretrial findings submitted by the prosecutor. The involvement of the victim just modifies the procedure to be

114 Article 409 (2) c.p.p.
115 Article 409 (4)–(5) c.p.p.
116 Article 414 c.p.p.
117 Ruggieri and Marcolini (2013), p. 393.
118 Article 415 (2) c.p.p. See Di Amato (2013), p. 169.
119 Grande (2000), p. 234.
120 Ruggieri and Marcolini (2013), p. 393. See Section 4.2.3 and 8.2.3, for more on the extortion of accusation in Germany.
121 Article 409 (5) c.p.p.
122 Di Amato (2013), p. 169.

undertaken in a more adversarial environment, forcing the judge to order a hearing to receive positions of all interested parties.

8.4.3 Authority for Discontinuing Investigations

In general terms, the Italian prosecutor is not free to decide on the discontinuation of the criminal investigation on her own. The final decision remains outside of the scope of prosecutorial powers and it is the GIP that will assess the prosecutorial request and issue such decision.[123] As discussed above, the prosecutor must be limited in her powers to discontinue criminal investigation in accordance with the legality principle. It is believed, that there must be an independent and impartial body evaluating whether the discontinuation of the charge would not represent a violation of the prosecutor's duty to pursue a criminal action.[124] And, at least in theory, the prosecutor lacks the power to settle criminal cases because every case must end in a judgement.[125]

In such case the question of the real amount of discretion must be raised. If it is the judge that decides to dismiss the case rather than the prosecutor, it seems that the prosecutor is left without any power regarding the decision to discontinue investigation. The judicial competencies seem broad, as the GIP may order continuation of investigation, enforce official identification of the suspect, or even mandate the prosecutor to file an accusation. However, one should remember that the GIP has no power to gather additional evidence and works usually only with the prosecutorial dossier, unless the victim wishes to get involved. Therefore, the scope of materials on which the judge decides on the prosecutorial request in the majority of cases will be rather in line with the prosecutor's view, which most likely would give not much room for interpretation. Finally the GIP will never be able to act *proprio motu*, which is certainly limits the judicial influence on the discontinuation of criminal investigation.

The prosecutorial control over the outcome of the investigation is even more visible when we take into consideration the mechanism of expiration of the investigation beyond which the case cannot be investigated further. Although it appears as a restrain on the prosecutorial discretion, in practice it gives a power to the prosecutor to decide on how the investigation should end despite the rigidity of the principle of mandatory prosecution. . The prosecutor may simply wait for the expiration of investigation and send the

123 Article 408 (1) c.p.p.
124 Di Amato (2013), p. 167.
125 Caianiello (2012), p. 262.

file to the GIP who will have, in such case, no choice but to discontinue the case.[126]

Finally, the power that the prosecutor retains over the decision to discontinue the investigation is significantly impacted by the police. Even though the police seem to be almost nonexistent in the procedure aimed at termination of investigation as prescribed above, in the light of previous considerations it cannot be underestimated.[127] Despite assuming control over investigation by the prosecutor in every case the system provides for quite a broad independence of the police in that regard. Therefore, the police may easily shape the investigation in a certain way without prosecutorial interference and submit the file aiming at discontinuation of the investigation. In particular, this will be the situation in cases of less severe offenses.

8.5 Discontinuation of Criminal Investigation in the United States of America

8.5.1 Threshold to Discontinue the Investigation

The informality of criminal investigation and prosecutorial discretion as an overarching principle of the US criminal process are determinant for the shape of the decision to discontinue criminal investigation. The former is discussed in Chapter 3;[128] the impact that the decision-making process in such aspects as initiation of investigation or refusal to initiate investigation is discussed in Chapter Four.[129] This section looks at the outcome of such analyses.

It is crucial to understand that in US criminal investigation the decision to discontinue the case is not considered as the final step in the course of criminal investigation as it is in the European countries discussed in this work. This partially results from adopting a concept of investigation with no ending point and with not even theoretically prescribed standard measures that should be undertaken during the course of investigation at conclusion of which an either-way decision must be made. This also means that at the various stages of the US criminal process such decision can be made. It can be done very early—just after arrest, as well as very late—just before trial and even during the trial itself. This leads to discussion on the nature of the decision to "discontinue criminal investigation" or rather to "discontinue the case."

126 Caianiello (2016), p. 12; Ruggieri and Marcolini (2013), p. 393.
127 See Sections 5.4.1 and 5.4.2.
128 Cf. Section 3.5.
129 Cf. Section 4.5.

But before addressing these issues, the terminological problems should be discussed. As on all other occasions throughout this book it can be stated that the US drive toward defining and categorization is not vivid. And as observed by Fairfax, "[w]hen a prosecutor declines to prosecute despite sufficient proof of guilt, we are unsure what to call it. Some might characterize it as an instance of prosecutorial nullification, while others may characterize it as a common or garden variety of exercise of prosecutorial discretion—a topic thoroughly explored through decades of thoughtful scholarly commentary."[130] The term "discontinuation of criminal investigation" is barely found in the US literature. Far more frequently "the decision not to prosecute"[131] or "decision not to charge"[132] and even "screening"[133] are used. Miller even suggested that we can differentiate between "the decision not to proceed further" and "the decision not to charge"[134] which is anything but homogenous. These terms suggest that the termination of criminal investigation is strongly associated with a decision not to charge. As discussed in an earlier chapter,[135] the "charging decision" is "a process consisting of a series of interrelated decisions"[136] which also makes the flip side of it i.e. "decision not to charge" quite ambiguous and impossible to pin down to one specific moment in the course of criminal proceedings.

In US criminal procedure another term is used very frequently to describe the termination of the case by the prosecutor. The decision not to prosecute a case after charges are filed with the court is called a *nolle* or *nol pros.*[137] This is short for the Latin *nolle prosequi*, translated as "not to wish to prosecute"[138] and defined as "the formal abandonment of a criminal charge by the prosecuting attorney."[139] In other words, as defined for example in the State of Connecticut, it is a "formal declaration by the prosecuting authority that it will not proceed further with an existing criminal prosecution"[140] or "a unilateral act by a prosecutor, which ends the 'pending proceedings without an acquittal and without placing the defendant in jeopardy.'"[141] This expression

130 Fairfax (2011), p. 1244.
131 Kamisar et al. (2015), p. 915.
132 Worrall (2012), p. 344.
133 Saltzburg and Capra (2010), p. 860; Boyce et al. (2007), pp. 1348–1351.
134 See Miller (1969), pp. 179 and 191.
135 Section 6.5.1.
136 Miller (1969), p. 11.
137 See Fairfax (2011), p. 1252, for an interesting discussion on the rarely used expression "prosecutorial nullification."
138 Garner (2000), p. 467.
139 *Webster's Legal Dictionary*, p. 173.
140 Spinella (1985), p. 621.
141 *Cislo* v. *City of Sheldon*, 240 Conn. 590, 599 n. 9 692 A.2d 1255 (1997); *State* v. *Anonymous* (1975), 32 Conn. Supp. 501, 502 (Super. Ct. App. Sess. 1975).

is also sometimes used interchangeably with the word dismissal[142] but there is reason to differentiate it since the "dismissal" is also sometimes understood as reserved only to judicial actions.[143]

With regard to the *nolle prosequi* mechanism, it should be made clear that it is a form of termination of a case by prosecutor that takes place after the formal charges in any of its forms have been filed with court. Therefore, the *nolle* refers only to charges that have been officially presented. If there is no charge, there is no necessity for the prosecutor to *nolle* the case because simply there is no case and no record of it. Before that, the prosecutor may decide that the case should end without even notifying the court. These discontinuations are not regulated, giving to the prosecutor, as well as to the police, a visible degree of freedom.

This brings us to the discussion on the diversity of such decisions which is vertical rather than horizontal. Since, in accordance with the nature of the US criminal process, the criminal investigation does not conclude upon filing charges with the court and can last beyond the commencement of the trial, three distinct situations must be considered. In general terms the decision to discontinue the case can take place at every stage of the criminal process: before the filing of charges, after charges has been filed but before the trial commences, and after the commencement of the trial, understood as after the jury is sworn and impaneled. During the early stages of criminal proceedings this decision seems to be undertaken in a very informal, and almost unregulated way, both by the prosecutor and the police; once charges are filed, it becomes much more formal. Since this work is devoted exclusively to the criminal investigation understood as the stage of the criminal process that takes place before trial commences, the last presented option—the decision to discontinue a case that happens after the beginning of the trial—will not be covered here. However, it will be necessary to devote some time to discuss the procedure concerning *nolle prosequi*. The discussion on the nature of the decision to discontinue the case by the prosecutor would not be complete without also referring to this type of termination of a case, since the charging process, as discussed before,[144] takes place very early in the course of proceedings and should not be considered as ultimately ending the investigation. So, even though the *nolle* resembles to some extent the withdrawal of the indictment as known from the Continental systems (beyond the scope of this book), the duality of the pretrial stage in the USA calls for at least a brief analysis of the *nolle prosequi* procedure.

142 See e.g. Rule 48 FRCP.
143 See Brown (2017), p. 408–410.
144 See Section 6.5.1.

On the other hand, the US system does not provide for the variety of forms of decisions to discontinue criminal investigation in a horizontal way as it is done in European countries. However, the law also gives an opportunity for the prosecutor to terminate a case by releasing the defendant to diversionary programs, which are comparable to conditional dismissals. It can be considered as an alternative to prosecution and "in its many forms has the great benefit of diverting cases out of the criminal justice system and into other, more acceptable programs."[145] Most commonly, the diversion takes place early in the process before the charges are filed or soon after, but it may occur at any stage prior to conviction. This is a well standing practice available to defendants in many states.[146]

The question of thresholds, reasons, and factors that the prosecutor must take into consideration when she decides on discontinuing a case is very likely to be the most problematic issue in the context of US criminal procedure.[147] The bottom line is that the prosecutor exercises discretion in making his or her decision to discontinue the case. This is equally true for the decision on what charges to bring against the defendant as well as whether to prosecute a case. In all of those decisions prosecutorial discretion is seen as wide, unreviewable, and unchecked. But at the same time prosecutorial discretion is considered as essential and indispensable.[148]

Therefore, among the most commonly invoked reasons to discontinue the case is the doubt that the prosecutor will be able to meet the burden of proof during the trial with the available admissible evidence.[149] Even though the threshold to charge a person with a crime is identified as probable cause, the decision to prosecute should encompass whether the prosecutor will be able to prove during the trial the case to a much higher standard, i.e. beyond reasonable doubt. Consequently, if the prosecutor is not convinced that it will be possible to prove the guilt of the accused, she should discontinue the case. This is supported strongly in the ABA Prosecution Function Standards, that encourages prosecutors to sustain criminal charges only if the prosecutor continues to reasonably believe that probable cause exists and that admissible evidence will be sufficient to support conviction beyond reasonable doubt.[150] It is also highlighted that the charges must be dropped

145 Jacoby and Ratledge (2016), p. 89.

146 See Kamisar et al. (2015), pp. 937–940. See e.g. a wide range of diversionary programs available in the State of Connecticut such as Alcohol Education Program or Family Violence Program in Practice Book §§ 39-11–39-17. See also Brown (2017), pp. 387–404.

147 The long list of reasons for discontinuing cases is presented in Frank W. Miller, *Prosecution. The Decision to Charge a Suspect with a Crime* (Boston: Little, Brown, 1969).

148 Cf. Section 2.5.2.

149 See e.g. Kamisar et al. (2015), p. 901; Worrall (2012), p. 340; Boyce et al. (2007), p. 1351.

150 3–4.3(b) PFS. See also on the role of ABA Standards with regard to charging decision in Gershman (2010), pp. 1259–1284.

if it is believed that the defendant is innocent, regardless of the state of the evidence.[151]

The second reason, strongly connected with the previous one, refers to the problems with witnesses that the prosecutor foresees as an obstacle to successful prosecution of the case. This might be an issue with the reluctance of the witness to testify at all, which in particular concerns victims, as well as doubts regarding the ability of the witness to present herself in a credible way. This also includes the cases in which the victim has directly expressed unwillingness to take part in proceedings or even asked that the suspect would not be prosecuted.[152] The prosecutor must take into account that the trial will be conducted in the presence of a jury, which is by its nature prone to the impression that the witness's personality and her behavior in the courtroom may provide. Therefore, the prosecutor may be reluctant to call some types of witnesses who might give an adverse impression while testifying and not assist the prosecutor's case. This is also partially reflected in the ABA Prosecution Function Standards that oblige the prosecutor to take into consideration when deciding to maintain charges the views and motives of the victim or complainant[153] and potential collateral impact on third parties, including witnesses or victims.[154]

Another important reason for discontinuing the case relates to economic concerns and maintaining the efficiency of the system. The system capacity and cost of prosecution are of vital importance here. the US system seems to openly admit that there are never enough resources to enforce every violation of the law,[155] and the prosecutor must take into consideration the cost of prosecution in relation to the seriousness of the offense[156] as well as the fair and efficient distribution of limited prosecutorial resources.[157] This stems from the "public interest" factor which calls for making the prosecutor "free to exercise his judgment in determining what [aims] prosecutions will serve."[158] As the Supreme Court underlined,

> [t]he decision to file criminal charges, with the awesome consequences it entails, requires consideration of a wide range of factors in addition to

151 3–4.3(d) PFS. Similar regulation can be found e.g. in NDAA National Prosecution Standards reading that "A prosecutor should file charges that he or she believes adequately encompass the accused's criminal activity and which he or she reasonably believes can be substantiated by admissible evidence at trial" (4-2.2 NPS).

152 See Miller (1969), pp. 173–178.

153 3–4.4(a)(vii) PFS.

154 3–4.4(a)(x) PFS.

155 Jacoby and Ratledge (2016), p. 14.

156 4-2.4 NPS.

157 3–4.4(a)(xiv) PFS.

158 LaFave (1970), p. 534.

> the strength of the Government's case, in order to determine whether the prosecution would be in the public interest.[159]

The reasons for discontinuing a case are sometimes described as assessed informally. For instance, when the police screening is taken into consideration some authors admit that the police may decide not to proceed further simply

> because the arrest was made for social control purposes that have been satisfied, as in separating combatants in a brawl or protecting a drunk on a cold night; or because the arresting officer's superiors regard the case as either unjustified or properly dealt with by citation.[160]

This only proves that the factors that must be taken into account when discontinuation of investigation is made are very complex, yet often very informally prescribed.

8.5.2 Procedure for Discontinuation of Investigation

The procedure on discontinuation of the case is regulated in detail when the defendant has been identified and officially charged. The law provides who, how, and when it can be decided. But there is almost no regulation regarding the procedure on discontinuation of investigation before the charges are filed with court. It is referred to as an "informal discontinuation" since the law does not force any formal decision to be issued. As discussed, the literature uses terms like "screening" of cases or "declinations" which underlines the distinction from the far more formal *nolle prosequi*.

At this very early stage of criminal investigation, after the person has been initially charged, the power to discontinue criminal investigation is vested in the police in the form of an informal police screening procedure and only if not undertaken, transferred to the prosecutor for her decision in that regard. It is therefore possible that when the detained suspect awaits court appearance the police may decide not to proceed further.[161] As reported, the decision to arrest may be easily reversed once the person has been brought to the police department for booking, but the practice regarding willingness to do so varies among the departments and only a very small percentage of felony arrests are likely to be rejected this way.[162]

159 *United States* v. *Lovasco*, 431 US 783, 794 (1977).
160 Boyce et al. (2007), p. 1348.
161 Boyce et al. (2007), p. 1348.
162 Kamisar et al. (2015), p. 10.

Equally elusive is the prosecutorial initial screening of cases after the arrest has been made but before the formal charging occurred. The statistics indicate that federal prosecutors decline roughly one-quarter of cases referred to them.[163] As discussed, it may happen for a variety of reasons but the form in which this is done remains unrecorded. However, the NDAA National Prosecution Standards try to provide for transparency, recommending basing the decision to decline prosecution on set factors[164] and to retain a record of it.[165] Moreover, the prosecutors are encouraged to promptly respond to inquiries from those who are directly affected by a declination of charges[166] which should be considered as enhancing public scrutiny over these secret and unreviewable decisions. And even though in the commentary to the NDAA Standards it is acknowledged that "screening decisions are the most important made by prosecutors in the exercise of their discretion in the search for justice"[167] the attention that this process receives is far from satisfactory. It is submitted that the process should also be regulated by internal office guidelines that provide for some scrutiny by the superior prosecutors of decisions not to charge. However, the public is rarely informed about the decision not to charge and only in high-profile cases do prosecutors explain their decision-making process.[168] One should not forget that in some cases it is even possible to hide behind the grand jury (in federal system and states that allow so) when such decision is being made in controversial cases e.g. the noncharging of police officers for their misconduct.[169]

The second level of discontinuation of the investigation is more regulated. Filing charges with court, which equals the decision to prosecute a person, never or almost never means that a case will go to trial. This is just the beginning of the long process that can end up in many different ways for the defendant facing these charges. He or she can be put on a trial in the future, but statistics show that it is more likely that proceedings will end differently. The defendant can end up filing a guilty plea accepting the penalty agreed upon with the prosecutor and therefore not face a trial at all. At that point some of the charges may disappear via plea-bargaining . Or the defendant may not enter a guilty plea but nevertheless the prosecutor can decide that charges filed won't be prosecuted at all.

163 O'Neil (2003), p. 271.

164 See 4-1.3 and 4-1.4 NPS.

165 4-1.7 NPS. Note however, that the wording of this standard is very soft and underlines that it can be done only when it is "permitted by law."

166 4-1.8 NPS.

167 NDAA NPS, 3rd ed., https://ndaa.org/wp-content/uploads/NDAA-NPS-3rd-Ed.-w-Revised-Commentary.pdf, p. 52.

168 Saltzburg and Capra (2010), p. 871.

169 See more in Section 5.5.3.

The discontinuation of the criminal process at this point also belongs to the prosecutor. The procedure concerning entering *nolle prosequi* after the charge has been filed with court will be explained using the example of the State of Connecticut. In that state, the announcement of entering *nolle prosequi* by the prosecutor must take place in an open court and must be recorded.[170] Even though in Connecticut the court has no actual power to approve or reject the prosecutorial decision, the prosecuting authority cannot make a decision to *nolle* a case without leaving a record of it. Whether practice shows it is done with the presence of the judge or sometimes even just when a clerk is present, is irrelevant, since the information on nulling the case must go on the record. This must be done officially in that form for the future reason of dismissing the case by the court. Therefore, the case will be almost automatically dismissed after 13 months from entering *nolle*.[171]

As the law provides, the decision to *nolle* a case shall be justified by the prosecutor when entering the decision.[172] Practice shows otherwise; the reasons for the *nolle* are seldom presented before the court. It shouldn't be surprising though that prosecutors are neither eager nor feel it is necessary to give reasons for their decision in this regard since there is no one who could object to the decision or appeal it. It seems like justification is given solely in controversial and publicized cases or when the court demands it because the media are present in the courtroom and in driving under influence cases where this need is particularly highlighted. There is no confirmation by the judge with regard to that issue. Moreover, there are no limits or guidelines provided by the legislature in Connecticut that would shape the practice of *nolle prosequi* there.[173] The scope of the powers of the prosecutor available in Connecticut to *nolle* the proceedings is rather unique, but remains in compliance with the old common law where it was long established that the prosecuting authority may enter a *nolle prosequi* in his or her discretion without having approval from the court.[174]

The decision not to prosecute, whether undertaken in the form of precharging screening or post-charging *nolle* is generally protected from judicial review, which means that it should be considered as a final resolution of the case in favor of the suspect.[175] In the case *Inmates of Attica* v. *Rockefeller*

170 § 39-29 CPB.

171 § 54-142a(c)(1) CGS.

172 § 39-29 CPB.

173 *Nolle Prosequi in Connecticut* (1971), p. 120.

174 *Confiscation Cases*, 7 Wall. 454, 457 (1868) ("Public prosecutions . . . are within the exclusive direction of the district attorney, and even after they are entered in court, they are so far under his control that he may enter a *nolle prosequi* at any time before the jury is empaneled for the trial of the case, except in cases where it is otherwise provided in some act of Congress").

175 Saltzburg and Capra (2010), p. 869.

the court affirmed that there is no possibility to compel the prosecutor in a form of mandamus to investigate and institute prosecution against an individual, which relies on the separation-of-powers principle which does not allow the judicial power to interfere with prosecutorial discretion.[176] The need to protect the independence of prosecutors in exercising their role to choose cases for prosecution strongly resonates in that mechanism. Although it must be admitted that there is no consensus whether the court should have a power to verify the prosecutorial decision not to prosecute despite the Supreme Court's view that decisions that the prosecutor makes "are not readily susceptible to the kind of analysis the courts are competent to make."[177] While in the federal system the government may enter the *nolle* with leave of the court and some states[178] follow that path, others do not require such approval .[179] A good example of the latter is again Connecticut. As one academic states: "it is doubtful whether in any jurisdiction in the United States the prosecutor has greater discretion in nol-prossing cases than in Connecticut and with less degree of restraint imposed on his acts."[180] The reason for that might be traced to the way prosecutors in Connecticut are chosen i.e. by the independent Criminal Justice Commission and not elected in popular vote.[181] This is also considered as the reason why the authority of the prosecutor to null a whole case without judicial review is not criticized in that state. Yet the necessity to present in open court the reasons for nulling a case by the prosecutor may also be considered assuring judicial oversight over limitless prosecutorial discretionary power.

8.5.3 Authority for Discontinuing Investigations

The main authority for discontinuing investigations is, then, the prosecutor. As famously stated by R.H. Jackson, former US Attorney General and Supreme Court Justice, "one of the greatest difficulties of the position of prosecutor is that he must pick his cases, because no prosecutor can even investigate all of the cases in which he receives complaints."[182] Therefore, this power is primarily vested in prosecutorial hands. Certainly, there are some forms of regulating that power such as internal guidelines within the office

176 See *Inmates of Attica* v. *Rockefeller*, 477 F.2d 375 (2d Cir.1973).
177 See *Wayte* v. *United States*, 470 US 598, 606 (1985).
178 Rule 48(a) FRCP.
179 Kamisar et al. (2015), p. 918.
180 Kosicki (1962), p. 164. See also Spinella (1985), p. 622. Note that Connecticut was one of the first states confirming that power of prosecution from even before the existence of the USA—see *State* v. *Lockwood*, 2 Kirby 19 (1787)
181 But the lack of judicial approval for *nolle* was also present in the past when state's attorneys were selected through the judicial appointment. See Kosicki (1962), p. 163.
182 Jackson (1940), p. 5.

or some more general, such as ABA and NDAA standards. But altogether the discretion of the prosecutor seems unlimited. This is particularly true for the very first stage of the criminal process, before the charges are filed, since it is not demanded by law to publish the prosecutor's reasons.

As discussed above, US law is not consistent as to whether the prosecutorial decision not to prosecute a case is subjected to judicial review. Such reluctance to give the power to the judge to verify the decision to discontinue proceedings might be somewhat surprising when it is considered that, at the same time, the decision to prosecute is subjected to careful scrutiny under the preliminary examination regime, which does not raise an eyebrow. The belief that compelling the prosecutor to present grounds for nulling a case on the record in an open court will prevent wrongful dismissals is rather naive. In jurisdictions where the prosecutor must file a *nolle prosequi* motion seeking judicial dismissal of the charges, such motion is reportedly almost always granted by the court.[183] This lack of judicial scrutiny over prosecutorial freedom not to charge or to *nolle* the entered charges has been critiqued.[184] But the reluctance of judges to assume responsibility for monitoring and controlling the work of criminal prosecutors is quite visible.[185] Therefore, if anything constrains the prosecutorial power to discontinue the case it is definitely not the judge through a very limited scope of mechanisms available to her in that regard.

The real limits remain within the scope of discretion exercised by the police. This is so since the prosecutor may only undertake the decision of whether to charge or not if the case is presented to her by the police. To that extent the prosecutor is dependent on the police, which in the USA possess extremely broad powers not to arrest even if the probable cause exists,[186] but also to screen out cases after the arrest has been made and to release the suspect without any further consequences. And, as Miller underlined 60 years ago "where, however, the police decide not to invoke the criminal process, effective methods of review and control are largely lacking, and this issue of the proper scope and function of police discretion is of great, current importance and difficulty."[187] This concerns, in particular, misdemeanors, and therefore the discretion to discontinue a case in these situations remains completely with the police and is not controlled by the prosecutor in any way.

183 Del Carmen (2004), p. 40.

184 See the overview of the case law in that regard in Loewenstein (2001), pp. 366–369.

185 Wright (2009), p. 587 ("When defendants invite judges to override prosecutor choices about the selection or pre-trial disposition of charges, judges view those requests through the lens of the separation of powers doctrine").

186 See more in Sections 4.5 and 7.5.

187 Miller and Remington (1962), p. 115.

8.6 Summary

The decision to discontinue criminal investigation in the four researched countries is vested, on the normative level, in prosecutorial hands. Since the prosecutor maintains the power to decide whom to prosecute, she also has competence to refrain from such a decision. Countries differ on whether the prosecutor should have full discretion in that regard or whether she should be constrained by the principle of legality. And even though the subordination of each system to the principle of mandatory prosecution has been discussed in Chapter 3, it is worthy of mention again that the countries allow the prosecutor to a distinct extent to discontinue the case based on discretionary grounds. The US prosecutor seems to be limited only by the soft law expressed in various guidelines, while German and Italian prosecutors should comply with the legality as a rule and may only under carefully prescribed circumstances resort to discontinuation of criminal investigation on public interest grounds. In the latter cases the discretion of the prosecutor is every time subjected to judicial scrutiny. At the same time Poland, through complex doctrinal concepts, rules out the possibility to terminate the case based on the public interest threshold.

But when it comes to the authority empowered to discontinue the criminal investigation it has been argued that the greatest impact in that regard is that of the police. The police maintain the power to discontinue investigations independently. While in Poland it is allowed for very minor crimes under certain conditions, in the USA the police power to primarily screen cases is acknowledged and accepted as a tool to maintain the efficiency of the system. But even in the cases of Germany and Italy, where officially such powers are not directly granted to police, the practice of nonreporting crimes exists, being a hidden form of discontinuing proceedings. The number of informal discontinuations of cases is nevertheless very hard to ascertain especially in those countries where there is no legal expectation that complaints will be carefully registered (the USA), but also in those countries where theoretically all should be put on the record (Italy).

However, as discussed throughout this book,[188] the police control materials presented to the prosecutor, for her to make the right decision in line with police expectations. And even if the final decision on discontinuation of criminal investigation must be undertaken by the prosecutor, this is the police that maintain broad powers to control the direction of the criminal investigation. In the majority of cases in all the researched countries the decision to decline investigation by the prosecutor is heavily influenced by the police. The case file may be prepared in such a way that the prosecutor

188 Cf. in particular Chapter 5.

will just follow the path desired by the police to terminate the case without questioning the material. And without the informed prosecutorial action the prosecutor just confirms the police suggestion. Therefore, it is safe to say that in at least less severe cases, the power of the prosecutor to discontinue criminal investigation is tempered if not disabled by the police. In Poland, where the prosecutor confirms the preliminary decision to discontinue investigation, it is perceived as a formality and a similar impression is derived from the Italian and German systems, where it is reported that the police "steer" the proceedings in the direction they intend. It seems that the USA is the fairest in openly admitting the police impact on the discontinuation of investigation.

It is doubtful whether the subsequent mandatory judicial verification could change the situation and provide more thorough control over such decisions. Especially, when such judicial scrutiny is based solely on the materials contained in the police reports and not challenged in the adversarial environment. Yet, if the police have such an overwhelming influence on criminal investigation, it should not be left solely for the prosecutor to eventually determine whether the criminal investigation should be discontinued. The prosecutor may work as an immediate first level of such verification while the judicial review can be considered as a second level. But here the researched countries differ the most. While Poland and Germany stick to the idea of judicial review triggered upon the victim's request, Italy provides for the mandatory judicial scrutiny over every single decision to discontinue the criminal investigation. This is done regardless of the victim's request, which, if submitted, only modifies the procedure, making it more adversarial in such case.

It is actually intriguing that the Italian criminal procedure forces the judge to decide on the discontinuation of the criminal investigation in each case while in Poland and Germany it happens only at the victim's request. The justification of the Italian approach is based upon the premise that the prosecutorial submission to the legality principle must each time be evaluated by the independent and impartial judge to be sure that the prosecutor did not violate her obligation to pursue the criminal action. But at the same time, Poland and Germany both respecting the principle of legality to a similar extent, did not adopt the same perspective, considering judicial review of the decisions discontinuing criminal investigation at the victim's request as a sufficient mechanism for verification of the accuracy of the prosecutor's decision. And even when Germany obliges the prosecutor to seek from the court the confirmation of discontinuation of investigation based on the public interest or undertaken conditionally, the mandatory judicial review is not perceived as resulting from the legality principle.

At the same time, the USA almost entirely excludes a possibility of verification of the decision to discontinue criminal investigation, providing arguments based on the separation of powers. This refers fully to the cases terminated prior to formal charging being done, but also applies to post-charging *nolle prosequi*. Even when in the federal system and throughout some states, the prosecutor is obliged to enter the *nolle* on the record in an open court, the competencies of the judge are very limited. The denial of the court approval for decisions to discontinue criminal investigation are rare and generally focus only on the most important cases. It is even argued that the efficiency of the system would be at stake if the judge wished too often to override such decisions.

Special attention should also be paid to mechanisms enforcing prosecution as available in some countries. While the USA does not provide any mechanism of such kind, making the decision not to prosecute reserved solely for the prosecutor, Continental countries present two resolutions to this end. Germany and Italy, the latter openly admitting that the German mechanism has been an inspiration to the resolution adopted in that country, grants the judge, at the victim's request, the power to enforce prosecution on the prosecutor. In the case of Poland, in a similar procedure the victim may oppose the decision to discontinue criminal investigation, but the final result is not aimed at forcing the prosecutor to bring the accusation but allows the victim to file her own "subsidiary" indictment and prosecute the case herself. It should be noted, however, that none of these mechanisms are of significant importance, since the numbers of such mandamuses and subsidiary indictments are in all cases quite low.

The analysis of the prosecutorial powers over the discontinuation of criminal investigation in the researched countries, despite the differences revealed between the systems, leads to one conclusion. On the normative level, the broadly prescribed prosecutor's competencies are in some cases limited by the judicial powers to review the decision but, in all systems are manifestly restricted, by the huge influence of the police on the shape of the criminal investigation, that determines the outcome of that stage of the criminal process. It is submitted that even in those countries in which normatively the judicial control over discontinuation of criminal investigation takes place, the impact of the police is much stronger and, unfortunately, frequently unclassified and therefore underestimated.

References

Boyce RN, Dripps DA, Perkins RM (2007) *Criminal Law and Procedure. Cases and Materials*. Foundation Press, New York.

Brodzisz (2015) Komentarz do art. 316 k.p.k. In: Jerzy Skorupka (ed) *Kodeks postępowania karnego*. Komentarz. CH Beck, Warsaw.

Brown RR (2017) Disposition without Trial. In: Schuman CJ (ed) *Connecticut Criminal Procedure*. Connecticut Law Tribune, Hartford, pp. 383–423.

Bulenda T, Gruszczyńska B, Kremplewski A, Sobota P (2010) "The Prosecution Service Function within the Polish Criminal Justice System. In: Jehle J-M, Wade M (eds) *Coping with Overloaded Criminal Justice Systems. The Rise of Prosecutorial Power Across Europe*. Springer, Heidelberg, pp. 257–284.

Caianiello M (2012) The Italian Public Prosecutor: An Inquisitorial Figure in Adversarial Proceedings. In: Luna E, Wade M (eds) *The Prosecutor in Transnational Perspective*. Oxford University Press, Oxford, pp. 250–267.

Caianiello M (2016) *Increasing Discretionary Prosecutor's Powers: The Pivotal Role of the Italian Prosecutor in the Pretrial Investigation Phase*. Oxford Handbooks Online, Oxford.

De Vocht D (2010) Poland. In: Cape E, Namoradze Z, Smith R, Spronken T (eds) *Effective Criminal Defence in Europe*. Intersentia, Antwerp, pp. 425–488.

Del Carmen RV (2004) *Criminal Procedure. Law and Practice.* Thomson, Belmont.

Delmas-Marty M, Spencer JR (eds) (2012) *European Criminal Procedures*. Cambridge University Press, Cambridge.

Di Amato A (2013) *Criminal Law in Italy*. Kluwer Law International, Alphen aan den Rijn.

Di Federico G (2008) Report on the Public Prosecution Service in Italy. In: Open Society Institute Sofia (ed) *Promoting Prosecutorial Accountability, Independence and Effectiveness*. Open Society Institute Sofia, Sofia, pp. 301–339.

Elsner B, Peters J (2010) The Prosecution Service Function within the German Criminal Justice System. In: Jehle J-M, Wade M (eds) *Coping with Overloaded Criminal Justice Systems. The Rise of Prosecutorial Power Across Europe*. Springer, Heidelberg, pp. 207–236.

Fairfax Jr RA (2011) Prosecutorial Nullification. *Boston College Law Review* 52:1243–1281.

Frase RS, Weigend T (1995) German Criminal Justice as a Guide to American Law Reform. *Boston College International and Comparative Law Review* 18:317–360.

Garner BA (2000) *A Dictionary of Criminal Law Terms*. West Group, St. Paul.

Gershman BL (2010) Prosecutorial Decisionmaking and Discretion in the Charging Function. *Hastings Law Journal* 62:1259–1283.

Gialuz M, Lupária L, Scarpa F (eds) (2017) *The Italian Code of Criminal Procedure. Critical Essays and English Translation*. Cedam, Milan, pp. 17–55.

Gilliéron G (2004) *Public Prosecutors in the United States and Europe*. Springer, Cham.

Grande E (2000) Italian Criminal Justice: Borrowing and Resistance. *American Journal of Comparative Law* 48:227–259.

Herrmann J (1974) The Rule of Compulsory Prosecution and the Scope of Prosecutorial Discretion in Germany. *University of Chicago Law Review* 41: 468–505.

Hofmański P, Jeż-Ludwichowska M (2015) Wzajemny stosunek pojęcia warunków dopuszczalności procesu i pojęcia przesłanek procesu. In: Jeż-Ludwichowska M, Lach A (eds) *System Prawa Karnego Procesowego. Dopuszczalność Procesu.* Volume IV. Wolters Kluwer, Warsaw, pp. 52–81.

Jackson RH (1940) The Federal Prosecutor. *Journal of Criminal Law and Criminology* 31:3–6.

Jacoby JE, Ratledge EC (2016) *The Power of the Prosecutor. Gatekeepers of the Criminal Justice System*. Praeger, Santa Barbara.

Jasiński W, Kremens K (2019) *Criminal Law in Poland*. Kluwer Law International, Alphen aan den Rijn.
Juy-Birmann R (2002) The German System. Delmas-Marty M, Spencer JR (eds) *European Criminal Procedures*. Cambridge University Press, Cambridge, pp. 292–347.
Kamisar Y, LaFave WR, Israel JH, King NJ, Kerr OS, Primus EB (2015) *Modern Criminal Procedure. Cases-Comments-Questions*. West, St Paul.
Kołodziejczyk A (2013) *Umorzenie absorpcyjne w polskim procesie karnym*. Wolters Kluwer, Warsaw.
Kosicki BA (1962) The Function of Nolle Prosequi and Motion to Dismiss in Connecticut. *Connecticut Bar Journal* 36:159–174.
Kruszyński P (2007) The Investigative Stage of the Criminal Process in Poland. In: Cape E, Hodgson J, Pranken T, Spronken T (eds) *Suspects in Europe. Procedural Rights at the Investigative Stage of the Criminal Process in the European Union*. Intersentia, Antwerp, pp. 181–209.
LaFave WR (1970) The Prosecutor's Discretion in the United States. *American Journal of Comparative Law* 18:532–548.
Ligeti K (ed) (2013) *Toward a Prosecutor of the European Union, Volume 1: A Comparative Analysis*. Hart Publishing, London.
Loewenstein AB (2001) Note, Judicial Review and the Limits of Prosecutorial Discretion. *American Criminal Law Review* 38:351–372.
Luna E, Wade M (2010) Prosecutors as Judges. *Washington and Lee Law Review* 67:1413–1532.
Meyer-Krapp E (2008) Das Klageerzwingungsverfahren, Dissertation for the purpose of obtaining a doctorate the Faculty of Law submitted to the Georg-August-University of Göttingen. Göttingen. https://d-nb.info/991096339/34. Accessed 12 July 2020.
Miller FW (1969) *Prosecution. The Decision to Charge a Suspect with a Crime*. Little, Brown and Company, Boston.
Miller FW, Remington FJ (1962) Procedures Before Trial. Annals 339:111–124.
Nolle Prosequi in Connecticut (1971) Comment. *Connecticut Law Review* 4:117–142.
Nowak C, Steinborn S (2013) Poland. In: Ligeti K (ed) *Toward a Prosecutor of the European Union, Volume 1: A Comparative Analysis*. Hart Publishing, London, pp. 498–509.
O'Neill ME (2003) When Prosecutors Don't: Trends in Federal Prosecutions Declinations. *Notre Dame Law Review* 79:221–290.
Pizzi WT, Marafioti L (1992) The New Italian Code of Criminal Procedure: The Difficulties of Building an Adversarial Trial System on a Civil Law Foundation. *Yale Journal of International Law* 17:1–40.
Rogacka-Rzewnicka (2007) *Oportunizm i legalizm ścigania przestępstw w świetle współczesnych przeobrażeń procesu karnego*. Wolters Kluwer, Warsaw.
Ruggeri S (2017) *Audi Alteram Partem in Criminal Proceedings*. Springer, Cham.
Ruggieri F, Marcolini S (2013) Italy. In: Ligeti K (ed) *Toward a Prosecutor of the European Union, Volume 1: A Comparative Analysis*. Hart Publishing, London, pp. 368–404.
Saltzburg SA, Capra DJ (2010) *American Criminal Procedure: Investigative. Cases and Commentary*. West, St Paul.

Siegismund E (2003) The Public Prosecution Office in Germany: Legal Status, Function and Organization. In: Effective Administration of the Police and the Prosecution in Criminal Justice. The 120th International Senior Seminar, Visiting Experts' Papers www.unafei.or.jp/publications/pdf/RS_No60/No60_10VE_Siegismund2.pdf. Accessed 12.07.2020, pp. 58–64

Stefański RA (2016) Rodzaje decyzji kończących postępowanie przygotowawcze. In: Ryszard Stefański (ed) *System Prawa Karnego Procesowego. Postępowanie przygotowawcze*. Volume X. Wolters Kluwer, Warsaw, pp. 1050–1135.

Spinella AP (1985) *Connecticut Criminal Procedure*. The Atlantic Law Book Company, West Hartford.

Trendafilova E, Róth W (2008) Report on the Public Prosecution Service in Germany. In: Open Society Institute Sofia (ed) *Promoting Prosecutorial Accountability, Independence and Effectiveness*. Open Society Institute Sofia, Sofia, pp. 213–246.

Webster's Legal Dictionary (1996) Random House, New York.

Weigend T (2007) Germany. In: Bradley CM (ed) *Criminal Procedure. A Worldwide Study*. Carolina Academic Press, Durham, pp. 243–272.

Weigend T (2013) Germany. In: Ligeti K (ed) *Toward a Prosecutor of the European Union, Volume 1: A Comparative Analysis*. Hart Publishing, London, pp. 264–306.

Worrall JL (2012) *Criminal Procedure. From First Contact to Appeal*. Pearson, Boston.

Wright RF (2009) How Prosecutors Election Failed Us. *Ohio State Journal of Criminal Law* 6:581–610.

Chapter 9

Redefining Prosecutorial Powers during Criminal Investigation

9.1 Criminal Investigation Remastered

The comparative research in this book has been devoted to the analysis of the level of engagement of the prosecutor in criminal investigation and establishing whether increasing the powers of the prosecutor at this stage of the criminal process is a desired response to the rising significance of criminal investigation.

Three assumptions are made to develop the arguments in this work. First, the role of the trial as a venue where the decision regarding the criminal liability of the accused is undertaken, constantly diminishes. Based on the statistical data it can be assumed that in some countries full trials are rare, if they have not vanished entirely. This is partially a result of the constantly growing criminalization of human behavior, which in consequence raises the number of cases entering the court system, causing a tremendous overload that somehow must be dealt with. It is no wonder that all criminal justice systems had to find other ways to resolve the backlog of criminal cases.

Second, the prosecutor' powers in the criminal process have increased remarkably in the sphere of decision-making, regarding the way in which the case will be resolved. To cope with the heavily overloaded system the prosecutor has been equipped with the power to bargain over sentences and, in some states, even over charges, that results in quick judgments in exchange for guilty pleas. Moreover, in other states, a variety of choices have been given to prosecutor when it comes to the form of deciding cases, such as penal orders or abbreviated proceedings. And in some cases the prosecutor is even allowed to take a part in adjudication, imposing quasi-punitive measures, as happens in the case of conditional dismissals of various kinds. The prosecutorial power to adjudicate criminal cases with little or no judicial oversight has become a trend on both sides of the Atlantic,[1] which, famously, has

1 Cf. Luna and Wade (2003), p. 1531.

made the prosecutor "a judge by another name."[2] None of these powers can be considered to be a mistake. But, as Brown explains, using the extreme American example of the overuse of negotiated mechanisms to dispose a case, broad prosecutorial discretion fits quite well in the system if, and only if, it rests on two features: adjudication occurs through trial; and the process is adversarial.[3] If adversariality becomes very limited and not engaging the judge, while full trials are almost gone, the system lacks the necessary checks-and-balances mechanism.

Third, the criminal investigation has been constantly evolving in the direction of sophistication caused by criminals using more and more advanced means to commit crime, frequently resorting to new technologies. The digital age has created new challenges for criminal investigation.[4] Cybercrime brings the investigation to a whole new level (without factoring in the problem of the transnationality of crimes). These developments demanded immediate specialization of the police in the field of new technologies and digital evidence that has changed the ways in which crimes are investigated. Moreover, the availability of methods involving online searches or wiretapping has put the rights of the individual in greater danger than ever before.

As a consequence of the decreasing importance of the trial, growing powers of the prosecutor in the sphere of adjudication, and challenges that the criminal investigation faces due to digitalization, the investigation has become more significant than ever. Since the materials gathered during criminal investigation are no longer tested during the trial for their admissibility and credibility, the verification of their relevance has to take place much earlier. While there are no signs that this trend will reverse, the answers and solutions for how to cope with this new environment should be sought.

Therefore, the research in this work has been driven by the important question: In the system in which the role of the trial is diminishing, and where the significance of criminal investigation is constantly growing, should the powers of the prosecutor at the early stage of the process be enhanced, taking also into account the already very influential role that the prosecutor gained during the criminal process? Put simply: do we need more or less involvement of the prosecutor in criminal investigation?

9.2 Prospects for Shaping Prosecutorial Powers during Criminal Investigation

As discussed in Chapter 1, when trials are diminishing and criminal investigations are growing in importance, it is tempting to adopt the

2 Weigend (2012), p. 383.
3 Brown (2012), p. 203.
4 See Caianiello (2019).

Continental scheme, having a long-standing tradition of reduced trials of an inquisitorial nature, where the evidence gathered during a long, formal, and official criminal investigation is usually read out or even admitted without being tested in an adversarial environment. In such a setting the close supervision of criminal investigation by the prosecutor, perceived as an impartial and objective figure controlling police action, is perceived as a necessary substrate of judicial verification of evidence during the trial. No wonder that the idea of *juge d'instruction* emerged in such a system. Therefore, the experience of centuries means that the practice which evolved in the Continental countries can serve as an example of the increased role of the prosecutor during criminal investigation. However, this should, in no way, mean that the only and appropriate solution for the proposed shape of prosecutorial powers during criminal investigation is an inquisitorial model. But there should be also no doubt that some of the solutions adopted in Continental states could be inspirational while others may be considered a warning.

The engagement of the prosecutor during criminal investigation may enhance the quality of investigation. As a lawyer and experienced litigator, she may quickly determine whether the evidence gathered through search or interrogation could be considered as valid as a basis for the judgment, and admissible during the trial. The arrests made as a result of consultation with the prosecutor have a chance to be more reasonable and less likely to be excluded as illegally conducted. Even the preauthorization of certain coercive measures by the prosecutor can be considered as a way of bringing a higher standard to mechanisms employed at the early stage of the process, especially when the prosecutor is positioned as a quasi-judicial figure. The prosecutor seems to be particularly predisposed to exercise control over the activities of law enforcement agencies when compared to the other actors in the criminal process. And by doing so, the protection of the individual is enhanced, preventing infringements against the suspect, as well as witnesses and victims. Also, when the prosecutor takes an active part in investigation, she may even participate in the conduct of such a measure or undertake it by herself. This all helps when the decision to charge a person with a crime is made based on her knowledge and own experience of the case, and not only on the police report and the case file. Trust in the evidence and belief in its reliability is stronger if she has taken part in its gathering and knows those who were doing this alongside and under her supervision. In a system where the careful examination of evidence during the trial is diminishing, this may seem an especially appealing construct.

Yet the flip side of this wonderland is the envisaged close bond created between the prosecution and criminal justice agencies through their constant cooperation. Instead of being a rigorous reviewer of the pretrial findings, the prosecutor almost changes into one of the investigators herself. It is also obvious that asking the prosecutor to conduct personally, or to supervise, investigative measures, is problematic, since the training she receives in this area is very limited and it is doubtful whether only legal experience can provide the necessary quality to such measures as searches, interrogations, or autopsies. When prosecutors become so close to the police, it is harder to look from a distance at their activities and evaluate them for the legality of measures undertaken by them and to trigger disciplinary action for their improper behavior. And building close relations with police officers makes it quite likely that the prosecutor's decisions will become biased. Moreover, being so engaged in criminal investigation on a daily basis results in acquiring the police perspective on the complaints and crimes, something that the prosecutor should not be a part of, if also subsequently asked to critically evaluate the outcome of such investigation. Such an engagement may create tunnel vision as to the responsibility of the defendant. It should also be added that the long history of prosecutorial misconducts does not show that this group is somehow immune from bias and prejudice. Making prosecutors a part of the investigation just enhances the probability of such cases. And as other studies show, the prosecutors are more inclined to control the formal conformity of the case file to the due process standard than its actual application.[5] Therefore, despite the advantages resulting from such a setup, the proximity of the prosecutor to the police and the investigation itself raise serious concerns regarding her ability to objectively evaluate the outcome of the investigation and to undertake the decision whether to prosecute.

It shall be also noted that if the prosecutor is burdened with the obligation to actively participate during criminal investigation, she is called to fulfill three independent roles during the criminal process. Originally, the prosecutor was designed to prosecute the case that is argued against the defendant during the trial. Throughout the evolution of the criminal justice system she gained a second role of negotiator and quasi-judge. And when the prosecutor is asked to supervise criminal investigation and even actively take a part in it, she is expected to be a quasi-police officer. Therefore, at the same time the prosecutor must be a qualified litigator, a reasonable adjudicator, and a crafty investigator. These roles are remarkably different. During the trial, the prosecutor is expected to be partisan, convinced that the defendant is guilty and deserves the punishment, and is called on to bring convincing evidence against her. While, during the criminal investigation, it is desired and frequently underlined, that the prosecutor should be objective and neutral in making her decisions, even focusing as much on exonerating as incriminating evidence. Even if trials are in decline and the first role is in

5 Soubise (2018), p. 615.

retreat, are we not demanding too much from one person? Is it possible to change perspective on a case from objectivity to partisanship?

In a discussion on the role of the prosecutor during criminal investigation, one can find voices that seek positives in the prosecutorial supervision over police actions. For instance, Rosenthal believes that the prosecutor is in the best position "to check excesses and potentially precipitous actions of the police" and "to consider and pursue hypotheses that may be inconsistent with suppositions adopted in the preliminary stages of the investigation."[6] Richman, calls for promoting teamwork between prosecutors and police (agents) "so long as each player orients to his distinct institution and professional culture, interaction presents less a risk of capture than an opportunity for both productive collaboration and mutual monitoring."[7]

The problem of assertion of objectivity by prosecutors being responsible both for investigating as well as charging and negotiating, has been addressed by Barkow, who observed that such duality of functions causes biases that prevent prosecutors from appropriately undertaking the decision whether to prosecute.[8] Subsequently she provided a solution in the form of separating investigative and adjudicative decisions of prosecutors by subdividing them to exercise these distinct functions with an aim to guarantee the objectivity of the final decision-maker when the evaluation of whether to prosecute or not is at stake. Although I fully agree with Barkow that the prosecutors who investigate a case are not in the desired impartial position to make a final assessment of guilt and to negotiate over the charges, the proposed solution seems less convincing. While such an idea was addressed by me on another occasion[9] I can only repeat that subdividing prosecutors to that regard would cause additional problems in the sphere of relocation of power within one prosecutor's office making the "adjudicating" group of prosecutors somehow reviewers of the work of their "investigating" colleagues. The latter group would therefore become more of legal advisors of police even if with some decision-making powers. It would also create unnecessary tension between both groups, especially when the first group could reject the prosecution when the other group did not bring convincing enough materials.

The question remains as to why it is so strongly believed that the "investigating" function should be conducted by the prosecutor, and not transferred fully to the police? Instead of demanding professionalization of the police in their activities and enhancement in their legal training, it is perceived that they should be left under the magical prosecutorial supervision that

6 Rosenthal (1998), p. 951.
7 Richman (2003), p. 813.
8 Barkow (2009).
9 Kremens (2014).

additionally also deprives them at least partially of responsibility for their actions. And by doing so we exculpate the police from observing certain rules by imposing fleeting and ineffective mechanisms for the inadmissibility of evidence as a deterrence mechanism, which in some cases will only work if a trial takes place.

Another solution has been also recently suggested by Weigend, who revoked the idea of granting the prosecutor equal status to judges.[10] This would allow the prosecutor to become eligible to decide on various measures during the investigation, that require judicial neutrality and impartiality, such as searches and seizures. In such case the position of the prosecutor seems to resemble excessively the famous *investigative judge*, the figure from which Continental countries are receding. Moreover, this refuses to answer important question how to maintain the objectivity of the prosecutor in evaluation of the outcome of investigation if she has been already engaged in it by deciding on coercive measures. Yet I fully share another of Weigend's views stated on the same occasion, that it is necessary to shift the investigative authority in full to thc police and make them wholly responsible for the investigation, which would add to fostering their professionalism.[11] Perhaps the biggest problem of the prosecutorial supervision of criminal investigation is the shared responsibility over that stage of the criminal process and its outcome. The police can in such a case simply hide behind the prosecutor when bold decisions must be undertaken. Moreover, such a setup does not encourage the professionalization of the police and does not enhance the desire to understand what activities may result in becoming the basis for the valid judgment finding the accused guilty.

It is also aptly argued that moving the criminal investigation entirely under control of the police, and making them fully accountable for their actions, would not necessarily make the investigation more partisan than it already is in those systems where the prosecutor is called to supervise the police at that stage.[12] As discussed in Chapter 3, despite the strict regulations on this, all systems admittedly fail to achieve that standard in practice even if the perceived as inherently objective prosecutor plays an important role during investigation. Perhaps we should stop believing that it is possible to achieve full impartiality in the case of investigation, as investigators, and not only them, are always affected by their personal views and backgrounds.[13] Especially since it is expected that the prosecutor will reserve her objectivity for the time when the decision as to what happens next with the case is

10 Weigend (2012), p. 390.
11 Weigend (2012), p. 380.
12 Weigend (2012), p. 380.
13 Panzavolta (2004), p. 585.

being made, infringing this expectation by asking the prosecutor to engage more in criminal investigation does not sound reasonable.

The powers of the prosecutor over the initiation of criminal investigation, regardless of the country in question, as discussed in Chapter 4, in practice are very narrow and artificial. Probably Continental lawyers should stop fooling themselves that it is possible to maintain full prosecutorial control over every investigation from the very beginning of each case. Germany, Italy, and Poland provide rules for the prosecutorial responsibility for each investigation, either by vesting in the prosecutor's hands the decision to initiate the investigation, or by being immediately informed about it by the police. Yet, the practice proves the contrary, openly going against the normative regulations. And even if the decision is very formal and carefully prescribed by law, the police, with prosecutorial silent approval, do everything to not immediately report the case, thereby circumventing these regulations.

It must be assumed, then, that obliging the prosecutor to participate in the initiation of criminal investigation will fail, if even right now, despite rigid rules, the practice goes so openly against them. Moreover, it should be considered to be an enormous waste of resources if the prosecutor is informed about every single case and called to control the enormous number of criminal proceedings resulting from complaints. Finally, if we agree that the prosecutor's engagement in criminal investigation is unnecessary to retain her objectivity for the sake of the future decision to prosecute the case, her knowledge of the case at such an early stage should not be considered as desirable.

What should be noted, however, is that the victim should be granted not only the information that the case has been opened by the police, which seems to be obvious, but more importantly, should have a right to appeal the decision if the investigation has not been initiated. Lack of supervision leaves unverified powers in the hands of the police. In addition, this deprives the victim, of a review of the legitimacy of such decision. This is not to say that each decision not to initiate an investigation should be automatically confirmed by the prosecutor or the court, but at least the victim should be eligible to be heard, and to be able to present the counterarguments in a similar way as is done in the case of discontinuation of criminal investigation.

The analysis of the four researched countries in Chapter 5 with regard to the powers of the prosecutor during the conduct of criminal investigation, provides for a strong disparity between normative regulations and practice, at least in Continental countries. Even though the supervision of the prosecutor over police actions is prescribed clearly, the freedom that the police retain in practice is remarkable. It is almost a customary rule in cases of minor crimes that the prosecutor receives the case file only at the end of the criminal investigation which makes her active supervision over the conduct of the investigation artificial. It is most often limited to accepting the outcome as proposed by the police without any serious revision of police actions. While this might still seem understandable concerning gravity of such offenses, one could expect that in case of more serious offenses it would be handled more carefully. Yet, even in such cases prosecutors often remain passive in directing the investigation and participating in it only as much as the law actually demands. The direction of the investigation is therefore determined outside the prosecutor's office, which significantly impacts undertaken measures.

Acknowledging that the prosecutor only artificially supervises the criminal investigation, which usually remains under police control, should work against proposals to enhance prosecutorial powers at this stage. However, the reasons why in some states the investigative autonomy of the police is reduced, at least on the normative level, should not be disregarded. As the German and Italian examples show, such an approach has been built as reaction to the traumatic World War II history when the overuse of uncontrolled police powers led to the most horrific consequences. The reluctance to employ police investigatory independence in practice and engaging the prosecutor to overlook police actions may be therefore justified. Yet, the belief that the prosecutor, even when normatively obliged to rely on the principle of legality, is able to objectively conduct and supervise all criminal investigations and evaluate its outcome afterwards, is a misconception. The diminishing influence of both principles on the criminal investigation seems to confirm it. It is true that the police in their actions are not usually focused on the legal necessities of undertaken measures, but much more on conducting a successful investigation.[14] However the prosecutorial supervision over criminal investigation is not necessarily the best remedy for such practice. Rather, this issue could be resolved by subordinating the police to the judicial authority when the decision interfering with rights and freedoms must be undertaken. It may be also achieved by proper education and training of police. Obviously, the prosecution may play an important role in that regard participating in such training. Still, the greatest influence on the quality of criminal investigation the prosecution may achieve by carefully verifying the outcome of investigation and not accepting results of improperly and illegally conducted investigations for the prosecution. This, however, may be fulfilled only by the objective entity aloof from the investigation.

Another argument can be made here against the calls for the reinforcement of the prosecutorial presence during criminal investigation. Thus, it is not only the problem of maintaining the necessary objectivity in making the decision whether to prosecute or not. The prosecutors are frequently

14 Trendafilova and Róth (2008), p. 241.

but falsely perceived as angels among devilish police officers and expected to become a remedy for the police incompetency and wrongdoing. Yet, it is true that the criminal justice systems failed on many occasions due to the proven prosecutorial misconducts concerning the coercive negotiations over plea bargains. Given that some prosecutors have compromised themselves while plea-bargaining, it is reasonable to ask whether they would raise the standard in criminal investigations in which they are supposed to engage. Perhaps we even demand too much of prosecutors. Standing with one foot in criminal investigation, actively searching for evidence, being expected to be objective and neutral providing checks and balances on the police, and with the second foot in deciding whether to prosecute and confidently arguing against the defendant at the trial is not a position that the prosecutors can handle without schizophrenia. Allowing prosecutors to devote themselves exclusively to one of these two tasks the criminal justice system may enhance the quality of their work. .

However, it should not be forgotten that police and prosecution do not work in the vacuum. The conduct of criminal investigation in each country is also substantially formed by the role that the suspect, and the victim, are assigned with by the criminal justice system at this stage of the criminal process. While in the USA they have almost no power to demand any investigative actions to be undertaken, the Continental countries give them a variety of choices in that regard, including granting them the right to formally request conducting certain measures. This is connected with the role of the criminal investigation, which in the Continental countries being conducted officially and formally, promising that the evidence will be gathered both for and against the accused to an equal degree, openly accepts such opportunities. But when one acknowledges that retaining full and pure neutrality during criminal investigation is simply impossible, the position of the participants should be reconsidered, calling for departing from the idea of relying on the goodwill and objectivity of criminal justice agents, but allowing and encouraging independent defense investigation.

Charging a person with a crime should be considered as a crucial moment in the course of the criminal process, when it is decided how the case will develop further. There is no doubt that this decision is, and should remain, in the hands of the prosecutor. This is, in fact, what the prosecutor is asked to do for the most part. But the shape of final charges undoubtedly feeds on the structure of informal preliminary charges being the basis of the criminal investigation when the suspect has been already identified. And as discussed in Chapter 6, the four countries differ significantly in the competence of the prosecutor to initially charge a person with a crime and how it should be done.

The more general question refers to whether the suspect should be entitled to receive, before the closure of investigation, a separate notification of her status as the suspect. This is of particular importance when the suspect has not been subject of a coercive measure such as arrest or search. There are valid arguments for such notifications, in particular connected with the right to defend oneself and having enough time to prepare for the case and to rebut the evidence collected by the police as early as during the investigation. This might not only prevent erroneous accusations but more importantly save the time of the criminal court. On the other hand, the inherent feature of the investigation is its secrecy and the right of the suspect to learn about her status should be balanced against that principle. Obviously, the full secrecy must be waived in case of coercive measures being imposed on the suspect, so she may defend herself against the evidence gathered by the criminal justice authorities justifying the use of the measure. This is, in particular, crucial when the liberty of the suspect is at stake due to the imposition of pretrial detention, however in case of wiretaps again the secrecy of criminal investigation should, at least temporarily, prevail. But aside from such cases, should the suspect have the right to be notified as soon as possible as to her status, or is notification at the end of criminal investigation, with a chance to counter the prosecution arguments, enough? The answer would be quite simple and confirmatory if not for the reported practice of police interrogating officially, or unofficially, the suspect as a witness, which may result in her revealing self-incriminating information, if not properly instructed on the right to remain silent. It becomes problematic since countries differ as to how the right not to incriminate oneself is triggered. They provide a variety of mechanisms, including the complicated structures of "custodial interrogations" as in the US case, or allowing every witness to refuse answering questions to which the answer would be self-incriminating, but not to refrain from participation in the whole investigation as Poland adopted. The case becomes even more complex when the obligation to appear and testify, which includes the witness, is introduced in the system. It is unclear how to differentiate between the witness and the suspect in such case, if both must appear and undergo the interrogation and only the latter may fully refrain from answering all questions, while the former may only refuse to answer some of them. And both interrogations are still not considered as custodial.

Although it is true that the suspect should be afforded information about the charges, so that she may conduct an intelligent defense, a proper balance should be achieved between the rights of the suspect and the inherent need of criminal investigation to be conducted in secrecy. If there are no coercive measures applied against the suspect, it can be argued that the knowledge that she is the subject of investigation could be revealed to the suspect at the end of that phase of the process. Save, that at the closure of investigation she will be notified about her status and will be granted the right to read the case file and be allowed to try to convince the prosecutor that pursuing the charges is unnecessary. This also should include giving the suspect enough time to prepare for her defense at trial. It should be clear, though it is not a rule in all researched countries, that whenever a criminal investigation is conduced into an individual, especially in the form of arrest, she must be treated as a suspect, with the rights applicable at that point) being notified to her.

The critical analysis of preliminary charging process as applied in the researched countries leads to conclusion that there is no place for the prosecutor to preliminarily charge the suspect with a crime. This should remain under the control of the police and for which the police should be held accountable. This must, however, remain an informal procedure resembling the Italian or US systems where the suspect is not subjected to coerced interrogations unless there is indeed a need to arrest her prior the trial. The Polish and German examples show that if there is a mandatory mechanism to interrogate a suspect during criminal investigation, she will be forcibly brought for such activity to be undertaken if unwilling to appear voluntarily, even if the grounds for arrest are not met. This should be considered as unacceptable interference in the rights and freedoms of the suspect. On the other hand, there should be nothing preventing the suspect from being interrogated if she demands it. A suspect can be even offered the chance to address the accusations by being invited to a nonmandatory interrogation in a presence of her lawyer upon demand.

There should be no doubt that ultimately the formal charging process should involve the judge. This is also one of the arguments against the very formal initial charging process occurring during criminal investigation that, as shown in the Polish example, replaced in practice the judicial encounter with the suspect. The charging process conducted before the court is all the more important in cases where, according to the intention of both parties, the trial is not to take place at all, i.e. where the parties have reached an agreement . The obligation for the suspect to indicate to the court that he is guilty and aware of the consequences of her actions, and to agree to submit to the penalty agreed with the prosecutor, ensures, as far as possible, the fairness of the procedure for determining the guilt of the accused outside the trial. Conducting this procedure before the court, and in the mandatory presence of the accused person, limits the activities of the prosecutor and improves the quality of the proceedings. The majesty of the court, the weight of statements made in such arrangement and the possibility to verify the evidence base of the decision proposed by the prosecutor, significantly increases the quality of decisions taken. Of course, one can argue, quoting many US examples, that such a setting is not free from abuses, including those in which the accused pleads guilty or is forced to plead guilty against the evidence gathered. However, it seems that when the charging takes place out of court and when the suspect's only contact with the criminal justice system is a meeting with a police officer during which her attitude toward the case is determined, is a much more inappropriate solution giving even more space for undesirable judgments. Therefore, to increase the protection of the rights of the accused and enforce the transparency and fairness of the charging process, especially in cases involving guilty pleas, conducting it orally before the court should be highly recommended as a proper check on prosecutorial powers.

Even more restrains should be imposed on the prosecutorial powers in the context of coercive measures. Although the convergence in that regard is perceived as particularly problematic,[15] in order to properly protect the fundamental rights of the individual, such as liberty or privacy the power to impose coercive measures should be entrusted solely to the judge (court). The prosecutor in a typical situation should be unable to authorize such a decision either prior to undertaking the measure or post factum. Since rights and freedoms are at stake, there is no place for compromise in the matter. Even in those countries where the prosecution is claimed to be a part of the judiciary, like in Italy, certainly the difference between the judge and the prosecutor are not entirely erased which makes the latter incompetent to put restrain on the rights of individual. The fact that in that country the prosecutor, despite her position of *magistrati*, is nevertheless unauthorized by law to decide on the deprivation of liberty and the use of wiretaps, seems to confirm that there is no equality between prosecution and judges.

In the proposed shape of criminal investigation where the police take the full responsibility of their actions, it is also undesirable that the prosecutor would participate in undertaking such measures either by personally requesting their imposition or even by transferring such request to the court. Primarily, if the judicial activity in that regard can already be considered as delaying the investigation, extending it even more by asking the prosecutor to review and forward the motion seems unreasonable. Second, expecting the prosecutor to intervene when coercive measures are imposed makes her a continuous supervisor of the police actions and involves her too much and too early in the case. Finally, since it is the prosecutor who must eventually evaluate the outcome of criminal investigation, her participation in such a procedure may infringe her capability to remain neutral and objective in doing so.

However, for obvious reasons aimed at the efficiency of criminal investigation the power of criminal justice authorities to conduct certain coercive

15 Cf. Ligeti (2019), p. 160.

measures, such as search and arrest, without judicial preauthorization in exigent circumstances should be preserved. It should nevertheless be recognized that such unauthorized measure should always be at least subjected to judicial review if not immediately presented to the judge for confirmation. For reasons discussed in Chapter 7, it is considered necessary to provide the person whose rights were allegedly infringed by an unauthorized coercive measure with the judicial review.

This should be recognized as more effective mechanism when compared with prosecutorial scrutiny that may immediately correct the illegal police behavior and help to establish the desired standard of police actions for the protection of the individual's rights. The judicial review at this stage of the process has an added value. Leaving the assessment of the lawfulness of the coercive measure conducted without a warrant at the trial stage results in no effective remedy for those whose cases never reach that stage. And since trials have become the exception rather than the norm, the adoption of a formula in which their conduct is verified during criminal investigation for their legality and validity, allows an individual to quickly assess her procedural situation in the context of the evidence already gathered against her at this stage of the proceedings. Moreover, immediate judicial recognition of the illegality of obtained evidence also allows the prosecutor to disregard such information in the process of making the decision whether to prosecute, or to discontinue the case. The judicial verification should also be considered as the desired form of verification of the measure especially when the measure did not result in seizure, or the case has been terminated by the prosecutor, since in such cases review of the measure during the trial will not even be available. Finally, it may be assumed that if the mechanism of verification will be designed properly and will work effectively, and coercive measures imposed without the prior judicial authorization will be subjected to careful judicial scrutiny, there is no place for the prosecutor to even get involved ensuring her desired objectivity when decision whether to prosecute is made.

Yet one issue leaves the problem of the imposition of coercive measures during criminal investigation still open. Since the measures understood as coercive for the purpose of this work require a different degree of intensity of interference with the individual's rights and freedoms, should they all be treated in the same way? Since the deprivation of liberty, when compared with the summoning of a witness, clearly entails distinct treatment, it should be further researched whether all coercive measures should be subjected to the same judicial scrutiny in every single case.

Since we currently operate within the "administrative" criminal justice system where the important decisions typically happen in charging and plea negotiations before the case even makes it to trial,[16] it is equally necessary

16 Lynch (1998).

to review decisions that enter the system as well as those that are decided to remain outside of it. The unfettered discretion of prosecutors and police officers not to proceed with a case must be put under judicial scrutiny. Such mechanisms as the obligation to give reasons for the decision to discontinue the criminal proceedings, to file it on a record in an open court and, finally, a right to interlocutory appeal available for the victim or complainant if the commitment of an offense concerns her rights, serve as useful tools to maintain control over unlimited prosecutorial powers.

Consequently, the decision to discontinue criminal investigation undertaken by the prosecutor should be eligible for the judicial verification.[17] Such revision should not have a mandatory character, but rather the victim should be granted the right to interlocutory appeal against the prosecutorial decision. Therefore, it should not be the court to confirm the decision to discontinue criminal investigation in every case, but whenever the victim desires the court will look into the case as a form of second check on the prosecutor's arguments against filing charges. In the adversarial environment of the court hearing, where arguments of the prosecutor encounter the victim's claims, the dispute between the two can be resolved in the best way.

Certainly, there might be valid arguments against the judicial scrutiny over the discretionary power of the prosecutor, based on the separation of power argument. But two issues should be raised to defend the necessity to provide for judicial verification in the case of discontinuation of criminal investigation. First, the reverse decision of the prosecutor—to bring the case for a trial, is not free from verification through various mechanisms, including probable cause hearings, and grand jury reviews. If the court is granted the power to decide whether to accept the accusation and verify its legitimacy, the decision on discontinuation of criminal proceedings should be understood in similar terms and likewise subjected to such assessment. Moreover, the judicial hearing provides for the possibility to hear the view of the victim, providing a distinct perspective which may only increase the accuracy of such decision. Second, even in those systems that do not grant the victim with the status of the party to proceedings, the enormous power that the prosecutor possesses to decline prosecution should not be left unverified if the victim recognizes such need. Especially where the prosecutor is allowed to bargain over charges and drop some of them in exchange for a guilty plea, the second opinion of an impartial adjudicator should be more than desired. Depriving the victim of an effective mechanism to review the decision not to prosecute may even lead in some cases to a miscarriage of justice. Situations where

17 Cf. Luna and Wade (2010), p. 1511.

the decision to prosecute has been incorrectly made, and situations where the case has been recklessly discontinued, are equally dangerous. In the first case the damage happens to the wrongly accused, and in the second the right to a court and to settling the case is taken away from the victim.

Also, the consequences of such judicial verification should be discussed. In this regard the researched countries make for interesting choices. Besides the possibility of obliging the prosecutor to reconsider the decision and reopen the investigation, the second request for review triggers the ultimate resolutions, such as forcing the prosecutor to file charges and prosecute a case (Italy and Germany) or allowing the victim to prosecute the case by herself (Poland). Accepting the first choice seems to be interfering too much with the prosecutorial competencies and even the countries that employ it in practice admit that judicial impartiality is at stake in such a case. Therefore, the prosecution by the victim could be considered as a choice. The requirement to be represented by a lawyer and especially the low number of such prosecutions in systems where it is already exercised, proves that this is not a mechanism that overloads the system.

Reflecting on the analysis on the role the prosecutor plays during the criminal investigation some final considerations should be made. The police taking exclusive responsibility for the criminal investigation brings an obvious dilemma. As the research of police practices in all countries presented within this work proves, the police, whether we want it or not, can shape the criminal investigation in the way they want to. The police reports, the dossier, and case files are always stamped with bias which might, but does not necessarily always have to, rely on objective evaluation of the facts. While it is tempting to provide for careful scrutiny of the police by the prosecutor to counteract this problem, for the reasons presented above it is not the right choice.

However, there are two things that can be done to counterbalance the threat of biased perspective that the subjective police report provides. First, it is necessary to allow for an independent private investigation to be conducted by the suspect and her counsel. And, at the same time, if the defense deems it necessary, the law should provide ways in which the defense would be able to discuss the evidence gathered by the police with the prosecutor when she plans to officially file charges with the court after the contents of the case file and evidence are revealed to the suspect. It would allow for the adversarial environment in which the arguments of both sides (the police and the suspect) are presented to the prosecutor. This should also apply to the court hearings when a decision on the pretrial detention or the discontinuation of the investigation is undertaken. And, as practiced in all the countries, the pretrial taking evidence in the presence of the judge in case of losing such evidence should be allowed.

Second, a great responsibility rests with those who control the police actions. It should apply equally to the court during the course of criminal investigation with regard to the imposition of coercive measures and the prosecutor at its conclusion. Since the police file can be one-sided, a cautious approach should be employed while evaluating its contents. Such a process should be accompanied by limited trust, criticism, and objectivity. Again, the adversarial environment is more than desirable in such case, but especially if there is no one to defend the perspective other than the one pushed by the police, the evaluation of the file should be even more careful. Due consideration should be given to the information gathered, and in particular the ways in which it was collected. This cannot be achieved only by law; rather, it requires boldness, sensitivity, and personal integrity in approaching the criminal cases. Undertaking decisions automatically, with a full trust to the materials presented, should be regarded as a mistake. It is particularly clear in well-documented cases in which the uncritical acceptance of negotiated deals leads to errors in establishing the facts, and often to wrongful convictions.

9.3 Concluding Remarks

This book aspires to answer the question of whether the prosecutor should be a *legal arm of the police* where her powers are focused on setting the direction of criminal investigation, conducting the investigative actions alongside the police, while at the same time verifying the need to employ coercive measures. Or rather, should she be focused on the objective evaluation of the outcome of investigation conducted independently by the police, overseen by the judge for compliance with human rights standards, and deciding on bringing charges and fully engaging in developing a just resolution of the case, either by negotiations or during an adversarial trial.

As argued in this work, there is more to lose than to gain when the prosecutor engages directly in criminal investigation. Certainly it is true that the prosecutor brings legal knowledge and litigation experience when supervising investigation, which might positively influence the collection of evidence by the criminal justice agencies. We can also agree that the prosecutorial presence at this stage may bring some restraint on hasty police actions, and an accuracy in undertaken decisions enhancing the protection of rights of individuals engaged in the criminal process. But the prosecutor should not become a Band-Aid for the misuse of police powers. Surely, adopting prosecutorial supervision of investigation takes the responsibility from the police, which is from then on shared between two entities not organizationally dependent on each other. Yet, more importantly, by taking part in criminal investigation, the prosecutor loses the objectivity so needed when the evaluation of evidence must eventually be done at the end of investigation.

Nonetheless, the prosecutor has other tools than a close supervision of criminal investigation to influence the police work. By rejecting cases where there are concerns about police misconduct or inadequately conducted investigations, the prosecutor maintains her role of the gatekeeper and guardian of the criminal justice system. Without her decision, no case, even those most carefully prepared by the police can enter the system. Indeed, the prosecutors are charged with a role to ensure that the system functions well and that all that have been engaged by the system—suspects, victims, and witnesses are sufficiently protected. Prosecutors can therefore continue to exercise these obligations by providing careful scrutiny of the police actions and their decisions. Thus prosecutors should retain their position of critical and bold reviewers of police work and not convert into police collaborators who jointly search for evidence with only one aim to win a case.

Precautions are necessary for a system to work properly in this a set up. First, when coercive measures are used in criminal investigation, judicial supervision is required. The control over the police when interfering with the rights of an individual by the judicial authority should be the standard we should be all looking for. Second, the protection of the rights of the individual during criminal investigation should be carefully secured. While the criminal process becomes more and more professionalized in its legal aspect, high-quality legal aid available to each suspect at the earliest stage of criminal investigation is a must. Third, the suspect should also be allowed to conduct private investigation and gather her own evidence independently to counterbalance the, too often, one-sided police files. Fourth, the police, made fully responsible and accountable for their actions during criminal investigation, should be properly trained and funded to provide the highest-quality work. The education, soft law, guidelines, and workshops conducted, also with the help of prosecutors, should be the highest priority. Finally, the verification of police decisions and control over their actions should be done transparently and objectively. Surely, the proper internal mechanisms preventing the overuse of police powers helping to avoid miscarriages of justice may not be replaced even by the most precise supervision of criminal investigation by the prosecutor

Although the emphasis in this work has been placed on redefining the role of the prosecutor played during criminal investigation any attempt to do so will be counterproductive if the independence of the prosecution from external influences, in particular politics, is not secured. This seems to be a necessary and fundamental condition for ensuring the integrity of criminal proceedings in general, regardless of the role that the prosecutor actually plays within the system. While it is less important whether the prosecution service formally remains a part of the executive or the judiciary, more pertinent is to consider the extent to which the prosecution service remains dependent on politicians and their decisions. Regardless of the criminal procedure model, the internal dependencies within the hierarchical structure of the prosecution service and the vision pursued by prosecutors, it is the influence of politics on this prosecution system that has the power to destroy the obligation of the prosecutor that is to ensure a fair criminal process for all.

References

Barkow R (2009) Institutional Design and the Policing of Prosecutors. *Stanford Law Review* 61:869–922.

Brown DK (2012) American Prosecutors' Powers and Obligations in the Era of Plea Bargaining. In: Luna E, Wade M (eds) *The Prosecutor in Transnational Perspective*. Oxford University Press, Oxford, pp. 200–213.

Caianiello M (2019) Criminal Process faced with the Challenges of Scientific and Technological Development. *European Journal of Crime, Criminal Law and Criminal Justice* 27(4): 267–291.

Kremens K (2014) Prokuratura wobec reformy postępowania karnego. Rozważania o rozdziale funkcji śledczych i oskarżycielskich na tle angielskiego procesu karnego. *Przegląd Sądowy* 5: 7–33.

Ligeti K (2019) The Place of the Prosecutor in Common Law and Civil Law Jurisdictions In: Brown DK, Turner JI, Weisser B (eds) *The Oxford Handbook of Criminal Process*. Oxford University Press, Oxford, pp. 139–163.

Luna E, Wade M (2010) Prosecutors as Judges. *Washington and Lee Law Review* 67:1413–1532.

Lynch GE (1998) Our Administrative System of Criminal Justice. *Fordham Law Review* 66:2117–2151.

Panzavolta M (2004) Reforms and Counter-Reforms in the Italian Struggle for an Accusatorial Criminal Law System. *North Carolina Journal of International Law and Commercial Regulation* 30:577–624.

Richman DC (2003) Prosecutors and Their Agents. Agents and Their Prosecutors. *Columbia Law Review* 103:749–832.

Rosenthal K (1998) Prosecutor Misconduct, Convictions, and Double Jeopardy: Case Studies in an Emerging Jurisprudence. *Temple Law Review* 71: 887.

Soubise L, Woolley A (2018) Prosecutors and Justice: Insights from Comparative Analysis. *Fordham International Law Journal* 42:587–626.

Trendafilova E, Róth W (2008) Report on the Public Prosecution Service in Germany. In: Open Society Institute Sofia (ed) *Promoting Prosecutorial Accountability, Independence and Effectiveness*. Open Society Institute Sofia, Sofia.

Weigend T (2012) A Judge by Any Other Name? Comparative Perspectives on the Role of the Public Prosecutor. In: Luna E, Wade M (eds) *The Prosecutor in Transnational Perspective*. Oxford University Press, Oxford, pp. 377–391.

Index

abbreviated proceedings 335
adjudication, prosecutorial participation in 335, 336

Brazzi, Marco 283
Bush, George HW 56

Clinton, Bill 56
coercive measures: categorization of 263–264; de facto police dominance of 294–295; judicial authorization, need for more of 346–347, 351; judicial review, need for more of 347; motions for review as remedy 295; overwhelming variety of 264–265; partiality of prosecutors 294; prevalence of warrantless actions 293; prosecutorial objectivity impractical 346; search and arrest as major forms of 265; terminology 262–263, 264; theoretical preference for warrants 293; *see also individual countries*
Committee of the Ministers of the Council of Europe 28–29
conditional disposals/dismissals 3, 221, 300, 302, 305, 306, 309, 335
conduct of investigation: de facto independence of police 197–202, 341–342, 349; exclusive powers of prosecutor 146, 198; federalist decentralization 197; judicial involvement 147, 200; minor vs. serious crimes 199, 201; objectivity of prosecutor, influenced by investigative role 146, 199; prosecutor–police relationship 145, 197–202; supervisory powers of prosecutor 145–146, 197–202; suspect's rights 146, 200, 343; time frame 146, 201; victim's rights 146, 200, 343; *see also individual countries*
Connecticut: appointment of state prosecutors 59–60; Constitution 53, 59, 65; Criminal Justice Commission 327; depositions 196; General Statutes 53; grand juries 101, 192–193, 195–196, 242n213; information and complaint 244n220; internal independence of prosecutors 65; *nolle prosequi* 320, 326, 327; Practice Book 53; prosecutorial discretion 103; supervisory powers of prosecutor 183; time frame for investigation 186–187
Consultative Council of European Prosecutors 29
criminal investigation: conclusion of in Continental systems 108; conclusion of in US 108; definition of 74–75, 107; discontinuation of proceedings 109; growing technological sophistication of 336; investigation upon complaint 109; mandatory prosecution 109, 110; prosecutorial control of impractical 339–340, 341, 349, 351; prosecutorial discretion vs. legality 75, 108–110; prosecutorial objectivity 75, 110–111; quality of evidence enhanced by prosecutorial involvement 337, 339, 350; *see also* inquisitorial vs. adversarial systems
criminalizing of human behavior, increase in 5, 335
cybercrime 336

defense investigation, need for 343, 349, 351

discontinuing investigation: definition of 299–301; horizontal variety of in Continental systems 322; judicial oversight minimal 330–331; judicial verification, need for more of 348; legality principle 329; minor vs. serious crime 330; police, broad shaping powers of 329, 331; prosecutors, powers of constrained by police 329, 331; public interest grounds 3, 110, 300, 329; separation of powers 348–349; vertical variety of in US 321; victim's right to appeal, importance of 348; victim's right to subsidiary prosecution 349; *see also individual countries*

European Convention on Human Rights (ECHR) 10, 209, 284
European Court of Human Rights (ECtHR) 29, 208, 209, 283–284

fascism 46, 66, 91
Florida 184
formal charging, judicial involvement in crucial 345–346

German Code of Criminal Procedure (StPO) 32–33, 118–119, 263; Section 100 155; Section 102 266; Section 103 267, 269; Section 112 267; Section 114 270; Section 115 270; Section 133 216; Section 136 218, 219; Section 151 210; Section 152 78, 79, 118; Section 153 301, 302; Section 160 118, 149; Section 161 153, 154; Section 162 220; Section 163 119, 151, 217, 220; Section 170 214–215, 301; Section 200 211
German coercive measures: authority for 270–272; judge for the investigation 268, 270, 271, 294; judicial oversight limited 271–272; judicial post-authorization of warrantless arrest 270, 271; low threshold for search 266; police, de facto power of 272; procedure for 268–270; prosecutor and police powers to order search 268–269; prosecutor's powers limited 272; provisional arrest 267–268; right of appeal against arrest 270, 271; right of appeal against search 269, 271; search and arrest not linked 266; search of suspect vs. non-suspect 266–267; search with warrant vs. without 267
German conduct of investigation: de facto police independence 150–152, 154; exclusive powers of prosecutor 154–155; federalist structure, influence of 147–148; general investigation clause 149–150; investigative officer status 148–149, 154; judge for the investigation 156–157, 176; "master of the investigation" 146, 150; Ministry of Internal Affairs 148, 149, 150; Ministry of Justice 148, 149; minor vs. serious crime 152, 153; police powers 153–154; prosecutor–police relationship 147–149; size of prosecutor's office 152; statute of limitation 153; supervisory powers of prosecutor 149–153; suspect's right to investigate 155–156, 200; time frame 153
German criminal investigation: administrative offenses 78; felonies 79; investigation upon complaint 79; judge for the investigation 77, 156, 220–221; legality principle 77–78, 79, 80, 109, 214; mandatory investigation 76, 78, 214; opportunity principle 79; outline of 75–77; private crimes 78–79; procedural economy 303; prosecutorial discretion 77–79; prosecutorial objectivity 80–81, 110
German discontintuation of investigation: authority for 305–307; conditional discontinuation 302, 305, 306; court's power to endorse discontinuation 306, 330; court's power to enforce prosecution 304, 305–306, 331; inappropriateness of the sentence 302; insufficiency of evidence 301, 304, 306; legality principle 301, 330; mandatory prosecution principle 301, 303; minor vs. serious crime 301, 302, 305, 306–307; offenses committed abroad 302; police influence on 306–307; procedure for 303–305; prosecutorial discretion, trend towards 303; prosecutor's powers relatively unconstrained 305–306; public interest grounds 109, 301, 304, 305, 306; suspect's right to be informed 303; threshold for 301–303; victim's right to

appeal 303–304, 330; victim's right to be informed 303
German initiation of investigation: authority for 121–122, 142; decision not to investigate 120; exceptions to legality principle 117–118; informal initial inquiry 119; legality principle 117; officiality principle 117; procedure for 119–120; suspicion 118; threshold for 117–119; victim's rights 120
German preliminary charging: authority for 210–211; failure to promptly inform suspect of status 213–214, 215; as final act of investigation 210; judicial interrogation 220–221; no formal designation of "suspect" status 211; penal orders 211; police interrogation vs. prosecutor interrogation 216–218, 255; police principal actors in 219–220; procedure for 215–219; scope of information given to suspect 217–218, 219; terminology 211–212; threshold for 214–215; timing of interrogation open to abuse 219, 255
German prosecution system: external independence of prosecutors 34–35, 66, 80; federal/state organization 36; internal independence of prosecutors 36–38, 68; mandatory prosecution principle 33; Minister of Justice 35, 37, 38, 68; sources of law for prosecution service 32–34
Germany: Code of Criminal Law (StGB) 79, 153, 218; Constitution (Basic Law) 33, 78, 266, 270–271; Court Constitution Act (CCA) 33, 35, 36, 148–149; Federal Constitutional Court 33, 35; Federal Court of Justice 215; Federal Criminal Police Office 148; German Judicial Academy 34; as inquisitorial exemplar 14, 76; Nazi period 66, 77, 342; State Court of Appeals 303, 304; vanishing of trials 3
Guide on the Status and Role of Prosecutors (United Nations) 28
Guidelines on the Role of Prosecutors (United Nations) 28

initiating investigation: informality of US discretionary system 141; legality principle 116, 141, 142; refusal to investigate 141; serious vs. minor crime 142; threshold for initiation 116; time frame 116; utopian formality of Continental systems 141; victim's rights 141, 341; *see also individual countries*
Innocence Project 8
inquisitorial vs. adversarial systems 9–13; adversarial system compromised by vanishing trials 11–12, 336; prosecutorial objectivity problematic in inquisitorial system 12–13, 337–338, 339, 340–341, 343, 350–351; *see also* criminal investigation
International Association of Prosecutors 28
International Covenant on Civil and Political Rights (United Nations) 10
International Criminal Court 6
investigative judges 16, 76, 83, 89, 100, 101, 156, 167, 176, 195, 340
Italian Code of Criminal Procedure (c.p.p.) 15, 45–46, 88, 91, 92, 168, 169, 174, 176, 177, 263, 279, 280, 283; Article 55 133, 172; Article 60 233, 235; Article 61 235; Article 131 315; Article 273 282; Article 274 282; Article 326 95; Article 327 171, 175; Article 329 236; Article 330 132; Article 331 131; Article 335 132, 133, 236; Article 347 133; Article 348 134, 171; Article 358 94–95; Article 370 171; Article 374 240; Article 389 282; Article 405 178; Article 407 132, 239; Article 408 314; Article 411 93, 314; Article 415 234, 235; Article 624 316
Italian coercive measures: arrest vs. detention 279–280, 281; authority for 282–284; Court of Cassation, appeal to 282; ECtHR criticism 283–284; joint constitutional regulation of search and arrest 278; judge for preliminary investigation, validation of arrest by 281, 282, 283, 284, 294; judicial supervision, weakness of 283–284; judicial review 280, 281; mandatory vs. optional arrest 279–280; partiality of prosecutors 283, 294; police, broad powers of 281; preventive detention 282; procedure for 280–282; prosecutorial authority, controversial nature of 282–284; prosecutorial

authorization of searches 280–281; prosecutorial post-authorization of warrantless searches 281; warrantless police search 279, 281
Italian conduct of investigation: defense's right to investigate 175–176; delegated authority 171; exclusive powers of prosecutor 173–174; judge for preliminary investigation (GIP) 173, 176–178, 283; judicial police 169–170, 172, 173; minor vs. serious crime 173; police interrogation vs. prosecutor interrogation 239; prosecutor–police relationship 168–170; special evidentiary hearings 177; statute of limitation 178; supervisory powers of prosecutor 171–173; time frame 173, 176, 177–178; victim's right to investigate 175–176
Italian criminal investigation: evidential hearings 90; investigation upon complaint 92–93; judge for preliminary investigation 89, 153; legality principle 91, 92–93, 109; mandatory prosecution principle 90; *notitia criminis* 90, 92, 93; outline of 88–91; preliminary hearings 89; pretrial detention 89; prosecutorial discretion 91–94; prosecutorial objectivity 94–95, 110; surveillance 89; time limit 90, 93, 130, 132
Italian discontintuation of investigation: authority for 318–319; judge for preliminary investigation, broad formal powers of 314, 315, 316–318, 330, 331; legality principle 314, 315, 317, 318, 330; minor vs. serious crime 319; police's power to shape decision 319; procedure for 315–318; prosecutor's power to shape decision 318–319; public interest grounds 109, 315; suspect's right to be notified 316; threshold for 313–315; time limit, manipulation of by prosecutor 318–319; victim's right to appeal 315, 316, 317–318
Italian initiation of investigation: alleged perpetrator's right to be informed 132–133; authority for 133–134, 142; legality principle 129; limitations to legality principle 129; medical reports 131; preparatory inquiry 130, 132, 134; procedure for 131–133; threshold for 128–130; time frame 130, 134, 172; victim's right to be informed 133
Italian preliminary charging: amendment of 235, 237; authority for 240–241; defense counsel's right to involvement as trigger for informing suspect of 237–239; judge for preliminary investigation (GIP) 234, 240–241; legality principle 236, 240; limited obligation to inform suspect of 234, 235, 236–237, 239–240, 256; no obligation to interrogate suspect 237; police, indirect influence of 240, 241; procedure for 237–240; suspect's rights 235–236; terminology 235; threshold for 236–237; as trigger for expiration date of investigation 234, 236
Italian prosecution system: diversity of charging instruments 233; external independence of prosecutors 46–48, 66; inquisitorial to adversarial shift 15, 45, 91, 94, 110, 283; internal independence of prosecutors 48–51, 68; legality principle 45, 47, 48, 50–51, 68; mandatory prosecution principle 91–92, 132; Minister of Justice 46, 47, 91, 169; *pubblico ministero* 31; sources of law for prosecution service 45–46
Italy: Constitution 45, 46, 50, 68, 91, 94, 109, 129, 169, 278, 280, 282, 283, 294; Constitutional Court 94, 170, 314; Court of Cassation 130, 282; fascist period 45, 46, 66, 91, 342; Judicial Regulations 94; National Anti-Mafia and Counter-Terrorism Bureau 49–50; obligation to report crime 131; organized crime 49–50, 239–240; over-criminalization 129; Rocco Code 89; state, military and judicial police 169; Superior Council of the Judiciary 47, 50, 68; vanishing of trials

Jackson, RH 51

legal aid, need for more of at early stage in investigation 351
Lenin, Vladimir 40
Lieberman, Joe 60

Michigan 242

negotiated case-settlement procedures *see* plea-bargaining
Nixon, Richard 56

Obama, Barack 56

pattegiamento: see plea-bargaining
penal orders 3, 211, 300, 335
plea-bargaining 2–3, 99, 182, 194, 207, 289, 299, 300, 325, 335, 336, 343, 350
Poland: Central Anticorruption Bureau 159; Constitution 40, 83, 87, 224, 278; National Revenue Administration 159; obligation to report crime 124; organized crime 86; Organized Crime and Corruption Department 43–44; Polish Prosecution Service Act (1985) 39, 41; Prosecution Service Act (2016) 39, 40, 42–43, 45, 88, 164; Soviet legacy 14–15; State Witness Act 86; Supreme Court 222, 226–227, 228; vanishing of trials 3
Polish Code of Criminal Procedure (k.p.k.) 39, 40, 81, 88, 159, 164, 224, 263, 272, 308; Article 2 82; Article 4 87; Article 10 83, 225–226; Article 17 308; Article 75 227; Article 170 166, 225; Article 183 226; Article 219 275; Article 244 277; Article 247 277; Article 306 310; Article 309 158; Article 313 223, 226, 227, 229; Article 322 307; Article 325 158; Article 326 160, 232; Article 335 230; Article 459 310
Polish coercive measures: arrest nonmandatory 273; authority for 276–278; judicial review of searches and arrests 276, 277; procedure for 274–276; prosecutorial post-authorization of warrantless searches 275; prosecutor's broad powers 276–278; search, definition of 272–273; search and arrest distinctly regulated 272; suspected person, arrest of 273–274; threshold for 273; warrantless police arrests 274, 275–276, 277; warrantless police searches 274–275
Polish conduct of investigation: Border Guard 159; de facto police independence 159–160; exclusive powers of prosecutor 163–165; inspection vs. inquiry 158, 159–160, 161, 162, 163; judicial involvement 164, 167–168; minor vs. serious crime 158; prosecutor–police relationship 158–160; statute of limitation 158; supervisory powers of prosecutor 160–163; time frame 162–163; victim's and suspect's right to request evidentiary measures 165–167, 200
Polish criminal investigation: court involvement 83; Customs Office 159; *ex officio* investigation 85, 165; *in rem* vs. *ad personam* 82; inspection vs. inquiry 81–82, 142; Internal Security Agency 159; investigation upon complaint 85; legality principle 83–86, 109; Military Gendarmerie 159; negotiated case settlements 86, 230; outline of 81–83; pretrial detention 83; private offenses 84; prosecutorial discretion 83–87; prosecutorial objectivity 87–88, 110; reasonable suspicion 84, 85; surveillance 83
Polish discontinuation of investigation: authority for 312–313; conditional discontinuation 309; insanity of the offender 309; inspection vs. inquiry 312, 313; interlocutory appeal against 310–311, 312; lack of social harm 308; legality principle 308; negative grounds 307–308; police initiation of 312; police's strong shaping influence 313; procedure for 309–311; prosecutor's broad formal powers 312–313; public interest grounds, lack of 86–87, 308–309; recorded discontinuation 312; subsidiary prosecution 311, 331; threshold for 307–309
Polish initiation of investigation: appealing refusal to investigate 125–126; authority for 127–128, 142; grounds for not investigating 123; immediate procedures 124, 231; legality principle 122; preliminary examination 123–124, 127; procedure for 124–127; reasonable suspicion 122–123; serious vs. minor crime 142; subsidiary prosecution 126; threshold for 122–124; time frame 123
Polish preliminary charging: amendment of charges 228–229, 254, 257; arrest separate from 231; authority for 231–233; compulsory attendance and interrogation of suspect 222, 227–228,

229–230, 254–255; EU directives and 224–225, 256; formal character of 227, 254; guilty pleas 230–231; informing the suspect 229, 254; inspection vs. inquiry 231–232, 256–257; interrogating the suspect 229–231; issuing the decision 228–229; lack of rights prior to 224; legality principle 225–226; motion for conditional discontinuation 221; motion to convict without trial 221; precise description of alleged crime 228; procedure for 227–231; suspected person vs. suspect 223–225; suspect's rights activated by 222, 223, 226; threshold for 225–227; written form of 221, 222; timing of manipulated by authorities 226–227, 254
Polish prosecution system: adversarial period 15, 87–88; external independence of prosecutors 40–42, 66; internal independence of prosecutors 42–45, 68; Minister of Justice 40, 41–42, 67, 68; *oskarżyciel* and *prokurator* 30–31; Soviet legacy 39, 40, 255; sources of law for prosecution service 38–39
politics, prosecutor's need for independence from 351–352
preliminary charging: definition of 208–210; diversity of methods 207, 254, 343; harm caused to suspect by 208; as main goal of criminal justice authorities 207–208; police, crucial role of 257, 345; protections afforded suspect by 208; required for coercive measures 208; suspect interrogated as witness 344; suspect's right to be informed vs. need for secrecy 344–345; *see also individual countries*
private prosecution 31, 79, 103
professionalization of police, need for 340, 342, 351
prosecution systems: executive vs. judicial affiliations of prosecutors 27–28; external independence of prosecutors 27–29, 66–67; internal independence of prosecutors 29–30, 68; prosecutor, definition of 30–32; *see also individual countries*
prosecutorial misconduct 8, 106, 338, 343
prosecutorial powers, study of: comparative 5–6, 13–14, 15–16, 17; country-related approach 17; criminal investigation as focus 8–9; descriptive 6; pretrial detention as focus 8; problem-related approach 7, 17–18; prosecutorial discretion as focus 7–8
prosecutorial misconduct as focus 8

Scalia, Antonin 288
Sessions, Joe 56
subdivision of prosecutorial powers, proposed 339

trials: alternative mechanisms 2–3; centrality in academic training 1–2; criminal investigation, increasing relative importance of 3–4, 5, 336; pretrial phase, greater relative importance of 4; public imagination of 1, 4; vanishing of 2–5, 335–336

United Nations 10, 28
United States: as adversarial exemplar 15; independent counsel 56–57; plea-bargaining 2, 99, 182, 194, 289, 325; prosecutor, definition of 31–32; vanishing of trials 2; *see also* Connecticut
United States agencies, departments and offices: Attorney General 54–56, 61–62, 63, 179; Bureau of Alcohol, Tobacco, Firearms and Explosives (ATF) 179; Criminal Division 140; Customs Service 179; Department of Homeland Security 179; Department of Justice 5–53, 54, 55, 57, 61, 62, 63, 102, 179; Department of Treasury 179; Drug Enforcement Administration (DEA) 179; Federal Bureau of Investigation (FBI) 61, 179; Immigration and Customs Enforcement (ICE) 179; Internal Revenue Service 179
United States case law: *Barker* v. *Wingo* 186; *Berger* v. *United States* 104–105; *Brady* v. *Maryland* 105; *Brinegar* v. *United States* 248, 292; *Chimel* v. *California* 286; *Coolidge* v. *New Hampshire* 291; *Costello* v. *United States* 191; *Dyson* v. *State* 287; *Illinois* v. *Gates* 248; *Imparato* v. *Spicola* 184; *Inmates of Attica* v. *Rockefeller* 326–327; *Johnson* v. *United States* 290;

Lafler v. *Cooper* 194; *Mapp* v. *Ohio* 293; *Miranda* v. *Arizona* 246; *Missouri* v. *Frye* 194; *Strickland* v. *Washington* 193–194; *Terry* v. *Ohio* 135, 249; *United States* v. *Dionisio* 190, 191; *United States* v. *Marion* 187; *United States* v. *Nixon* 54; *United States* v. *Wade* 105; *United States* v. *Williams* 191; *Wolf* v. *Colorado* 285
United States coercive measures: authority for 290–292; case law exceptions to warrant requirement 286–287; exigent circumstances 287; Fourth Amendment protection against 284–285, 286, 287, 290; *Gerstein* review 289, 291; judicial review of searches inadequate 288–289; neutral and detached magistrates 290–291, 293; no coherent regulation of 263; particularity requirement for searches 288; police, wide discretionary powers of 292; probable cause 285, 286, 287, 288, 290, 291; procedure for 287–290; reasonable suspicion 286; remedies inadequate 289–290, 295; search incident to arrest 286–287; search warrant requirement largely circumvented 287–289; stop and frisk 286, 289–290
United States conduct of investigation: defense's duty to investigate 193–195; depositions 196; early arrest 182; exclusive powers of prosecutor 187–193; federalist structure, influence of 179; grand jury proceedings 188–193, 199; inadequate police reporting 182–183; inspectors hired by prosecutors 183–184, 197; interception of communications 187–188; judicial involvement 195–196; minor vs. complex crime 184, 185; no separate investigative police 179; prosecutor–police relationship 179–181; supervisory powers of prosecutor 181–187, 197–198, 199; time frame 186–187
United States Constitution: Fourth Amendment 96, 136, 191, 245, 247, 263, 284–285; Fifth Amendment 96, 100, 191, 242, 245, 246, 250; Sixth Amendment 186, 187, 244, 245, 246, 250; Fourteenth Amendment 52, 103, 186
United States criminal investigation: arraignment 99; constitutional protection of suspects 96; difficulty of defining 96; discontinuation of proceedings 99; felonies vs. misdemeanors 97–98; grand juries 98, 100, 184, 187; initial appearance hearings 98–99, 182, 183; inquisitorial character 97; institutional constraints on prosecutors 102–104, 110; judicial influence on 100; *Miranda* rights 190, 246, 250–251; outline of 95–101; pretrial phase, overlap with 99–100; proactive vs. reactive 98, 135; prosecutorial discretion 101–104, 109–110; prosecutorial misconduct 106; prosecutorial objectivity 104–107, 111; public harm, degree of 102; resource constraints 103; selective and vindictive prosecution ban 103–104
United States discontinuation of investigation: authority for 327–328; difficulty of pinpointing 320–321; diversionary programs, release to 322; economic motives 323; grand juries 325; informality of before charging 321, 324; judicial review, lack of 326–327, 331; *nolle prosequi* 320–321, 326–327, 328, 331; police discretion not to arrest 328; police post-arrest screening 324; probable cause 322, 328; procedure for 324–327; prosecutor's broad discretionary powers 322, 327–328; prosecutor's pre-charge screening 325; public interest grounds 323–324; reasonable doubt 322; separation of powers 327, 331; witness credibility 323
United States initiation of investigation: arrest as commencement of 135, 136; authority for 139–141; discretion almost unlimited 137; lack of formal procedure 137–138; pre-arrest investigation 135, 139; probable cause for arrest 136; procedure for 137–139; standard of proof for 136–137; threshold for 134–137; unreviewability of refusal to investigate 138–139
United States laws, rules, and guidelines: Act to Establish the Department of Justice 52–53; Code of Law (USC) 53, 138; Federal Rules of Criminal

Procedure (FRCP) 52, 53, 102; Federal Rules of Evidence 52; Judiciary Act 52, 61; Justice Manual 53–54, 55, 102, 140; National Prosecution Standards (National District Attorneys' Association) 54, 103, 105, 140, 180–181, 292, 325, 328; Speedy Trial Act 186; Standards for Criminal Justice (American Bar Association) 54, 105–106, 194–195; Standards on Prosecutorial Investigations (American Bar Association) 97, 103, 106, 136–137, 180, 185, 322, 323, 328; *see also* United States Constitution

United States preliminary charging: amendment of charges 243; arrest as preliminary charging decision 246; arrest warrant 243–244; authority for 252–253; commencement of prosecution phase as moment of formal charging 244, 250; complaint 243–244; custodial interrogation 246, 251–252; diffuse nature of 241–242, 243, 246; Fifth Amendment rights of suspects 246, 250–251; grand juries 242–243, 247, 252; indictment vs. information 242–243; initial appearance 250; legality principle 249; police, crucial role of 252–253; probable cause for 247–249; procedure for 249–252; reasonable suspicion 249; severe consequences of arrest for suspect 247; *see also individual countries*

United States prosecution system: election of state prosecutors 57–59; external independence of prosecutors 54–60, 66, 67; federal/state organization 51–52; internal independence of prosecutors 60–66; sources of law for prosecution service 51–54; unparalleled discretionary power of prosecutors 60–61, 64, 65, 68, 101

United States Supreme Court 52, 62; arrest as starting point of investigation 135; consequences of arrest 247; defendant's rights activated by commencement of prosecution 244–245; defense's duty to investigate 193–194; discretionary powers of prosecutors 61; due process 96; executive's right to prosecute 54; exigent circumstances 287; Fourth Amendment protections 285–286, 289, 290, 292; grand juries 191, 242; judicial review of discontinuation of prosecution 327; *Miranda* rights 251; objectivity of prosecutors 104–105; probable cause, definition of 136, 248, 285; public interest in prosecution 323–324; reasonable suspicion 249; search incident to arrest 286–287; separation of powers 67; time frame for criminal investigation 186, 187; warrant-issuing authorities 291

Watergate 56

World War II 45, 66, 77, 342

For Product Safety Concerns and Information please contact our EU
representative GPSR@taylorandfrancis.com
Taylor & Francis Verlag GmbH, Kaufingerstraße 24, 80331 München, Germany

www.ingramcontent.com/pod-product-compliance
Ingram Content Group UK Ltd.
Pitfield, Milton Keynes, MK11 3LW, UK
UKHW022347190926
475702UK00015B/2149

* 9 7 8 0 3 6 7 6 5 5 5 8 7 *